THE WISDEN PAPERS

1969–1990

THE WISDEN PAPERS

1969–1990

MIXED FORTUNES

EDITED BY BENNY GREEN

Stanley Paul

LONDON SYDNEY AUCKLAND
JOHANNESBURG

Stanley Paul & Co. Ltd

An imprint of Random Century Group
20 Vauxhall Bridge Road, London SW1V 2SA

Random Century Australia (Pty) Ltd
20 Alfred Street, Milsons Point, Sydney 2061

Random Century New Zealand Limited
PO Box 40–086, Glenfield, Auckland 10

Century Hutchinson South Africa (Pty) Ltd
PO Box 337, Bergvlei 2012, South Africa

First published 1991

Set in Times by Speedset Ltd, Ellesmere Port
Printed and bound in Great Britain by
Mackays of Chatham PLC, Chatham, Kent

British Library Cataloguing in Publication Data
The Wisden papers 1969–1990
1. Cricket. History
I. Green, Benny 1927–
796.35809
ISBN 0 09 174602 7

Photographic acknowledgement
The author and publishers would like to thank
the following photographers and agencies for
permission to reproduce their copyright photographs:
Patrick Eagar, Hulton-Deutsch Collection, Press Association
and Sport & General

CONTENTS

PROLOGUE

This final volume of *The Wisden Papers* covers what is sadly the modern, sulphurous age of cricket, in which the fortunes of the game have too often been thrust into the background by considerations of financial, legal and political expediency. Tragic though the process may have been, it is remarkable that the crises did not arrive sooner, and that, by sheer obduracy, sometimes inspired, sometimes unfortunate, cricket administrators contrived to delay the days of reckoning for so long. Until 1968, even the most grievous calamities to do with cricket had been purely cricketing calamities, issues of interpretation of the rules, gentlemanly conduct on the field of play, and so on. After 1968 this was no longer the case. Cricket was suddenly flung, with alarming lack of ceremony, into the world arena, from the back page to the front page, obliged to fight battles which had no faint connection with the origin of the googly or the blandishments of the one-day game. Indeed, so deep was the rift caused by the events of 1968 that, to this day, the repairs remain undone.

The events of eleven years later, although they brought about an eruption of truly sensational proportions at the time, can now be seen as having been parochial by comparison, and were merely concerned with money. But they too damaged the fragile infrastructure of the game, destroyed careers, brought all sorts of moralities into question. Because there was a genuine ethical issue involved in the first crisis, and none to speak of in the second, it was 1968 which produced its heroes and its villains, while 1977 could offer nothing more edifying than a bunch of buffoons and an expensive juridical farce. The second crisis could probably have been avoided, the first probably not, but it is revealing that in neither case was the world of cricket remotely prepared to weather the challenge of the new, intemperate climate. Yet again, Wisden proves as reliable a guide as any through the minefields of contention and recrimination. An almanack dedicated to the chronicling of cricketing lives found itself obliged at last to peep over its ancient pallisades at the outside world. In retrospect, it will be seen to have peeped with commendable perception.

THE D'OLIVEIRA CASE [1969]

Cancellation of South African Tour

BY MICHAEL MELFORD

The die was cast twenty years before. At the end of the 1948 season an England touring party under the leadership of F. G. Mann set sail for South Africa. Among the platoon of communicators accompanying the cricketers was Leslie Thomas John Arlott, whose voice was already beginning to be recognised as a national treasure. A policeman turned poet, a staunch advocate of the joys of Liberalism, an honest radical in practical affairs, he was, and is, a richly gifted man, a natural charmer whose light has sometimes been hidden under the bushel of his countryman's burr and an outer aspect of bluff regional insularity. In truth he is a highly sophisticated, deeply compassionate man, never likely to mince words for the convenience of the moment. On arrival in South Africa for the first time, Arlott found himself ordered to complete a questionnaire for the edification of the local functionaries. One of the questions asked: 'Race'. Arlott filled in the answer: 'Human', from which moment his relations with South Africa arrived at a point of no return and the seeds of the controversy of 1968 fluttered unnoticed to the ground.

Among the many aspects of South African life repugnant to Arlott was the crude mockery of its sporting arrangements. A culture which invested almost too much importance in sport, and yet a culture with no conception of sportsmanship. The contradiction might have seemed comic had it not been so tragic. Potential sporting masters were obliged to fritter away their promise on tenth-rate grounds, to make do with makeshift equipment, and, in the absence of adequate coaching facilities, to teach themselves as best they could. There is no way of calculating how many hundreds of outstanding sportsmen were flung to the dogs of bigotry and oppression in South Africa. One or two renegade historians of cricket had dropped a few broad hints, and the heretical Roland Bowen, in his brilliantly perverse Cricket, a History, *had named chapter and verse. But ever since the acceptance of South Africa into the family of Test-playing nations in 1888, issues of racial equality on the playing fields had been swept under the imperial carpet by a succession of administrators intent on preserving a status quo which, at any rate since the end of the Great War, had ceased to exist. But it was not until the melodramas of 1968 that the carpet of concealment was suddenly swept away by the winds of change.*

It is revealing that in the years following his first and last visit to South Africa Arlott, unlike a great many more flamboyant crusaders, had mounted no soap boxes, espoused no revolutionary political causes, was never reported in the press for something he might have said about the in-

congruities of apartheid in sport. He continued to write and commentate on South African cricketing tours to England, and enjoyed personal friendships with more than one of the Republic's star players. Long after the affairs of 1968 had passed into history, and Arlott into retirement, he told an interviewer, 'I was so happy in the commentary box, and, as far as I know, I didn't make any enemies.' Which was a modest man's way of conceding that he was perhaps the best and most widely loved man in the game. The affronts of 1948 had never been forgotten, but he kept his own counsel.

One day in 1958 he received a letter from a man he had never heard of, a Mr. B. D'Oliveira, containing a request for advice and the writer's cricketing career figures. It was difficult to assess the worth of these figures, for they had been achieved by someone designated in the polychromatic madhouse of the Republic as a Cape Coloured. That is to say, he wasn't black and he wasn't white, but sufficiently off-white to constitute a potential threat to the state. Which meant that he had never had the opportunity of playing any first-class cricket, never been allowed to measure his ability against the great players of his own land. Even so, when a man scores eighty centuries, when he takes nine wickets in an innings for two runs, when he scores 225 in seventy minutes, he cannot quite be an insignificant player. Arlott decided to respond to the letter by investigating the prospects for its sender of cricketing employment in England. After sending the letter, D'Oliveira toured Kenya and East Africa with a non-white representative side and emerged with a batting average of 46.

In the meantime, Arlott had passed on the letter requesting work to John Kay, a sports writer with the Manchester Evening News *and well-placed to know the workings of league cricket. Kay's brother was the secretary of the Middleton club, and inquiries were made. It appeared that Middleton already had enough of professionalism in its ranks in the form of that wild and woolly West Indian Test bowler, Gilchrist. On January 14th, 1960, Kay wrote to Arlott that 'there was no hope of a league post in 1960'. Seven days later, the arrangement with Gilchrist having suddenly collapsed, Kay wrote again, passing on Middleton's offer to D'Oliveira to play for the club in the coming season for a fee of £450. The offer was niggardly, but D'Oliveira, now 25 years old, recognised it as his one hope for some sort of a future. His fare to England having been raised by a series of raffles and collections, he set foot in England on April 1st, 1960, later making the pointed remark, 'The fool had arrived.'*

At first the strange playing conditions so disconcerted him that he was unable to make runs. But, after a week or two of depressingly low scores in which he doubted the wisdom of the whole enterprise, he began to adapt, and by the end of the season came out top of the Central League batting averages. Garfield Sobers finished second. A year later D'Oliveira returned to England, this time with his wife and small son. He bought a house and soon became a respected member of the local community. But he had still not realised his dream of playing first-class cricket. Attempts to interest the Lancashire County club failed after that deep thinker Cyril Washbrook dismissed the recruit as a 'Saturday afternoon slogger'. D'Oliveira then signed for Kidderminster in the Birmingham League, at which point there entered the second of his great benefactors, Tom Graveney, at that time rebuilding a fractured career. After a long association with Gloucestershire, Graveney had resigned after a dispute over the succession to the captaincy, and had moved over to Worcestershire, where he was to enjoy championship medals and a rejuvenated international career. Always eager for any opportunity to strengthen his new county, Graveney saw that Basil D'Oliveira would be a great asset to the club. By the time D'Oliveira's first season with Kidderminster had ended, Graveney had already made the diplomatic overtures which would clear D'Oliveira's path to the Worcestershire side.

When he made his first-class debut, against the Australian tourists at Worcester, in May 1965, D'Oliveira was past his thirtieth birthday. Most first-class players are beginning to think of retirement at that age. He was just beginning. It way all a desperate and perhaps foolhardy gamble which was to result in a storybook triumph. In his first season D'Oliveira hit six Championship hundreds, and by 1966 was on the brink of the England side. The West Indies, captained by Sobers, won the first Test by an innings, with the usual consequences. The England selectors made wholesale changes for the Lord's game, including Boycott for Russell, Graveney for Mike Smith and—D'Oliveira for Allen. In the third Test, won by the tourists, D'Oliveira made scores of 76 and 54 and took four wickets. He had established his place as England's all-rounder. In 1967 Wisden selected him as one of the Five Cricketers of the Year. The general public too knew all about him, from television coverage of the Tests, recognising him as a batsman of quiet, neat practicality who defended against the good ball and severely punished anything loose. He had almost no uplift but used powerful forearms to punch the ball to the boundary. His medium-pace off-spin, which reminded some old stagers of the style of the old Middlesex and England player, J. T. Hearne, looked innocuous enough, but in the 1967 domestic season he took nearly sixty wickets. All these facts were tempting far-seeing followers of the game to speculate on the possible scenario now beginning to take shape.

At the end of the 1968 season an England side was due in South Africa. Already it looked as though that side would not be at its best without D'Oliveira. A few ostriches buried their heads in whatever patches of sand they could find, privately hoping that a loss of form on D'Oliveira's part might absolve them from the task of doing something positive. For a while it seemed as though their prayers were answered. Towards the end of that summer, with England struggling to defeat the Australians, a loss of form cost D'Oliveira his place in the national side. But then the pendulum swung back when the selectors called him back for the final Test at the Oval. As if following his cue, D'Oliveira now vindicated himself with his finest innings since arriving in England. He made 158 brave and brilliant runs and had surely booked his passage for the Cape. The sequence of events which followed remains difficult to countenance even after all these years, and is perhaps best recounted in the form of a chronology:

August 27th: The England Selection Committee convenes a meeting to discuss the compositon of the touring party to South Africa.

August 28th: Team for South Africa announced. D'Oliveira not selected.

August 29th: Questions are asked in the House of Commons. Resignations from MCC members begin to arrive by post.

September 4th: Club members demand an Extraordinary Meeting.

September 6th: The Rev. David Sheppard joins the protest.

September 8th: The News of the World *signs D'Oliveira to cover the South African tour.*

September 11th: The South African Prime Minister says that 'Guests who have ulterior motives usually find that they are not invited.'

Here was the first official acknowledgement that the selection of an England cricket side had become a prime issue in South African politics. Had D'Oliveira been passed over because of his political unacceptability to the government of his homeland? Had the England selectors allowed extra-sporting considerations to cloud their judgement? If they had not, what about his wonderful century at the Oval? Did that count for nothing when weighed in the balance against the politics of Apartheid? Members of the Selection Committee grimly insisted they had chosen the best side to the best of their ability, and had allowed no extraneous factors to influence their choices. The debate might have rumbled on and faded away had it not been for the next unexpected twist in the story. Tom Cartwright, the Warwickshire all-rounder who had been preferred to D'Oliveira, injured his shoulder. On September 16th Cartwright announced his withdrawal from the touring party and D'Oliveira was named as his replacement. How convenient, said the cynics, many of whom suspected that Cartwright's convenient injury had been merely diplomatic, a tactful gesture to ease the embarrassment of the England selectors, who could now scuttle to salvation. But in belatedly absolving themselves from any charge of political expediency, the selectors now found themselves in much deeper waters. On the day after the announcement of D'Oliveira's selection for the tour, the South African Prime Minister made one of the most maladroit speeches in the history of his country:

It is not the MCC team. It is the team of the Anti-Apartheid movement. We are not prepared to accept a team thrust upon us. It is a team of political opponents of South Africa. It is a team of people who don't care about sports relations at all.

With which extraordinary outburst Mr. Vorster resolved the complexities of the case, simplifying the issues so utterly as to take the argument out of the ethical back into the sporting context, offering a heaven-sent bolthole to those who thought that a cricket match was more important than the humanitarian issues surrounding it. Suddenly, with Mr. Vorster's words, all the confusions of racial justice, of political allegiance, were swept away, and it became blindingly clear that, on purely cricketing grounds, a tour of South Africa was inconceivable. For the thinkers of conservative thoughts who abhorred the idea of severing connections with a Test-playing country but who suspected that the treatment of D'Oliveira was scurrilous, for the progressive lobby which wanted no part of anything South African, for the hapless administrators of cricket caught up in a maelstrom, everything had overnight become simple and straightforward again. How can you have a game of cricket with opponents who insist on the right to select your team? This ludicrous situation was resolved when on September 24th it was announced that the tour of South Africa had been cancelled.

What is most revealing of all about this extraordinary sequence of events is that it presented nothing new, nothing that had not happened before, nothing previously unknown to English selection committees. What was quite new was not the South African government's obduracy but the way in which it had instantly become a public issue. The cricketing morals of England had not always been so exposed. In 1929 the South Africans sent a party to tour England. Among those chosen to play in the first Test at Birmingham was the Sussex star K. S. Duleepsinhji. The tourists objected to Duleep's presence in the side and made their feelings known to the selectors, who obligingly omitted him from the rest of the series, leaving the tourists to return home with their purity unsullied. In the following summer Duleep returned to the England side against the Australians at Lord's, scoring 173 and 48. In the words of Roland Bowen:

> Duleep never toured South Africa, but those were the days when it was not necessary to send the best team to that country. In later years, when serving as Indian High Commissioner in Australia, he stated that he had agreed to stand down, not wanting to cause trouble; he was always a gentle creature, not like his uncle, who was ever ready to stand on his rights and his dignity and who was furious over the whole affair.

But evidently not quite furious enough to make the issue public. By 1968 cricket had become democratised, comparatively speaking, and the brand of genteel blackguardism which removed Duleepsinhji from the firing line was no longer viable. The implications of the D'Oliveira affair were to echo down the decades which followed. To this day, twenty-two years later, South Africa remains beyond the cricketing pale.

THE bitterness engendered by the sequence of events leading up to the cancellation of M.C.C.'s proposed tour of South Africa only six weeks before the scheduled starting date made a sad end to the 1968 English season. Almost from the moment that England walked off the field at The Oval with a rare victory over Australia to their credit, English cricket was caught up in a whirlpool of acrimony and political argument such as it can seldom have known before. The culmination, on September 17, was the refusal by the South African Prime Minister, Mr. John Vorster, to accept Basil D'Oliveira, a Cape Coloured, as a member of the M.C.C. team, and the M.C.C. Committee's consequent cancellation of the tour.

Since D'Oliveira came successfully into English cricket, and even before he played for England in 1966, it had been evident that a delicate situation might arise if he were selected for this tour of his native country. However, what appeared to be a relatively simple problem of whether he was acceptable or not had been greatly complicated when the time came, especially by his original omission from the team and the outcry which greeted it.

When the New Zealand Rugby Board were refused permission to bring their Maoris to South Africa in 1967 by Mr. Vorster's predecessor, Dr. Verwoerd, they cancelled the tour with so little rancour that it was soon being replanned for 1970 with the ban removed. Cricket, however, ever more exposed to publicity, had to endure charges and recriminations of a passion which resounded far outside the sporting world. Not until December, when, at a special general meeting of M.C.C. the Committee defeated three resolutions put forward by dissident members, was relief in sight from a period of unpleasantness which must have been a nightmare to the ordinary sensitive lover of cricket.

By a coincidence, M. J. K. Smith's M.C.C. side, managed by the secretary, S. C. Griffith, was in New Zealand in March 1966 when the New Zealand Rugby authorities were about to cancel their tour of South Africa. Mr. Griffith was asked what action he thought his committee would take in similar circumstances and he replied unequivocally that no other course but cancellation was conceivable.

In the following winter Mr. Griffith visited South Africa at the invitation of the South African Cricket Association. With one other cricket correspondent, Louis Duffus of the Johannesburg *Star*, I interviewed Mr. Griffith and the then President of the S.A.C.A., Mr. Boon Wallace, in Cape Town at the end of the visit. Asked if the case of D'Oliveira had been discussed with the S.A.C.A., Mr. Griffith said that naturally it had in principle and he had made M.C.C.'s position abundantly clear. They had considered the broader question of non-European cricketers in general as members of M.C.C. sides. In view of the number of cricketers of West Indian descent likely to be playing in English domestic cricket in the future, the discussions had not concerned only one player.

Later in January 1967 a reporter of the Johannesburg *Sunday Express* put a similar question by telephone to Mr. P. Le Roux, the Minister of the Interior, one Saturday night. The reply, as given in next day's paper, stated the law as it existed at the time and the inference was drawn that D'Oliveira would not be acceptable. Though to most people in South Africa at the time this seemed far from an inspired statement and to be running against the tide of the Prime Minister's policy, it excited public criticism in Britain and the West Indies. In one quarter it induced questions in the House of Commons and in the other the withdrawal of an invitation to three South Africans, the Pollock brothers and Colin Bland, to play in Barbados.

After a week Mr. Denis Howell, the Minister with special responsibility for sport, in a statement in the House, scotched suggestions that M.C.C. might give way. 'M.C.C. has informed the Government that the team to tour South Africa will be chosen on merit. . . . If any player chosen were to be rejected by the host country, then . . . the projected tour would be abandoned.' This was what Mr. Griffith had told the New Zealand Rugby Board a year before.

On April 11, 1967, Mr. Vorster, speaking in the House of Assembly in Cape Town, clarified the position of coloured sportsmen in teams visiting South Africa. Visiting teams of mixed race would be able to tour the country if they were teams from countries with which South Africa had 'traditional sporting ties' and 'if no political capital was made out of the situation'.

Superficially this appeared to make the way clear for any non-European to visit South Africa with an M.C.C. team, but D'Oliveira, as a native of South Africa, might be considered likely to be the focus of political influences where others would not. M.C.C. therefore wrote to the S.A.C.A. in January 1968 asking for an assurance that no pre-conditions would be laid on their choice of players. At about the same time Sir Alec Douglas-Home, the previous year's President of M.C.C., talked to Mr. Vorster in Cape Town during a tour which he made as Opposition spokesman on foreign affairs.

M.C.C. had received no firm answer to their question by late March and had then to decide whether to cancel the tour or to go ahead as planned, leaving the matter of a player's non-acceptability until it happened. On Sir Alec Douglas-Home's advice they decided to go ahead and for much of the summer the issue seemed unlikely to arise.

D'Oliveira had toured West Indies with Colin Cowdrey's team but without success. He had played in the First Test against Australia at Old Trafford in June and had made 87 not out in the second innings, but he had been left out at Lord's in favour of a third fast bowler. England almost won at Lord's and as their fortunes improved without him, D'Oliveira lost form for Worcestershire with the bat. Though he took plenty of wickets later in the season, they were mostly on imperfect pitches and were not obvious recommendations for a Test place.

However, after the team for the Fifth Test had been chosen on August 18, R. M. Prideaux, one of the opening batsmen in the prolonged absence through injury of G. Boycott, dropped out through bronchitis. He was replaced by D'Oliveira, an unexpected choice, made partly to help the side's balance and partly, perhaps, on a hunch.

The hunch came off. D'Oliveira, though little used as a bowler, made 158. England won and that night, August 27, the selectors sat down to pick the team for South Africa. When it was announced next day that this did not include D'Oliveira, the chairman of the selectors, D. J. Insole, explained that the selectors regarded him 'from an overseas tour point of view as a batsman rather than an all-rounder. We put him beside the seven batsmen that we had, along with Colin Milburn whom we also had to leave out with regret.' This explanation of a selection was no new departure and followed the selectors' practice over the last fifteen years.

To the non-cricketing public, however, D'Oliveira's omission immediately after his innings at The Oval was largely incomprehensible. It was easy for many to assume political motives behind it and a bowing to South

Africa's racial policies. More knowledgeable cricketers were split between those who agreed that on technical grounds D'Oliveira was far from an automatic choice and who were doubtful if he would be any more effective in South Africa than he had been in West Indies, and those who thought that after his successful comeback to Test cricket, it was 'inhuman' not to pick him.

Some holding the latter opinion were also ready to see non-cricketing reasons for the omission, refusing to believe Mr. Insole and Mr. Griffith, who publicly stated that none existed. Much was said which was regretted later—four out of nineteen members of M.C.C. who resigned in protest applied for reinstatement within a few days—and Lord Fisher of Lambeth, the former Archbishop of Canterbury, was prompted to write to the *Daily Telegraph* condemning a leader 'which appeared to cast doubt on the word of the selectors'. A group of twenty M.C.C. members, the number required to call a special meeting of the club, asserted this right, co-opting the Rev. D.S. Sheppard as their main spokesman. For three weeks the affair simmered like an angry volcano.

During this period the *News of the World* announced that it had engaged D'Oliveira to report the tour in South Africa. This did much to antagonise Government opinion in South Africa, as had several events unrelated to the team's selection. One of these was M.C.C.'s refusal in June to include Rhodesia in their itinerary. Two others, outside M.C.C.'s province, were the rejection of a mixed South African Olympic team and the turning-back of Colin Bland at London Airport in August because he had a Rhodesian passport.

Though the *News of the World* emphasised that D'Oliveira would only be reporting the cricket and though there were precedents (Wardle in 1958 and Close in 1967) for players left out of M.C.C. teams being sent by newspapers, suspicion of English motives and of political intrigue was undoubtedly increased in South Africa. When so many voices in England were discussing the political side of the affair, it was hard for any one at a distance who did not know them to believe that D. J. Insole, A. V. Bedser, P. B. H. May and D. Kenyon, augmented by G. O. Allen and A. E. R. Gilligan and the captain, M. C. Cowdrey, were impervious to political influences and were picking a side purely on cricketing qualifications.

It was harder still after the final readjustment of the team on September 16. Cartwright had been unfit when picked originally but the assurances given by specialists of his imminent recovery had been provisionally accepted and he had bowled ten overs for Warwickshire on September 14 without apparent discomfort. However, the subsequent medical report ruled him out and D'Oliveira was chosen to replace him.

In view of Mr. Insole's previous statement that D'Oliveira had been considered only as a batsman, his substitution now for a bowler must have been the final proof to the South African Government that political influences were at work. Mr. Insole's explanation that the balance of the side had had to be entirely reviewed made little impact. No replacement of Cartwright's type or experience did in fact exist in England in the unavailability, for different reasons, of B. R. Knight, R. Illingworth and others.

On the following evening, Mr. Vorster said that South Africa was not prepared to receive a team which had been forced upon her by people 'with certain political aims'. It was one of many unhappy chances that he should be speaking in Bloemfontein where cricket has probably a less enthusiastic following than anywhere else in a country where it is generally booming. A dignified speech of regret might have done something to heal the wounds but Mr. Vorster broke the eighty-year-old links between English and South African cricket in a speech for internal political consumption—in 'crude and boorish words', as the *Daily Mail* leader put it—and with a harshness which can have won him little sympathy outside his own party.

It only remained for the M.C.C. Committee to make the formal cancellation of the tour, which they did on September 24. At the meeting, the Committee discussed future cricket relations between the two countries with two members of the South African Board, A. H. Coy and J. E. Cheetham, who had flown overnight from Johannesburg.

The special general meeting of M.C.C. was fixed for December 5 at Church House, Westminster, with the President, Mr. R. Aird, in the chair. A vote was asked for on the following resolutions:

1.   That the Members of M.C.C. regret their Committee's mishandling of affairs leading up to the selection of the team for the intended tour of South Africa in 1968–69.
2.   That no further tours to or from South Africa be undertaken until evidence can be given of actual progress by South Africa towards non-racial cricket.
3.   That a Special Committee be set up to examine such proposals by the S.A.C.A. towards non-racial cricket; the M.C.C. to report on progress to the Annual General Meeting of the Club; and to the Governing Body for Cricket—the M.C.C. Council.

The meeting, which lasted nearly four hours, was attended by over 1,000 members and, through a special decision of the Committee, by the Press. The main speakers for the resolutions were the Rev. David Sheppard and J. M. Brearley and for the Committee, D. R. W. Silk and A. M. Crawley.

Those putting the case for the resolutions said that their main concern was to debate future policy rather than to analyse past events, but they maintained that the Committee had acted weakly and irresponsibly and should have insisted on a definite answer from the S.A.C.A. in the spring to the question 'Would D'Oliveira be acceptable as an M.C.C. tourist without conditions?'. Had the answer been a public 'Yes', the selectors' disinterestedness in choosing the team in August could not have been challenged. Had the answer been 'No', or continued equivocation, then, reluctantly, the tour should have been called off. Those who protest, they said, are frequently charged with bringing politics into cricket. 'It is, of course, South Africa which organises its sport on political grounds and intrudes its politics upon all teams which visit the country.'

The Committee said that they were motivated by a continuing desire to foster cricket wherever it is played. Over the years M.C.C. had never thought it the collective function of its Committee to act as inquisitor-general into the domestic attitudes towards race-relations, immigration, political orientation or anything else of the governments or governing bodies of their respective opponents. They had accepted Sir Alec Douglas-Home's opinion that to confront the South African Government with individual possible selections was wrong and would undoubtedly result in a refusal to answer hypothetical questions. To have pressed for an immediate answer to their letter would have appeared to be not only hypothetical, but politically inspired. The England captain, Colin Cowdrey, stated that the selectors had never been put in an 'intolerable position', as was suggested. 'We were quite free to pick the best team on cricketing merit,' he said.

The first resolution was defeated by 4,357 to 1,570, the bulk of the votes having been recorded by post. The Committee had a 386 to 314 majority in the hall. The second resolution was lost by 4,664 to 1,214 and the third by 4,508 to 1,352. The voting in the hall on these two resolutions was 516 to 137 and 474 to 155 respectively.

After the meeting, Mr. Sheppard said that the vote made clear that a large proportion of the M.C.C. membership cared about the issue. 'What is more important than votes, however, is that ideas have been ventilated. Nothing will be quite the same in English cricket after the debate.'

Mr. Aird, the President, said that he was pleased that most members of the Club still saw cricket as a game to be played wherever and whenever possible. 'We shall strive for the welfare of all cricketers both in South Africa and wherever the game is played.' Mr. Aird also paid tribute to the 'great dignity which Basil D'Oliveira had maintained throughout the whole business'.

WATERY REFLECTIONS FROM AUSTRALIA [1969]

BY JACK FINGLETON

Understandably, everything which happened in 1968 was overshadowed by the late flowering ironies of the D'Oliveira Affair. Not even the visit of an Australian touring party attracted much attention by comparison. The depressing effect of the summer's weather is well enough defined in the rueful title which Jack Fingleton gives his essay, and for anyone to have achieved a balanced account of events from May to September would have been difficult although perhaps not impossible. It must therefore be accounted a sad deprivation that Fingleton should have abandoned his attempts to produce a book on the summer campaign. Not only was he a Test player of wide experience and considerable achievement, he was also a trained journalist whose sequence of books on the battles for the Ashes, beginning in 1948 with Brightly Fades the Don, *have become required reading for all students of the game. It was typical of his blunt candour that he should have made a public display of his failure to complete his assignment even if his reasons read unconvincingly.*

'Nobody', *says Fingleton,* 'wanted to read the dreary story of rain over England's cricket fields.' *In retrospect the wrongheadedness of that remark causes the reader to despair. Rain may deter the cricketers but it cannot dampen the ardour of those who write about them; someone should have reminded Fingleton of Neville Cardus's recollection that some of his best reports for the* Manchester Guardian *were composed on days when not a ball was bowled. As for the assumption that there are too many cricket books Fingleton was, for all his assumption of tough realism, too modest to say what he really meant, which was that there are too many bad cricket books and that the exceptions will always be welcome. What would we not give today for that book which Fingleton should have written but did not?*

His dismissal of English pitches is irrefutable, his contempt for the County championship less so, his suggestion that the cricket at Lord's should be turned through an angle of ninety degrees unintentionally comic. While his plan is not quite so hare-brained as Conan Doyle's propositon for the abolition of lefthandedness, and not nearly as insane as R. A. Young's suggestion that the fielding captain be allowed to pour eighty gallons of water on to the playing area at a moment of his choice, the idea that there should be bowling from the Mound Stand end is wild enough. He was on much firmer ground in castigating fast bowlers who spend half the day walking back to their marks, and probably misguided in his insinuations that Gleeson had been diddled out in England by biased umpiring.

But it is on the theme of D'Oliveira that Fingleton disappoints us most. He offers one fresh insight when he suggests that perhaps if D'Oliveira had surfaced a generation earlier there might have been no trouble; history is against Fingleton here, but it is at any rate an opinion which nobody else offered at the time. But in his pose as the hardened man of affairs he ignores the moral issues completely, almost as though he believed that ethics as well as politics ought to be kept out of the game. Intentionally or not, he conveys the impression of a man who believes that things might have been done differently, and with a less calamitous ending, but he never says exactly what it was that was or was not done.

The most priceless section of the essay deals with the witchery of the bizarre Mrs. Doris Munday, a West London harridan who telephoned the secretary of the MCC claiming to possess the power to control the weather. There seems to have been a healthy respect for Mrs. Munday at head-quarters, but whether the drowning of the cricket of 1968 was the work of the vengeful Mrs. Munday Fingleton never says.

THOUGH I feel there are too many cricket books, it was my intention for some time to write one on the 1968 Australian tour of England. My publishers were keen and had offered a most generous contract. I had known, on preceding tours, what an exacting task it is to maintain a daily outflow to newspapers and, at the same time, keep up to date writing a book of the tour's happenings. This imposes a big strain during, say, a tour in Australia or South Africa, but in those countries there is only one match a week whereas in England there are two and sandwiched between, a tiring consideration, are the two trips that have to be made most weeks.

A book on an English tour must be written from week to week, or, as some do, even nightly after the day's play. There always seems to be a scurry to have the first book out (although I believe most things are better dealt with in retrospect) and woe betide the writer who gets too far adrift as the tour progresses. As well as in a writing sense, he gets mentally snowed under. So, then, I set out to write a book on this tour and I was amused to notice the keen attention that my friend, Bobby Simpson, took in the progress of my book. Simpson is as keen a writer as ever came from the field to the Press-box—and his work is done splendidly by himself and by his own two fingers on his typewriter. You rarely get all this from a former Test player. He was constantly asking how I stood and would tell me with rare pleasure that by the end of each night his book was up to the end of that day's play.

By the end of the second Test at Lord's I, too, was well up on the summer's doings, but I decided to knock my book on the head. It seemed to be a repetition of rain, pitch covers, delays, drawn games and disappointing cricket. Nobody, I was convinced, wanted to read the dreary story of rain over England's cricket fields. It was the worst summer for weather I had known in England since 1938 and so I decided that the book, like many of the tour matches, would be best abandoned. And I did that, deserting it after the second Test at Lord's, but it must have been the sadistic side of my character that would not let me admit immediately my decision to Bobby Simpson. He kept eyeing me as warily in the Press-box as he did the English bowlers over those three days at Old Trafford in 1964 when he made 311. When Simpson asked me the inevitable question, I would nod mysteriously and admit nothing. I hope, the next time he sees me, he thanks me for keeping him up to the writing mark. And I know his book will be a good one because he brought enthusiasm to his task, a knowledgeable mind and nice descriptive typewriting.

The 1968 tour of England by the Australians was not worth many books. It was, as I have written, an abominable summer and cricketers cannot do themselves justice if the sun does not shine or if the game is being constantly interrupted. To some of the new Australians, having their first experience of English pitches, cricket must have seemed a game from another planet. The ball, for the bowlers, was often heavy and slippery; barely two pitches were alike in bounce and pace and many, indeed, were not up to the standard required for first-class cricket. Indeed, it was later reported by a committee that Old Trafford was not up to the standard necessary for Test cricket.

So, in making assessments, one must also make allowances. That is very important. I saw pitches on this tour that were a poor compliment to a touring side, which is always expected to play brightly and will get a critical caustic cane if it does not. Many problems pose themselves to English cricket—as, indeed, most do to world cricket—but I saw nothing more detrimental to good cricket on my 1968 tour of England than the pitiable pitches provided by many grounds. County cricket is another matter. I have sensed for many years now that the present system of county cricket is archaic, and simply not worthwhile, but no matter what the type of cricket, a good pitch is fundamental to a good game and many games in England can never get off the ground because of the inadequacy of the pitches on which they are played.

Six-days-a-week county cricket has been the vogue now for many decades, so modern groundsmen cannot blame incessant play for poor pitches because the past would deride them. But, indirectly, the incessant play *is* the cause of poor pitches—or so I think. On the final day of a game, one will often see another pitch cut for a new game beginning on the morrow. This, I believe, is the inherent fault of the system. A new pitch can be cut but, because of the current play, it cannot be watered and, for all the technical knowledge and mechanical means that groundsmen now possess to make pitches, I do think that watering and rolling are the main necessities for good pitches, granted that the soil and grass are proficient.

At Nottingham on the Sunday of the touring match, Richie Benaud and others travelled to Luton for a friendly match. Benaud told me next day he had seen the best pitch in England of the whole summer. Simpson concurred. 'They had an ardent enthusiast in their groundsman there,' said Benaud, 'and he worked odd hours on his pitch. But, basically, all he did was water and roll it, water and roll it.'

I recall, and still with misgivings, how we played for several seasons on our club pitch at Waverley, in Sydney, with the ball spitting, kicking, shooting and doing all manner of unorthodox things. It was as dry, as Bill O'Reilly once put it, as a hymn-book. The groundsman of the time did not believe in watering his pitch. The one before him, 'Boss' Reid, a wonderful old Edwardian gentleman with a beard like Dr. Grace, used to water his pitch as late as Saturday morning and then roll it with a heavy roller and let the sun dry it out. It was on Reid's pitches that Alan Kippax became the Trumper of his generation.

Nobody—and Bradman, Jackson and McCabe never got runs at Waverley in my time—could overcome the later 'dusty' one and batsmen became highly suspicious of it. No batsman can do himself justice on a dry, dusty pitch, although many a bowler, as we have seen in England, can forge a fictitious reputation on them.

I thought the Lord's pitches in 1968 were uncommonly indifferent. One expects something better at the headquarters of the game and it was, for the Australians, a blessing in disguise that rain so often intervened there, or else the Australians would have suffered several more defeats on their tour. I was watching play there one day, with the ball bringing up dust, when the idea occurred to me how little use is made of the middle of a pitch, which gets just as much rolling as the business-ends. My thoughts led to imagining a pitch made up of 'middles' which, at the very least, would be thickly turfed with no bare spots—and I suggested this in the London *Sunday Times* as an experiment well worth trying.

One of Lord's assistant secretaries, Jack Bailey, was absent in Holland at the time I wrote my suggestion, and I still think it had much merit and the spirit of experiment in it. It would have turned play about, with the bowlers running from Father Time one end and the late Tavern the other. Even the traditions of Lord's, I thought, could have withstood what would have been an interesting innovation. But Mr. Bailey seemed to think I had gone beserk when he approached me about my suggestion. He thought I was not taking Lord's seriously.

The county system apart, the quality of pitches is England's biggest problem. Some special committee seems to scurry here and there to inspect, when a pitch gets a bad report, but what are lacking are watering (even in England's climate!) and rolling when the pitch is malleable.

I prefer not to mention names in this little story but I was once admonished by several very good English friends for writing some captious comment on over-coaching. We stood, one Sunday morning, on the cricket field of a famous English school while the 'lesson' was read to me. I was not very interested in it. The sun was shining brilliantly and the pitch was wet from over-night rain. My critic was in charge of cricket and I thought: 'What a lovely pitch this will turn out later if the heavy roller is put on it now.' The school first eleven had a game that afternoon and, later, I asked my lecturer how the game went. 'Oh, it was disappointing. The pitch was absolutely spiteful.' And so it would have been; the marks on it drying under a hot sun had remained unrolled.

I never seem to have luck with my suggestions in England. The Lord's pitches apart, I have been hammering for years that fast bowlers and particularly alleged fast bowlers should be restricted in their run-up to, say, sixteen yards. Keith Miller, fast enough to displease any batsman, ran ten yards and sometimes twelve. A run-up, surely, is to enable a bowler to get up momentum. Those who know the science of athletics can say how long it takes a one hundred yards sprinter to reach top speed after his take-off. It would not, I guess, be very far and yet I constantly see in first-class and Test cricket a bowler travelling forty yards who is running as fast after ten yards as he is after thirty-five yards. Indeed, I have seen some worthies even lose pace in their run as they come near delivering the ball.

At the time of writing, Charlie Griffith and Wesley Hall are in trouble with some Australian umpires for taking too long to bowl an over. Griffith, timed at seven minutes for an eight-ball over, was advised in Melbourne to take a taxi, so long was he in getting back to his far-distant mark. This long run, with its official sanction, is the most nauseating absurdity of all cricketing time. How we put up with it, year after year, is beyond my comprehension. Next time, I invite you, when you see one of these dreary runners in action in a first-class game, to look at the faces of those around you and see how bored they are. The poor batsman, who stands there in frustration, awaiting a ball a minute—and that often delivered pretty wide of the mark—generally incurs the wrath of the critic and the slow handclap of the spectators when these condemnations rightfully should be directed at some innocuous bowler whose only attribute is that he clamps down the scoring rate. He does that by holding up play and not delivering smartly. I see no genius in that.

I saw a bowler at Kennington Oval in 1968 who trudged into the distance and then put foot after foot in a dull manner for forty yards to deliver a ball about as fast as a London bus going up Fleet Street.

It was a piece of fulsome, unexciting running. I would not mind so much if such a bowler turned a catherine-wheel for variety in the middle of his run. It would not, I am sure, affect the speed of the delivered article; it hurt more than ever when somebody said the same bowler, on the Sunday, had cut his run by half in a time-limit game. I broached this pet hate of mine to an important member of Surrey and he floored me by saying the tactics in a long run were to catch the batsman in between the taps of his bat on his mark! I think he was pulling my leg. But while I continue in this berating mood let me call down a murrain on all fast bowlers, seamers and alleged fast bowlers who walk back into eternity and take an eternity to emerge from it. And a bigger murrain on officials who allow them to do it, to the great boredom of the cricketing public.

There is one other blot on modern cricket—padding-up—and M.C.C. showed its obvious concern with this malady during the summer. The habit existed with some English professionals as far back as I can remember but it developed new proportions after the amendment of the lbw rule in the 'thirties. This amendment, permitting lbw to a ball breaking from the off, encouraged a rash of in-swing and off-break bowlers and the modern batsman believes he can offset this part of the rule by thrusting his front pad up the pitch at the ball, in the belief that no first-class umpire will give him out lbw so far away from the stumps.

I think the remedy here is with the umpires. Instead of giving the batsman the benefit of the doubt, they could give it against a man who negates the spirit of the game. It is interesting at the time of writing that the West Indians in Australia are befuddled by John Gleeson's flick-spin. The English largely nobbled Gleeson by pushing their front pad at him, attempting no stroke. Gleeson appealed often but couldn't get lbw's. I could well imagine the thoughts of Gleeson the batsman when he several times in England emulated his opponents by pushing his front pad up the pitch at an off-break—and was given out lbw! But Gleeson was a number ten batsman.

I often thought umpires paid too much respect to the names of some avid pad-pushers. Alec Bedser told me in England this summer that on his home pitch he constructed a paper frame to represent a front pad down the pitch and, time after time, on breaking through the paper-frame, he knocked over the stumps! All umpires, please note!

M.C.C. arranged a fine dinner to mark the 200th Test match—which, fittingly, happened at Lord's—between England and Australia. I was chatting with an old foe, Sir Leonard Hutton, before dinner when a young man, obviously Australian, on his first visit to England, asked Sir Leonard a question. 'How,' asked the young visitor, 'would you say the present generation of cricketers compares with yours?'. It is a question only an inexperienced cricketer would ask. Sir Leonard did not answer directly. He looked at me. 'Jack,' he said, with that lovely arch look so typical of him, 'there were county players in my day who never looked like playing for England and who would walk into this present English side.'

The young man invited the rebuff—the natural answer to such a question to a cricketer of other days. The English team was not a good one. It was patriarchal in the field and, at Lord's and at Edgbaston, much batting time was lost when the situation demanded urgency. England in batting and bowling merit deserved to win the series by a wide margin, but there was much to admire in Lawry's tactics at Old Trafford when his batting initiative against Pocock put Australia into a winning position almost before the English appreciated it. Lawry took Pocock by the scruff and Walters, Sheahan and Chappell followed their skipper's lead. 'I had never batted against Pocock before and I knew he must have had doubts in his mind about me. So I decided to charge him,' said Lawry afterwards.

It was this initial 'charge', winning the Old Trafford Test, that eventually drew the series. It is always hard to win a series from a side that wins the first Test. A winning skipper can take command of the general situation, set the tempo, so to speak. This has often made many series drab between England and Australia, in both countries, and it induced Jarman, while Lawry watched, injured, from the Leeds balcony, to decide on safety-first tactics to impose in the Fourth Test. Jarman had to bear the brunt of many ironical remarks from his fellow-Australians on the field as he passed them. Here was a pitch made for spinners and for the Australians to win another Test and so offset the suggestion that rain had saved them in the series. But Jarman, who may have been his off-field master's voice, would not use spin, nor give Gleeson the end which Snow had so mutilated with his sprigs.

Rain, in the long run, beat England for the series. It beat, also, the nationalism of Mrs. Doris Munday, of West London, who rang Lord's when the famous ground was covered in hailstones during the Second Test and said: 'I am responsible for this storm. And there will be many more until the Australians pay their debts.'

In telling me this story on the night of the M.C.C. 200th Test dinner, Mr. Donald Carr, an assistant secretary at Lord's, said Mrs. Munday, a hypnotherapist, claimed that she had occult powers as far as weather was concerned and would continue to use them because several years ago she had broken a seven-years drought for the Australians who had thanked the aborigines and had refused to pay Mrs. Munday. 'The woman said she was not fooling and over the phone she began to put an occult spell upon our Jean, who felt dizzy and cut the caller off,' said Mr. Carr.

Mrs. Munday, who also claimed to have broken droughts in India, China and the United States, did not let up on the Australians and it became the wettest tour in history, although Mrs. Munday seemed to have relented later. In the bushfires of the Blue Mountains, N.S.W., in November, 1968, she offered her occult powers to put them out.

This Australian team was, I thought, the poorest batting and bowling side I had seen in action under the green caps. The poor pitches have to be assessed in the batting failures, although so many Australians were lacking in primary technique. Yorkshire, under the brilliant captaincy of Fred Trueman—and I saw no better leadership in England during the summer—diddled the Australians completely, beating them by an innings and 69 at Sheffield, an ignominious defeat for a touring side against a county. The Yorkshiremen rubbed it in also, through Ken Taylor, by winning the long-distance throw at the end of the cricket!

I must pay tribute, too, to the second successive win of Glamorgan over the Australians on a good pitch in one of the best games of the tour. And in Alan Jones I saw one of the very best batsmen in Britain.

Of that defeat by Yorkshire I wrote in the London *Times*: 'Some Australian players came early and easily into Test cricket and not through the crucible that tempers skill with temperament—too many at Sheffield under baggy green caps bent and withered in an un-Australian manner.' In the tours to come, Australian teams must always regard the match against Yorkshire as another Test. Yorkshire, in the field, looked an infinitely better team than the English Test one. And Trueman's captaincy was full of fight, shrewd moves, and colossal Yorkshire bluff. I like the 'Tykes' because they are never false to their nature. When Trueman's team came into the dressing-room, I afterwards learned, they did not indulge themselves in any wild paeans of self-praise. Far from it. They got stuck into a first-class row as to whether individual money prizes . . . the 'brass' . . . should go into a communal fund!

Trueman, sadly, will be seen no more on the first-class cricketing field. He was, in very truth, a wonderful character. I met him first when George Duckworth gave the pair of us a lift back to Lymm from Old Trafford. Trueman, then twelfth man for England, talked of himself all the way back. He is Yorkshire to his boot-heels and an unforgettable character on the field. I loved him most at Adelaide one Australia Day when the artillery on the parade ground opposite the Oval broke out into a salute. Fiery Fred dived to earth immediately and waved his white hanky fiercely in surrender.

I've written before of how wrong I think it is that the best of the international blood of other countries should be sucked dry by England in trying to keep alive the out-moded, incongruous county cricket system. International cricket will suffer, as the West Indians seemed to be suggesting at an early stage in their Australian tour. They are tired of cricket before a tour begins. They are played out. In trying to insist that there is still a future for six-day county cricket, the supporters of the system fail to realise the effect upon attendances of the deaths of hundreds of thousands of cricket lovers since World War Two. This applies not only to England. The lovers of cricket, if not the game itself, are dying out. It is a sober thought to be measured for the future.

It is interesting for me to note the upset over D'Oliveira. I went to the Press conference at Lord's on the evening Mr. Griffith announced the team and Mr. Insole, chairman of selectors, presented himself for questioning. Mr. Griffith read the team for South Africa in alphabetical order and it was not until he got to Knott that the penny dropped and the Press realised D'Oliveira was not in the side. Then there was a mad scramble by some through the door to get the news flashed over the air.

Asked about the non-selection of D'Oliveira, Mr. Insole gulped, said, 'Uh, well,' paused, and then went into a long and involved explanation. I noted several things about the D'Oliveira case—particularly how one or two played politics in their writings when accusing others of exactly the same thing—but, knowing South Africa well and the general situation there, I found it none of my business and refrained from asking Mr. Insole questions that might have been asked. Generally, I found it more than strange that selectors should present themselves for questioning on their actions. I can imagine what Sir Donald Bradman would say if anybody asked him for *HIS* reasons. But the oddest thing of all in this distressing imbroglio was the incredible demand by one who has had a long cricket career, that the way the selectors voted on D'Oliveira should be made known to their various counties so that members would then know how to vote on their selectors. A crazy world, indeed!

I know South Africa well and think that the South African Government would have accepted D'Oliveira had they been sure that the tour would have gone off, in his presence, with no incidents, but many of those who so strongly rushed into print with virulent attacks on all and sundry in the D'Oliveira case showed little cognisance of a political situation that was bound to arise in certain circumstances and which would have been exploited by some who never saw a cricket ball bowled. Nor did many voluble critics show much knowledge of the realities of South African life. One can like or dislike South Africa and its ways, but the one who pretends that any activity is inseparable from politics in most countries these days is a political innocent. It was the 'innocents' who got most publicity in the D'Oliveira affair.

So 1968 ended with the best string of young batsmen in the world, the South Africans, forced into inactivity and because, however inadvertently, of a cricketer that the South Africans had greatly aided in pursuing his career in England. On how slender a thread, at times, hangs destiny. Had Barry Jarman held a catch from D'Oliveira at The Oval when he was 31— he made 158—the hullabulloo would never have arisen, nor would it if Roger Prideaux had not developed pneumonia on the eve of the match and let D'Oliveira into the side.

If I could see little merit in the all-round batting and bowling ability of the Australians, I must not fail to pay tribute to their fielding. In agility, in throwing, I think it was the best international team in the field I have seen. Against that, has to be set the poor record at The Oval when catch after catch went down, but The Oval is a notoriously difficult ground on which to make catches. The background of the flats there makes it very hard to judge a ball in the air and I think it will be found that more Test catches are dropped at The Oval than on any other Test field.

I must, too, warmly acknowledge the very good batting of Redpath and Chappell. Redpath was an interesting study. On the preceding tour he made a glorious century against Oxford at the Parks and one thought he would move on to a very high niche in Australian cricket. Then he became bogged down in his crease to off-spin bowling and there were early signs in 1968 that the same fate would befall him. Of a sudden, however, he sent a message to his feet and they began to twinkle and Redpath emerged once again into near-greatness. It was footwork that made Bradman great— among other things—and footwork is the basis of good batting. One or two other Australians began to copy some Englishmen in poking their front pad at the ball—one of the ugliest sights in cricket. Yet the further this tour progressed, and on so many dubious pitches, Redpath became a model to others in his footwork.

Chappell, too, came on apace. He had breeding in his cricket—from grandfather Vic Richardson—and I do believe his batting jumped ahead immediately he decided that he would stand up straighter in his stance. He, too, forsook somewhat the dominance of his lower hand in his strokes— what a wonderful lesson golf teaches in the importance of the top hand in swinging a club! And the more the tour progressed the more he drove with power. Some day, I hope, he will take his hands higher up the handle and then we really will see something memorable from this cricketer who, like V.Y.R., is full of guts.

One very good book emerged this summer and that was by my *Sunday Times* colleague, Ian Peebles. It did not get the prominence it deserved. It had not the hot meat of the several current controversies yet it dealt with throwing which, several years back, gave us cricket's most bitter controversy, once inducing the hurried presence at Lord's, specially summoned from Australia, of Sir Donald Bradman and Mr. W. J. Dowling. Peebles called his book *Straight from the Shoulder*. It is, by far, the best book, *the* definitive book, written on the subject. Peebles delved deep and backed his case with some surprising photographs. I see no argument against his logical case that the arm, when it reaches the level of the shoulder in the delivery action, shall not be bent until the ball is delivered. This cuts away all the verbiage and all the doubt. Why officialdom dallies in accepting the Peebles law is beyond my comprehension. This book kills throwing for all time.

AND GILLIGAN LED THEM OUT [1970]

BY ROWLAND RYDER

One of the most extraordinary essays ever published in the almanack turned up in 1970. The title's biblical overtones should have sounded warning bells for those readers who naturally assumed they were about to be entertained by a sentimental reminiscent sketch of Arthur Gilligan's long-gone cricketing days. Instead, the piece, by Rowland Ryder, proved to be a blatant propaganda exercise on behalf of the Church of England, showing that cricket and Christianity, being so inextricably intertwined, it was impossible to know where one ended and the other began. In an attempt to justify this astonishing tomfoolery, Ryder displayed a few testimonials from players who subscribed to it, no faint hint of salvation being offered to the likes of Asif Iqbal, Majid Khan, Younis Ahmed, Mushtaq Mohammad or Farokh Engineer, all of whom had for some time been performing in the County championship without noticeably lowering the ethical tone of the proceedings.

In truth, Ryder's view had once been fashionable, but not for generations. There had indeed been a time when the well-intentioned English gentleman-cricketer, combining presumption with imbecility, had assumed a symbiotic relationship between Christ and the Captain of the Eleven. L. C. B. Seaman, one of the more perceptive of modern imperial historians, wrote in Victorian England, that:

> Cricket was associated with religion: just as freemasons referred to God as the Great Architect of the Universe, young cricketers were taught to think of Him as the One Great Scorer and almost to regard a Straight Bat as second in religious symbolism to the Cross of Jesus.

One cricketer who certainly believed all this was the Cambridge, Middlesex and England missionary C. T. Studd, who, after disappearing from the first-class game in order to convert the indigenous population of Africa to his opinions, built a church in the jungle whose aisle measured exactly twenty-two yards, thoughtlessly leaving the Deity no room for a run-up. That sesquipedalian oddball Albert Knight used to ease the pain of opening the batting for Leicestershire and England by praying for God's assistance before facing his first ball. Walter Brearley, who opened the bowling for Lancashire without, it may be said, benefit of clergy, regarded this as cheating and complained of it to the M.C.C. It is hard to know which of the two men betrayed the more uproarious gullibility: Knight, who assumed that God cared a fig for batting averages, or Brearley, who evidently believed He cared enough to assist the batsman. And then there was Neville Cardus, who so relished the remark of the Yorkshire professional Ted Wainwright regarding Ranjitsinhji's batting style: ''E never played a Christian stroke.'

But anecdotage is one thing, solemn sermonising quite another. It might have been more redolent of the Christian spirit had the editor commissioned a twin essay by some devout atheist, in which the writer might have shown how Christianity had mitigated the England bowling tactics in the winter of 1932–33, had tempered the tendency of Ian Chappell's Australians to go sledging, had influenced the conduct of the Yorkshire committee in withholding from its greatest player and finest captain the leadership of the side. The absurdity of Ryder's premise is doubly surprising in view of the excellent form he had shown in previous editions of the almanack. In 1968 he had contributed an eminently readable essay called 'Warwickshire the Unpredictable'. Now, having succeeded within the span of a few pages in insulting the majority of the cricketing members of the Commonwealth, he might well have preferred as his title, 'Ryder the Ecumenical'.

On Saturday, Monday and Tuesday, May 17, 19 and 20, 1924, Warwickshire played Sussex at Edgbaston, and won what was very nearly a rain-ruined match by nine wickets. They were lucky to get a result. Warwickshire made 201 in reply to Sussex's 120, but there was only an hour and half's play on the Monday, and no play before 3.30 on the third day: 'Sussex had to bat under difficult conditions on Tuesday afternoon', says *Wisden*, 'the sun shining down on a wicket drenched by rain on the previous evening'.

Sussex soon lost seven wickets in their second innings, but thanks to Col. A. C. Watson, who made a blistering 32 in less than no time, they eventually made 94, leaving Warwickshire 14 to win with nearly an hour left for play.

But rain, which was never far away from Edgbaston in the early summer of 1924, returned at the end of the Sussex innings, and within a minute of the players reaching the pavilion it was pouring with rain. A hundred or so bedraggled spectators glared at the heavens in frustration; about fifty of them left the ground. There could be no play now, that was obvious; nonetheless, some fifty of us stayed on, hoping for a miracle to happen. A miracle *did* happen. Suddenly, the tolling of the pavilion bell was heard— we looked at one another in astonishment and faintly flickering hope; surely it was a mistake?—and the rain came down more heavily. But there was no mistake. The umpires came out, and behind them, laughing and chatting as they threw the ball to one another, for all the world as though they were about to start a homely knock-about on some sun-drenched Sussex hay meadow, came Gilligan and his men—his own brother A.H.H., Col. A. C. Watson, A. J. Holmes, J. K. Mathews, E. H. Bowley, George Cox, Tommy Cook, H. E. Roberts, W. Cornford, and—the knowledge-able said he would one day play for England—a fast-medium bowler named Maurice Tate.

Warwickshire lost one wicket for eight runs in six overs from Gilligan and Tate; the former then put on his picnic bowlers and the match was over. The Sussex team returned to the pavilion with their heads high. They were soaked to the skin, but there was sunshine in their smiles. The spectators rose to them—all fifty of us. 'Well played, Mr. Gilligan,' called a voice in a rich Birmingham accent. We buttoned up our mackintoshes and went home in the never-ending rain, and warmed by the sunshine of Sussex.

By the middle of June it had actually stopped raining, and Tate and Gilligan were back at Edgbaston. They skittled out South Africa for 30 in the first Test Match; Gilligan took six for 7 and Tate four for 12—was this achievement a reward from providence?

Gilligan's gesture at Edgbaston was typical of a great many cricket teams, whatever their standard; typical of cricket. It also seems to be an example of something more than mere sportsmanship, an example of Christianity itself. Sporting gestures are still—thank heaven!—commonplace on the cricket field, but there was more to it in this Warwickshire-Sussex match of 1924. Gilligan had obviously said to his team that Warwickshire deserved to win, and, rain or no rain, Sussex should give them the chance: it is obvious, too, that he had full support from his side. 'I always like to think that cricket and Christianity are closely allied', he wrote (October 18, 1968) in a letter referring to this particular match.

Another Sussex and England captain, E. R. Dexter, discussed the subject of cricket and Christianity with Colin Cowdrey in a wireless broadcast ('Subject for Sunday', April 1968). Dexter's own view is that Christianity comes into the actual playing of cricket—literally into batting and bowling: 'I feel that Christ has an opinion about the use of bouncers and how much you appeal to the umpire, and whether you walk when you've hit it, and whether you are a selfish or an unselfish player.' He quoted John Arlott's statement: 'If you are to understand Colin Cowdrey you have to understand Colin Cowdrey's Christian faith and the way it affects his life.'

Cowdrey himself goes deeply into the subject: 'I was in some state of confusion on leaving Oxford as to whether one was justified in giving one's life to cricket. One of the tenets of the whole Christian faith is that life is a service, and could one honestly justify standing at first slip for two days of a Test Match and touching the ball three times and then making nought and one and taking a week over it, and then in the evenings having the good fortune to meet with gifted people in other walks of life—perhaps a gifted surgeon who had just saved three lives and worked nine hours a day sweating flesh and blood in a tremendous life of service.' Cowdrey recounted that he went to see Cuthbert Bardsley, the present Bishop of Coventry, who was then Bishop of Croydon, for advice. 'One of the things he did say was that this [cricketing ability] surely must be one of the gifts that I'd been given, and that if I were to play cricket for a certain number of years then I must give myself a hundred per cent to it.'

Cowdrey also made this vividly evocative statement: 'Batting in a Test Match, the build-up, the waiting for two or three hours at Melbourne, I think that's a picture which comes to mind with 70,000 Australians clamouring for an English wicket, or perhaps two or three wickets fall quickly and you are not the next one in, but the next after that, and the tension is built up, the radio's on in the home and you know that 20 million at home are listening in. . . . One is terribly alone. And I think these are the moments when one desperately needs this abiding Christian faith which brings, I think, a mastery of oneself . . . without that feeling I think you are desperately on your own. I think you are in the jungle.'

The Right Reverend David Sheppard, of Sussex and England, for twelve years Warden of the Mayflower Family Centre and now Bishop of Woolwich wrote (1961): 'I have often been asked if religion and cricket can mix. Brian Booth, one of Australia's great batsmen, was taken to task by a newspaper for saying that God wielded his bat for him. I believe that by leaving out other things he said at the same time they made this appear to mean something he did not intend. Brian is a great friend of mine and we have discussed this at length. Certainly as a Christian he believes, and I believe, that health, strength, quickness of eye, all come from God. Success comes from God—and so too can failure. If I say my prayers faithfully this is no guarantee that I shall make a hundred next time I go in to bat. I may make a duck. But I can make duck or hundred to the glory of God—by the way I accept success or failure.'*

Ted Dexter feels the same: 'Cricket, perhaps more than any other game, has its ups and downs for the individual,' he writes (October 17, 1968). 'A hundred one day, nought the next. A brilliant catch is followed by dropping a "dolly". Keeping a sense of proportion and a level head is half the battle and I find that it helps to remember Christ in these separate moments of elation and distress.'

Returning to David Sheppard, it is interesting to learn that as a cricketer he found himself talking about the Christian faith with other cricketers. These were not only convinced Christians, like Brian Booth, Colin Cowdrey and John Dewes, but many who had half a faith or none, but wanted to see what Christianity had to say to their situation.

I asked him now that he is Bishop of Woolwich what he has learned from his cricketing years; 'It was through cricket that I began the process of learning to respect other men for what they are and not for the colour of their skin or for the school they went to. Living for the last fourteen years in inner London, Islington, Canning Town and now Peckham, that process has been accelerated. I hope that I have learnt much more to meet all people on level terms. More than ever I believe that Christ calls in question all our attitudes and actions. If God is the God of all the earth, there can be no dividing our life into compartments which we label "sacred" and "secular".'

Another cricketing clergyman—of a previous generation—is the Reverend Canon J. H. Parsons, MC., Hon.C.F., who was born in 1890 and was a member of the Warwickshire championship side of 1911. He joined the Warwickshire Yeomanry as a Trooper in August 1914, served in Egypt, Gallipoli and Salonika, took part in the last charge ever made by a British cavalry unit, played for the Players against the Gentlemen and for the Gentlemen against the Players; scored 39 centuries in first-class cricket, hit four 6's in succession against the West Indies (1928), became ordained in 1929, as a Senior Chaplain he was torpedoed in the Second World War, arrived at last on land, he gave Holy Communion to 1,200 German P.O.W.'s. At the age of 70 he played against Solihull School—and scored 65 in 45 minutes.

'I like to look back on the early days of cricket,' he writes, 'to the days when it first started on the village greens of this lovely England of ours, for

* *Parson's Pitch*, by David Sheppard. Hodder and Stoughton.

that is where it undoubtedly started, later it spread to the Rector's Glebe and the Squire's Home Meadow, and as someone once said 'Cricket was invented by gentlemen, gentlemen born in a cottage as well as in a castle.' One has only to go back within one's own lifetime to remember village cricket teams usually had the Rector or Vicar of the Parish playing, and in long vacation his sons home from school and the University also joining in. The church was very much to the forefront of cricket in those days, and it is my firm conviction that on those old village greens of England the great principles of the Christian religion were inculcated into the great national game of cricket.

'Those of us who played County cricket at the beginning of this century were privileged to experience cricket as it should be played, which gave tremendous enjoyment both to those who played and to those who watched.

'The most remarkable thing about all that was the complete absence of fuss about rules and regulations. The game was played by people who were only concerned with playing the game according to the principles of the game.

'That is obviously not so today. In fact it appears to be all a question of what new rules and regulations can be introduced to bring "life" back to the game. What we have to relearn, both in our cricket and our Christianity is how to hit straight sixes and revive the great principles of life, as laid down by Christ.'

Cricket, of course, like *Punch*, is not what it was: it never has been. We see cricket today and sigh for the days of Hobbs and Sutcliffe, of Tate and Gilligan; in the 1920s we told each other that the game had sadly deteriorated since 1902, and we talked of Trumper and Noble, and Jessop and Fry and Ranji—and so on, working backwards, to the time of the Hambledon men. But though the implements and the rules of cricket have changed, I believe that, in general, the attitude of cricketers has always been very much the same, so that the expression 'It isn't cricket'—with its obvious implications—has become part of the language. The cricketer 'must be cool-tempered, and in the best sense of the term, MANLY, for he must be able to endure fatigue, and to make light of pain', wrote Charles Cowden Clarke in his introduction to John Nyren's classic, *The Young Cricketer's Tutor*, and isn't what he said in 1833 very similar to what Cowdrey and Dexter and Sheppard have told us today?

Christianity and good sportsmanship cannot be equated; on the other hand it is difficult to draw a dividing line. Perhaps it is fair to say that whereas all good sportsmanship has its roots in Christian behaviour, the intention behind an action—and the attendant circumstances—is more important than the action itself. Here are some incidents connected with the cricket field that are not only examples of good sportsmanship but can also be acclaimed as instances of Christian behaviour.

H. L. Higgins, playing for Worcestershire v. Somerset, was 'on a pair' in his first county match, in 1920. John Daniell, the Somerset captain, said to him: 'Hit one to me and run.' H. L. Higgins did so, and John Daniell successfully fumbled the ball. David Sheppard was in a similar position in *his* first county match playing for Sussex v. Leicestershire in 1949. 'Les Berry, the Leicestershire captain, said, "There'll be a run for you on the off-side if you want it." I said, "Thank you very much." All the fielders went back a few yards so that I could push an easy single.' Colin Cowdrey recalls a similar incident: 'When the West Indies Test batsman, George Headley, was recalled from England in 1953/4 to make a comeback against Len Hutton's M.C.C. team, he was cheered all the way to the wicket on his return appearance in Test cricket. Tony Lock was the bowler. Len Hutton pushed the cover field back, asking Tony Lock to bowl a half volley, wide of the off stump, so as to give Headley one run off the mark. This spontaneous action was warmly appreciated by the crowd.'

The cricketer often observes the spirit rather than the letter of the law. H. L. Higgins found himself again in luck, this time against Gloucestershire. 'After playing forward and missing a ball outside my off stump, and lifting my back foot to re-take my stance, I heard Col. Robinson [the Gloucestershire captain] say, "Don't lift your foot until I have returned the ball, or I shall *have* to stump you".'

A superb example of this kind of incident took place in the England v. Australia Test at Nottingham in 1964.

'Just before the Duke of Edinburgh piloted his helicopter round the ground,' says *Wisden*, 'the Australians raised the biggest cheer of the day's cricket for a genuine act of sportsmanship. Grout could have run out Titmus when Boycott placed Hawke towards mid-on and both batsmen dashed for a quick single. Hawke dived for the ball and in the process knocked Titmus over from behind. Titmus was far from home when the ball landed in the wicket-keeper's gloves, but Grout let him reach the crease and England were credited with a single.' By a sad coincidence, Colin Cowdrey wrote about this gesture on the very day of the late Wally Grout's death, stating that he 'paused for a moment with his hand over the wicket and then threw the ball back to the bowler without removing the bails. It was a marvellous example of the true spirit of cricket.'

Playing on in the rain—as Gilligan did—so that a side that has deserved to win can actually do so, is another example of a Christian attitude being part of cricket. Colin Cowdrey recalls a similar occasion during Peter May's M.C.C. tour to the West Indies in 1959–60, when the team were outplayed by Barbados, who needed 58 to win in their second innings. 'With twenty runs to make it was a downpour, but Peter May and I felt that their victory had been deserved and we stayed out in conditions where one would have been justified in coming off.'

These incidents do not always follow stock patterns, there is an infinite variety. I shall never forget the occasion when C. L. Vincent, the South African Test player, was caught by T. Collin of Warwickshire, at Edgbaston. Vincent had made a terrific cover drive, Collin had managed to half stop it, the ball flew into the air, and Collin caught it as it fell, with his hands behind his back! It was C. L. Vincent, half-way down the pitch, who put down his bat, and led the applause.

And a story I love is that of Fleetwood-Smith showing a special, secret grip, I think, to Verity. When one of his team mates suggested that such actions wouldn't do Australia any good, Fleetwood-Smith replied simply 'Art is universal.'

But cricket isn't always fun. 'It was in the last Test match of the M.C.C. tour of West Indies in 1934–35,' writes R. E. S. Wyatt, 'that I was hit in the jaw by a ball from Martindale. It was not a bouncer but was short of a length and lifted quickly. I sustained a double compound fracture of the jaw (actually broken in four places). . . . I do remember that the day I was injured I was quite unable to speak and was supposed to be replying to a toast at an official dinner. Errol Holmes deputised for me and I sent a message to Martindale emphasising that it was a fair ball and that I attached no blame to him and had the greatest respect for him as a cricketer. This message, I was told by Errol, brought tears to his eyes.' A few days later Wyatt was taken straight from hospital to the boat at Port Antonio: Martindale was there to see him off.

'The Church and the Game have been close down the years', writes Leslie Deakins, the Warwickshire secretary; there is plenty of evidence to prove his words. The Reverend James Pycroft spent sixteen years of research (1835–1851) in compiling his classic *The Cricket Field*, thus rescuing much of the early history of the game from oblivion, and it was he and Bishop Ryle who in 1836 revived the Oxford and Cambridge match. Famous cricketing families like the Lyttletons and the Studds have been active in the cause of Christianity: the game is charged with the Christian ethos.

The examples quoted in this article are examples only—any cricket lover will be able to think of plenty more—but they are, I think, typical of the attitude that has pervaded the game from the time of John Nyren to the present day.

THE MIDWINTER FILE [1971]

BY GRAHAME PARKER

Most essays in the almanack make interesting reading, but occasionally one turns up which, in addition to being diverting, constitutes a priceless addition to the stockpot of the game's history. Such a contribution appeared in the 1971 edition, when the then secretary of the Gloucestershire County Cricket Club, having access to documents unseen by the public eye for almost a century, was able to tell one of the most entertaining stories any lover of the game could desire. The story had everything: excitement, surprise, great humour, the distance in time which lends enchantment, and most important of all, two great men at the heart of it.

Any account of any sequence of events which casts fresh light on the figure of that most neglected of all the eminent Victorians, W. G. Grace, is to be welcomed with eager arms. To describe the Doctor as neglected may sound perverse to those within the fold of cricket, but so far as the world at large is concerned, less is known about him than any of his contemporaries. While we know enough, and perhaps more than enough about the private lives of Gladstone and Disraeli, Tennyson and Browning, Darwin and General Booth, we remain in the dark about Grace's home life, his favourite foods, his standing as a lover, husband, father. We know only a few scraps about his career as a doctor, nothing at all about his daily routine when he wasn't playing cricket—for all of which reasons, a rounded biography of the man remains an impossibility. At least in the 1971 essay we see him at close quarters, embroiled in a huge row, writing letters and struggling to bring his powers of diplomacy to bear on a problem which may have seemed serious at the time to those involved in it, but which, to posterity, represents one of the very best joke-episodes in cricket history.

But at least Grace is celebrated. The figure of William Evans Midwinter (1853–1890) is, in stark contrast, an ambivalent one, even though he invented, singlehanded, one of the most brilliant ploys ever accredited to any cricketing thinker. The incidents described by Parker are connected only tenuously to Midwinter's one moment of blinding perception, which was that there is no reason for that lugubrious concept, the last day of the season, ever to come about. Two generations before English county cricket became the receptacle for the great cricketers from other countries, Midwinter turned himself into the world's first commuting cricketer. And, being the first, his status remained necessarily undefined. Although more than a century has now passed since he established his awesome record, there has never been, nor ever will be, the slightest chance that anyone will equal it; the reader of the almanacks of the present day can look up the 'Records' section and see for himself that while there have been a few players who represented two different Test countries, there is nobody who has remotely aspired to the riotous triumphs of Midwinter, the only man ever to play for Australia against England, then for England against Australia, and then for Australia once again against England. Of the serpentine nature of his temperament, of the bewilderment of the cricketing authorities of both countries, of the prominent role played in Midwinter's affairs by the Grace family, of Midwinter's place of honour as the first ever to commute between continents, there is much which remains to be said, but for the purposes of extracting full enjoyment from this memorable account of a fragment of ancient history, all the reader needs to grasp are the following facts.

That Midwinter, an authentic Gloucestershire man, born in the Forest of Dean, emigrated to Australia with his family when he was ten years old; that W. G. Grace, on the famous honeymoon tour of 1873–74 to Australia, played against Midwinter and was much impressed by two aspects of the case, his all-round ability and his impeccable bona fides as a Gloucestershire man; that in 1877 Midwinter arrived in England and became a regular member of the Gloucestershire side; that in 1878 a party of Australian tourists arrived in England; that among the tourists selected by them was

Midwinter; and that Midwinter, thereby obligated to two paymasters at the same time, soon ran himself into the ridiculous impasse which he must surely have known was inevitable.

The narrow puritanism of some writers on the game might impel them to dismiss the melodrama of Billy Midwinter's amazing career as being too remote to be much more than an old Victorian joke. If this is so, then the puritan lobby is wrong, because the figure of Midwinter raises issues still unresolved in the cricket world a century later, especially those two vexed questions, whether or not overseas international stars should be invited to enter the County Championship, and to what extent the professional cricketer ought to be allowed to be the captain of his own financial fate. There is one other quaint circumstance which qualifies the Midwinter fracas, not as a musty antiquarian legend, but as an event whose physical setting survived into the modern world. The first of the letters penned by the Australian manager was written at the Horse Shoe Hotel, in Tottenham Court Road, a huge hostelry which was still functioning even as Mr. Parker was compiling his essay. I crossed its threshold only once, in its very last days, when a pianist of my acquaintance dragged me up to its first-floor hall one sunny afternoon so that I could hear his latest composition. Knowing as I did of the great affairs which had once been conducted under its roof, I was too distracted by the thought of the anger of a long-dead colonial to pay much attention to the music. The Horse Shoe no longer functions, but the story of William Midwinter, of which the following episode is little more than a passade, remains as lively a proposition today as it was on that lost morning when cricket turned itself into a horse race.

W E. Midwinter has a unique place in cricket history. He was Gloucestershire's first full-time professional, was the only cricketer to have played for Australia and England in Test Matches against each other, eight for Australia and four for England, and the first of the inter-hemisphere cricket commuters.

This is a piece of research that grew out of a reference in Haygarth's Cricket Scores and Biographies, Volume XIV, page 24:—'He (Midwinter) was born in the Forest of Dean, near Cirencester.' Throughout the last months of 1968, and during 1969, this reference grew into a file of correspondence and information an inch thick. The primary qualification in the early days of County Cricket was by birth and I felt sure the geographical inaccuracy concealed another piece of 'Grace gamesmanship'. I was wrong.

The cricket record books report that William Evans Midwinter was born on June 19, 1842. While England is on his death certificate, and Cirencester on his marriage certificate, there is much confusion over his place of birth. He himself told W.G. he was born in a village near Cirencester, but claims have been as diverse as Yorkshire, Gloucester, Melbourne, Bendigo, as well as Haygarth's 'Cirencester in the Forest of Dean'. Perhaps we should not read too much into these nineteenth century inconsistencies. The details on his birth certificate are clear enough, 'born June 19, 1851 at St.

Briavels, Forest of Dean'. His father, William John Midwinter, Farm Bailiff, of Clays Lane End, near Coleford, and his mother, Rebecca Evans, a daughter of William Evans, a farmer of the Lower Meend, St. Briavels, were married at nearby St. Paul's Church, Parkend by the Rev. Henry Poole on October 13, 1849. His father was born at Chedworth, near Cirencester and his mother at St. Briavels.

Cirencester in the Cotswolds, 50 miles to the east of the Forest of Dean, is Midwinter country. Perhaps there was an itinerant streak in the father that was later to be strongly exhibited by the son, for there is no reference to William John Midwinter in the Forest censuses of 1841, 1851 and 1861.

We next hear of the Midwinters through a cricket reference to young William. They were in Australia at Sandhurst, present day Eaglehawk, on the Bendigo goldfields. The middle years of the last century saw much unemployment among the Forest of Dean coal miners, and many emigrated to the Colonies or tried their luck in gold rushes. Father Midwinter was first a gold miner and later a butcher.

William John Midwinter (38), gamekeeper, Rebecca Midwinter (36) and sons William (9), John (5) and daughter Jane (7), sailed from Liverpool on February 2, 1861 as unassisted passengers in the *Red Jacket*—2,035 tons. Her Master was William Billing, she carried a crew of 65, 216 passengers and a cargo of sundries. She arrived at Melbourne on April 24.

William grew into a tall, rough, athletic boy at Sandhurst, and began a lifelong association with H.F. (Harry) Boyle, who at 15 was already showing the cricket skill and organising ability that was to make him famous as an Australian cricketer and administrator. He was playing for Sandhurst and young 'Mid' for the California Gully School. Boyle formed a club of young cricketers at Sydney Flat, two miles from Sandhurst. There were only thirteen of them, but they cleared and levelled a patch of bush among the mine dumps, and it was here that Boyle, Midwinter and many other famous Victorians played their first cricket. The Midwinters lived five miles away at California Gully in a wooden, stone slab floored shack, separated from a piece of open ground by a stone wall. The boy helped his father on his butcher's rounds but they found time to practise together here and, as with the Graces in their Downend orchard, it was the dog who did most of the fielding! In the 1890s the area became a cricket ground, appropriately named Midwinter's Oval. The shack was still standing but had been demolished progressively for firewood. Even today some rough open ground still remains, much of it occupied by two tennis courts and bungalows.

There is an unverified report that when still quite young he made 256 in an innings. The first definite reference in his cricket career is the fact that during the 1864–65 season, young Midwinter left the Sydney Flat Cricket Club for Bendigo United and although only 13, held his place in the senior club. In 1870 the Carlton Cricket Club travelled the sixty miles to Bendigo and were so impressed with Midwinter and Boyle that they invited them to play in Melbourne. During the following season they both played in a single wicket match for the Bendigo VI that surprisingly defeated Charles Bannerman's New South Wales IV. In 1873 Midwinter's name first appeared with the Melbourne C.C.

W.G. took a team to Australia for the 1873–74 season. Although the party included the recently married Mrs. Grace and three other Gloucestershire cricketers, G. F. Grace, J. A. Bush and W. R. Gilbert, it could not have been a happy tour. Towards the end the Englishmen were extremely unpopular with the Australians, who felt they were being fleeced, particularly in payment to W.G. It was almost twenty years before he could be enticed back. Midwinter played against them twice. Before Christmas 1873, in a game at Melbourne that drew 40,000 spectators in three days, he was caught Bush, bowled Grace, for 7. It was the second match the following March, when amid great excitement, he bowled both W.G. and G. F. Grace, that no doubt activated W.G.'s shrewd and fertile imagination.

Midwinter played his first of nine inter-state games in 1875. He was now 6ft. 2½in. and 14 stone, a hard hitting batsman, a medium pace round arm spin bowler, a fine outfielder with a strong arm, one of the best quarter milers in Victoria and a fine shot and billiards player, variously nicknamed the Sandhurst Infant or the Bendigo Giant. He played in the first All Australia v. All England game in Melbourne during the James Lillywhite tour of 1876–77. Spofforth, the great Australian fast bowler, refused to play in the game because his usual wicket-keeper, W. L. Murdoch, had not been selected. Surprisingly England were defeated for the first time in an even-handed game against Australia. Haygarth blamed the travelling and the 'high living' to which the tourists were subjected, but Charles Bannerman's first innings, 165 not out, had set up the Australian victory. Midwinter's match analysis was 6 for 101. He had now proved he was an international cricketer and decided to try his luck in England.

There is some confusion over his first journey back to England. An article written in *Cricket*, January 27, 1891, just after his death, reports his arrival at Plymouth on Tuesday, May 5, 1877. The next day the ship disembarked at London and with a rough diamond friend, Denmark Jack, he was on his way to the Oval where W.G. was playing.

In fact he sailed from Melbourne on April 21, 1877 in the S.S. *Durham*, Master F. Anderson. She was one of a line of steam and sailing ships operated by Money Wigram & Sons of Blackwell Yard, London, and on this journey she carried 246 passengers, amongst whom is listed 'W. Midwinter, male, 25 years, cricketer, English'.

W.G. was probably expecting him, for he soon had him playing in his United South of England XI at Birmingham, Holbeck and Barrow-in-Furness. The Gloucestershire minutes of 1877 make no reference to his arrival with the County, nor do they record his departure in 1882. He played in the combined Yorkshire/Gloucestershire team which drew with a Rest of England XI at Lord's on July 17, but his first full Gloucestershire appearance was in one of the most famous games in the County's history when England were beaten at the Oval by five wickets. Midwinter's contribution was a significant 7 for 35 and 4 for 46 in the two innings. W.G. took him in hand and added a defensive dimension to his aggressive batting. This was prominently evident during the Yorkshire match later in the season, where he saved the day with a four-hour 68. A collection was taken during his innings and Mrs. Grace presented him with £15. This happened to be another of those Grace testimonial games. With brotherly solicitude, E.M. raised the gate charge from 6d. to 1/– without informing his committee. Later in the season Gloucestershire beat Nottinghamshire in one of the Cheltenham Festival games early on the third day. The County then played a local XI. With broomsticks they made 299, E. M. Grace 104, Midwinter 58, to which Cheltenham, using bats, replied with 50 for 2 before time ran out. The County had been Champions in 1876 and also again—for the last time since!—in 1877.

1878 saw the first Australian tour of England. They arrived with eleven players and picked up Midwinter in this country. He had already played for the United South of England, an England XI and England v. M.C.C. before joining the Australians at Trent Bridge on May 20. They lost by an innings and 14 runs but he batted through their second innings for 16 not out in two and a half hours. The next game was the first Australian visit to Lord's. It was completed in 105 runs between 12 and 6.20 p.m. on the first day! M.C.C. 33 and 19, Australia 41 and 12 for 1. Midwinter was top scorer with 10.

The Australian press reports of a following game against the Gentlemen at Princes, record an interesting comment that the 'so-called Gentlemen Cricketers, Messrs. W. G. Grace and W. R. Gilbert received the sum of £60 for their services, and when Mr. Conway raised an objection to it, it was asserted that W. G. Grace, G. F. Grace and W. R. Gilbert were invariably paid for playing'.

And so we come to a fateful day. On Monday, June 20 the Australians were playing at Lord's. They had lost the toss and had been put in to bat. Their opening pair, Bannerman and Midwinter, were padding up, unaware that a storm was approaching them through the cloudless summer sky. On the other side of London at the Oval, W. G. Grace had found his Gloucestershire team a man short. The Champion, 6ft 2in., wicketkeeper J.A. Bush, 6ft 2½in. and the Coroner, E. M. Grace, 5ft 8in.—to do the talking no doubt—burst into Lord's, 'persuaded' Midwinter he should be playing for Gloucestershire, bundled him into the waiting carriage and were gone. Much later Midwinter regretted what had been done, but before they had reached the Edgware Road he must have wondered how fate had dropped him into that hot, uncomfortable seat. The dust had hardly settled in the St. John's Wood Road when an Australian posse set off in pursuit of the Gloucestershire hijackers. In the posse were the Australian Manager, John Conway, Midwinter's friend, Harry Boyle and David Gregory, the captain. An 'unhappy altercation' took place at the Oval gates where W.G. in front of bystanders, called the Australians 'a damn lot of sneaks'.

The Australians were deeply hurt. Letters of increasing acidity passed between them and the County during the following weeks. The first was despatched by John Conway on June 22 from the Horse Shoe Hotel, Tottenham Court Road, and was read at the Gloucestershire Committee meeting of July 1: 'Unless Mr. W. G. Grace apologises for his insulting behaviour . . . we shall be compelled to erase the Gloucestershire fixture from our programme'. The Committee drafted a reply regretting this fact, but added 'Mr. W. G. Grace did not for a moment intend his remarks to apply to Mr. Conway and Mr. Boyle'. This brought a stinging reply from David Gregory at the Albion Hotel, Manchester. They still refused to play at Bristol. 'I may state that he (W.G.) publicly insulted the whole of the Australian Eleven in most unmistakable language'. He now introduced for the first time the initial cause of the storm '. . . moreover we are averse to meeting Midwinter, whose defection from us we regard as a breach of faith'.

The long Gloucestershire reply tried to spread some oil on the disturbed waters, but set out their version of the Midwinter affair:—

Midwinter is a Gloucestershire man, he returned to England last year and played in all the matches which were played by Gloucestershire after his arrival in England. This year he has already played in the Colts match at Bedminster and had promised Mr. Grace to play in all our County matches. This engagement of his was well known all over England, and can hardly fail to have been known to you. Mr. Bush discussed this with Mr. Conway at Princes on Monday and Tuesday, the 17th and 18th of June. With the knowledge of Midwinter's engagement staring you in the face you attempted to induce him to break his promise, desert his County, and play for you by offering him a much larger sum than we could afford to pay him. Such proceedings are to say the least uncommon and go far, in our judgment, to palliate Mr. Grace's stormy language at the Oval.

The Australians would not leave it there. In a letter from Leicester dated July 15, David Gregory still refused to bring his team to Bristol, but was 'willing to overlook Midwinter's defection though they consider they have first claim to him, as before he came to England he asked Mr. Conway to keep a place for him in the team. We started from Australia relying upon his joining us.'

E. M. Grace, as Secretary, dutifully transcribed all those letters in the Minutes Book, but the page continuing W.G.'s eventual letter of apology contains only the heading 'Mr. W. G. Grace wrote a letter apologising to David Gregory and the Australians'! After a long search the contents of this letter came to light in an Australian report of the tour:-

The Cottage,
Kingswood Hill,
Bristol.
July 21st.

Dear Sir,
    I am sorry that my former expression of regret to the Australian

cricketers has not been considered satisfactory. Under the circumstances, and without going further into the matter, I wish to let by-gones be by-gones. I apologise again, and express my extreme regret to Conway, Boyle and yourself, and through you to the Australian cricketers, that in the excitement of the moment I should have made use of unparliamentary language to Mr. Conway. I can do no more but assure you that you will meet a hearty welcome and a good ground at Clifton.

Yours truly,
W. G. Grace.

The matter closed with W.G.'s apology. The Australians received the warmest hospitality at Bristol. Midwinter did not play against them, he had a split thumb. The Australians, with Spofforth in full blast, thrashed the County. It was Gloucestershire's first ever defeat on a home ground.

Midwinter was paid £56 for his seven games in 1878. The Gloucestershire Minutes report that he was perfectly satisfied with this arrangement. He played in all the 1879 games at the same rate of £8 a match. He had the chance of the Middlesex or Lancashire game at Clifton for his benefit and unluckily chose the latter, which was ruined by rain. It was proposed he should receive £100 as some compensation for his ruined benefit. An amendment was carried that he should receive a further £100 at the end of the 1883 season. He did not accept the bait. E.M.G. had to send this sharp reminder:—

Dear Sir,

The Committee are very much surprised and annoyed that you have taken no notice of my letter to you in which I said the Committee had passed the following resolution:—

'That W. Midwinter be paid the sum of £100 at the end of the season and £100 at the end of 1883 provided he plays for Gloucestershire when required to do so.'

I am, yours faithfully,
Edward Mills Grace.

The reply came two days later:—

Prince of Wales Hotel.
31st May 1880.

To the Committee of the Gloucestershire County Cricket Club.

Gentlemen,

I beg to return you my sincere thanks for the very liberal sum of money you have kindly agreed to give me, and also to thank the Gentlemen of Gloucester C.C.C. for the very kind treatment I have received from them since I have had the honour of playing for them.

Your obedient servant,
W. Midwinter.

In 1880 he joined the M.C.C. staff of bowlers at Lord's. During this season he made his highest score, 103, and only century, for Gloucestershire against Surrey at Cheltenham. The Australians were again in this country and he played against them at Clifton.

He commuted between England and Australia from 1880–1882 to play six successive seasons of cricket. After completing the 1880 season for the County he returned to Australia. He sailed from London on September 29, in the *Lusitania*. The passenger list refers to him as W. Midwinter, 29 years. He travelled back to England in the same ship from Melbourne, April 26 1881, now listed as W. Midwinter, Gent. He was in Shaw's 1881–82 England tour of Australia and played in four Tests. Back to England for 1882, he suddenly gave up his M.C.C. bowling appointment although he had recently taken part in a quite remarkable stand for the M.C.C. Club and Ground against Leicestershire. During his stay at the wicket the score rose from 19 for two to 472 for three in five and a half hours. He scored 187 and Barnes 266 and it is reported tht he never once lost count of their joint scores. At the end of 1882 he played his last game for Gloucestershire at Clifton against—the Australians! He returned home with Murdoch's triumphant Ashes team and stood umpire for them in their games in the United States.

On his arrival home he claimed he had ceased to be a professional cricketer and 'considered himself an Australian to the heart's core' and 'objected to being called an Anglo Australian'. These patriotic sentiments failed to impress the hard-hearted Australian critics and Censor in the *Sydney Mail* asked:— 'Are the cricketers of the Colony, and especially those of Victoria, to submit to another season of vagueness from this very slippery cricketer? One day he is an Australian and the next day an English player.' All was quickly forgiven and he was soon in action for Australia against the Hon. Ivo Bligh's 1882–83 touring team. In March 1883 he was presented with a gold watch for his 92 not out for Victoria against England at Melbourne.

He returned to England with the Australians in 1884, played for them in three Tests and against Gloucestershire at Clifton and Cheltenham, on both occasions bowled out by his old friend, Woof. He was to play two more Tests for Australia against Arthur Shrewsbury's team in 1886–87. In all he played eight Tests for Australia against England and four for England against Australia.

After six years of association with the Gloucestershire amateurs it was a more refined Midwinter who finally returned to Australia than the one who had set out so hopefully in 1877.

He married Elizabeth Frances McLaughlan at St. Peter's Church, Melbourne, on June 4, 1883. Her father, a carrier from Paisley, Scotland, and her mother Mary Dowling of Kilkenny, Ireland, were married at Kyneton, Victoria, January 13, 1857.

After an unsuccessful attempt at stockbroking, he became landlord of the Clyde Hotel, which still stands at the corner of Elgin and Cadogan Streets in Melbourne. Mr. Christopher McCaffin, now 92, remembers as a boy being chased away from the horse drinking trough by the tall, fair-haired Billy Midwinter. He continued to take an active part in the affairs of the Carlton Club, setting a fine example to the Club's young cricketers.

His keen perception and his humorous entertaining conversation were held in high esteem. He was invited to tour England with the 1888 team, but declined on business grounds. He had moved to the Victoria, Bourke Street, but his eyesight was beginning to fail and he retired from active cricket.

The family bereavements that were to break his heart struck whilst they were living at the Victoria. First his ten month old daughter, Elsie, died of pneumonia on November 22, 1888; next, August 23, 1889, his wife Elizabeth, of apoplexy and, finally, on November 2, three year old Albert Ernest.

He loved his family dearly and these sudden domestic tragedies were more than he could bear. In June 1890, whilst staying with his sister and brother-in-law, Mr. and Mrs. H. Hicks, at Sandhurst, he became so violent that he was removed to the Bendigo Hospital and, on August 14, to the Kew Asylum in Melbourne. He became paralysed from the waist down. Happily one of his brief periods of consciousness on November 21 coincided with a visit from his old friend Harry Boyle, on his return from the Australian 1890 tour of England. He recognised him and spoke admiringly of W.G., Arthur Shrewsbury and of Woof. He was delighted to hear that his old County had twice beaten Nottinghamshire. He died at 11 a.m. on Wednesday, December 3, 1890, aged 39. The funeral took place on Friday, December 5, attended by a great many cricketers and sportsmen among whom was a Gloucestershire representative, W. O. Tonge, who had played with Midwinter in two County matches at Clifton College during August 1880.

He was buried in the Roman Catholic compound of Melbourne General Cemetery beside his wife and children. The grave, No. L286, is difficult to find, it has no tombstone and the area surrounding it is untended.

The last word, as the first, belongs to Haygarth, in his biography of Midwinter, Vol. XIV:- 'May the death of no other cricketer who has taken part in great matches be like his!'

RESHAPING LANCASHIRE CRICKET [1971]

BY JOHN KAY

The publication of 'The Midwinter File' alone qualifies the 1971 almanack as one of the best of the post-war period, but it was only the first among several glories whose corporate effect was to transform the edition into something which would surely have delighted the Pardon brothers, a good read. There was a useful summary of the career of Peter May, a memorable obituary of Herbert Strudwick by Neville Cardus (see 'The Wisden Papers of Neville

Cardus'), an appreciation of Syd Buller by someone who might be defined as his long-standing colleague, Frank Lee, and at least three longer essays deserving of a place in any anthology. The ground they covered could hardly have been more widely dispersed; a county history, a sober analysis of the South African game of political cricket and a riotous fragment of arcana concerning what its author defines as 'the dreaded Cypher'.

The county history concerns the affairs of Lancashire, a club which was currently enjoying a revival of fortune, especially in the new-fangled one-day game. If there is a modern hero of the history it is certainly Jack Bond, the veteran captain of the county side who welded the eleven into a formidable organisation which made a strong bid for the championship and made itself into something of a specialist team when it came to the limited-overs tournaments. Among the entrancing lights cast on the backstage realities of the county game is the mention of Bond's attitude to statistics. The essay was written by the same John Kay who had played such a vital hand in the D'Oliveira Affair.

ALTHOUGH the Lancashire County Cricket Club was not officially born until 1864 there are plenty of records to prove that cricket had been played at county level in the earlier days of the century and in 1842 the Manchester Cricket Club, the forerunner of the county club itself, sent a side to Lord's to play the Gentlemen of the M.C.C. They were overwhelmed and gave up the match when the opposition reached 200 after tumbling their visitors out for 59 in the first innings. A bad start—but no deterrent to the future of a club that has been a power in the cricketing world since the beginning of the twentieth century, some eighty years after the formation of the Manchester Club whose part in formulating the Lancashire side was marked by the original title: The Lancashire County and Manchester Cricket Club, a description maintained until midway through the 1950s when the Manchester Club as such ceased to exist and Lancashire took overall command.

ALL-ENGLAND BEATEN

Lancastrians could look with pride upon the early achievements of a club that was eventually to become the county one. In 1844 the club met and defeated an all-Yorkshire XI and later an All-England side led by the redoubtable George Parr and from 1849 until the official formation of the club, fifteen years later, there were regular matches against Yorkshire before the club moved to its present ground at Old Trafford, which was to become an historic cricketing venue and the scene of many stirring Test Matches. When the lease was officially signed at an agreed purchase price of £1,100 it was pointed out, with some degree of pride, that 'underneath the pavilion is an excellent wine cellar'. Old Trafford is now much changed and the wine cellar has been put to other uses but it remains the home of the Lancashire County Cricket Club and has played a memorable part in cricket history at both test and county level.

A club that had its beginnings, first in Salford and then in Hulme, established itself in what was then the 'countryside' adjacent to the city of Manchester, but few even today link Manchester with Lancashire from the cricketing point of view. Old Trafford is synonymous with cricket the world over. Down the years tributes have been paid to the near-perfect amenities. Players commend the state of the pitch and the high quality of the light. Official visitors praise the hospitality they encounter and the ordinary man in the street sings praises because of its ability to house a crowd with comfort and afford every spectator a good view of the game. But Lancashire has more to offer than Old Trafford.

The club's history is liberally sprinkled with names of players who have made their mark in all the cricketing parts of the world and from the administrative point of view Lancashire has provided its share of leading officials who have maintianed a link with M.C.C. and Lord's that was finally cemented this winter when the Marylebone Club held one of its rare 'outside' functions at Old Trafford—a dinner for its North-West members. Need it be said that the official verdict after a memorable night was that Lancashire and Old Trafford had excelled once again.

NOTED SECRETARIES

The strength of Lancashire cricket lies in the names of the men who have made it famous. Some of those present at the foundation of the club in 1864 boasted names that have been synonymous with good cricket and astute administration. First and foremost among them was S. H. Swire who became the first and only honorary secretary, doubling his duties off the field with occasional effort as a batsman in the middle and remaining in office until 1906 when it became apparent that the growth of the club and the ever-increasing popularity of the county club called for full-time administrators. Since that year five men have served in the secretarial capacity and each has made a name for himself in one direction or another. T. J. Matthews was in office from 1906 to 1921, when H. Rylance took over and continued until 1932 when he gave way to Captain Rupert Howard. Captain Howard eventually became Major Howard, managed two M.C.C. touring sides in Australia and New Zealand, and made himself one of the most respected officials in cricket before passing on an onerous post to C. G. Howard of Surrey, who served from 1949 to 1964 and also managed M.C.C. touring teams in Australia and India before returning to The Oval and being succeeded by the Yorkshire-born J. B. Wood, a man who has contributed much to the recent emergence of Lancashire as a cricketing power after years in the doldrums from a playing point of view.

ILLUSTRIOUS PLAYERS

The club's list of captains, from E. B. Rowley in 1866 to J. D. Bond in 1971, contains an illustrious band of famous players, several of whom played also for England and led their country in Test matches at home and abroad. Talk of Lancashire cricket in the early days and the names of the Hornby family vie with those of the Rowley brothers—all distinguished administrators as well as players. Few would argue against the age-old belief that when one discusses Lancashire captains, the name of A. C. MacLaren means most. A majestic figure on and off the field, captain of Lancashire and leader of England, the mighty MacLaren gathered round him a county side that included the master bowler, S. F. Barnes, the stylish amateur batsman, R. H. Spooner, the first of the famous Tyldesleys, Johnny of run-scoring fame, and the devastating fast bowler, Walter Brearley. This, it was said, was Lancashire's vintage time and when the county was at full strength, it was a vintage team.

TRIPLE CHAMPIONS

Certainly, Old Trafford was a well populated spot in those far-off and historic cricketing days, but there are many, and some of them are still to be seen on the ground, who reckon the team led by Leonard Green in the middle twenties was a better cricketing combination. It contained the graceful Australian fast bowler, E. A. (Ted) McDonald, the incomparable Cecil Parkin of whom it was said that he could bowl a different delivery with each of his six balls in the over, the perspiring spinner Richard Tyldesley and his namesake Ernest Tyldesley, brother of J.T. but no relation to Dick, who scored more runs (some 34,000) than any other Lancashire batsman. In addition there was the dour Harry Makepeace opening the innings along with the stylish Charles Hallows and the incomparable George Duckworth behind the wicket. This was the team that claimed three of the eight Championships won by Lancashire to date. Leonard Green led his side to the County Championship three years in succession, in 1926–27–28, and few will deny his right to be classed with the county's great captains and his team to challenge for the title of the club's 'best-ever'.

The County Championship was won again in 1930 and 1934 under the leadership of P. T. Eckersley, but since the war only one joint share of the Championship has gone to Old Trafford—in 1950 when N. D. Howard led a side that finished level with Surrey in a summer bedevilled by bad weather and suspect pitches. Lancashire, like all other county clubs, closed down during the period of World War II and saw Old Trafford bombed and battle-scarred before cricket was resumed in 1945 with a victory Test against a powerful Australian Services side ushering in a new cricketing decade.

POST-WAR PROBLEMS

Forced to recruit players from up and down the country in 1946, Lancashire lost more than most to the ravages of war. Paynter, Oldfield, Nutter and Farrimond refused to accept terms or risk the physical consequences of five near-idle years but there remained Washbrook, Place, Pollard and Wilkinson of the old brigade to reshape the future of a proud club. W. H. L. Lister, in charge when play was suspended in 1939, was not available. T. A. Higson, son of the club chairman and a 'stand-in' for Lister in pre-war days, was also unable to continue playing and the choice of captain provided much thought. Eventually it went to J. A.

Fallows, son of the club honorary treasurer and a club-cricketer with some Minor County experience before the war. Fallows had a distinguished Army record and, although by no means a good player, he did a responsible job in 1946.

His first task was to re-establish team spirit. He leaned heavily on the experience of Washbrook and Pollard, though the latter, who was still in the Services, could play in fewer than half of the matches; he also encouraged the newcomers, J. T. Ikin, left-hander of great pugnacity, G. A. Edrich, recruited from Norfolk, B. P. King, from Worcestershire, T. L. Brierley who was signed from Glamorgan to plug the wicket-keeping gap. Among home-produced players were Place, Wharton, Roberts, Price and Garlick and had it not been for some bad luck with the weather and the toss Lancashire might well have started the new decade by winning the Championship. That they failed was no reflection upon Fallows or his team. Yet the club committee was not satisfied. Fallows had contributed little from the batting or fielding point of view but had done a superb job behind the scenes. Yet he was summarily dismissed and, unfortunately, learned of his dismissal through the Press before being officially informed. It was an action that incensed Fallows, upset his players, and did much damage among the members, though they welcomed his successor Kenneth Cranston as a stylish and promising all-rounder.

The chairman, T. A. Higson, was much criticised but he rode the storm and continued to rule the committee with an iron hand. Cranston captained Lancashire for two years and delighted all with the grace of his batting and the power of his bowling. He narrowly failed to do the double of 1,000 runs and 100 wickets in his first year and won England caps in what was a brief but colourful career in the first-class game. When Cranston went Lancashire were faced with the problem of maintaining the old order or breaking away from the traditional demand that the captain should always be an amateur. On hand, as senior professional and one of the most successful batsmen of the post-war period, was Washbrook, first choice for England and a prolific scorer for both county and country, a man with vast experience and an impeccable reputation on and off the field. But the old order was maintained and N. D. Howard, son of the club secretary and a very promising batsman, was appointed to succeed Cranston. Under him Lancashire enjoyed considerable success. They shared the Championship with Surrey in 1950, and came third in each of the three remaining years of Howard's captaincy, a run of success which they were not to emulate for many years.

WASHBROOK CAPTAIN AT LAST

Howard retained office until the end of the 1953 season when business demands forced him to go. In 1954 Lancashire broke with tradition and appointed Washbrook the county's first-ever professional captain. He did his utmost to see the young players' point of view and never once spared himself in the cause of Lancashire cricket but he found the going hard and the necessity to constantly pacify players with legitimate complaints about pay and working conditions proved too much for him.

Washbrook continued to play and lead Lancashire until the end of the 1959 season, playing on against his real inclination, until the side showed signs of settling down and a new leader appeared. It did not happen. The gulf between players and committee widened visibly season by season. Two amateurs, R. W. Barber and J. F. Blackledge, held the captaincy for brief spells. In 1960 Lancashire came second in the Championship under Barber, who was first picked for England in this same season. But unfortunately their improved form was not maintained.

Good players were recruited from the vast reservoir of talent in the leagues, but a lot more were allowed to by-pass the county (Frank Tyson and Keith Andrew had earlier been two very prominent 'escapees') and things were allowed to drift on. The public, disappointed with results on the field and mystified by decisions off it, gradually forsook Old Trafford. K. J. Grieves had been appointed as the Club's second professional captain in 1963, but it was a sad wind-up to the club's centenary year in 1964 when the news 'leaked' that the services of Marner, Clayton and Dyson had been dispensed with and that Grieves had been relieved of the captaincy.

The summer of 1965 saw Statham given control after the club had unsuccessfully advertised for a captain—another example of committee reasoning baffling to members and public alike. It was a move that eventually led to a group of members demanding a special meeting to pass a vote of no confidence in the committee. It also coincided with the departure of the secretary to Surrey and the appointment of J. B. Wood, who found himself taking over with things in turmoil. Resigning but seeking re-election, the old committee surrendered six seats to young and enthusiastic newcomers and although one or two fell by the wayside in the reorganisation so badly needed it soon became apparent that Lancashire were turning the corner.

STATHAM TAKES OVER

Statham did his best to reshape the playing side. His skill and popularity as the most successful pace bowler in the history of the club and his mighty deeds for England at home and abroad ensured him the full support of the youngsters who were drafted into the side. A more sympathetic committee, mindful of the need for a new relationship and more security for the players, encouraged the side to better things and the public, at last given evidence of good intent by the new officials, began to return to Old Trafford. What was of equal importance was the committee's determination to move with the times without showing a lack of respect for the past.

NEW IDEAS

New sources of revenue were essential and the bold step of selling part of the club's ground for building purposes on the grand scale was so successful that at the end of the first of a three-phase plan it was possible to call a halt to the possible 'disfigurement' of Old Trafford as a world-class cricketing venue. For years Lancashire had taken little part in the government of the game. Always at Lord's they had been regarded as staunch supporters of the establishment, eager to maintain old standards and showing no great desire to break away from old ideas and ideals. In a word Lancashire had been content to drift along. All this was changed with the upheavals of 1965.

AN INSPIRING CHAIRMAN

Old Trafford became the focal point of several new cricketing ideas. The county proposed and supported the move to introduce overseas players into the English cricketing scene and made a bold bid for the services of the man who had most to offer—one, G. S. Sobers! Winning the fight to introduce leading cricketing figures from overseas, Lancashire made it quite clear that their own reasons were for merely stop-gap purposes. They wanted time to find and encourage the next generation of native-born players and signed Farokh Engineer and Clive Lloyd to that end. The Indian and the West Indies left-hander have proved admirable signings and the failure to agree terms with Sobers has caused few regrets at Old Trafford where, with the advent of C. S. Rhoades as a live-wire chairman of committee great things are happening.

It would be folly to credit Mr. Rhoades with all the praise and responsibility for all that has happened in Lancashire cricket in recent years. But he has made his mark not only with his own committee but with his players and with the powers-that-be at Lord's and elsewhere in the cricketing world. His commanding presence, infectious enthusiasm and determination to succeed, have broken down barriers hitherto regarded as unscalable.

One of the major tasks was to win back the essential goodwill of the smaller cricketing powers in Lancashire. The county has long been the home of the most powerful and world-famous cricketing leagues. Within 20 or 30 miles of Old Trafford have been playing the best cricketers in the world, delighting league crowds and attracting more publicity than the county game itself. Lancashire's new chairman made it his job to go round the county. He has won back the faith and the confidence of minor cricketing officials who were often ignored or unknown at Old Trafford. In doing so he has done much to achieve a united front in Lancashire cricket.

BOND BEGINS HIS REIGN

The new secretary, J. B. Wood, has also been a great help in this respect and with the appointment of J. D. Bond as captain to succeed Statham in 1968 there was forged the third link in a chain that has seen Lancashire emerge as trend-setters of the new cricket and pullers of the new crowds that are now watching the game. Bond's appointment was greeted with reserve by many Lancashire followers. They had seen him come and go as a batsman capable of pleasing but seldom conquering. He was a little man with limitations as a batsman, but now a cricketer who has found his forte in leadership. Do not be misled by the apparent reserve of this little man from Bolton. He has the happy knack of making friends and keeping them.

He has wielded Lancashire into a strong and attractive side by the simple but all-important belief that no one man is more important than the other. He ignores averages and has banned their publication on the dressing-room notice board until the end of each season.

He has earned respect instead of demanding it. He praises and criticises with equal fervour and will fight hard in support of each and every player—in form or out of it. Whimsical at times but deadly serious when the occasion demands, Bond accepted the introduction of the John Player League as a means of 'letting off steam'. He knew the only way to win back the crowds was to play the Sunday cricket happily. Ignoring the threat to take away the players' only day off, he gathered the Lancashire side around him and said: 'This new league can be the making of cricket. We may not like sacrificing first-class principles in order to provide a spectacle but it is worth a try. Let us go out there and enjoy ourselves; if we do that the crowds must surely enjoy themselves, too.'

Bond's assessment of the new order was correct. Lancashire threw themselves into the hurly-burly of Sunday cricket with great enthusiasm and no little skill. Their attitude was the correct one. They have been Champions two years in succession and last summer extended their honours by winning the Gillette Cup for the first time. Finishing third in the County Championship, Bond and his men were disappointed that the 'big one' got away, but they are confident that Lancashire now have their priorities right. They have won back the crowds and entertained them. In response the club committee have made cricket a worthwhile career for the players by giving them top wages and long-term security.

DECENT CONTRACTS FOR PLAYERS

Newcomers have been attracted to the game not only because of the money they can earn but also because Lancashire now link cricket with industry and commercial life by also ensuring their youngsters employment all the year round. Long-term cricketing contracts and worthwhile jobs in the winter coupled with schemes to help finance business ventures when their playing days are over have done much to break down the barriers that held Lancashire in bondage for so many years. There is still much to be done and there are still critics of the way Lancashire play the game and sustain it. But they are outnumbered and last summer Old Trafford housed big crowds. Not only did they come on Sundays but also on Saturdays and in mid-week, too, and seldom did they go away disappointed. It is true that Old Trafford's once sacred turf was trodden underfoot by masses of cheering cricket followers, that beer is now drunk openly on the pavilion side, and that many a member feels he is entitled to remove his collar, and sometimes his shirt, to enable him to watch the game in comfort. Old ideas and ideals have been sacrificed in certain respects, but Lancashire cricket is now vibrantly throbbing with enthusiasm and skill. Old Trafford is no longer a neglected sports venue. It is alive with incident and crowded with eager spectators.

It may well be a long cry from the dignity and grace of the days when

MacLaren and Spooner stroked their way to majestic centuries and Barnes and Brearley wreaked havoc with their pace and swing. But who can deny that Bond and his merry men have also got something to offer? An hour of Clive Lloyd at his best must still remain one of cricket's major joys. That Lloyd is not Lancashire born may worry the few but not the masses. Cricket today has broken down age-old barriers and Old Trafford has figured prominently in the transformation. Who could ask for more?

THE DREADED CYPHER [1971]

BASIL EASTERBROOK

One of the rarest joys of cricket is the engaging lunacy of certain episodes in its history. If the genius of a Trumper or a Compton at the apex of its glory can justify dithyrambic excess from the aesthetes, then at the nadir the sublime absurdity of some of the more obscure matches invites the gratitude of all, from social historians to collectors of arcana to seekers after slap-stick humour. Nobody who has ever seen the scorecard for that Victorian masterpiece of a match, 'One-Arm versus One-Leg', can ever be sure again that a Test match is the highest expression of the cricketing arts. Nobody familiar with the fancies of James Matthew Barrie can ever forget the tactical acumen of long leg in a ladies' match who, instead of returning the ball, 'ran smartly with it to the stumps and put it personally into the wicket-keeper's hands'. And what are we to make of the contents of Wisden for 1879, which contains reports of the matches on ice played across an England gripped in the iron fist of a smaller Ice Age, when games were contested on the Duke of Devonshire's pond, on the meadow at Grantchester, at Gateshead, at Sheffield and at numerous other venues unlisted by the almanack only because notice of the event had not been forwarded to the editorial office? Never was the patrician gesture more beautifully exemplified than by the Marquis of Abergavenny, who, in that gelid time:

> . . . with that considerate courtesy characteristic of his race, had the gates of his park thrown open to all who chose to enter and witness the grand Fete on the frozen water of the great lake at his Lordship's seat, Eridge Castle . . . Lord Henry Neville being frequently applauded for the command he evinced over skates and bat.

Predictably there were eight Run-Outs in the match, but amazingly, only one batsman failed to score. The fortunes of batsmen are not always so benign, as Basil Easterbrook demonstrates in his masterly 'The Dreaded Cypher'.

A pair in a Test Match! Can anyone imagine a worse fate befalling a batsman, especially when he is fighting for a place in the M.C.C. team in the Final Test at The Oval where his middle stump was sent flying for 0 by Procter with the third ball of the first innings and again for 0 with the first ball of the second innings. It set me pondering on this subject of 'The Dreaded Cypher'.

Suppose it had happened to him on his debut for England in the first Test two months earlier at Lord's. Would the selectors have looked at him again? They cast aside Alan Jones, Sharpe and Denness for their failures in that match. Luckhurst was sensible enough to prove himself first; so he did go to Australia with my best wishes and I will tell you why.

Wisden's first edition in 1864 at one shilling for 112 pages in notebook size to slip into the slimmest pocket was the best bob's worth on the bookstalls.

On the flyleaf was a note addressed to the reader: 'In offering our first edition of the Cricketers' Almanack to the patrons of the Noble Game, we have taken great pains to collect a certain amount of information, which we trust will prove interesting to all those that take pleasure in this glorious pastime. Should the present work meet with but moderate success, it is intended next year to present our readers with a variety of other matches, which the confined nature of an almanack precludes us from doing this year.' A little enough acorn but what an oak grew from it!

In passing one wonders how John Wisden and Company, offering their literary sprig at their warehouse in the Haymarket, would have reacted to the 1969 edition of 1,055 pages. The original publication's collection of matches was drawn from games anywhere in the first half of the 19th century. For example, you could inspect the scorecard of a game at Lord's in July, 1806, a bare nine months after Trafalgar on page 30 and a game at The Oval in 1863, when W. G. Grace was a lad of 15, a few pages further on.

We live now in a dreary age of specialisation and the 1,000 page monsters of the 1960s deal with nothing but cricket but in 1864 you could study *Wisden* and become a mixture of Datas and Leslie Welch. On one page alone you were told the dates of the eight Crusades ranging from 1097 to 1270, the venues of the twelve battles of the Wars of the Roses, a précis of the trial of Charles the First and a final paragraph which ran 'A brass bell weighing 17 cwt cast in 1699 at Woolwich Arsenal used to call and disperse the labourers, was cleft by the hammer while ringing, from the effects of the severe frost on January 4, 1861.'

On another page was a potted history of English coinage going back to 1302 and all the canals in Britain above 30 miles in length. If you needed to know how to go quoiting or play Knur and Spell, or when China was first visited by Europeans, the winners of the principal horse races, the rules of the game of bowls, how to bet on cricket like a gentleman, or what time the British Museum closed, then *Wisden* 1864 was a volume you could not afford to be without.

Seen through the corrupt eyes of the second half of the 20th century, it was of course a time of innocence but the original compilers knew where their main duty and purpose lay and they also had an eye for the romance

and drama of the game. Now for all cricketers like the writer who made
more ducks than he has eaten baked dinners, the originators of the world's
holy writ on cricket started a section called 'Extraordinary Matches', which
amid all the welter of feats and records has been allowed to lapse by their
distinguished successors. They gave details of a match which made a man
like myself feel he had his rightful place in the game without relying on the
second prize of writing about it for that place. In August, 1855 the Second
Royal Surrey Militia met Shillinglee in Sussex at the seat of Earl
Winterton. The scorecard of the Militia's first innings was as follows:

Private Dudley b Challen junior	0
Private Plumridge b Heather	0
E. Hartnell, Esq. b Heather	0
A. Marshall, Esq. b Challen junior	0
Private Ayling b Challen junior	0
Lieut. Pontifex b Heather	0
Corporal Heyes	0
Lieut. Ball b Heather	0
Major Ridley not out	0
Sgt. Ayling run out	0
Private Newberry b Heather	0
Extras	0
TOTAL	0

It was No. 10 who nearly ruined the whole thing. He hit one to cover
point and set off like an Olympic sprinter going for the tape. Major Ridley
rent the pastoral scene with a stentorian voice of command— 'Go Back
Sergeant.' Sgt. Ayling, pulled up all standing, fell base over apex and was
run out by 15 yards. There were those who accused the gallant Major of
moral cowardice, but I see him as a man with a sense of history. There is
something aesthetically perfect about that scorecard—no catches, no
stumping, no LBWs and no runs.

The Militia made 106 in their second innings, but who wants to bother
with that?

From that time *Wisden* has increased tenfold in size, thirtyfold in price
and a hundredfold in status, but the Pardons, Stewart Caine, S. J.
Southerton and the Prestons who have built the greatest monument of
print in all sporting history all stand arraigned for a serious sin of omission.
They have become so intoxicated with faithfully preserving for posterity
the feats of THEM, that is the handful of lucky blighters who play first-class
cricket from April's end to September that they have almost completely
ignored US namely, The Rest, who do not.

Individual scores of 300 or more, hundred on debut in England, most
individual hundreds, they are all there in the record section extending for
nearly as many pages as there were altogether in the original *Wisden*. It's
sickening. Every year you are told that J. B. Hobbs hit 244 hundreds in all

cricket and W. G. Grace 217 and there are columns of names running from Sir John Berry Hobbs to Brian Valentine of chaps who made 35 or more centuries in first-class cricket.

Even a young fellow like Boycott has got his name into the list obsessed with batting his life away instead of learning to pick four notes from the strings of a guitar and earning himself £1,000 a week.

Because, let's face it, *Wisden* has made us obsessed with runs, a charge I substantiate by a reference to the simple fact that nearly 20 pages of the record section are devoted to such improbable events as C. J. Eady scoring 566 for Break-O'-Day against Wellington at Hobart in the winter of 1901–2 before a mention is made of bowling feats. And of the considerable achievement of making a duck nothing in all the 1,000 or more pages. It came to me in a blinding flash of intuition that *Wisden* is a vast conspiracy dedicated to the proposition of creating a totally false image of the game.

Any mug with enough talent and concentration can make a hundred. It requires the soul and tenacity of a martyr to score nothing and continue to score nothing. Once in 1935 at Dartmouth I made 16 out of a total of 43 against the Royal Naval College but in self defence I would point out that even Homer nodded and that if you go to the crease often enough there comes a day when you will get some runs regardless of what you do. I have remembered this innings for 35 years for I believe this is as far as I got from the circular cypher in one innings.

How much colour and interest have been withheld from lovers of cricket by Wisden's refusal down the years to publish a section devoted to the nought. There was Ian Peebles, for example, on an overseas M.C.C. tour who went into the scorer's book 'absent bathing 0'. Hutton might easily have been one of US instead of THEM. He began with great promise—a duck in his first innings for Yorkshire seconds, a duck for the first eleven at Fenner's in 1934 and a duck in his first innings for England, against New Zealand. He deteriorated so far that he made 129 centuries and in June, 1949 by scoring 1,294 made more runs in a single month than anyone else.

Hammond made 0 in his first match against Lancashire at Cheltenham in 1920 but he slipped further than Hutton, ending his career with 167 centuries with only Hendren 170 and Hobbs 197 ahead of him in the all time list of century makers.

Philip Mead, the world's No. 4, with 153, made a duck in his first match against the Australians at Southampton in 1905. Frank Woolley, No. 6 with 145, made 0 a year later in his debut against Lancashire at Old Trafford. He soon got the taste for notoriety by making 64 in the second innings and was lost to US from then on. Old Trafford remained one of his favourite grounds and it is said that on one occasion he square cut Ted McDonald for six and the ball struck one of the pavilion towers with such force that when it rebounded back into the field of play at a tangent McDonald took it first bounce as he was walking back, said, 'Good shot, Frank,' turned and ran in to bowl the next delivery. W. G. Grace, 126 hundreds, failed to score in his first game for the Gentlemen of the South v. Players of the South at The Oval in 1865 but even at 17 he had no sense of proportion as he showed by taking thirteen wickets for 84 runs in the match.

Tom Graveney, the leading century compiler of current players, began with 0 in The Parks against Oxford in 1948 but he was another who could not keep it up.

All these with the exception of Hutton lacked the stamina to make a serious bid to be regarded as US rather than THEM, but there were players who later degenerated into household words who for a brief season did splendidly. George Dews of Worcestershire was bowled by Eric Price in both innings at Old Trafford on his debut against Lancashire and notched a notable 'hat-trick' by failing to score in the first innings of his next match against Warwickshire at Dudley in 1946. Johnny Douglas, when beset by the worries of the England captaincy must more than once have pondered ruefully on how different life might have been, for, like Dews, he too started his career with a 'hat-trick' of ducks. He was bowled by George Hirst in each innings in the Essex v. Yorkshire match at Leyton in 1901 and failed to score in his next innngs against Gloucestershire at Clifton. Morton, a Derbyshire stalwart in the early years of the century, did even better.

At Edgbaston in 1901 against Warwickshire he was clean bowled by Charlesworth twice. In his next game at Lord's he was castled a third time before he had scored and in the second innings he was run out trying to get off the mark. M. J. K. Smith got a duck for Leicestershire against Northamptonshire in his first match at Leicester in 1951 and another in his second against Derbyshire at Burton-on-Trent.

I showed this list with what I felt to be justifiable pride to a friend of mine, Michael Fordham, the well-known statistician. He looked at me pityingly and said, 'My dear old lad, you have barely scratched the surface,' and in short order came back to me with the following string of names— Ewart Astill, Sonny Avery, Wilf Barber, Gordon Barker, Les Berry, Hon. F. S. G. Calthorpe, W. A. Brown, A. W. Carr, Sam Coe, Bernard Constable, George Cox senior, A. J. Croom, Dai Davies, George Dawkes, E. W. Dawson, Ted Dexter, Desmond Eagar, George Emmett, C. B. Fry, R. A. Gale, George Geary, S. E. Gregory, J. Gunn, Arnold Hamer, Lord Hawke, A. Hearne, Clem Hill, Errol Holmes, Martin Horton, J. C. Hubble, E. Humphreys, D. R. Jardine, A. S. Kennedy, Ray Kilner, Billy Neale, Charlie Oakes, Sir T. C. O'Brien, Edgar Oldroyd, Jack Parker, Eddie Paynter, Bobby Peel, Winston Place, J. M. Read, R. R. Relf, D. W. Richardson, Jack Robertson, Water Robins, Neville Rogers, Eric Rowan, Bishop David Sheppard, A. Shipman, Reg Sinfield, Denis Smith, Ray Smith, Arthur Staples, Harold Stephenson, W. Storer, Jack Timms, Les Todd, Victor Trumper, J. Tunnicliffe, Clyde Walcott, Sir Pelham Warner, Everton Weekes, Alan Wharton, Bert Wolton, Stan Worthington and Norman Yardley. I lost a sheet or two of Michael Fordham's painstaking research so the list is not complete. It is, however, a grim enough catalogue. Of all this legion who could have swelled the ranks of US not one of THEM made less than 10,000 runs in first-class cricket. It is odd to reflect that of the 46 men who made a hundred instead of a duck on their first appearance in top-class cricket half of them made no further mark on the game and five never played at first-class level again.

We are tending perhaps to get too involved in the sheer mechanics of our theme.

There are many of cricket's best untold stories in the making of a duck. I remember one occasion when Yorkshire were playing Oxbridge. A wicket had fallen. Slowly gracefully from the pavilion emerged a slim willowy figure most beautifully attired—the next man in. His flannels could only have been cut in Savile Row; his boots were new, his pads spotless. On his head set at a carefully cultivated devil-may-care Beatty angle was a multicoloured cap. Clipped round his neck to protect his throat from the rude winds of early May which do not spare even university towns, was a silk scarf. On his way to the crease he played imaginary bowlers. With wristy cuts and flicks, perfectly timed drives, and daring late glances and hooks he despatched the imaginary ball to all parts of the ground.

The Yorkshire players watched his approach in silence. He eventually arrived at the wicket and looked all about him imperiously, like a king, come to his rightful throne. He took guard, and then spent a full minute making his block hole, shaping and patting it until it was to his satisfaction. Another look around the entire field—and he was ready to receive his first ball.

Freddie Trueman bowled it and knocked two of the three stumps clean out of the ground. As our young exquisite turned languidly and began to walk away, Freddie called to him sympathetically, 'Bad luck, Sir, you were just getting settled in.'

Makers of ducks have always been subject to the occupational hazard of being dropped but one of the unfairest dismissals from a team I personally encountered was down in Devon before the war. The captain of the side decided that a certain individual was failing to make runs because he was, in the skipper's choice of words, a bookworm. He wrote him a letter which began 'I have decided to leave you out because it has come to my notice that midnight frequently finds you immersed in Jane Austen.'

There can be mystery too in the making of a duck. One wet week-end when cricket was out of the question I played 24 frames of snooker at the Royal Hotel, Ashby-de-la-Zouch with the late Jack Bartley, the Test Umpire.

In his playing days Jack had opened the bowling for Cheshire and in one Minor Counties fixture against Yorkshire Seconds he clean bowled the opposing captain, Col. Chichester-Constable, for a duck.

'I did it again in the second innings. The Colonel walked towards me on his way to the pavilion. As he drew level with me he grinned and looking over my shoulder addressed a greeting to a fellow called Shorthouse. The strange thing was that I do not recall a player of that name in either team. Now wasn't that odd?' said a puzzled Bartley.

The idea of writing a treatise on the making of a duck is not original. The late R. C. Robertson-Glasgow penned one of his delightful and all too brief essays on the subject over a quarter of a century ago. In it he wrote this passage: 'Even *Wisden* so rich in the scattered cypher, *Wisden* which has garnered cricket's yearly harvest, has left us to glean the 0's as best we may. They have to be picked out, like a few pearls from legions of oysters.

'True, we may read at rare intervals of whole teams shot out for 0, not even a bye flicked off the stomach past the stumper; and that is admittedly remarkable, even though, as we are apt to suspect, the outgoing side consisted of subnormal batsmen assailed by a crazy sergeant major who was bowling on a pitch of broken glass. Remarkable, yes; but not exclusive; for eleven 0's, even if one of them be perforce 0 not out, are ten too many; like eleven pies thrown by eleven comedians in one act.'

Dear Crusoe, he took me under his wing when I was a fledgling cricket writer and I shall be eternally in his debt. How or when he first became Crusoe is a matter for historical research. Most of the evidence points to a day at The Parks in 1920 when Charles McGahey of Essex returning to the pavilion was asked by his skipper J. W. H. T. Douglas how he lost his wicket. McGahey replied, 'I was bowled out by an old —— I thought was dead 2,000 years ago, called Robinson Crusoe.'

It was in that year that Crusoe first played for Somerset under John Daniell who, at the end of the season said 'Come again next summer, but don't wear that bloody straw hat.'

What would Crusoe have thought about the Gillette Cup and the Player Sunday League? He would have liked them, I think. Certainly he would have entered into the spirit of the thing. But he would never have supported the throwing over of the three-day county match. 'First-class cricket cannot be made just snappy. It is not a wisecrack, but an old and mellow story.'

He intended to write again on the art, colour, drama, humour and heartbreak of making a duck but he never did. He gave me a few jottings on the subject once after we had dined together at a riverside hotel at Gravesend nearly 20 years ago—or perhaps it is over 20 years. 'You might find them useful sometime when you have more experience and when you are less solemn about cricket,' he said.

During that meal he showed me that a duck could be large and illustrious as well as an embarrassing spasm.

Miles Howell was long before my time but apparently he was playing for Surrey against Yorkshire at The Oval and Rhodes was bowling at his deadliest. Howell was just then at the top of his form, and he played the Yorkshire bowlers, mostly Rhodes, during forty-three mortal minutes, firmly and in the middle of the bat—for no runs. 'Any spectator who entered the ground at any point in that innings and failed to observe the scoreboard might reasonably have thought that Howell was in the comfortable thirties or forties. But that ball would not pierce those fielders,' said Crusoe. 'And then he was run out, bravely answering a call from his rash partner. Run out nought; with the sweat of battle pouring from his forehead. As he remarked in the pavilion: "Not a run; not even a little one, dammit; and I feel as if I'd sprinted to the House of Commons and back!" '

Rockley Wilson was master in charge of cricket at Winchester where he was on the staff for forty years. One day he grew mildly exasperated with a boy in the nets. This boy played across the ball and over the ball.

He played either side of it and going down on one knee to sweep played under it. Wilson who made a century in his maiden first-class match and came back out of club cricket to play for Yorkshire during school vacations in his forties said: 'My dear boy, you must play one ball in the middle of your bat before you meet your Maker.' This made such an impression on the boy that under Wilson's guiding hand he reached a stage where he could go to the wicket and make 15 or 20 runs every third or fourth innings.

So another promising recruit for US was lost even if he could never hope to aspire to THEM. It was a classic example of the inherent dangers of coaching. For half-way house in cricket is equivalent to the old fashioned conception of a fate worse than death. Crusoe knew that. I have before me as I write, some papers of his, yellowing a little now, and I quote again— 'There are those who fancy that it is something to have scored 1 or 2 or some other disreputable and insignificant digit. They are wrong; it is nothing, or, rather, worse than 0. They have but enjoyed a span too short to show a profit, long enough to show their ineptitude.

'They have but puttered and poked and snicked in wretched incompleteness. No; give me the man who makes 0 and doesn't care. As numbers go, he has achieved nothing; but equally, because he has never started, he has left 0 unfinished.'

Crusoe once whiled away a tedious train journey by compiling a list of innings of a Mr. O. E. Jugg, as unlikely a character as Tootling C.C. for whom he played. Jugg's place in the batting order at No. 10 was described as a singular promotion. Crusoe's scratch pad showed Jugg's previous six visits to the crease as:

1. v. Gas, Light and Coke Company (Home) 0
   (3rd ball, snooted by a double bouncer)
2. v. St. Luke's Choir (Away) 0
   (without receiving a ball; fast asleep and run out by an old tenor)
3. v. G.P.O. (Home) 0
   (c and b by the head sorter)
4. v. The Pirates (Home) 0
   (1st ball; shattered by a long hop)
5. v. St. Luke's Choir (Home) 0
   (2nd ball; LBW from behind)
6. v. Gas, Light and Coke Company (Away) 0
   (1st ball; run out, after a quarrel)

Yes, Crusoe, who once said of his old friend and snicking partner Jim Bridges that they never made a century between them but they made a devil of a lot of them for other people, either bowling, or criticising from the pavilion, was *SYMPATICO* to all of US who have ever walked to the wicket with the air of men who have left lighted cigarettes in the dressing-room.

The great thing about US is that we wear our ducks like a row of medals but the other first-class lot are inclined to be terribly stuffy. Crusoe once said to one of THEM, 'Ah, Prendergast, my dear fellow, how did you enjoy your duck at Lord's yesterday? I arrived just in time to see you in and out.' Telling me this over coffee and cigars after that fondly remembered meal at Gravesend, Crusoe gave that great, triumphant bellow of laughter of his and said with the emphasis he did so well, 'A brittle silence fell as if a bottle of the old and nutty had exploded in my pocket at a temperance rally.' And off he went into another crockery-shaking guffaw. What a wonderful man he was!

Gone but not forgotten. It could be said of him as of few others, 'We, his fellows, loved him—and he made us laugh.' What better epitaph could any man be given in this sad and sorry 20th century of ours?

Turning back to *Wisden* for a final riffling through of the batting records, I am convinced beyond a peradventure (whatever that phrase means) of the justice of my plan to be represented in this section of the almanack. Look at the chaps who have made 35 or more centuries. There must be nearly a couple of hundred and that means there must be thousands who have made between 10 and 30 and probably millions who have made one or two. As for those who have scored their 50s and 60s it does not bear thinking about.

We would have it no other way for it gives US that warm inner glow that comes from belonging to an exclusive brotherhood. To make my point, permit me one final dip into Crusoe's cricket Thesaurus.

'The essence, the aristocracy of 0 is that it should be surrounded by large scores, that it should resemble the little silent bread-winner in a bus full of fat, noisy women. Indeed, when the years have fixed it in its place, so far from being merely the foil to jewels, it should itself grow, in the fond eye of memory, to the shape and stature of a gem.'

That, as Mr. Alf Garnett might say, is yer actual true philosophy of the duck.

THE SOUTH AFRICAN TOUR DISPUTE [1971]

BY IRVING ROSENWATER

The 1971 edition had more still to offer. English cricket, having drifted into the muddied waters of politics through the D'Oliveira Affair, was now expending prodigious energies on drifting out of them, finding in the process that to enter the arena is far simpler than to leave it. The attempts of the various organisations seem in retrospect to have been so maladroit as to defy belief. Of the stances adopted by the Cricket Council in England and by the lobby represented by Jack Cheetham in South Africa, it has to be said that the arguments put forward by each of these factions were logical, fair and eminently sensible, but only in the world of 1935. Neither Mr. S. C. Griffith nor Mr. Cheetham seemed to have any faint grasp of the extent to which England had changed since pre-war days. Cheetham's touching faith in what he referred to as 'the British public' is almost as naive as the TCCB's 'respect for the rights of those who wish to demonstrate peacefully'. The point which nobody discussed but which was in the minds of all embroiled in the debate was the ease with which a mechanism as delicate as a cricket match may be disrupted, and the impossibility of policing against it.

To be fair to the cricket administrators of both countries, circumstances had pushed them into a position for which they were prepared neither by environment nor experience nor inspiration. The committeemen of both nations in their desperation began playing the ancient game of Pass the Buck, to the politicians, who, in the persons of the Prime Minister and the Home Secretary, promptly passed it back. Again the world of cricket returned it, and this time Mr. Callaghan did what he should have done weeks before and cancelled the tour. Most people breathed a sigh of relief and privately marvelled at the insularity of most professional cricketers, who had firmly supported the South African visit from the first exchanges to the bitter end.

There was a final crushing irony to come. The TCCB, suddenly finding itself bereft of a touring side for the coming summer, hastily improvised a series billed as 'England versus the Rest of the World', an emergency measure which, in the event, was to produce much memorable cricket. And that same insularity which had prevented the cricketers from grasping the simplest moral precepts now worked in reverse, for the good of the game. The Rest of the World included five of the South Africans who had originally hoped to represent their country in England that summer, and five West Indians, whose cricketing board had so adamantly opposed the idea of South Africa playing anybody. The repugnance at the South African government's stance is well brought out by the Wisden essay, but it is in the Editor's report of the Tests that we find the irony at the heart of all the ironies:

> So far the only disappointing performer for The Rest had been Graeme Pollock, but in the final Test at the Oval he played gloriously for 114 and thousands of white and coloured spectators cheered him and Sobers (79) while they indulged in a memorable stand of 165.

And so, through the collapse of cricket under the pressures of an uncongenial world, there came together the two greatest left-handed batsmen of the modern age, in an alliance which could never have come about at all had not international cricket been reduced to chaos. In describing so emotive a sequence of events, the chronicler, Irving Rosenwater, kept an admirably level head. He was not to repeat the act the next time the challenge came around.

CRICKET as a way of life has been a feature of British society ever since the game emerged in its present recognisable form something like two hundred years ago. Poets have sung its praises, and its charm and influence and its appeal to the emotions have been invoked in aid of all that is good in life and play. Cricket is a liberal education in itself, said Andrew Lang, and did not Professor Trevelyan once surmise that if the French *noblesse* had been capable of playing cricket with their peasants, their *châteaux* would never have been burnt?

Whether cricket is an art, an exercise, an interest, a cult or a philosophy, it was never meant to do a mischief, let alone cause strife. But the bitter, emotional—sometimes hysterical—aura that hung over English cricket in 1970 divided the nation, cricket lovers or not, into impassioned camps, each clinging firmly to its principles: the one anxious, for a variety of reasons, to welcome the South African Cricket Association side to England; the other as anxious, indeed desperately so, not to welcome it.

Sport has given rise to conflict before. Ill-will may stem from a mere lapse of amiability—or be a positive expression of ideology, and cricket of course had its moments of passion before 1970. Personal rivalries on the field have sometimes (but fortunately only rarely) grown into feuds. There have been allegations of unsportsmanship, bad umpiring, and heated arguments about bowlers with doubtful actions. The 1932–33 tour of Australia strained Anglo-Australian relations in quarters far beyond those of cricket. But all these disputes were *technical* ones—and even Larwood in the course of time was forgiven by a once hostile and outraged Australian populace.

The bitterness of 1970 was not technical at all. It was moral, political, personal, ideological. Confusion and hate were brought into cricket together with prejudices of race, creed and colour—brought into the very sport which had shown perhaps the greatest tolerance of all sports in the passage of history, and where friendly, civilised competition had for so long been paramount. The overtones and undertones were such that most men found it terribly difficult to be dispassionate. The summer of a General Election did not help to cool matters, either. How thankful must have been the village, club and school sides of England who happily played their cricket last year with their traditional blend of innocence, zest and good fellowship.

Before the distaste and disquiet of last year can be properly understood, it is necessary to consider briefly something of the history preceding it. The South African government's attitude towards mixed sport within South Africa was dealt with at length by the Prime Minister, Mr. B.J. Vorster, in the House of Assembly in Cape Town on April 11, 1967, when he said unambiguously that the policy inside the country was that there would not be mixed sporting events, no matter how good were the participants. 'In respect of this principle we are not prepared to compromise, we are not prepared to negotiate, and we are not prepared to make any concessions.' Fundamentally it was this uncompromising—and in some ways curiously obtuse—defence of apartheid put up by Mr. Vorster that led directly to the events of last year. Political attitudes struck thousands of miles away in England were, arguably, unhelpful in the struggle against injustice; and, anyway, Mr. Vorster's views by no means religiously reflected the moral heart-searching among his more thoughtful supporters and among many of South Africa's leading cricketers. But while opportunities for white and non-white cricketers were unequal, and while they could not take part together in trials and other matches to test their respective abilities, a case against South Africa's sporting system existed.

Mr. Vorster at the same time made one other relevant statement, not frequently quoted: 'The demand has been put to us that our Springbok team would not be welcomed unless it includes members of all race groups. If that demand is made a condition of the continuation of sports relations, I say we are not prepared to meet it because it is our affair and ours alone.' The tone brooked no argument, but it was noted in many parts of the world. So far as cricket teams visiting South Africa were concerned—as well as any other sporting side from a country having 'traditional ties' with South Africa—Mr. Vorster made it clear that mixed teams would be acceptable provided politicians did not interfere to harm relations between countries or between groups inside South Africa.

How Mr. Vorster in September 1968 rejected an M.C.C. side that included Basil D'Oliveira is well enough known, and the seething discontent that arose from that episode never subsided until May of last year, having by then reached a dangerous boiling point such as sport in this country had never known.

Without fuss or heroics the South Africans' programme for their English tour was released in September 1969—a full season's fixture-list from May 2 to September 8, including five Tests and matches against all the counties. The news at first went almost unnoticed—until Mr. Denis Howell, the then Minister with responsibility for Sport, declared on television on October 19 that the South African team 'should stay away from Britain'. The same night Mr. Jack Cheetham, president of the S.A.C.A., at once rejoined by saying that South Africa had no intention of withdrawing from the 1970 tour. The battle was on. Mr. S.C. Griffith, Secretary of M.C.C. said, not for the last time, that 'the Cricket Council have stated, and still feel, that more good is achieved by maintaining sporting links with South Africa than by cutting them off altogether'. It was this policy of 'open bridges' that was in due course to be attacked so vehemently by the tour opponents.

With a South African Rugby Union tour of Britain about to start on November 5, the seeds of controversy were dangerously apparent. People were beginning to take sides: it was easy to forecast that passions could be aroused to split the nation.

Meanwhile a new name had entered the lists—that of Peter Hain, a 19-year-old white South African and first-year engineering student at Imperial College, London. From a liberal Pretoria family and with opinions formed during his youth, he had been in England only three and a half years when he organised and launched the Stop the Seventy Tour Committee in September 1969, and was its chairman throughout. During the summer of 1969 he had taken part in demonstrations against Wilfred Isaacs' South African touring side. His committee—much to Hain's surprise—began to make an increasingly strong impact. He was committed to non-violent protest, from which platform he doubtless derived the support he obtained.

In South Africa talks got under way between the white and non-white cricket bodies in the hope of improving relations, but they quickly broke down in a flurry of charge and countercharge of 'insincerity'. In these exchanges it was important for the observer to remember that S.A.C.A. officials could only go as far as their government would allow. But matters were not helped when Mr. Arthur Coy, convenor of the S.A.C.A. selectors, announced there was no question of non-white players being included in a South African team.

The rigorous police control necessary at the South African Rugby matches—troubles and nasty incidents were encountered in England, Wales, Scotland and Ireland: by mid-December alone 68 policemen had been injured—began to convince cricket officials of the impossibility of protecting cricket grounds in 1970 without counties facing enormous bills. The ease with which play could be disrupted by determined demonstrators was not underestimated. The South African Rugby players themselves were suffering considerable distress from the intensity of the demonstrators' actions. In this atmosphere Messrs. Cheetham and Coy flew into England in November for talks at Lord's to finalise the tour arrangements. (When the South African Rugby team left England, their manager, Mr. Corrie Bornman, said: 'The last three months have been an ordeal to which I would never again subject young sportsmen. . . . The players were really fed up. . . . Mercifully, no one was hurt, but the violence we have seen leaves me in no doubt that any future South African team in Britain will be in danger.')

The decision confirming the continuance of the cricket tour was taken by the Cricket Council at Lord's on November 27, and a confidential letter was sent to all county clubs asking them to consult police and other authorities to assess the security arrangements for the South African games. Lord's officials were also in touch for the first time with the Home Office about arrangements. Figures of between £7,000 and £10,000 (and even—later—£18,000) were being quoted to protect a three-day match, and the size and strength of the continued Rugby demonstrations were no comfort for those who cherished the hope that anti-South African activity would diminish before the cricketers arrived. The actual cost at a South African Rugby match at Manchester in November 1969, when 2,300 police were on duty—29 of them were injured and there were 93 arrests—was £8,985.

Such a bill would have wiped out completely the anticipated profit of £7,000 each county could have expected from the tour. Security arrangements for the South Africans' two scheduled visits to Birmingham were expected to total about £250,000, mostly to be borne by ratepayers. The newly consecrated Bishop of Woolwich, the Right Rev. David Sheppard (who had refused to play against the South Africans in 1960), while unwaveringly opposing the tour, warned demonstrators against disruption and violence, which could 'destroy the whole cause of anti-apartheid'. The trade unions were also beginning to agitate, and more than 100 Liberal and Labour M.P.s signed a letter to M.C.C. saying they had every intention of joining the protestors if the South African team came to England.

The T.C.C.B. had plenty on its plate for its two-day meeting at Lord's on December 10–11, 1969. Jack Cheetham, in Johannesburg, 'pinned all hopes' on the tour proceeding, and the Lord's meeting issued the following statement:

> *The Test and County Cricket Board, comprising representatives from all first-class counties and the minor counties, have confirmed unanimously their recommendation that the South African tour will take place.*
>
> *In re-affirming this decision, they repeat their aversion to racial discrimination of any kind. They also respect the rights of those who wish to demonstrate peacefully.*
>
> *Equally, they are unanimous in their resolve to uphold the rights of individuals in this country to take part in lawful pursuits, particularly where these pursuits have the support of the majority.*
>
> *A sub-committee has been appointed to deal with all matters relevant to the tour and to report to the T.C.C.B.*

Four days later Jack Cheetham, in Cape Town, announced that future South African sides would be selected 'on merit' alone, 'irrespective of colour considerations'—which drew the immediate riposte of 'empty words' from Mr. Hassan Howa, president-designate of the non-white South African Cricket Board of Control. Mr. Cheetham's announcement and the T.C.C.B.'s decision pleased as many people as it angered others, and thenceforth there was little peace in the land on the vexed and emotional tour issue. On the one hand the T.C.C.B. had made a representative and honourable decision; on the other a tragic and irresponsible one.

The sequence of events thereafter became so crowded, with individuals and organisations in England and abroad voicing impassioned pleas for both factions, that even the salient happenings came thick and fast. The East African section of M.C.C.'s proposed tour there and to the Far East early in 1970 fell an early victim after Uganda accused the Cricket Council of having 'double standards' by playing both all-white South Africa and coloured teams; a referendum by the Cricketers' Association in January showed that just over 81 per cent of English first-class players were in favour of the South African tour; on the night of January 19–20 co-ordinated action saw anti-apartheid attacks directed at a dozen county grounds; an eight-man delegation from Lord's conferred with Mr. Callaghan and Mr. Howell at the Home Office; Messrs. Cheetham and Coy flew in for further confidential talks; a shortened tour of 12 matches (on fairly 'defensible' grounds) was announced by the Cricket Council; South Africa duly anounced their 14-man side under Ali Bacher—all white—to tour England; and the Prime Minister, Mr. Harold Wilson, in a hotly criticised television interview on April 16, considered that M.C.C. had made 'a big mistake' in inviting the South African team—'a very ill-judged decision'. He said, with the proviso that any protests must not be violent: 'Everyone should be free to demonstrate against apartheid—I hope people will feel free to do so.'

Money—and lots of it—seemed one way of saving the tour, though the true cost of protecting grounds was absolutely unpredictable. On April 23 'The 1970 Cricket Fund', with a minimum target of £200,000 and with the approval of the Cricket Council, was launched at Lord's under the chairmanship of Lt.-Col. Charles Newman, v.c. and with a distinguished list of patrons who included the Duke of Norfolk, the Duke of Beaufort, Viscount Portal, Lord Wakefield, Judge Sir Carl Aarvold, Sir Peter Studd, M. J. C. Allom, Alec Bedser, Brian Close and Colin Cowdrey. Money for financing the tour had been arriving well before this date, but the chairman made it clear that no donations would be accepted from South Africa. But on the very day the fund was launched the Supreme Council for Sport in Africa (which includes 36 countries in its membership) threatened the withdrawal of 13 African countries from the British Commonwealth Games in Edinburgh scheduled for July: all depended on whether or not the tour was called off, and this Commonwealth Games issue became yet another major factor in the saga.

The Fair Cricket Campaign also came into being in April, with its first objective to stop the tour. It made no secret of its intention to organise 'a massive and peaceful march of conscience past Lord's on Saturday, June 20'—the Saturday of the Lord's Test. The Bishop of Woolwich was chairman, and his vice-chairmen were Sir Edward Boyle, m.p. (now Lord Boyle of Handsworth) and Mr. Reginald Prentice, m.p. The Bishop of Woolwich and Sir Edward Boyle were major speakers urging cancellation at the M.C.C. Annual General Meeting last year, when the potential danger to race relations and to international sport was also ventilated. The great majority of M.C.C. members, however, were in favour of the tour proceeding, and the A.G.M. in fact had no real influence on the situation at all. The T.C.C.B. meanwhile took the precaution of writing to players to say that those English cricketers appearing in the five Tests and for the Southern and Northern Counties sides would have their lives insured for £15,000. Lancashire's two overseas players, Clive Lloyd and Farokh Engineer, had previously been threatened with violence (and their families too) if they did not withdraw from the county's proposed match against the tourists.

A rare event in British life—a House of Commons emergency debate on a sporting topic—took place, at the instance of Mr. Philip Noel-Baker, on May 14, when for three hours the tour issue was passionately thrashed out. (No vote was to be taken.) Mr. Denis Howell declared that never in his experience had he had to deal with a question 'where the issues were as deep, as emotional and as involved as in this one'.

Mr. Howell said that the proposed tour raised deep feelings, and four questions of great public importance had to be considered by the Government and by the Cricket Council. First, the effect of the proposed tour upon racial harmony; secondly, questions of law and order; thirdly, the implications for the Commonwealth Games; fourthly, the long term interests of sport.

Mr. Howell dealt with the points in turn and announced the latest resolution of the Sports Council for Great Britain (of which he was chairman) which 'strongly urged' the Cricket Council to withdraw the 1970 tour invitation 'because it believes the consequences of the tour taking place will have harmful repercussions on sport, especially multi-racial sport, extending far beyond cricket itself'.

Mr. Reginald Maudling, then Deputy Leader of the Opposition, argued that:

> *It is a positive gain to encourage people to come here and play games with us so that they are able to see the freedom and tolerance in this country. Let them learn from our system, a system that is based on merit. Let them play with teams here who are always chosen on the basis of merit and not on grounds of race, creed, religion or politics.*
>
> *. . . I believe our basic principle must be that any man is entitled to do what is lawful and to expect that the State will protect him from unlawful interference. This must be the first duty of government. . . .*
>
> *Once a man is denied the right to do what is lawful because other people at home or overseas may disagree with his views, it would be striking at the roots of freedom under the law. Once we admit the right of people to enforce their views by violent means with impunity—and there are many examples in the world today—democracy is at risk.*

Sir Edward Boyle explained to the House why he had agreed to become a vice-chairman of the Fair Cricket Campaign:

> *I did so because, as someone who utterly deplores and opposes violence and disorder, I had come reluctantly to the view that the South African cricket tour was likely to be bad for community relations in this country, bad for the future of cricket, bad for the future of sport generally, bad for the Commonwealth, and bad for law and order in Britain.*
>
> *. . . Many hon. Members believe that this summer will be unpleasant but that, somehow, we will get through and that international sport within the Commonwealth will then go on as before. I hope they are right, but I ask the House to seriously consider the possibility that it may not prove so simple as that. It would be tragic if one wrong decision now were to undo all the fine work which the M.C.C. has done over the years to promote integration in sport.*
>
> *. . . This is an apt moment to pay tribute to the work of the M.C.C., whose members are justly proud of what they have achieved. I also take this opportunity to thank personally the members of the M.C.C. and the Cricket Council for all the courtesy that has been shown by them to me and to other visitors who have discussed this matter with them recently.*

The Home Secretary, Mr. James Callaghan, referred to the 'unparalleled crescendo of opposition' to the tour, and went on:

When I hear the list of organisations who oppose the tour, when I consider the possible damage that could be done. . . . I repeat to the Cricket Council that it is for it to consider . . . whether its judgement to proceed with this tour is right.

What I fear is that there will be damage done to racial relations and other matters. But I have to weigh that, in the discharge of my duties, against imposing my judgement that the damage to be done is so grave that I should interfere with the traditional rights of people to carry on a lawful pursuit, even though it is an unpopular pursuit. So far, I have reached the conclusion it would not be right to do that. . . .

I believe that that is correct and that it is not unfair to throw the responsibility upon the Cricket Council. It invited the South Africans; it can uninvite them if it chooses to do so. If it does, I promise the Council this: no one will construe it, because he will not be correct, to mean that the Council will be bowing to the forces of lawlessness or disorder, or the demonstrators in this country.

It seemed at the time that if there were to be a watershed at all before the scheduled arrival of the tourists on June 1, then it would be the Commons debate. Up to that point the Cricket Council insisted, come hell or high water, that the tour was on. On the evening of May 14 they had parliamentary pleas on which to pause and ponder. If there was any chink of dissension discernible within the Cricket Council, it had come only via whispered rumours: the public face of the Council was carefully presented as solid and unified. But in all conscience there was a vast and simmering edifice of responsible opinion, building itself into a more powerful and insistent structure each day, that was hammering on the portals of the Council. The gathering momentum of the demonstrators was now joined by a corpus of opposition to the tour that took as its common theme an appeal to the Cricket Council 'to demonstrate their sense of responsibility as citizens, and at the same time their concern for the future of international cricket' by cancelling the tour invitation.

This was the text of a letter in *The Times* on May 6 signed by seventeen prominent persons, among them the Bishop of Woolwich, Lord Constantine, Fr. Trevor Huddleston, Jeremy Thorpe and Sir Edward Boyle. Whether it was letters such as this, Mr. Callaghan's words, the more responsible elements of the press, the Commonwealth Games issue, the potential antagonism of some I.C.C. countries, the attitude of the Church, of the Sports Council or of the Race Relations Board, or even the apparently lukewarm response to the 1970 Tour Fund, the Council had food for thought (and much of it unpalatable) from every quarter. It is as well to record that the anti-tour movement attracted a fanatical fringe as well as a large body of ordinary, sincere people. Its more militant allies had motives that were probably as questionable as their tactics were reprehensible, but as the campaign progressed these voices became less audible than those of other elements carrying more weight.

Hot on the heels of the Commons debate came the shattering news for

South Africa of her formal expulsion from the Olympic movement—the first nation ever so expelled since the Olympic movement was revived in 1894: in a secret ballot in Amsterdam the International Olympic Committee—with the names of Basil D'Oliveira and Arthur Ashe well in their minds, it is said—made perhaps the most momentous decision in sporting history. '*It will be noted*', said a spokesman at Lord's. The expulsion made a much stronger impact on most people than the many resolutions against apartheid dutifully passed at the United Nations. On the same day the Royal Commonwealth Society, with its impeccable record of good sense and responsibility, expressed 'great concern at the harm that would be done by the tour to multi-racial sport and good relations within the Commonwealth'. In Cape Town, Jack Cheetham made a last desperate plea to keep the tour alive. The Fair Cricket Campaign (with new recruits in Sir William Robson Brown, M.P. and Mr. Nicholas Scott, M.P.) stepped up its activities by sending out 20,000 invitations to organisations and individuals to stop the tour. The Archbishop of Canterbury and the Chief Rabbi added their voices to the wave of opposition. It was even made public that, according to unofficial sources, the Queen, in her personal capacity, was opposed to the tour. It seemed that the mightiest and the humblest in the land, and all those in between, were committed one way or the other. (An announcement from Buckingham Palace, by the way, said that the South African cricketers would not be received there; nor was there to have been a Royal visit to Lord's for the Test match—as there had likewise not been to Twickenham for the England-South Africa rugger match the previous December.)

What a great section of the public—both pro and anti the tour—considered would be an eleventh-hour reappraisal came at Lord's at a special and secret meeting of the Cricket Council on the evening of Monday, May 18. The meeting was a long one, deep into the night, and what agonies of conscience were experienced will only be known by those who were there. It did not transpire until the following day that the meeting had taken place—a critical meeting, to be sure, and held, incidentally, on the same day that the Prime Minister announced that the General Election would be held on June 18. (This date was the scheduled start of the Lord's Test, and visions of race riots on polling day could not have been a welcome thought to any political party.)

In Barbados, a statement from the West Indies Board of Control set out its positive opposition to the tour, adding that 'irreparable harm' would come from it. P. D. B. Short, the Board secretary, said that the Board fervently hoped that the direct representations that had been made would result in cancellation. The West Indies Board had also been asked that the forthcoming tour of England by the West Indies Young Cricketers (in July-August 1970) be called off if the South Africans toured. Mr. Mark Bonham Carter, chairman of the Race Relations Board, who had spoken eloquently at the M.C.C. A.G.M., expressed his further concern in a private letter to Mr. G. O. Allen, vice-chairman of the Cricket Council. The council of the 14,000-strong Inner London Teachers' Association deplored the prospect of the tour and the 'inevitable repercussions' in schools. And a last-minute petition to halt the tour was presented to M.C.C. on behalf of several hundred people living near Lord's.

It was against this background—and there were many more pressures too numerous to enumerate—that the Cricket Council came to their decision on May 18. At 7 p.m. the following evening, after a day of somewhat wild speculation, and while protest groups with banners paraded outside the Grace Gates, a crowded Press Conference in the Long Room at Lord's received the following statement from Mr. Griffith:

At a meeting held yesterday the Cricket Council—representing all grades of cricket in the United Kingdom—were given a full report by the Executive Committee on all matters relating to the South African tour which had arisen since the Council's last meeting on April 23. The Council weighed carefully the strength of opinion both for and against the tour. This full statement of the Council's deliberations is indicative of their concern and of their awareness of the responsibilities with which they were faced.

The Council have decided by a substantial majority, that this tour should proceed as arranged. It has always believed that cricket in South Africa should be given the longest possible time to bring about conditions in which all cricketers in their own country, regardless of their origin, are able to play and be selected on equal terms. The South African Cricket Association have taken the first step by announcing that all future touring teams will be selected on merit. The Council have confirmed the present tour in the hope and belief that this intention will be capable of fulfilment in the future. It is for this reason that the Council, while confirming finally their invitation to the South African Cricket Association to tour this summer, wish to make clear their position regarding the future.

They have informed the South African Cricket Association that no further Test tours between South Africa and this country will take place until South African cricket is played and teams are selected on a multi-racial basis in South Africa.

In this increasingly complicated issue the Council felt that they should first reassess their responsibilities. These they confirmed as being contained in the following broad headings:

1. To cricket and cricketers both in the United Kingdom and throughout the world;
2. To other sports and sportsmen.

It should be stressed that the Council have taken into account other matters of a public and political nature, but they consider these matters to be the responsibility of the Government who are best equipped to judge and act upon them.

In reviewing their original decision to confirm the invitation to the South African Cricket Association, the Council had to consider whether the desirability—so often repeated—of maintaining contact with South

Africa had in any way changed. It was agreed that in the long term this policy was in the best interests of cricket, and cricketers of all races in South Africa.

The Council had also to consider its responsibilities to cricket and cricketers throughout the world, taking into account the opposition to the tour from certain quarters and the effect on other cricket-playing countries if the tour proceeded. The Council sympathised with those Boards of Control who had themselves been put under considerable pressure in regard to this tour but felt that the long term effects upon cricket could be disastrous if they were to succumb to similar pressure.

The Council also had to consider whether cricket would be a practical proposition if played amidst all the stresses and strains which have been threatened and predicted. The Council were under no illusions as to the risks of disruption at the matches to be played. They had also to consider the recent statement of the Home Secretary in the House of Commons on May 14 that 'there need be no fear in anybody's mind that the police are incapable of handling this kind of demonstration'. They also noted his assurance that it would be the duty of the police to prevent a breach of the peace and bring them (the offenders) before the courts.

The Council discussed the question of the Commonwealth Games in Scotland and deeply regretted the attitude of those countries who had threatened to withdraw if the cricket tour took place. The Council acknowledged a degree of responsibility to other sports and recognised the problems with which the organising bodies are faced. They hope, in view of their statement as to the future, that these countries will reconsider their attitude.

Two other issues which have already been mentioned should perhaps be further elaborated.

First, the question of community relations. The Council recognise that there has been a growing concern in the United Kingdom with the unacceptable apartheid policies of the present South African Government. The Council share this concern, but wish to re-emphasise that cricket has made an outstanding and widely acknowledged contribution to the maintenance of good relations between all people among whom the game has been played.

Secondly, the question of freedom under the law in this country. The Council do not consider it the duty or responsibility of cricket to campaign for freedom under the law at the expense of the game itself. But the Council and its constituent members are aware of the dangers of a minority group being allowed to take the law into their own hands by direct action. However distasteful to this minority group, the South African tour this summer is not only a lawful event, but as shown by the outcome of recent opinion polls, it is clearly the wish of the majority that the tour should take place.

Thus the 1970 tour was still 'on'. And so was the hubbub against it. Meanwhile, what was the attitude in South Africa of the S.A.C.A.?

South Africa's cricket future was in jeopardy, and rightly or wrongly the S.A.C.A. believed that cancellation of the tour—for which they had been preparing since the original invitation was extended by M.C.C. in July 1966—would mean the isolation of South African cricket for a very long time ahead. The reluctance of the S.A.C.A. to take any step in cancelling the tour was bolstered, too, by the fact that the 1968–69 M.C.C. tour of their country was cancelled as a result of interference by the South African government. The ordeal likely to face their players in Britain was never minimised, but they expressed much faith in what they trusted would be the 'good sense and fair play' of the British public. In the midst of the furore Jack Cheetham declared: 'I have said it before, and I say it again, that the British public will, as ever, stand by visitors to their country. I place my confidence in this.'

While these protestations of faith were being sent across the world, objectionable tactics to disrupt the twelve tour matches were being carefully hatched, estimates were being bandied about of between 10,000 and 50,000 demonstrators who would converge on Lord's on June 6, and barbed wire and artificial pitches (if the natural pitch were maliciously damaged) were being laid at cricket grounds to withstand the expected intrusions. But by the third week-end in May, with a feeling of shock and disappointment in South Africa over the Olympic decision, and the Sports Minister, Mr. Frank Waring, lamenting that 'politics have triumphed over sport', many realists in the Republic believed the cricket tour to be impossible. This was despite a South African poll which showed that only one-fifth of these questioned were against the tour taking place. South African newspapers showed dramatic pictures of Springbok wives depicted as 'the women who wait and pray'. The influential *Rand Daily Mail*, a persistent supporter of the tour, said that even if Bacher's side did make the journey to Britain, it was 'difficult to see them getting very far with the business of playing cricket'. The paper added that only 'a clear, unambiguous statement by our cricket authorities on the principle of non-racialism in sport' could help the tour. Those who recognised this as South Africa's own problem had long awaited such a statement. It had not been forthcoming, and it was not forthcoming now.

An unequivocal statement against sports segregation by either the captain, Ali Bacher, or the tour manager, Jack Plimsoll, would have been welcomed in the absence of one from the S.A.C.A. itself. But presumably they regarded apartheid as the national policy and not the responsibility of sportsmen (so far as public pronouncements went, at any rate). It is true that neither of them was completely silent, but—before the cancellation, at least—their words were very guarded. Bacher, a doctor working in a hospital for non-Europeans near Johannesburg, soon after his appointment as captain for the English tour, said he would welcome multi-racial cricket in South Africa 'as soon as the Government finds it practical'. He was at all times behind his governing body in supporting the tour, and consulted Dawie de Villiers,the rugger captain, to find out what his team might expect to encounter in England. 'I would always speak to a demonstrator,' said Bacher, 'provided he was polite.' But he was firm in urging that demonstrators must not be allowed to break up the tour, lest there be 'dire consequences' for world sport. 'We are not politicians,' he said early in May. 'We are going to England to play cricket.'

Bacher and the other 13 members of his team—not one of whom, incidentally, ever considered withdrawing because of the potential threats—had come under attack from the Stop the Seventy Tour Committee for not declaring themselves against apartheid sport and thus seeming to condone it. Bacher and Peter Pollock were quick to reject this: the reticence of cricketers on the issue of apartheid did not of course mean that they were necessarily in favour of it. Bacher, indeed, publicly recognised the right to stage demonstrations, provided they were peaceful and did not disrupt a match—precisely the view held, though they were on opposing sides, by both S.C. Griffith and David Sheppard, and expressed by them in October 1969.

As the tour drama was reaching its climax Jack Plimsoll, up to then silent about the controversy, said in an interview that he was not against mixed sport in South Africa. 'There are a lot of non-white cricketers who, in better company, would improve with increased competition and could force their way into a Springbok side,' he said. But this did not amount to a plea for the breaking down of the barriers.

Exactly two weeks before the South Africans were due to land in England, the S.A.C.A. Board of Control, after a week-end meeting in Johannesburg, unanimously reaffirmed that it was proceeding with its plans for the team's practices in Durban and subsequent departure for England. The announcement came as world-wide controversy seemed to be reaching a peak, and amidst fresh criticism from even within South Africa, where Kevin Craig in the Johannesburg *Sunday Times* warned the S.A.C.A. that unless they called off the tour they would 'expose our cricketers to physical danger and maybe death'. In South Africa, as in Britain, there had been speculation whether the government might not step in and call off the tour. At a political rally at Uitenhage on April 11, Mr. B.J. Schoeman, the Minister of Transport and number two in the South African cabinet, said that if he had his way he would not send the side to Britain. 'Why should we allow our boys to be insulted by those long-haired louts?' he asked. He stressed this was a personal view, but at no time—so far as one can ascertain from governmental and S.A.C.A. sources—was there any approach from the South African government to S.A.C.A. to reconsider the tour.

After the Cricket Council's statement of May 19, events moved swiftly to their climax. Outrage and determination to increase demonstrations was the reaction of the anti-tour groups, but those who cared about liberty and law and order felt greatly in debt to the Cricket Council. There was relief in South Africa, even though the Council had admitted there was something grossly wrong with cricket selection there.

Almost at once Mr Callaghan invited the Cricket Council to meet him at the Home Office on May 21. The chairman, Mr. M. J. C. Allom, and the secretary, Mr. S. C. Griffith, attended a three-hour meeting at which the Home Secretary requested that the tour be cancelled 'on the grounds of broad public policy'.

The Home Secretary's letter to the Chairman of the Cricket Council read:

> *When you and Mr. Griffith came to see me this morning, we discussed the statement issued on behalf of the Cricket Council on May 19 about the South African tour.*
>
> *You explained that the Council had come to their conclusion that the tour should go on after reassessing their own responsibilites, which were limited to the impact of the decision on cricket and cricketers, both in the United Kingdom and throughout the world, and on other sports and sportsmen. You emphasized however that although the Council were naturally concerned with various other matters of a public and political nature which had been brought to their notice and had taken them into account, at the same time they felt that these matters fell outside their own responsibilities and that it was beyond their competence to judge what significance to attach to them. This, they felt, was the responsibility of the Government, who were equipped to judge and act upon them.*
>
> *I accepted this distinction.*
>
> *The Government have therefore been very carefully considering the implications of the tour, if it were to take place, in the light of the many representations that have been received from a wide variety of interests and persons. We have had particularly in mind the possible impact on relations with other Commonwealth countries, race relations in this country and the divisive effect on the community. Another matter for concern is the effect on the Commonwealth Games. I have taken into account too the position of the police; there is no doubt as to their ability to cope with any situation which might arise, but a tour of this nature would mean diverting police resources on a large scale from their essential ordinary duties.*
>
> *The Government have come to the conclusion, after reviewing all these considerations, that on grounds of broad public policy they must request the Cricket Council to withdraw their invitation to the South African Cricket Association, and I should be grateful if you would put this request before the Council.*

This amounted to a government directive, and faced with a formal request of this kind, the Cricket Council had little choice but to agree. They bowed to *force majeure*. Not even a vote was taken.

The cancellation came on May 22. The final statement on behalf of the Cricket Council read thus:

> *At a meeting held this afternoon at Lord's, the Cricket Council considered the formal request from Her Majesty's Government to withdraw the invitation to the South African touring team this summer.*
>
> *With deep regret the Council were of the opinion that they had no*

alternative but to accede to this request and they are informing the South African Cricket Association accordingly.

The Council are grateful for the overwhelming support of cricketers, cricket lovers and many others, and share their disappointment at the cancellation of the tour. At the same time they regret the discourtesy to the South African Cricket Association and the inconvenience caused to so many people.

The Council see no reason to repeat the arguments, to which they still adhere which led them to sustain the invitation to the South African cricketers issued four years ago. They do, however, deplore the activities of those who by the intimidation of individual cricketers and threats of violent disruption have inflamed the whole issue.

Thus the sorry saga—apart from the inevitable series of reactions both in England and abroad—was at an end. It had been distressing and distasteful. Cricket, and especially Mr. Griffith at Lord's had been subjected to pressures never experienced in the game before. Let us hope that cricket will never know such conflict again.

A LIFETIME WITH SURREY [1972]

Stealing Singles with Jack Hobbs

BY ANDREW SANDHAM

The dominant thought raised by the essays in the 1972 almanack was probably Time, and the frightening rate at which it passes. Two essays in particular emphasised the point, the recollection of a cricketing life by Andrew Sandham, and a look back at Denis Compton's record-breaking year by Basil Easterbrook. By the time he wrote down his memories, Sandham was already old enough to surprise a great many younger readers who might have been pardoned for thinking he was dead. In fact he lived on for some years after the publicatiton of the essay, becoming one of that extraordinary breed of ancient virtuosi who survived into their nineties, who included his team-mate Herbert Strudwick and the two master bowlers Wilfred Rhodes and Sydney Barnes; perhaps none of them quite matched the durability of Frank Woolley, who emigrated in his 85th year, remarried, and finally departed, as he had so often done in his playing career, in the nineties. Sandham sounds acutely conscious of the time factor in the lives of cricketers, and is quick to chastise those commentators who were babes in arms when the events on which they pontificate were taking place. In view of Sandham's love of the Surrey club, it is surprising that he makes no mention of the most astute of Surrey captains, Percy Fender, yet another of Sandham's generation destined to become a nonagenarian.

Sixty years, which is the total time spanned by my career with Surrey County Cricket Club as player, coach and scorer, is a very big slice out of a life-time, but I have no regrets about it. Whatever the differences in method, tactics and so on between my day and the present, I am glad that I played when I did, for I consorted with some of the 'greats' and we all enjoyed the game. Cricket has been good to me in that I have met so many friends and have been enabled to visit so many countries which I would otherwise never have seen.

My keenness on cricket began at an early age. After leaving school, I turned out for my father's club, Streatham United, on Streatham Common at the age of 16. A Mr. Raphael, father of J. E. Raphael, who played cricket for Oxford and Surrey, and also got a Blue for Rugby and represented England in nine Internationals between 1902 and 1906, used to watch our team occasionally and he mentioned my name to the Surrey County authorities. As a result I had annual trials at The Oval nets for three years. I remember that the first coach to see me was the famous Bobby Abel, a kindly man. Then E. H. D. Sewell became coach and later on, in 1946, when I, too, took up the position of coach, I looked up an old coaching report-book to see what he had said about me. It read: 'A fair bat and a promising bowler,' but I was rarely called upon to bowl in first-class cricket.

When 18 I went to Mitcham C.C. and a Surrey Committee-man, a Mr. W. W. Thompson, spoke about me to the then County Secretary, the late W. Findlay. In December 1910, Mr. Findlay strongly advised me not to become a professional cricketer; but I told him that I was sure that, if given the chance, I would make good. So I joined the County staff in 1911 at a wage of 25s a week—one golden sovereign and two half-crowns. I think my winter pay was £1 per month! But I was happy, though when I watched Tom Hayward, Jack Hobbs, Ernie Hayes and Co., I thought I would never reach their high standards. There were, if I recall, 30 players on the bowling staff, which meant that, quite apart from the first eleven, one had to be very good to get a place in the second team.

In those days when the first team were playing away, and even if a second eleven match was taking place at The Oval, members came to the nets for practice (half an hour a time). This meant that the 'left overs' were continually bowling at them and at the end of the day were rather tired. We had a 'kitty' and sometimes we picked up eight or ten shillings each, which at that time was a fair sum.

I was allowed to turn out for Mitcham on Saturdays and in four consecutive matches I scored a century—for Mitcham, the Young Players of Surrey, Surrey Club and Ground and Surrey second eleven against Wiltshire. As a result, I was given a game for the county eleven against Cambridge University and, in my very first first-class match, I scored 53. There was at that time a public house with a flat roof over on the gas-works side of The Oval, with six or seven tiered seats for customers who could see cricket for nothing. As the pubs were then open all day long and the beer was both cheaper and stronger, the customers by the afternoon got a bit 'under the influence' and frequently gave us 'the bird'. I got it on my first appearance and I thought it rather hard, for I naturally wanted to do well and took only two hours for my 53. All this, too, from people who were not in the ground!

We lesser lights had to put in our own practice with the coach at 10 a.m. and then wait for any visiting players and our own first eleven players who came out for a knock and bowl to them. I remember rushing to bowl against G. L. Jessop, but after he played 'forward' and the ball narrowly missed my head, I had sense enough to bowl at his legs.

Soon after my 'baptism' against Cambridge, I was as usual bowling at the nets when, ten minutes before the start of a match with Lancashire, I was told that I was playing, Tom Hayward having dropped out. This was such a shock that I nearly dropped, too. In those days there was a telegraph-office on the ground and, having seen the batting order, I sent my father a wire telling him the news. My father, who was a Lancashire man, had taken a few hours off from work and come to The Oval, so that he missed my telegram. He told me that he was sitting in the crowd, but had not got a score-card. So he turned to the man next to him and asked: 'Who is this lad coming in to bat?' He was shaken when he was told: 'It's a second eleven lad named Sandham.' I scored 60 and my father said that after I was out he left for home. I remember being nearly run out at 49 by that splendid batsman, R. H. Spooner. Come to think of it, it seems rather silly to risk a run out at 49 or 99.

In this connection, I have often been asked how Jack Hobbs and I managed to steal so many sharp runs. I guess I must have run hundreds for him, for I never called him for one! As a matter of fact, he used not to call, for I knew from his push-stroke to the off that he wanted to run. I was always a yard or so down the pitch after the ball had been delivered and as I was rather fast between wickets, he knew I would make it. I remember Herbert Sutcliffe talking to me after being in with Jack for the first time about 'these short runs'. I said: 'Well, I know when he wants a quick run without calling, so I run.' Herbie said something to the effect that he was not going to run any; they had got to stop; but I noticed that he found that he had to when coupled with Jack in Tests—and a jolly good job they made of it, too.

Incidentally I read in a newspaper article last summer the view that 'Hobbs and Sutcliffe never took a chance with their running'. I cannot agree with this. The fact was that, like Jack and myself this pair developed such an understanding that, though the element of risk remained, it was reduced to a minimum. I wondered at the time how the author of the article, who was born less than two years before the close of Jack's playing career, could have written with such authority. I also heard of a retired former player who said in a speech at a club dinner that 'Hobbs and Sandham wouldn't have made the runs they did in these days.' Well, perhaps I would not have done, who knows; but to say that Jack would not is a bit much! I looked up the person concerned in *Wisden* and I see from his birthday that he was 12 years of age when Jack retired in 1934. I fancy that, being the great batsman he was, Jack would have coped.

In 1913, I made my first first-class century, 196 against Sussex at The Oval. Curiously enough, I hit the last of my 107 centuries also against Sussex, at Hove at the age of 47 in my final game before retiring.

Many people have asked if any particular person taught me. The fact is that I must have had a natural aptitude for batting and I always watched the established players. I was always on the players' balcony to see Tom Hayward and Jack Hobbs open the innings for Surrey. Tom was my idol then, though later on he frightened me, for when I was twelfth man away from home and he had made a good score, he would bark at me to get him a whisky and soda. I would say 'Yes, sir,' but was afraid to ask him for the money. My own fault, I suppose, but Tom had many a whisky and soda on me! He was the senior professional and 'well in' with the various captains Surrey had, and what he said went.

The 1914–18 War finished Tom's career and I was destined to take his place in 1919. I wonder how many centuries Hobbs would have made during that break in first-class cricket, for I once asked him when he considered he was at his best and he said: 'Before the 1914 War broke out.' My association with him was broken for a time in 1921 when he was taken ill with appendicitis during a Test at Leeds against Australia. That season was a bad one for English batsmen, who had no experience against fast bowlers of the pace of Jack Gregory and Ted McDonald. What a pair for any opening batsman to face! Incidentally, I consider that McDonald had the most graceful action I have ever seen in a fast bowler. As a result of Jack's illness, many openers were tried for England and I think about 30 men turned out for the country that year. I got my chance in the last Test at The Oval, going in at No. 5 and making 21. Being an opener, I found it rather nerve-racking to have to sit and wait until five minutes past six to take my turn at the wicket.

Odd things stick in the memory. I recall in 1921 an amateur named T. J. Moloney, who bowled under-arm, appearing in one of our trial matches. Well, he was bowling against Jack, who jokingly advanced down the pitch, only to miss and be stumped by Herbert Strudwick. A few weeks later 'Struddy' said that was the worst thing he ever did, for later on Moloney played in one or two county matches and, as his mode of bowling was down the leg-side, 'Struddy' experienced many narrow escapes from batsmen swinging their bats and just missing his head. 'Struddy's' friend was included in the side when we went to Trent Bridge for the Whitsun Bank Holiday match, for which in those days the ground was always full before the start.

Notts batted and after a while Moloney was put on to bowl. His was a new Surrey name to the crowd and they were curious. Well, you never heard such a howl of laughter as that which followed his first delivery. When quiet was restored and just before Moloney bowled his next ball, a man just behind me on the boundary shouted: 'Keep him on, Fender. I'm going home to fetch my old woman.' In actual fact, Moloney had the last laugh, for I think he took three wickets for eleven runs, all caught on the boundary.

We then went to Leicester and in due course Moloney was brought on. He bowled one ball down the leg-side wide enough for Lord, the opening batsman, to turn right round and try to hit it to the fine-leg boundary. He hit it all right, but straight to the tummy of Strudwick, who caught it as much in self-defence as anything. After that game, 'Struddy' said: 'If Moloney plays again, I won't,' so we never saw that bowler again.

In reference to under-arm bowlers, there was one, G. H. Simpson-Hayward, of Worcestershire, who was good enough to be chosen to go with the M.C.C. to South Africa. A tall, very strong man with powerful fingers, he could spin the ball either way. The following season, when Surrey were playing Worcestershire, there was talk in our dressing-room about how to deal with him. 'Struddy' said: 'Well, I know which way the ball will turn, for I kept to him in South Africa.' When 'Struddy' went in, he was out first ball—lbw to a full-pitch!

I was a member of the 1922–23 M.C.C. team to South Africa where at that time cricket was played on matting wickets, there being no grass pitches as now. Coming out from grass pitches, we took a long time to get used to the matting, but Jack Russell did very well and he made two separate hundreds in the last Test at Durban, a feat the more remarkable as he was far from well during that match. We were captained by one of the nicest men I played with, F. T. Mann.

In 1924–25 I was honoured again, being in the team to Australia. Though I scored a good many runs on the tour, my Test record read thus: lbw, caught on the leg-side, played on and, finally, run out. The only time I made two centuries in the same match was when I got 137 and 104 at Sydney against New South Wales during that trip. M.C.C. were captained by A. E. R. Gilligan and he again led the side when I went to India with M.C.C. in 1926. We played 32 matches and I missed only four of them. That was a tiring business, for there was no flying then and India was not divided, so that there were long train journeys. Nevertheless, because of this, I probably saw more of India than many people living there.

After India came a visit to the West Indies under the Hon. F. S. G. Calthorpe. I understood that the West Indies asked if M.C.C. could send some of the older England players and Wilfred Rhodes, George Gunn and the late Joe Hardstaff (as umpire and baggage-man) were in the party. Our first Test was at Barbados on the fastest pitch I ever batted on, a view shared by the 'veterans' I have mentioned. I remember the first 'bouncer' I received from Learie Constantine and though I did not mind fast bowlers, I was a bit lucky to get away with this one, for I mistimed it and just cleared short-leg. Other 'bouncers', which came frequently, I let go!

Meanwhile George Gunn, then 47 or 48 years old, who opened with me, put out his tongue at Learie every time he bowled him a 'bouncer'. George made a modest score and left me and the others to deal with an infuriated fast bowler, thoroughly roused in front of his own people! Over the years I have enquired of players who subsequently visited the West Indies how they found the pitch in Barbados. Their reply has been: 'It may have been fast in your time. It isn't now.'

Why are there no fast pitches in England today? In my early days it was agreed that the Leyton pitch and that at Taunton were the fastest in the country and allowed fast bowlers and batsmen who liked fast bowling to come into their own. Nowadays fast bowlers seem to get little reward for their skills and energy. In last season's Tests with Pakistan and India, they bowled with the new ball and then gave way to the spinners, who operated from then till the end of the innings. Surely at the start of a match the batsmen and fast bowlers are entitled to expect a fast pitch to play on if there has been no rain about.

Reverting to the West Indies tour, in the last Test—also the final match of the tour—England scored 849 and 272 for nine and the West Indies 286 and 408 for five. Then it rained for, I think, two days and the game was abandoned as a draw. It was in this match that I made my highest score ever, 325; but I would not have done so but for Joe Hardstaff, who was umpiring. I started with sore toes and after reaching 100 I said to Joe: 'I'm off now.' But he said: 'No, you stay here and talk to me. I don't know anyone out here.'

Starting next day at 150 not out, I duly got to 200 and then told Joe: 'I'm going now,' but he always found an excuse. This time it was: 'There's a new ball due. See that off.' Or else there was an interval due. Anyway, by tea-time on the second day I had scored about 250 and somebody had been looking up the record by an Englishman in the West Indies. It was around 260 and Joe said: 'Stay here and beat that.' Having managed to do so, I asked: 'Are you satisfied now?' and he replied: 'No, go on and make it 300'—and that's how I made my biggest score! This was all very well, but whenever a wicket fell at the other end, a sprightly newcomer came in and ran me off my feet. One of them was Les Ames, who made 149, and he was no slouch between wickets.

The following winter I went to South Africa with A. P. F. Chapman's M.C.C. team, but unfortunately, after two matches, I was involved in a car accident—about which I knew nothing, for I was looking out of the back window at the time—and I played no more on the tour. This was a considerable misfortune for the side, for it meant the loss of an opener.

I visited The Oval only occasionally in 1971, but I did go there on the last day when Glamorgan were the visitors and Surrey were trying to get another six points to win the Championship. At one time I saw a West Indian and a Pakistani batting for Glamorgan and a Pakistani bowling to them, and I thought: 'Where do the young lads in the various county second elevens come in?' Mind you, I have nothing against imported cricketers, either white or black, and over the years I enjoyed playing against their countrymen. But what must county coaches think when they have a promising youngster ripe for the first eleven, an imported player is invited and the lad loses his chance? If young English cricketers are to be encouraged, surely there should be a limit to importations and I am glad this has now been done.

Another thing. Bowling tactics have changed from my early days. The advent of 'in-swing' cut out off-driving and cutting, so that on-side play became the main method of scoring and drives through the covers became few and far between. This, with brave fielders standing in very close at short-leg, coupled with slower pitches, has cramped batting and no doubt bored spectators.

Fielding, I think, may be better than in my time—maybe because we played till later in life and were not termed veterans at 39 or 40. It must, however, be remembered that we had to chase the ball to the far-distant boundaries, for the 75-yards boundary was not then the vogue. I remember before the 1914 War, when I was in and out of the county side, I played in a game against Oxford University at The Oval. In those days three or four of the eleven were rested for such matches and the likes of me given the chance. Tom Rushby had asked for a rest but was refused and, no doubt fed-up, did not try too hard when put on to bowl. I was at mid-on when he bowled from the Vauxhall end of a pitch well over on the gasometer side. The other boundary was a very long way away and when Tom was hit to the deep I chased the ball, thinking: 'I wonder how many these lively young men have run.' In fact they ran six! I had scarcely regained my position at mid-on than I was off again next ball to the same place, and again they ran six. Slightly annoyed with Tom and also out of breath, I had to pursue the next ball in the same direction though they only ran five that time! It was on my third journey that the Secretary, Mr. Findlay, looked out of his office window. Next morning he sent for me and said chidingly that he was surprised to see me not running very fast—though he did apologise when I pointed out that I had chased the two previous balls while twelve runs were scored! I think this makes clear that the old-time boundaries were very long on most grounds and one had to be a tremendous thrower to get the ball back to the wicket-keeper. At present, with a fast out-field, fielders possess little chance of cutting off the four. This is a pity, because there are few things better in the game than the sight of a speedy out-fielder after the ball and picking it up near the ring. Of the many fast out-fielders of my day, I would say that Johnny Arnold, of Hampshire, was the best Englishman. He also had a fine throw.

I remember, too, those two great Australian out-fielders in 1921, namely, 'Nip' Pellew and J. M. Taylor. They were very fast and must have saved hundreds of runs on that tour.

Surrey in the end took the Championship last season, though I must say that I do not feel altogether happy that they got home over Warwickshire simply because they won more matches. A clear-cut points margin would have been more satisfactory all round. In the same way, I think Worcestershire's success in the Player League leaves something to be desired, for they got there by a minute fraction of a run per over averaged over the whole season. This seemed to me to be a bit rough on Essex, who scored the same number of points, even if it is in accordance with the rules of the competition. If two counties finish equal on points at the top of the table, would it not be better to have a play-off match?

COMPTON'S RECORD SEASON [1972]

It Happened 25 Years Ago

BY BASIL EASTERBROOK

If Andrew Sandham's essay on himself stressed the longevity of so many of the great players of his time, Basil Easterbrook's on Denis Compton most alarmingly reminded every reader of the headlong pace at which Time was proceeding. Could it really have been twenty-five years ago that Denis attained his godhead? Could a quarter of a century have slipped away? It seemed impossible when there were thousands of men, including the present writer, still in the habit of dropping in at Lord's on some aimless afternoon, to find themselves so conscious of what they had once seen there that they felt almost as though about to waken from a dreary dream to find Denis striding out to the wickets with that slightly hobbling gait of his.

Mr. Easterbrook's essay draws heavily on Robertson-Glasgow, substantially on John Arlott, but he makes several valid points of his own. In only two regards might the reader take exception. One of the more miraculous aspects of the record-breaking year was the fantastical accelerando of the latter part of the season. Between July 12th and September 17th Denis scored 2074 runs, including twelve centuries, for an average of 109, which explains how it was that for the first half of the summer it was his partner Bill Edrich who stood at the head of the averages. The other slip is perfectly understandable, for when Mr. Easterbrook tells us that we shall never see the like again of 1947, he was probably right. But it is always a dangerous game to write off the cricketing present; the events of 1981 were not remotely comparable to the supreme grace, wit and gallantry of what Denis achieved, any more than the crescendo of 1947 bore even vestigial resemblance to the lusty giantism of Ian Botham. But the effects on the population at large were not, after all, so very different. This is not to compare one man with the other, for both were incomparable.

THE cricket season of 1947 came to us like a late October day of golden sunshine just before the setting in of a dark, drear Northern winter from which at times there seems no escape. In the quarter of a century which has followed we have seen cricket in decline. Before the 1960s had run their course recognised England batsmen like Cowdrey and Graveney barely topped 1,000 runs for a whole season's endeavours without causing many eyebrows to be raised. On reflection, this was perhaps not to be wondered at, for those most closely connected with first-class cricket were kept occupied with rows and wrangles embracing politics, colour, the seeming impossibility of the creation of fast, true pitches, the change in public tastes; the apparent determination of first-class players to live in a cloud-cuckoo land of their own devising.

The game which above all other human pastimes has inspired noble thoughts and words in profusion, has been invaded and pervaded by the general bitchiness which for all the technological advances made in a breathtakingly short space of time is, alas, the accepted pattern for living in the second half of the twentieth century. Adventure, boldness and joy had largely gone from the game. Teams are more concerned with stopping the other lot doing anything than winning themselves. There was a term for this when I was a boy. It was dog in the manger. When the spirit grows mean and over cautious inevitably performance suffers in direct ratio and this is precisely what has happened in cricket.

It helps to explain why Australian sides, technically no better than England's and in some respects often not as good, have in the past twenty years survived series after series when they should have been beaten into the earth. Sunday Leagues and knock-out competitions, splendid in their way, are only palliatives not cures. If the first-class game becomes extinct the Sunday League would immediately have identical status with the long established Saturday Leagues of the North and Midlands. We shall be a nation of club cricketers as well as a nation of shopkeepers and shop stewards.

The crowd-pulling power of the Sunday League, the Cavaliers, the Gillette Cup, comes from the fact that the players are first-class from a background of three-day and five-day cricket. Robertson-Glasgow put it neatly when he tried to show the impossibility of always concentrating three days' cricket into one— 'It is as if you approached a famous opera singer and said, "See here, madam, we are going to cut the opera from three acts to one and we want you to sing a lot faster and a lot louder to make up for the other two."'

The first-class complex concerns only 17 teams and no more than 200 players are involved at any one time. If ways and means to do this cannot be found in an island of over 50,000,000 inhabitants then it is time we stopped talking nonsense about British ingenuity and all the other qualities we pride ourselves on including a sense of history, and encouraging of all the arts and crafts known to mankind.

Of course, one likes to see cricket played against the background of a big crowd rather than a sparsely filled or virtually empty ground, but this is beside the point. First-class cricket has never been a game for a mass following and I say that in no derogatory sense. The English climate and personal economics have always made it virtually impossible that this should be so.

Nevertheless, first-class cricket is something which should always be there. The interest in a Test Match is great enough for the telephone service to provide a special number for people to ring who want to know the state of the game. That one fact alone is enough to justify the survival of the first-class game as it stands.

Cricket may have several ills but you do not cure a patient by killing him off. It is a change of heart we need rather than a change of system, for if we scrap the system which permits our best players to perform on their terms instead of being wound up like clockwork toys for over 40 overs then we sell the pass to days that are over and done. There will be no records like Compton's 3,816 runs and 18 centuries in 1947 to aim at because there will be no opportunity for any aiming to be done.

One of these years we may get another glorious summer of weather like we did in 1947 and if we do I hope our contemporary players will answer the warmth of the sun on their backs the way the boys did then. Walter Keeton, George Emmett, Jack Crapp and Denis Brookes all made six centuries, Leslie Todd, Joe Hardstaff, and Leslie Ames seven, George Cox eight, Winston Place ten. Then came Hutton and Washbrook with 11 each, Jack Robertson and Bill Edrich 12 each and far above them all on some dizzy, improbable Parnassus—Compton with 18.

Compton's Annus Mirabilis began with no real hint that it would be that. He made 73 and 7 for the M.C.C. against a somewhat experimental Yorkshire side who were soundly beaten by 163 runs at Lord's on May 6. A drawn game with Surrey followed and Compton in two useful innings for M.C.C. contributed 52 and 34. Joining Middlesex the following day, he did little with the bat in two matches, the first of which was won by Somerset by one wicket in what will always be remembered as Maurice Tremlett's game. The second against Gloucestershire was won by Middlesex in two days by an innings and 178 runs. Compton's three innings in those games were 6, 25 and 22. Compton had so far played all his cricket at Lord's and when Middlesex headed for Birmingham and their first away game Compton stayed at headquarters to help M.C.C. beat the South Africans by 158 runs. Lindsay Tuckett got him for 18 in the first innings and caught him in the second off Ossie Dawson when Denis needed just three more runs for a hundred after a typical display of free cutting and driving.

Compton had got the taste and he took apart first the bowling of Worcestershire and then Sussex, the next two visitors to Lord's. Going in second wicket down he took out his bat for 88 in a total of 207 and in the second after a stand of 118 in eighty minutes with Bill Edrich, went on to 112 before Dick Howarth bowled him. Rain caused a long hold up on the last day but Middlesex claimed the extra half hour and Worcestershire's last two wickets to win by 234.

Whitsun brought perfect weather and 46,000 paying spectators to Lord's for the two days the game lasted. Walter Robins took the extra half hour on the Whit Monday and Middlesex scored the 21 runs they needed from their second innings without loss. Of the 380 Middlesex made in their first innings Compton scored 110 before Charlie Oakes bowled him, and his running mate all down the length of that glistening season, Bill Edrich, made 106.

When I asked Compton if he could account for his astonishing feats in 1947 he replied 'Oh, don't expect me to go into a long-winded technical dissertation. I was as fit as a flea, I did what came naturally and I enjoyed myself. Yes, that is what I remember best, how I loved every minute of that season.'

Lovable, laughing, harum-scarum Denis, it was silly of me to expect any other kind of reaction than the one I got. I will endeavour to convey what a fantastic phenomenon this man was with a bat in his hand just after World War Two before that accursed soccer injury, and the weight problems which the approach of middle age brought with them, by trying to recall just one incident in the August of 1947. Doug Wright was bowling on a Lord's pitch which had 'dusted up' and was taking spin. It was the last afternoon and Middlesex were trying to chase a target not far short of 100 runs an hour. I know Middlesex did not make it but Compton scored well over 150 before he holed out to Wright on the boundary. When Wright bowled the delivery previously mentioned Compton went out of his crease like a whippet, gambling on it being a leg break and shaping to drive through the offside field. Only it wasn't a leg break. When it pitched it was as beautifully a disguised wrong 'un as the heart could wish for and I heard a voice behind me shout 'Comp's gone'.

It seemed a case of stating the obvious for Compo checked, reared and fell on to his chest like a demolished building—but as he did so his bat came round in a lightning sweep to send the ball, spitting in viciously from the off, to the leg side rails. That was the measure of Compton's greatness. He could do the right things superbly but when he broke all the rules the ball still ended up at the fence.

There is no better word picture of Compton than the one painted by John Arlott in his book *Vintage Summer: 1947*. 'In technique, he was deficient in the straight, or near straight drive. But his control through the two wider arcs was such that he would tantalize a slow left arm bowler's cover field, or the leg side setting of an off spinner, with a degree of control few men have ever bettered. At need, he had all the strokes and, if his left foot often seemed further from the ball than the purists would approve, that gave him greater room to power his strokes, and his superb eye kept him out of such trouble as would have beset lesser cricketers who thus deviated from the text book. . . . By 1947 he had thickened physically. Before the war he had been comparatively slight: in subsequent years he developed a tendency to inconvenient weight.

'In that summer he had come to maximum power with unimpaired mobility; powerful of shoulder and trunk, muscular in arms and legs, yet with a lazy looseness of movement and, for all his negligent air, quick and balanced on his feet. No part of his equipment was more deceptive than his speed—particularly in readjustment. He would move out to drive through the covers; the ball would, unexpectedly, move on to him and, with a mock-desperate wrench of body and arms, he would flick it down to long leg. Or, in impish mischief, he would rock on to his back foot and, with an immensely powerful twist of the forearms—or, in even narrower space, of the wrists—drive a ball coming into his leg stump through the covers. At need he could be decorous in defence; that was never any trouble, for the germ of orthodoxy was in him, even at his most unorthodox; or, when he had abandoned the anchors, his superb natural eye and balance would retrieve the situation for him. He was an instinctively perfect timer of the ball. But the facet of his cricket which went to the heart of the average club player who watched him was his improvisation, which rectified such error as, in ordinary men, would have been fatal.'

Compton ended May where he had spent it, at Lord's, playing for Middlesex against the South Africans. He had already taken 97 off them in the second innings of their game with M.C.C. and he went out to bat on June 2 facing a total of 424 of which centuries by Bruce Mitchell and Viljoen accounted for more than half. Robertson and Brown were soon disposed of, but Compton with Edrich added 147 and then a further 103 with his brother Leslie. He was eventually stumped jumping out at Athol Rowan after four hours of sheer delight for 154 in which he hit nineteen 4's. Rowan bowled him for 34 in the second innings on a worn pitch but a not- out 133 by Edrich saw Middlesex save the match without too much difficulty.

Hampshire came next to Lord's to be beaten by an innings and 49 and Compton's contribution to a Middlesex total of 429 for six declared was a madcap 88 at two a minute. He lost his wicket to, of all people, Johnny Arnold, being stumped when running down the pitch and trying to hit the seventh bowler used by Hampshire, out of the ground.

Compton's next task was as far removed from this kind of frolicking as it could possibly be. At Trent Bridge, England in the face of South Africa's first innings 533 collapsed for 208 of which Compton made 65. Following on 325 behind on a still beautiful batting wicket England lost four wickets for 170 so that when Norman Yardley joined Compton 155 were needed to save the innings defeat and apart from Godfrey Evans there was no real batting to come. Compton and Yardley added 108 in the last hundred minutes of the day and on the final morning Yardley called for an hour's concentrated net practice from the surviving batsmen.

Yardley should have gone after adding only six to his overnight score but he was badly missed at first slip by Mitchell and he and Compton went on to a partnership of 237. When Compton gave Mitchell a slip catch off 'Tufty' Mann, he had made 163 and held up South Africa for nearly five hours. It was an innings which underlined Arlott's statement that he could be decorous. Compton's critics tried to blow up to larger than life size the playboy side of his character but this was as great an innings for side as opposed to self as has yet been played in the cause of England. The tail, inspired by his example and able to take advantage of the toll in sharpness and calm that Compton's defiance had extracted, took England's score to 551. It left South Africa less than two and a half hours to get 227 to win and although Alan Melville made his second century of the match they never really attempted the task.

If they could have seen what lay ahead of them they might have been tempted to stake everything on winning this Test for they were to win none of the remaining four. Compton's next appearance for Middlesex was against Yorkshire where the potential champions had to be content with first-innings points after seven consecutive victories. Middlesex, in their only innings, declared at 350 for two when Compton was 50 not out.

Then it was Lord's Test time with the weather perfect and thousands having to be turned away on the first day after South Africa's surprising opposition at Nottingham. This time they lost the toss and the match was decided by a mammoth third-wicket stand of 370 between Edrich and Compton. Edrich made 189 and Compton 208, his second highest score of 1947. England had a long tail and when Hutton and Washbrook went with less than a hundred on the board the responsibility for a match-winning total lay heavily upon Edrich and Compton. They faced a determined attack, splendidly supported in the field, and for a considerable time the struggle was tense. Then the Middlesex pair mastered their tormentors and *Wisden* used a phrase it has kept in cold storage these many years—'a sparkling exhibition of fluent stroke play'. Compton used everything in his complete and considerable repertoire.

Still living in the memory are his brilliant sweeping of slow bowling and his powerful lofted pulled-drive. Not until twenty minutes after lunch on the second day did South Africa part the pair the popular dailies inevitably dubbed 'The Terrible Twins'. Edrich fell 11 short of a double century but Compton went on to 208 and was not dismissed until England's score had reached 515. He had batted ten minutes short of six hours and made his runs out of just over 400. Once again Compton had proved completely that while the stories of his forgetfulness and irresponsibility off the field grew and were not denied, when out in the middle it was very much a case of the professional soldier's belief in 'on parade, on parade'.

England declared at 554 for eight and although Alan Melville made 117, his fourth successive Test century against England, South Africa could do no better than reach 327. They had to follow on 227 behind and with 15 scored in their second innings play was held up for twenty minutes while the players were presented to the King and Queen and the Princesses Elizabeth and Margaret. Whether such a representative gathering of royalty intimidated the South Africans or inspired Edrich will probably always remain a matter of opinion, but on the resumption Edrich flattened Melville's middle stump with his second ball.

Two overs later he picked Viljoen's stump clean out of the ground. South Africa were clearly on the way to defeat which 80 by Mitchell and 58 by Nourse could only delay. Eventually, they made 252 which left Hutton and Washbrook the formality of going to the crease to score 26 for victory by ten wickets.

Compton rejoined Middlesex at Leeds for Bill Bowes's benefit match. The big fast bowler won the toss for Yorkshire and put Middlesex in. Compton failed twice on a pitch which retained a lot of moisture after being saturated on the Friday, the ball frequently rising alarmingly. He was caught by Hutton off Coxon for 4 and caught Coxon bowled Wardle for 15 in the second innings. Bowes's gamble backfired for although Middlesex were put out for 124 Yorkshire collapsed for 85 and Middlesex were batting again after tea on the first day. Edrich made 102 on the second day and the task of making 274 to win on a damaged surface was 88 runs out of Yorkshire's reach. It was all over in two days but it was anything but a financial failure. Over 41,000 paid around £3,000 to see two dramatic days of cricket and the popular Bowes ended the season with a benefit that topped £8,000. Compton, having failed with the bat, made a major contribution with his left arm mixture returning four for 23 and three for 28. He took the last wicket through a catch in the deep by his brother Leslie, Fred Price keeping wicket.

Denis had four days break after this match before resuming his massacre of South Africa's bowlers at Old Trafford. The Third Test was played in dull, cold thoroughly unpleasant weather. On the Saturday a bitterly cold north westerly wind blew straight down the pitch, and when I say blew, I mean strongly enough to topple one of the sight screens as well as frequently lift the bails from their grooves. South Africa had every reason to feel proud of a total of 339 in one of Manchester's most unattractive moods. They were a good side, those 1947 South Africans. Not so well equipped with all round ability as those of the sixties but very little behind. That cannot be stressed too much or too often for it puts the feats of Compton and his partner Edrich into true perspective. Nine of England's men contributed no more than 162 when their turn to bat came, but the total was 478—191 from Edrich and 115 from Compton, his third century in three Tests. Thus four of his first six hundreds had been taken off the Touring side and all four in succession.

Despite their lead of 139 England were a long way from victory. Nourse made a grand century when South Africa batted a second time and rain lopped three hours from the third day. In the end England had to get 129 in two and a half hours and they made them for the loss of three wickets, one of whom was Compton who, trying to keep out a nasty left arm leg break from 'Tufty' Mann, hit his wicket after scoring only 6.

Compton's seventh century came at Grace Road, Leicester, in a match which Middlesex won by ten wickets. An easy one-sided affair for a great team on their way to the championship, you might assume. It was in truth a titanic achievement by Middlesex and by Compton and Edrich especially. The home side were put in to bat by Edrich, who was captaining Middlesex for the first time, and made 309, the Australian, Vic Jackson, scoring 117. Middlesex replied with 637 for four—Edrich 257, Compton 151. The two were in partnership for two hours ten minutes in which they scored 277 runs. Needing 328 to avoid an innings defeat Leicestershire refused to die gracefully. Les Berry hit 154, Maurice Tompkin 76, there was a forty here, thirties there and when the last wicket fell they were only seven short of 400.

At lunch time on the last day Leicestershire led by 17 and had six wickets standing with only eighty minutes left for play. Middlesex dropped those six wickets for 48 in thirty-five minutes and Compton did it, being easily the most successful bowler with five for 108, the last man falling to the first ball of his thirtieth over.

This left Middlesex just twenty-five minutes in which to score 66 runs. Edrich took Compton in with him and they got them in twenty-one minutes off seven overs. On the second day of the match 663 runs were scored.

Compton's next match was Gentlemen v. Players, a fixture which could still draw 15,000 to Lord's in indifferent weather for a day's play. It fizzled out into a hopeless draw and in his only knock Compton was caught at the wicket by the present secretary of the M.C.C., Billy Griffith, off the bowling of Trevor Bailey for 11. He stayed at Lord's for the visit of Essex who gave Middlesex a good scrap for three days before losing by 102 runs. Scores: Middlesex 389 for seven declared and 356 for five declared; Essex 350 and 293. Highest individual score of a fine match was Compton's 129 in the first Middlesex innings which ended when he gave Peter Smith a return catch. He was at the crease a fraction under two hours. There was just time before the fourth Test at Leeds for Edrich and Compton to help Middlesex win at Northampton by eight wickets. Middlesex declared at 464 for five after their numbers 3 and 4 had put on 211 for the third wicket. When Compton was bowled by Partridge for 110, Edrich went on to the highest score of his career, 267 not out.

For once the Middlesex terrors played modest supporting roles to Hutton and Washbrook at Headingley. Hutton got 100 and Washbrook 75 compared with 43 by Edrich and 30 from Compton, but South Africa's batting failed twice for the first time in the series and England won by ten wickets in three days.

So Compton came to August and unknown to the world and himself nine centuries still lay ahead. He hit the first of them in Jim Langridge's benefit match at Hove which Middlesex won by nine wickets. Walter Robins declared at 401 for four as soon as Denis completed three figures for the tenth time that season. After hitting thirteen fours Denis and his 'Chinamen' played the main part in putting out Sussex for 195 and making them follow on. His haul was four for 90 in 21 overs.

Lord's, Trent Bridge, Old Trafford, Hove, noble grounds all, had been fitting stages for Compton to display his genius and now he added Canterbury. Five days play at the 1947 Canterbury Festival drew 46,756 paying spectators; over 13,000 of them were there on the Thursday and they saw Compton make 106 out of a Middlesex total of 225. When Middlesex followed on Compton was caught by Leslie Ames off Harding for only 4, but Robertson and Edrich struck hundreds and the prospective champions declared. They set Kent two hours to get 232 and dropped six of their wickets to come close to winning from a near hopeless position.

Next came The Oval and the defeat of Surrey by an innings and 11 runs. The gates were closed on Saturday and 54,000 saw the three days cricket in which Compton strode the world famous enclosure like the Colossus of cricket he was. When Middlesex declared at 537 for two he was 137 not out after adding 287 in 165 minutes with Edrich without being separated. Of the four men who batted Syd Brown's 98 was the lowest score. Surrey replied with 334 and 192 and the match did nothing for the reputations of no less than thirteen bowlers. The exception was the slow-left-arm, unorthodox-over-the-wicket Compton, whose work with the ball on this occasion outstripped his batting. He took six for 94 in the first innings and six for 80 in the second, sending down nearly 53 overs. This remember was the second week in August in a season in which Compton had been the key batsman for both England and the champion county, yet neither Compton nor Robins his captain saw any reason why at such an advanced stage of the campaign he should be nursed. It is, to me, at least, a grain of comfort that in our own post-war period there were still men of giant capacity in cricket. In that match Alf Gover, Alec Bedser, Stuart Surridge, Laurie Gray and Jack Young took just three wickets between them!

Back across Westminster Bridge went Middlesex to a defeat by 75 runs by Kent that would have been much heavier had not Compton scored a glorious 168 in the fourth innings on a dusting pitch, a knock I have already touched upon. And just to make certain Compton earned his corn 'Robbie' made him bowl another 55 overs in the match which brought him four more wickets!

It was now time for the fifth Test at The Oval and South Africa after three resounding defeats ended the series as they began it by coming close to victory. After four days of wonderful, fluctuating cricket the Springboks were 28 runs short with three wickets left. Bruce Mitchell on his farewell Test appearance in England made the match his by scoring 120 in the first innings and 189 not out in the second, but Compton put his stamp on the series in which great things had been done by the batsmen of both sides with innings of 53 and 113.

The series was over but a lot of cricket was left for Compton. He retraced the familiar route to Lord's for the games with Surrey and Northampton-shire which finally saw off the magnificent challenge made by Gloucester-shire. Middlesex scored 462 for seven declared on the first day—thirty-five minutes were lost because of bad light. After seeing Robertson, Brown and Edrich sent back for what in 1947 Middlesex considered low scores, Compton carefully shielded F. G. Mann through a shaky start. Then the pair cut loose and in three and a quarter hours put on 304. Compton's 178 was a bewitching mixture of orthodox strokes and his own inventions. It was as if by this time he had to amuse himself with improvisations on a well worn theme to keep his interest and concentration from going altogether. Jim Laker, who was to earn his own immortality some nine years later, got him in the end, one of two wickets which cost him 105 runs. Surrey put totals of 202 and 309 in the book, but the wicket was broken when Middlesex went in to score 50; Gover got Brown for 0 and Edrich for 2, and then Compton went in to hit off the runs with Jack Robertson—after bowling 48 overs in the two Surrey innings.

Next, Northamptonshire were annihilated in two days by 355 runs, Compton playing innings of 60 and 85. This victory ensured Middlesex finishing top. The Championship secured, the season ended on a note of anti-climax for Middlesex with Lancashire coming to Lord's and winning, by 64 runs to finish third in the table for the second season running, but their win was overshadowed by Compton's feat of equalling Hobbs' 1925 record of sixteen centuries in a season. Spin and flight beat Compton early in the first innings, John Ikin bowling him for 17 but in the second, with Middlesex chasing nearly 400, Compton was at his greatest. Confined to defence for long periods against bowlers who had the sweet smell of victory over the Champions, Denis fought his way grimly to three figures after spending half an hour in the nineties.

The season had brought out all the shining facets of his many sided cricket character and what could be more appropriate than that he should sign off at Lord's having made 139 and kept Lancashire from their prize for nearly three and a half hours when finally Price drew him out for Barlow to stump him. In this match watched by 60,000, he had bowled another 35 overs and added another five wickets for 95 runs to his considerable haul, but this last appearance of an unforgettable season for all connected with Lord's cast more than the first shadows of the approaching autumn.

On the first day he had to leave the field. A call to the dressing-room from the press box brought the reassuring reply 'Oh, it's nothing to worry about. Denis has got a spot of knee trouble and is having some manipulative treatment.' Nothing—except the first hole in the dyke.

Compton went to Hastings where on Sepember 5 at the Central Ground the South Africans gained victory by nine wickets over the South of England, but as at Lord's a few days before the performance of a team was forgotten because of the innings of a batsman in the losing team. Compton set a new all time individual record by scoring 101—his seventeenth century of the season. It was his twelfth hundred in 25 innings and when he reached it the game was held up for five minutes as crowd and players including his Middlesex colleagues, Edrich and Robins, went on to the field to congratulate him. It was a century to rank with the other sixteen, for the South Africans understandably were not going to give this man anything. He had already taken five centuries off them before this game and when he added another 30 in the second innings before Athol Rowan bowled him he had brought his season's aggregate against South Africa alone to 1,187 runs.

Without any comment I would like to add that over 20 years on in the enlightened era of the 1970s with its rockets orbiting to the Moon, its cannabis, its 7½ per cent bank rate, Graveney's aggregate for a whole season was 1,130 and Cowdrey's 1,093. As the man said—I suppose you cannot have everything.

The late A. A. Thomson once said to me: 'Of all the seasons I wished could go on forever 1947 was the one.' It is not hard to understand how 'Tommy' felt. At The Oval on September 13, 15, 16 and 17, 1947, for the first time in twelve years the Champion County played The Rest of England. For only the third time the champion county won it and for the first time a side other than Yorkshire, successful in 1905 and 1935, succeeded. Middlesex began badly, losing three wickets for 53; then Compton coming in at number five instead of his customary four, joined Edrich and they proceeded to take apart an attack comprising Harold Butler, Alec Bedser, Doug Wright, Tom Goddard, and Dick Howarth. Oddly enough, both Edrich and Compton were stumped by Godfrey Evans off Goddard, Edrich for 180, Compton for a season's best 246. In their innings both batsmen beat Tom Hayward's aggregate of 3,518 runs in a season which had stood since 1906.

It was also Compton's highest innings in this country, but even in this supreme hour which lifted Compton on a pedestal in company with such as

Bradman, Grace and Hobbs, the gods gave a warning that they were soon to foreclose savagely. After he had helped Edrich to add 138 on the Saturday, Compton had to retire with a recurrence of knee trouble. He resumed his innings on Monday and as the runs cascaded from his bat even those who knew just how heavily strapped his knee was found it almost impossible to accept that his freedom of movement was already restricted and would never be quite the same again although he was to thumb his nose at pain and difficulty for another seventeen years. Middlesex declared at 543 for nine; bowled out The Rest for 246 and 317 and knocked off 21 for the loss of Robertson in the first hour of the fourth day. What is remarkable is not so much the result but that Compton ignoring the knee which had driven him from the field for the second time in just over a fortnight bowled 34 overs and 4 balls and took six wickets in the match for 141 runs—the second most successful bowler in the contest!

It is among the more hackneyed phrases in sport that records are made to be broken but I wonder whether Compton's figures of 1947 will ever be surpassed. He played 50 innings, was not out in eight of them, scored 3,816 runs, made 18 centuries and had an average of 90.85. He bowled 635.4 overs and took 73 wickets. He also held 31 catches, three in one innings, for example, when Gloucestershire, the runners up, came to Lord's.

When the time came for *Wisden* to pay tribute to Compton and Edrich in their 1948 edition they turned unerringly to Robertson-Glasgow. Crusoe put them together in English cricket as Gilbert and Sullivan go together in English opera. Nor was the analogy a careless one for, as he pointed out, in the art of giving pleasure to an English audience, both pairs lacked rivals. Crusoe of course did not give a damn for figures. He saw the great Middlesex pair as champions in the fight against dullness and the commercial standard.

It is what they were that mattered to him far more than what they had done. In those wise and humorous eyes which I always thought to be the most striking feature in a striking whole, Compton and Edrich (and they cannot be spoken of apart in 1947) were the mirror of hope and freedom and gaiety; heroic in the manner of heroes of school stories; the inspiration, and quarry of the young because, in a game that even then was threatening to become old in the saddest sense, they did not outgrow the habit, the ideals, the very mistakes of youth.

'Most cricketers enjoy doing well, though I could name great ones who had a queer way of showing their enjoyment,' wrote Crusoe. 'But Compton and Edrich are of that happy philosophy which keeps failure in its place by laughter, like boys who fall on an ice slide and rush back to try it again. . . . And they seem to be playing not only in front of us and for us, but almost literally with us. Their cricket is communicative.'

That such players should break records was in Crusoe's opinion inevitable rather than relevant. It was never the slightest use trying to impress this man of many brilliant parts with statistics. I remember making the error in my salad days as a cricket writer and he made me realise the gap in our generation and our background by replying 'More people have listened to Frank Sinatra than Caruso, Clark Gable received more letters of homage than Sir Henry Irving. Numbers can be such silly things.' The sort of thing which delighted Crusoe was when, with easy vehemence, Compton would persuade a ball of fairish length on the leg stump to the extra cover boundary.

Robertson-Glasgow admired Edrich for his talent and his unquenchable pugnacity. He was the first to pay tribute to a cricketer who, in his words, started with a number of talents and increased them into riches. Compton was different, a cricketer apart. 'Denis has genius, and, if he knows it, he doesn't care.'

In his essay in *Wisden*, 1948, Crusoe wrote the following passage: 'Compton cannot help it. He has the habit of batting as the sun has the habit of journeying from east to west; and the fielders are his satellites. Hardest worked of them, and most perplexed, is cover point. Other batsmen of our time have been severer on the stroke. Walter Hammond could leave the nimblest cover motionless or just flickering as by token, could use cover's toe caps as an echoing junction for the boundary; but Compton uses cover point as a game within a game, tantalises him with delayed direction and vexes him with variety. He is for ever seeking fresh by-products of the old forward stroke and has not yet, I fancy, come to the end of experiment. He finds it so amusing and so profitable. He outruns the traditional and discovers new truth. Compton is the axiom of tomorrow.'

Alas, for all of us, Crusoe, you were wrong in your final sentence. Nothing in cricket that followed 1947 has remotely approached it in either stature or weather. One all time great as a writer on the game, he saw two all time great exponents of it as adornments to something that was meant not as an imitation of, but as a refreshment from the worldly struggle.

Cricket in the two decades that followed proved unworthy of all three of them. It was to become as fearful, as joyless as so much of the world that surrounded it and its shame was greatest at the highest level of all. In the Brisbane Test of December 1958 between Australia and England a full day's play produced 106 runs and even that was not the nadir for nearly two years earlier at Karachi in a Test between Australia and Pakistan the result of a full day's labour was 95 runs. It seems that we could not possibly be talking about the same game that Percy Fender played when he scored 113 in forty-two minutes at Northampton in 1920 or when Alletson at Hove in 1911 went from 50 to 189 in half an hour.

But then, even 1947 and the Compton that enthralled me along with millions of others is already overlaid with the mists of antiquity. Compton, fielding near the wicket in a bending posture, hands palm down on his knees as if waiting for some kindred spirit to leapfrog over him—was it all a figment of my imagination?

Shortly before I wrote this article my teenage son read a piece by Cardus on Compton. He drew my attention to a sentence which ran 'on the field of play, at any rate, Denis's hair was unruly beyond the pacifying power of any cream, oil or unguent whatsoever'. He looked up and shaking his head said: 'I'm surprised that a writer as good as you keep telling me Sir Neville is, should find it necessary to pad out an article like that.' It was, I realised, another example of the generation gap. Paul had never seen Compton's portrait on hoardings up and down the land, advertising a nationally famous hair dressing, so the adroit, gentle allusion to it by Cardus was entirely without meaning for him.

When I meet Denis now, a busy, bustling character in his early fifties for ever flirting with rotundity as once he flirted with everything be it a good length, passing fair or loose as a decayed tooth, I am momentarily saddened to think that once 'panting Time toiled after him in vain'. Then I see him move sideways and laugh uproariously at a joke he has just told me and I know that inside he is the same person who many aver was the worst judge of when or when not to take a run the game has ever known.

I see him again with the eyes of 1947, as he was at Lord's and on the bill posters, England in a pair of pads, dark, competent, unflustered and I am glad that the most runs and centuries concentrated into one marvellous summer will remain for all time in his keeping. For once, the gods chose right.

DENIS COMPTON 1947

1.	112	v. Worcestershire	Lord's
2.	110	v. Sussex	Lord's
3.	154	v. South Africans	Lord's
4.	163	v. South Africa (1st Test)	Trent Bridge
5.	208	v. South Africa (2nd Test)	Lord's
6.	115	v. South Africa (3rd Test)	Old Trafford
7.	151	v. Leicestershire	Leicester
8.	129	v. Essex	Lord's
9.	110	v. Northamptonshire	Northampton
10.	110 n.o.	v. Sussex	Hove
11.	106	v. Kent	Canterbury
12.	137 n.o.	v. Surrey	Oval
13.	168	v. Kent	Lord's
14.	113	v. South Africans	Oval
15.	178	v. Surrey	Lord's
16.	139	v. Lancashire	Lord's
17.	101	v. South Africans	Hastings
18.	246	v. Rest of England	Oval

LORD CONSTANTINE [1972]

The Spontaneous Cricketer

BY JOHN ARLOTT

The death of Learie Nicholas Constantine drew an obituary tribute from John Arlott, who was as well equipped as any living writer could be to strike a balance between his subject's prodigious cricketing gifts and his uplifting subsequent career as barrister, politician and statesman. To those of my generation, who had little opportunity of seeing him in action on the field, the lighthearted improvisations of wartime cricket at Lord's were a priceless bonus. Constantine, by then in the last days of his playing career, led assorted gallimaufreys of cricketers in a succession of one- and two-day matches, never failing to excite the huge crowds which rolled up to watch him while the chance was still there. It is somehow typical that my most vivid memory of him is to do with a controversial dismissal. Even in adversity Constantine was the type of man to dominate the proceedings. Batting at the Nursery end he hit a huge steepling straight drive which seemed destined to scatter the greybeards on the pavilion seats, when Leslie Compton, fielding on the boundary, inched back as he awaited the arrival of the ball. At last it came down, and Compton, arching his back but keeping his feet within the playing area, brought off a wonderful catch. There was an undercurrent of protest, but as Compton's feet had remained inside the boundary line, the catch was of course perfectly legitimate. Nobody knew this better than Constantine, who trotted out towards Compton and the pavilion, while the crowd roared its appreciation of inspiring cricket.

The first inkling most of us had in those days that Constantine was something more than a great cricketer came during the incident which Arlott mentions concerning a notorious test case of the period involving a hotel which by a rare coincidence happened to be no more than two hundred yards from where I lived. By involving himself in the social politics of the district in this way, and winning his fight, Constantine seemed to me to have, as it were, joined our borough. He was indubitably a great man, and Arlott is judicious in his mention of the key to this greatness, C. L. R. James, Constantine's lifelong comrade who, in that masterpiece, Beyond a Boundary, *described in passionate prose the struggle that Constantine accepted in his steady rise through the ranks of society.*

LORD Constantine, M.B.E. died in London on July 1, 1971. The parents of the child born in Diego Martin, Trinidad, almost seventy years before, may in their highest ambitions have hoped that he would play cricket for the West Indies. They cannot have dreamt that he would take a major share in lifting his people to a new level of respect within the British Commonwealth; that along the way he would become the finest fieldsman and one of the most exciting all-rounders the game of cricket has known: and that he would die Baron Constantine, of Maraval in Trinidad and Tobago, and of Nelson, in the County Palatine of Lancaster, a former Cabinet Minister and High Commissioner of his native Trinidad.

Learie–or 'Connie' to forty years of cricketers—came upon his historic cue as a man of his age, reflecting and helping to shape it. He made his mark in the only way a poor West Indian boy of his time could do, by playing cricket of ability and character. He went on to argue the rights of the coloured peoples with such an effect as only a man who had won public affection by games-playing could have done in the Britain of that period.

Learie Nicholas Constantine, born September 21, 1902, was the son of Lebrun Constantine, a plantation foreman who toured England as an all-rounder with the West Indian cricketers of 1900—when he scored the first century for a West Indies team in England—and 1906. In 1923 they both played for Trinidad against British Guiana at Georgetown, one of the few instances of a father and son appearing together in a first-class match; both of them long cherished the occasion. In constant family practice the father insisted on a high standard of fielding which was to prove the foundation of his son's success.

The younger Constantine had played only three first-class matches before he was chosen for Austin's 1923 team to England when he distinguished himself largely—indeed, almost solely—by his brilliance at cover point. On that visit he learnt much that he never forgot, by no means all of it about cricket: and he recognised the game as his only possible ladder to the kind of life he wanted.

As C.L.R. James has written 'he revolted against the revolting contrast between his first-class status as a cricketer and his third-class status as a man'. That, almost equally with his enthusiasm for the game, prompted the five years of unremitting practice after which, in 1928, he came to England under Karl Nunes on West Indies' first Test tour as an extremely lively fast bowler, hard-hitting batsman and outstanding fieldsman in any position.

Muscular but lithe, stocky but long armed, he bowled with a bounding run, a high, smooth action and considerable pace. His batting, which depended considerably upon eye, was sometimes unorthodox to the point of spontaneous invention: but on his day it was virtually impossible to bowl at him. In the deep he picked up while going like a sprinter and threw with explosive accuracy; close to the wicket he was fearless and quick; wherever he was posted he amazed everyone by his speed and certainty in making catches which seemed far beyond reach. His movement was so joyously fluid and, at need, acrobatic that he might have been made of springs and rubber.

Although he did little in the Tests of that summer he performed the double and in public esteem was quite the most successful member of the party. He provided splendid cricketing entertainment. Everyone who ever watched him will recall with delight his particular parlour trick—when a ball from him was played into the field he would turn and walk back towards his mark: the fieldsman would throw the ball at his back, 'Connie' would keep walking and, without appearing to look, turn his arm and catch the ball between his shoulder blades; no one, so far as can be ascertained, ever saw him miss.

Crowds recognised and enjoyed him as a cricketer of adventure: but the reports alone of a single match established him in the imagination of thousands who had never seen him play. At Lord's, in June, Middlesex made 352 for six and West Indies, for whom only Constantine, with 86, made more than 30, were 122 behind on the first innings. When Middlesex batted again, Constantine took seven for 57—six for 11 in his second spell.

West Indies wanting 259 to win were 121 for five when Constantine came in to score 103 out of 133—with two 6's, twelve 4's and a return drive that broke Jack Hearne's finger so badly that he did not play again that season—in an hour, to win the match by three wickets. Lord's erupted: and next day all cricketing England accepted a new major figure.

That performance confirmed the obvious, that Constantine was, as he knew he needed to be, the ideal league professional—surely the finest of all. He wanted a part-time living adequate for him to study law. England was the only place, and cricket his only means, of doing both. His batting could win a match in an hour; his bowling in a couple of overs, his catching in a few scattered moments. This was the kind of cricket nearest his heart: and he expressed himself through it. No man ever played cricket for a living—as Constantine needed to do more desperately than most professional cricketers—with greater gusto. Any club in the Lancashire leagues would have been grateful to sign him. Nelson did so with immense satisfaction on both sides. Constantine drew and delighted crowds—and won matches: Nelson won the Lancashire League eight times in his ten seasons there—an unparalleled sequence—and broke the ground attendance record at every ground in the competition. Less spectacularly, he coached and guided the younger players with true sympathy. Among the people of Nelson, many of whom had never seen a black man before, 'Connie' and his wife, Norma, settled to a happy existence which they remembered with nostalgia to the end. In 1963 the Freedom of the Borough of Nelson was bestowed on the man who then was Sir Learie Constantine.

Because of his League engagements he played little more than a hundred first-class matches, in which he scored 4,451 runs at 24.32, and took 424 wickets at 20.60. In eighteen Tests between 1928 and 1939 his overall figures were poor—641 runs at 19.42; 58 wickets at 30.10. On the other hand he virtually won two important Tests and shaped a third. At Georgetown, in 1930, when West Indies beat England for the first time, George Headley made a major batting contribution; but it was Constantine who twice broke the English batting with four for 35 and five for 87, figures not approached by any other bowler in the match. At Port of Spain in 1934–35 he levelled the series—which West Indies eventually won by one match—when, after scoring 90 and 31, he took two for 41 and ended his second innings three for 11 (in 14.5 overs) with the master stroke of having as great a resister as Maurice Leyland lbw with only one ball of the match remaining. In his last Test, at The Oval in 1939, when he was 37 years old, his five for 73 took West Indies to a first-innings lead.

As he grew older he grew more astute. As his pace dropped—though he was always likely to surprise with a faster ball or deal a yorker of high speed—he developed a superbly concealed slower ball; and at need he was an effective slow bowler with wrist or finger spin. He continued to play in charity matches well through his fifties when he could still make vivid strokes, bowl out good batsmen and take spectacular catches.

In his younger days some thought him bouncy or unduly colour conscious; if that were so, Nelson warmed him. It would have been strange if so dynamic and effective a cricketer had not bubbled over with confidence. Certainly, though, he gave unhesitating and helpful counsel, and generous praise to his amateur colleagues in the Nelson team. Meanwhile he fought discrimination against his people with a dignity firm but free of acrimony.

Half Learie Constantine's life was spent in England and, although his doctors had long before advised him that a lung condition endangered his life if he did not return to the warmer climate of the West Indies, he died in London. He remained in England during the Second World War as a Ministry of Labour welfare officer with West Indian workers. In 1944 he fought one of the historic cases against colour prejudice when he won damages from The Imperial Hotel in London for 'failing to receive and lodge him'.

He was deeply moved—and never forgot it—when the other players— all white-skinned—elected him captain of the Dominions team that beat England in the magnificent celebratory, end-of-war match at Lord's in 1946. He rose to the occasion in a fine forcing partnership with Keith Miller and his shrewd captaincy decided a narrow issue with only minutes to spare.

By then, however, his serious cricketing days were drawing to an end. He did occasional writing and broadcasting. Among his books are *Cricket in the Sun, Cricket and I, How to Play Cricket, Cricketers' Carnival, The Changing Face of Cricket* (with Denzil Batchelor), and *Colour Bar*. Years of dogged study were rewarded when he was called to the Bar by the Middle Temple in 1954. Returning to Trinidad he was elected an M.P. in his country's first democratic parliament; became Minister of Works in the government and subsequently High Commissioner for Trinidad and Tobago in London from 1962 until 1964. He was awarded the M.B.E. in 1945; knighted in 1962; made an honorary Master of the Bench in 1963; and created a life peer in 1969. He served various periods as a governor of the B.B.C., a Rector of St. Andrews, a member of the Race Relations Board and the Sports Council.

A devout Roman Catholic, of easy humour and essential patience, he lived a contented domestic life with his wife and his daughter, who is now a school teacher in Trinidad. His outlook was that of a compassionate radical and he maintained his high moral standards unswervingly.

To the end of his days he recalled with joy the great moments of his cricket and the friends he had made. His wife survived him by barely two months: and Trinidad posthumously awarded him the Trinity Cross, the country's highest honour.

SHILLINGS FOR W.G. [1973]

Looking Back Eighty Years

BY SIR COMPTON MACKENZIE

For the 1973 edition the editor had an inspiration. Why not select some distinguished literary figure old enough to remember a certain prestigious Victorian event and invite him to reminisce? The choice of Sir Compton Mackenzie was truly inspired. For one thing he was famed across the entire province of literature as the possessor of a phenomenal memory. He could claim total recall of events witnessed in infancy, and always insisted on the recollection of some rabbits shown to him by a solicitous nursemaid when he was ten months old. More to the point, Mackenzie had lived through a schoolboy addiction to the almanack and the doings of famous cricketers. In a wartime broadcast for the BBC, contemplating the latest edition, he recalled:

Here's old *Wisden* at eighty-two, whom I first bought before he was thirty and used to say over to myself like a breviary year in year out all through the nineties. I'm under the impression that a very fat *Wisden* cost only two bob in those days. Today a *Wisden* thinned by the austerity of war costs six and sixpence. That'll test the pockets of schoolboys even in these days of alleged schoolboy affluence. A. C. MacLaren was a young cricketer of the year in one of those *Wisdens* of long ago. In this year's almanack I read his obituary.

Mackenzie put his boyhood idolisation of the great cricketers of the day into his best-known novel, Sinister Street, *capturing the statistical essence of schoolboy interest in a few lines:*

Cricket was in the same way made a mathematical abstraction of decimals and initials and averages and records. All sorts of periodicals were taken in—*Cricket, The Cricketer, Cricketing* amongst many others. From an exact perusal of these, Michael and the Macalisters knew that Streatham could beat Hampstead and were convinced of the superiority of the Incogniti C.C. over the Stoics C.C. With the collection of cricketers' portraits some of these figures acquired a conceivable personality; but, for the most part they remained L. M. N. O. P. Q. Smith representing 36.58 at innings and R. S. T. U. V. W. Brown costing 11.07 a wicket. That they wore moustaches and lived and loved like passionate humanity did not seem to matter compared with the arithmetical progression of their averages. When Michael and Norton (who was staying with him at St. Leonards) were given shillings and told to see the Hastings Cricket Week from the bowling of the first ball to the drawing of the final stump, Michael and Norton were very much bored indeed, and deprecated the waste of time in watching real cricket, when they might have been better occupied in collating the weekly cricketing journals.

But it was something else which Mackenzie happened to say in passing during his radio talk which must have given the compilers of the almanack their bright idea. In recalling the amazing feat of A. C. MacLaren in 1899 in scoring 424 in a county game, Mackenzie had this to say:

Even the achievement of the immortal W. G. Grace in making 1000 runs during the previous May was dimmed for a while by this stupendous new record. We had all of us stumped up our bobs for the *Daily Telegraph*'s shilling testimonial fund to W. G.; but if we had been called upon to stump up another bob to show our admiration of that 424 of Archie MacLaren's we would willingly have done so.

With which recollection the reader is now armed to appreciate the essay which follows, the only addendum being that Sir Max Beerbohm also sent his shilling to the fund, attaching a note explaining that his generosity reflected, not his love of cricket but a loathing of golf.

Wisden is privileged to have received the last article by Sir Compton Mackenzie. It arrived a week before he died in Edinburgh on November 30, aged 89. In the last few years of his life Sir Compton was almost blind and only last summer he had a spell in hospital which left him with periodic fatigue. During his life he wrote about one hundred books. His work included novels, biographies, histories, travel books, essays, stories for children, besides numerous broadcasts and television appearances. He was born Edward Montague Compton in West Hartlepool and was educated in London at Colet Court and St. Paul's School before going to Oxford University. After coming down he studied law before turning to writing and then he assumed an old family name, Mackenzie.

CRICKET is a pastime I have always enjoyed. I do not suggest that I was ever a good cricketer. I suffered, in my opinion, from the handicap of being a left-handed bowler and a right-handed batsman. I could bowl without disgracing myself, but as a batsman I was hopeless.

How well do I remember the summer of that sunblessed year, 1893. I was ten years old and eager for fun. There was the cricket match between the small boys of Broadway and the visiting team of small boys in which I took five wickets. This was a pure accident. So much embarrassed was I when put on to bowl that I concentrated on bowling straight and in order to do this I thought the surest way was to swing my arm directly over my left shoulder. The result was a series of half volleys which an experienced batsman would have hit over the boundary by stepping out and treating the delivery as a full pitch. As it was, the inexperienced batsmen I bowled against stepped back and their stumps were spreadeagled. I was entirely at a loss to understand my success as a bowler and not in the least elated by it. Only when I held a tough catch at cover-point at the very end of the innings, which left the boys of Broadway victors, did I feel elated. The echo of that 'well caught' from the spectators still rings in my mind's ears from eighty years ago.

I recall the Scarborough cricket week of 1893 when I was taken by Frank Goodricke, the eldest son of the manager of the Spa, to see the South of England eleven playing Yorkshire. Well do I remember the venerated figure of W. W. Read, the Surrey batsman, in his chocolate coloured cap; we were too much in awe of cricketers eighty years ago to pester them for autographs. I recall dark handsome Tom Richardson, the Surrey fast bowler, and fair handsome Lockwood; I recall the burly figure of Sir Timothy O'Brien making terrific swipes off the redoubtable Yorkshire bowler Peel; I recall F. R. Spofforth, the 'demon' bowler, with his heavy drooping moustache; finally, I recall J. J. Ferris of Gloucestershire, a small left-handed bowler from Australia who only played a couple of seasons for Gloucestershire and went back to Australia in 1895. I have an impression that he took the wicket of the famous J. T. Brown; I certainly saw him take one Yorkshire wicket.

I fell into disgrace with Frank Goodricke because from where I was sitting in the pavilion I could see a football match going on. I can hear him now turning to me and saying 'This is the last time I'll bring you to the Scarborough cricket week if you want to look at football.' Frank Goodricke did not know that the ten-year-old boy looking at football, when the paragons of cricket were performing, was anticipating what the whole of the British public would be doing twenty years later. Two years earlier Somerset had been added to the eight first-class cricket counties. It was the bowling of S. M. J. Woods, or as we kids called him 'Sammy Woods', and the perfect batting of the brothers L. C. H. and R. C. N. Palairet which kept Somerset as a new first-class county.

The summer of 1894 I spent in Brittany with several other small boys to be coached for scholarship examinations and for entrance to H.M.S. *Britannia* for the Royal Navy. What I recall from that wet summer was the destruction of my butterfly collection by the customs officials who insisted on my opening the cigar boxes, in which I was carrying them back, and scattering them all over the wet ground. So wet a summer was it that we felt we had not lost much cricket but I do recall our surprise that the top of the batting averages was Brockwell of Surrey with 39 runs an innings.

However, the year 1895 was to become a remarkable one in the history of cricket. The prodigious performance of W. G. Grace in scoring over 1,000 runs in twenty-two days in the month of May inspired the whole country with a tremendous interest in cricket and cricketers. There had been nothing like it and, moreover, more than thirty years passed before it was repeated by another Gloucestershire stalwart, W. R. Hammond, in twenty-five days.

There must have been three or four periodicals produced in 1895 devoted to cricket records and the personalities of the various cricketers. It may have been due to this interest at this time that, as I remember, five were promoted to first-class counties that year. These were Hampshire, Derbyshire, Warwickshire, Leicestershire and Essex.

It was a batsman's year. W. G. Grace was in his forty-eighth year and he had taken considerable pains to get himself into the best physical condition possible. He was by far the heaviest player taking part in the great matches and he was in his thirty-first season in first-class cricket. Moreover, he played many long innings without a mistake: 288 against Somerset at Bristol in five hours, twenty minutes; it was his hundredth century; 257 against Kent at Gravesend and The Champion was on the field during every ball of the match.

Enthusiastic crowds flocked to see him wherever he appeared and he finished that memorable summer in making 2,346 runs, the largest aggregate of the year. He was entertained at banquets in London and Bristol; a National Testimonial was organised and the *Daily Telegraph*, the paper with which I was later to have some connection, collected £5,000 by means of a shilling subscription. Schoolboys all over the country were invited to contribute. I can still recall from eighty years ago our determination not to let our pocket-money of sixpence per week be given to cigarettes until we had the necessary shilling for W.G.

One summer's evening in mid-July of this year of W.G., when I was in the Recreation ground a friend came along Gliddon Road and shouted to me to open the gate for him.

'Archie MacLaren has made 424 against Somerset,' he announced as he passed through the gate.

'You liar!'

'No, really he has, and Lancashire have made 801.'

I was speechless and stood gazing at the hands of the golden school clock nearing eight on that golden evening. Lancashire 801! Archie MacLaren 424! What a chap Archie MacLaren must be! It was always our custom to talk of some famous cricketers by their Christian names—Archie MacLaren, Sammy Woods, Bobby Abel, Tom Richardson and of others by their initials—L.C.H. and R.C.N. (Palairet), W.W. (Read), and of course the mighty W.G. A year or two later when Worcestershire was added to the first-class counties, thanks to the redoubtable batting of old Malvernians like H. K. and R. E. Foster it was considered a great joke to call Worcestershire, 'Fostershire'.

Sadly for me I did not see any of the cricket of the Scarborough Festival of 1896 because I succumbed to what was called at that time inflammation of the lungs, which meant the agony of being painted with iodine and the irritation of being told by the doctor that I was imagining the pain. My mother at the time decided to buy a bungalow called Canadian Cottage on the outskirts of Alton in Hampshire; instead of going back to school in September I went down with her to Canadian Cottage and I felt myself well rewarded for the pain of that wretched iodine by the pleasure of reading at last three or four schoolboy weeklies, among them, *The Captain*, later edited by P. G. Wodehouse. A redoubtable player called Jessop was making large scores for Beccles College in East Anglia. G. L. Jessop! How lucky Gloucestershire and Cambridge University were to have him whom we used to call 'The Croucher'. Another of our heroes of that time was C.

J. Kortright of Essex whom we believed to be the fastest bowler who ever bowled a ball.

Now with the memory of K. S. Ranjitsinhji and C. B. Fry batting at Hove and of what seemed Ranjitsinhji's ability to make it look as easy to hit the ball to the boundary as it was back to the bowler, I shall move on to 1901 when I went up to Magdalen College, Oxford. It was now being realised that golf was a menace to cricket. Instead of practice at the nets, members of the Varsity XI were going off to play golf at some place called Hinksey. At the same time junior cricketers were playing golf at Cowley long before Cowley became the heart of the Morris motor works. Then on top of the threat of golf for the future of cricket came the addition of lawn tennis, which we used to call pat-ball in those days, real tennis still being considered the only kind of tennis fit for recognition. When a half-blue was awarded for lawn tennis, professional cricket did not seem to have anything to fear from either golf or tennis.

In 1939 when war with Germany was obviously drawing nearer the second National Government invited various people to speak round the country to step up recruiting. I was invited to address the City of Bradford with Herbert Sutcliffe as my partner. I had been warned by Auckland Geddes that Bradford could be as difficult an audience as Manchester had been for him the previous week when it kept chanting 'Tripe! Tripe!' When I stepped forward on the platform of the Alhambra on that Sunday evening I said I hoped the citizens of Bradford would not suppose that I was a representative of the National Government: 'What I think of the National Government could not be said on any platform or in any pulpit on a Sunday evening.' When I sat down Herbie Sutcliffe turned to me and said:

'Oh my, how I wish I could speak like you.'

'You don't wish nearly as much that you could speak like me as I wish I could bat like you,' I replied.

As I bring to a close these reminiscences of cricket as I recall it from eighty years ago I hear on the radio that Rhodes is drawing near to a century of years and I am back hearing of the feats of Rhodes and F. S. Jackson for the White Rose of Yorkshire against the Red Rose of Lancashire.

NORFOLK AND THE EDRICH CLAN [1973]

A Special Tribute to Bill Edrich

BY BASIL EASTERBROOK

Understandably the rosy glow of Mackenzie's essay made the rest of the 1973 essays seem warmed-over in comparison, but the composition by Basil Easterbrook on the Edrich family remains essential reading. There are a few whimsical deviations from the promise of the title, brought about, it would seem, by the author's straining to thrust his cultural bona fides under the reader's nose. Swinburne might have been amused to see his verses being recruited in the cause of a game whose headquarters are located in St. John's Wood, in which purlieus Swinburne himself played a rather more lurid game with certain lady entrepreneurs. The quoting of the Harrow School song might strike a note of comical incongruity in the context of Bill Edrich's career, but because the words have been so widely adapted for all sporting occasions since Bowen wrote them, perhaps the ploy is justified. But the presence of Shakespeare, Bacon and the Virgin Queen puts one in mind of those unfortunate players on England tours who never perform any function more exciting than bringing out the drinks. The essay wavers uncertainly between a celebration of the Edriches and a history of the county of their origins, but no doubt Mr. Easterbrook would defend himself by saying that the two are virtually the same. Nobody who recalls the time when Edrich centuries were being made simultaneously for Middlesex, Lancashire and Kent will make any complaints.

NORFOLK cricket and Bill Edrich—and surely strawberries and cream are not more synonymous—have in common an abiding endurance. There are some threads of evidence that a cricket club existed in Swaffham as far back as 1700 which means that the game has been played in this part of East Anglia for about 275 years. Nearly 100 years later Swaffham was just one of the many cricket clubs in the county—Castle Acre, Downham, Norwich, Lynn, West Lexham, Brinton, Dereham, for a generous half dozen.

David J. M. Armstrong of Holt, son of the Rev. H. B. J. Armstrong, one of the most notable of Norfolk cricket enthusiasts and a legend at Lakenham for his anecdotes and humour, privately published a history of Norfolk County Cricket in 1958 in which he records a team calling itself Norfolk taking the field for the first time as far back as 1797. The match was played on Swaffham Racecourse 'in the presence of an immense number of spectators from all parts of the Kingdom' between England and 33 of Norfolk. The county, despite their preponderance in numbers, were beaten by the eleven England cracks by an innings and 14 runs and in the two Norfolk innings there was but one solitary double-figure score of 14 and as many as 35 ducks!

This monumental humiliation of local talent served only to whet the appetite for cricket in Norfolk and the first quarter of the 19th century was a tale of continuing growth culminating in the formation of the County Cricket Club on January 11, 1827, at the Rampant Horse Inn, Norwich, with Lord Suffield as president. Mr. Armstrong's opening chapter of early days in Norfolk cricket is studded with tales of club matches played for side stakes, some of them distinctly peculiar. One match in 1811, for example, was played for 22 bottles of cider and 22 pounds of cherries, another in 1823 between eleven married and eleven single ladies for eleven pairs of gloves. Three years before this second game Norfolk went up to Lord's to play

M.C.C., and included in their team a man whose name had become immortal—Fuller Pilch.

At the formation of the County Club it was agreed to start with four matches the following summer, one each at Norwich, Yarmouth, Swaffham and Gunton. So great was the enthusiasm that just over five weeks later some ardent cricketers at Diss took time by the forelock and opened their season on February 20. The mere at Diss was gripped by a frost of unusual severity and two teams played what was reported as a *bona fide* match on skates! The game drew a crowd of several hundred, began at 10 o'clock in the morning, and was continued until half past five.

By 1831 Norfolk were described in one periodical of the day as 'Now the next club to the Marylebone'. Certainly the previous summer both Norfolk and Norwich had beaten the M.C.C. at Lord's, although M.C.C. won the two return matches at Norwich and Dereham.

There came an historic moment in September, 1833, when Yorkshire played their first-ever game and their opponents were Norfolk. The match took place at Sheffield and the Tykes immediately established the habit of winning that was to bring them 31 outright championships. The scores were Yorkshire 138 and 196; Norfolk 67 and 146. A year later Yorkshire were soundly thrashed at Norwich by 272 runs, Fuller Pilch making 87 not out and 73 in the two Norfolk innings. In 1835 the match with Yorkshire was left drawn because of rain but not before Pilch made 157 not out in Norfolk's second innings.

Now came an unexpected swing of the pendulum. The public at Yarmouth and Gunton withheld their support and in 1836 Pilch was lured away to Kent on the promise of £2 a week throughout the year. He took with him another leading Norfolk player called William Stearman. Next, Lord Suffield was thrown by his horse and killed and the drive faltered both on the field and in the committee room. The decline in the 1840s was unchecked and the County Club folded up in 1848. It was revived briefly in 1862 but by 1870 it had failed again.

It is perhaps necessary at this point to digress slightly and consider the character of the East Anglian. Local patriotism is strong in all parts of England but it is doubtful if the people of East Anglia are not the proudest of all. Progress has done less to destroy the essential character of Norfolk, Suffolk, Essex and Cambridgeshire than any other part of the United Kingdom. Their landscape, villages, churches and great country houses still retain the qualities for which they were valued in earlier centuries and even the towns are generally traditional and unspoiled.

Blickling Hall and Castle Acre Priory—where else would architectural monuments be found to surpass them? It was an early cricket match at Blickling Hall that inspired some forgotten poet to pen the lines:

> *Weary of play, some summer eve perchance*
> *You will come running in from dewless lawns*
> *The long day's sunshine on your countenance.*

But there is more to Norfolk than stately piles and old monuments. The ancient wind and water mills, the harvest fields in autumn, the fishing fleet leaving or entering Yarmouth, the Broads—and driving the iron into the soul of the Norfolkman—the sea; an ambivalence brought about by a remoteness and isolation which can be both cherished and deplored. This is still splendidly evoked by Swinburne's lines:

> *A land that is lonelier than ruin;*
> *A sea that is stranger than death;*
> *Far fields that a rose never blew in,*
> *Wan waste where the winds lack breath;*
> *Waste endless and boundless and flowerless*
> *But of marsh-blossoms fruitless as free,*
> *Where earth lies exhausted, as powerless*
> *To strive with the sea.*

For me, the foregoing makes it clear why two failures were brushed aside and the dogged, uncompromising men of Norfolk started up their country cricket club once more on October 14, 1876. It certainly makes the Edrich clan entirely realistic and acceptable.

John Edrich in his book *Runs in the family*—one of the better cricket book titles—begins his first chapter with this paragraph:

'My grandfather, Harry Edrich, of Manor Farm, Blofield, a village near Norwich, spent his days farming, cricketing and raising 13 children. One of his sons became my father, Fred, and another the father of Geoff (Lancashire), Brian (Kent and Glamorgan), Eric (Lancashire) and Bill (the famous 'W.J.' of Middlesex and England).'

What odds, one wonders would the newly arisen betting parlours on our first-class grounds offer against some future family providing players for five of England's first-class counties with two of them becoming Test stars? The greatest of them, notwithstanding John's admirable service to England, is Bill.

Lack of inches never stopped him from doing the things he set his heart on. Playing, flying, living, he extracted the last ounce from all of them, with enough success to make any two normal men envious. To see him come through the gate at Lord's and walk out to the middle was to see the personification of self-confidence and aggressiveness. There was nothing of the brute in his intelligent features but the pugnacity was unmistakable. He walked with chest thrust out like the human fighting cock he was, but as light on his feet as a girl going to her first dancing class.

He might have been a star winger with Tottenham Hotspur but his talent at cricket was so outstanding that he wisely soon gave up his soccer. He did not play professionally for Middlesex until 1937 but in less than a season he established himself as one of the most promising players in the country in a period when there was no shortage. His fleetness of foot and his utter fearlessness made him the kind of batsman we have so often sorely needed in the years since he returned whence he came, to Norfolk, where, as late as 1970, coming up to his middle fifties, he played 18 innings and easily topped the county's batting averages.

The bowling could be nasty, fast and the ball rising but Edrich either hooked it off his eyebrows or got right behind it.

Wes Hall and Charlie Griffith would not have got under Bill's skin although I fancy he might well have got under theirs. In the war he became a pilot in Bomber Command and won the D.F.C., for a daylight attack—not the easiest way to earn this major decoration. Between establishing himself in first-class cricket and the outbreak of the Second World War, Bill Edrich was granted just one year—1938, the year of Munich. Edrich seized his solitary chance characteristically to make 1,000 runs before June 1st. He was the sixth man to achieve it and to date the last. Perhaps it will never be done again, although Edrich's feat was the fifth of its kind in the space of eleven years. FIN DE SIÈCLE?

There were two other remarkable facts about it—it was done in the same season that Bradman did it for the second time, the one occasion it has been performed twice in the same May, and all Edrich's runs were made at Lord's. His innings included 104 for M.C.C. v. Yorkshire, 115 for M.C.C. v. Surrey, 182 for Middlesex v. Gloucestershire and 245 for Middlesex v. Nottinghamshire. When he was out against Nottinghamshire he needed just 19 more runs for his 1,000 with eight days of May still stretching ahead of him. Nottinghamshire were beaten by an innings and Middlesex did the same in the next match against Worcestershire. For Edrich it was three wasted days.

He hit a return catch to Bob Crisp the South African without scoring—his first failure in what was, for those who set store on such things, his thirteenth innings of the season. That left him two possible chances of getting the 19 runs he required, for Middlesex met the Australians on May 28, 30 and 31. All Saturday the players watched the rain falling as straight as stair rods and it did not let up on the Sunday. On the Monday play was possible all day but these were no conditions for batsmen.

The Australians, who had made six scores of over 500 in seven innings, were put out for 132 and Middlesex, battling all the way, reached 188. Edrich's share of obtaining this lead of 56 was 9. He was then bowled neck and crop by O'Reilly and when Bradman and McCabe came together in the second innings in what was the Australians' only real stand of this rain-riddled fixture Edrich seemed certain to end the month with 990 runs. Then with less than half an hour to play out the formalities of a hopelessly drawn game, Bradman declared and said to Edrich: 'See if you can get those 10, Bill.' There was just time for half a dozen quick overs shared by McCabe and Waite and Edrich got those 10 and helped himself to 10 more for luck. He had made 1,010 by May 31, with an average of over 84.

Edrich had his detractors, especially for the extended period he was given in the England team before he succeeded at Test level. They, the ubiquitous 'they', said it was only because of his Lord's background. Well, perhaps Lord's did help him, perhaps if he had played for Somerset or Glamorgan his path to the top would have been longer and thornier, but that he would have got there in the end there can be no doubt.

The watcher from the ringside, however diligent, is always open to at least two charges, *(a)* that he has his favourites and *(b)* that he never played at top level and therefore his judgement is open to doubt.

Speaking personally, I accept those charges even if the motives behind them are often malicious so I sought a friend of both Edrich and myself who had played with him and against him. No one, I think, would question Trevor Bailey's status as a player or deny that he is a shrewd assessor now that he has become a writer on the game.

'I have always maintained that seeing this little man hook Ray Lindwall was one of the most exhilarating sights I have ever witnessed on a cricket ground,' Bailey told me, adding that he rated Edrich as a great player who would have been an automatic choice for a world eleven at his peak.

'In company with most small, nimble batsmen Bill was very quick on his feet against the spinners and his cutting was of the very highest order. He also preferred a lofted stroke wide of mid-on, which was a cross between the on drive and the 'cow shot' which brought him a vast number of sixes on even the largest of grounds. As the years went by Bill lost some of his freedom and though, because of his sound technique, he was never easy to dismiss, it was possible to keep him relatively quiet by bowling a full length on and just outside his off stump—something which could never have occurred during those memorable days of 1947.'

Memorable days indeed with Middlesex winning the Championship by continuous all-round cricket of brilliance and character. It was, although none knew it at the time, the last great pyrotechnic display before the game was overtaken by our egalitarian times. 1947, when Compton, Robertson and Edrich scored 32 centuries between them for Middlesex alone. 1947, when a county fixture could draw 20,000 for a day's play.

The memory of that exceptional summer of weather as well as cricket reminds me of a day when a modern player of some renown was at considerable pains to explain to Jim Sims how much more scientific the game had become since his playing days.

'Yes, mate,' replied Jim Sims, 'but we drew the crowds.'

And why did they draw the crowds? Did they come content just to watch Compton, Edrich and the rest making their big scores? No, for while they scored heavily they still believed in the feasibility of having 400 on the board shortly after tea. Edrich was a man who knew instinctively about time and its value. Were not the last words of Elizabeth the First reported to have been: 'All my possessions for a moment of time.'? And there was Shakespeare lamenting 'I wasted time and now doth time waste me.' Whether batting all day or providing the impromptu cabaret at an all-night party, Bill Edrich believed with Bacon that a man that is young in years may be old in experience if he has lost no time. Or as Quarles ended a famous passage—One to-day is worth two to-morrows.

Edrich was always for me the living symbol that a man does not have to stand six feet two in his stockinged feet to be a great cricketer. I think that it was no accident that when he finished with first-class cricket Edrich made a clean cut. Other great players like Compton, Benaud, Brown, Dexter, Yardley, Peebles, Bowes, Fingleton, Laker, Bailey and Gover—an eleven of nearly all the talents—kept in touch by writing, broadcasting or commentating on T.V.

What Edrich did do, most logically and sensibly was to combine a life in commerce with playing and captaining Norfolk in the Minor Counties Competition. To give what you have to give in the right place at the right time is surely the art of living. As recently as 1970 the memories come rushing back when he made a brief reappearance at Lord's when Norfolk came to H.Q. on Gillette Cup business.

Cardus, of course, has not permitted such a player as Edrich to escape his matchless pen. 'Edrich the born fighter, battling on with his batting, a great little driver who, on his day, could bowl fast. He would run so fast to bowl that after release of the ball his follow through propelled him somewhere near, or between, cover and gully—as though he had been sucked forward by the wind or draught of his own bowling. He was the most gallant and fearless of batsmen, whose only misgiving was that Denis Compton might any moment run him out.'

Sir Neville, like myself, never had to bat against him or bowl to him and as Trevor Bailey put it as he cast his mind back more than a quarter of a century—'I did and Bill did not exactly inspire lyrical prose in my breast at the time. In those days bowling against Middlesex was more of a problem than bowling against many Test teams. Bill was a complete batsman with a magnificent defence. Few in my experience have watched the ball so closely. And, it goes without saying, he had a very wide range of attacking strokes. The harder you hit him, either with the bat or ball, the greater became his determination. I never remember him flinching.

'It is hardly surprising to know he had a distinguished career in the war, not in some quiet little sinecure far removed from the main scene of the conflict but at the sharp end.

'When hostilities ended Bill, with his D.F.C., a decoration never lightly awarded, returned to Middlesex and after one season decided to become an amateur. It was the early days of the social revolution when it was still considered essential to have an amateur captaining England. At that time it seemed quite probable that Bill, who was an automatic choice as player, might lead England when Wally Hammond retired. For a variety of reasons, including a disregard for the hierarchy, a certain wildness and impetuosity, and an unconventional outlook he never achieved this particular honour. However, his decision to join the amateur ranks undoubtedly cost him at least a ten thousand tax free benefit.

'Bill lived hard and played hard. He believed that life was for living and was prepared to let to-morrow take care of itself, a view which his experiences as a combat pilot had helped to develop. I always felt that he needed a 36-hour-day and inevitably there were clashes with authority from time to time, because he was a colourful, controversial and sometimes headstrong individual. I remember how he upset one rather sedate selector who simply could not understand the ethical gulf that divided the two of them, and never would. This selector was utterly and completely dedicated to cricket, to Bill it always remained a wonderful game, but he never allowed it to interfere unduly with his private life. As a result England went to Australia in 1950-51 without him, and this piece of selectorial folly could well have cost us the Ashes.

'Bill loved parties and he brought to them the zest and enthusiasm which epitomised his cricket. He was also firmly of the opinion that a good one should never end before dawn. His party piece took the form of either a vocal, or a conjuring act.

'He had acquired his repertoire of songs during long forgotten nights in the mess and I think it is fair to say that his memory of the lyrics was considerably more impressive than his voice which was, fortunately, unique in my experience. It was an off beat, husky whisper but sufficiently penetrating to reach everyone in the room. He also had another favourite party piece involving an egg which was always far more entertaining when it failed than when successful, a view not shared by one distinguished cricket correspondent whose white tuxedo never looked quite so immaculate again.'

When Trevor's fascinating reminiscences of a brother tourist came to an end I steered him carefully back to Edrich the cricketer. He saw nothing beautiful about his bowling action. A quick scurry up to the wicket followed by a slinging action (it reminded Bailey of a catapult) but he conceded Bill did propel the ball through the air at a considerable speed and with enormous zeal. Bailey, who took 2,082 wickets in something like 22 years in the first-class game, 132 of them for England, felt Edrich was essentially a shock bowler, to be used in short bursts, when he was always liable to surprise the batsman by his speed.

'His lack of height combined with his action ensured that he did not achieve much lift, in fact he tended to skid off the wicket.' Bailey, a man not given to overstatement or facile praise, then added with a note of genuine admiration, the salute of one great craftsman to another—'but for a few overs he was genuinely quick'.

Bailey had now dealt with his contemporary as a batsman, a bowler and an individual. To dot the i's and cross the t's did he have anything to add on Edrich as fielder and captain?

'Originally a cover and a good mover, as one would expect from a professional soccer player, Bill gradually developed into a very effective and unspectacular first slip.

'His captaincy was in a similar mould to his slip fielding, sound rather than showy. He did not miss any tricks, but he was always willing to take a gamble if there was the slightest hope of victory.'

This then was Bill Edrich who played 39 times for England and made six of his 86 centuries in Tests. In all first-class cricket he scored 36,965 runs and as in the case of his 'twin' Denis Compton, Wally Hammond and Len Hutton one inevitably muses on what his figures would have been if he had been able to play at this level between 1940 and 1945. In the case of Edrich the years he lost covered the period between his 24th and 29th birthdays and he might well have retired in the company of names like Sutcliffe and Grace if not Hobbs, Woolley and Hendren. Robbed by fate as he was, he still accomplished not one but two seasons which will make his name imperishable as long as 22 men somewhere on the earth's surface can be found to play the game of cricket. Only three actual playing seasons after he achieved the now legendary feat of 1,000 in May he scored in 52 innings the remarkable aggregate of 3,539 runs which included twelve hundreds with an average of over 80. The fact that Denis Compton scored 3,816 in two innings less at an average of nearly 91 takes nothing from Edrich's marvellous follow up to 1938.

When he played his last first-class season in 1958 he was already half-way to his 43rd birthday and few could have visualised him carrying on into his middle fifties as an adornment to Minor Counties cricket. As year followed year and his name and performances continued to shine out from the middle reaches of *Wisden* those of us to whom he had given such unadulterated pleasure at Lord's were glad to know the little war horse had a whinny or two left in him.

If he has a regret it is that on his return to the county that had sired him and given him his first chance he was unable to lead Norfolk to the championship of the competition it has not won for 60 years.

The Minor Counties Championship was inaugurated in 1895 and in its first year Norfolk headed the table, sharing the title with Durham and Worcestershire. Ten years later Norfolk were outright champions after a wonderful season. Losing their first match and held to a draw in their second Norfolk, captained by the Rev. G. B. Raikes, won their remaining eight fixtures. Raikes was still captain in 1910 when Norfolk took the championship again and G. A. Stevens made 201 in the challenge match.

In 1912 Michael Falcon became captain, an office he held until the end of the 1946 season. Norfolk won seven of their eight matches but the championship was left unawarded as floods prevented the challenge match with Staffordshire being played. Ironically Norfolk with a far less impressive record won the title the following year. In a wonderful game against Staffordshire, Norfolk won by 35 runs, despite a certain Sidney Barnes taking nine for 31 in their first innings.

The outbreak of World War I caused the Minor Counties' programme to be abandoned in 1914 and it was not resumed until 1920. Between the wars Norfolk, in the opinion of its able historian Mr. Armstrong, was at its strongest. Like all cricket lovers he succumbed to the temptation to pick his best eleven. In this case it is from the sides that represented Norfolk in the thirties and it comes as no surprise that three of the first six bear the name Edrich. All eleven of this team played first-class cricket at sometime or other, and here it is:

(1) D. F. Walker, (2) W. J. Edrich, (3) G. A. Edrich, (4) M. Falcon (captain), (5) M. R. Barton, (6) E. H. Edrich (wicket-keeper), (7) D. C. Rought-Rought, (8) R. C. Rought-Rought, (9) C. S. R. Boswell, (10) T. G. L. Ballance, (11) G. R. Langdale.

In this period Norfolk played 96 matches of which they won 33 outright and a further 27 on the first innings. Only 12 were lost. Yet the title at the end of the season always eluded Norfolk. Not for the first time fate took a hand against them in 1933 when, just as in 1912, the county reached the top of the Minor Counties table and in the words of the understandably disappointed Armstrong 'only to be robbed, perhaps, of the title (who can tell!) by a misfortune over the challenge match, this time due to a miscalculation of points'.

This is what happened: Yorkshire Second XI were credited with full points in a match with Staffordshire, when they should have had first-innings points only, the match having been reduced by rain to one day, and there having been a misunderstanding as to which of the two days had been rained off. These extra points had put Yorkshire in second place and they had then played and beaten Norfolk in what was supposed to be the Challenge Match. As a result of this victory, Yorkshire Second XI were put at the top of the table.

When the final table was being checked for insertion in *Wisden* it was found that the columns did not tally and on investigation the error was discovered. Wiltshire and not Yorkshire should have had the right to challenge Norfolk. The title was therefore left 'Undecided' with Norfolk placed at the top of the table, champions in all but name.

Bill Edrich, a product of Bracondale school, made 20 out of a total of 49 against the 1932 Indian touring side and in 1935 distinguished himself against the South Africans whom he was to put to the sword in company with Compton 12 years later. At Lakenham he scored 111 for Norfolk in 165 minutes and two months later when selected for the Minor Counties he took a further 79 off the Tourists.

The degree of Edrich's virtuosity is surely plain to later generations when they learn that he continued to play for Norfolk until the end of 1936—just two years before he scored 1,000 by the end of May. Although the title continued to elude them, sometimes by maddeningly narrow margins, Norfolk went from August 25, 1932 until July 1, 1937 without losing a single Minor Counties fixture.

When 1946 came Norfolk faced the task of building an almost new side. Walker and Ballance had been killed in action in the Second World War, Geoff Edrich and Eric Edrich had become Lancashire professionals, R. C. Rought-Rought had retired.

After one season Falcon's wonderful career came to a close. From 1906 to 1946 he took 727 wickets and scored 11,340 runs—tremendous figures for a competition so limited in fixtures as the Minor Counties.

Norfolk soldiered on into the fifties without being able to gather together a side capable of making a serious bid for honours but Eric Edrich had returned from Lancashire and in 1955 John Edrich, soon to leave for Surrey and a professional career as distinguished as Bill, topped the batting averages. As a fitting finale to the season a Norfolk XI played an All Edrich XI in which W.J. hit a century.

Before the decade was out the same W.J. Edrich was back at Lakenham. He polished off the fifties, shone steadily through the sixties and greeted the seventies by finishing top of the Norfolk batting with an average of over 35 and second in the bowling, sending down 238 overs and taking 25 wickets. He was then 54 years and seven months old. The summer of 1972 marked the 40th year since his entry into county cricket. 1972 also happened to be the centenary of the writing of the immortal song of Harrow School—'Forty Years On' by Bowen. Noble words, a haunting tune and no Harrovian of my acquaintance would object I feel sure if I quote the first verse here in tribute to one of the outstanding cricketers of my time.

> *Forty years on when afar and asunder*
> *Parted are those who are singing to-day*
> *When you look back and forgetfully wonder*
> *What you were like in your work and your play*
> *Then it may be there will often come o'er you*
> *Glimpses of notes like the catch of a song*
> *Visions of boyhood shall float them before you*
> *Echoes of dreamland shall bear them along.*

WHEN THREE-DAY CRICKET WAS WORTHWHILE [1974]

BY C. T. BENNETT

It may well have surprised some readers of the almanack that as late as 1974 there were still advocates of the good old days who wrote about the joys of Gentlemanly Cricket. C. T. Bennett had first won his place in the Harrow eleven in the year of Passchendaele, since which time he had been obliged, like the rest of his generation, to stand by and witness the relentless erosion of the lifestyle, on and off the field, which is so passionately cherished. His essay is a confusing mixture of blimpish blundering and cool perception, veering from a castigation of those thieves who have engineered a fall in the number of overs per hour, to the foolishness of his demand for the return of 'glorious adventure' to a game long since commercialised down to its fulsomely endorsed bootstraps; perhaps the plea might have carried more weight had its author shown a little more tendency to glorious adventure in his own play, which, in eighty-five first-class innings, produced no centuries.

Mr. Bennett's idolatry of F. S. Jackson oversteps the bounds of discretion when it tells that Jackson was an example to all 'on and off the field'. Presumably this is a passing reference to Jackson's political career when he became chairman of the Unionist Party. Bennett's suggestion that Jackson was incapable of an act to which the world could respond with 'that's not cricket' might make a useful theme for a Wisden *essay on the ethics of party chairmen who preside over affairs as grubby as the Zinoviev Letter of 1924.*

But even as Bennett exasperates us with his comic imperceptions, he retains our interest with the anecdote involving Lionel Tennyson in the West Indies, and goes on to win our approval by regretting the tendency of some players to drift from county to county. Having re-established his bona fides, he then destroys them again by expressing approval for the Yorkshire county club's refusal to traffic in players born outside the county limits. There is much to be said for retaining the regional aspect of the County Championship, but not in the case of Yorkshire, which has persisted in making itself the butt of the cricket world by stubbornly refusing to shift from a principle rendered hopelessly bogus by the fact that its first advocate, Martin, Lord Hawke, was born in Lincolnshire. Bennett misses the chance for laughter here, but compensates with three vital passages. The first offers some rare insights into the links between cricket and horse-racing, the second with Bennett's curt dismissal of racial discrimination, and the third, the gaffe of a well-intentioned young lady spectator at the University cricket match. The latter anecdote recalls one other, the sequence in one of Leslie Stuart's Edwardian operettas where the heroine attends the Varsity match and attempts to prove her grasp of affairs by postulating that Oxford batted at one end and Cambridge at the other.

'Tris' Bennett was in the Harrow XI for five years, 1917 to 1921, being captain in the last year. He gained his Blue at Cambridge for cricket in 1923 and in 1925 when he was captain. He also kept goal for Cambridge in the Association football University match of 1925.

WHY is first-class cricket losing its power of attraction to the British public? Sometimes I hark back to the days, not, at any rate to me, so far distant, when Surrey or Middlesex against Yorkshire used to be played before 'full houses', with the gates closed against many hundreds of would-be watchers. Nowadays such games draw little more than a handful of spectators and those mainly members or Yorkshire 'exiles'.

The reasons for dwindling attendances are many and various. Firstly there is the difference of approach to the game by the participants compared with the old days. Few could deny that there is an almost entire lack of glorious adventure, as evidenced by the general unwillingness of captains to take a chance of bringing off a victory should there be at the same time a risk of suffering defeat. We need some leaders with the outlook of Percy Fender, Beverley Lyon and Stuart Surridge, great skippers of years gone by.

There is, too, an absence of 'characters' such as we used to have in such men as George Gunn, Leonard Braund, Cecil Parkin, 'Patsy' Hendren and Alec Skelding, to name but a few. In my time a leavening of professionals with the great amateurs was for the good of cricket. For that reason I have never ceased to regret the passing of the best match of all, Gentlemen v. Players at Lord's.

The current prevalence of 'gamesmanship' is often exposed by the leisurely rate at which overs are bowled, with unnecessary pow-wows between captain and bowler and time wasted over minute alterations in field-placing. In this regard, too, I cannot help feeling that the tremendously long run-up of some bowlers is more for psychological reasons than anything else, for the pace at which the ball is delivered is nothing commensurate. My 1925 Cambridge team, described by *Wisden* of the period as 'probably the best sent up to Lord's by either University since the War', maintained an average of about 20 overs an hour, though I admit that we possessed no bowler of great pace. Now it is deemed necessary to impose a fine upon counties averaging fewer than 18½ overs an hour during a season. How odd that players should, for fear of losing money, be virtually forced to do what should come naturally to them—and what an implied commentary upon the moderns!

One great personality of the past who could not have tolerated the unethical approach to cricket of today was Sir Stanley Jackson, immortalised in the Harrow song-book by 'A Gentleman's A-bowling'. He was an inspiration and an example to all both on and off the field, especially to Harrow, Cambridge and Yorkshire, to say nothing of England, for whom he played in 20 Test matches between 1893 and 1905. He was the greatest cricket aristocrat of them all. I feel sure that many of the problems of the game would be solved if a man of his character still graced our cricket fields.

It is a long time ago, but I think that I am right in saying that it was about 1918 or 1919 that Sir Stanley played his last match, when he captained I Zingari against Harrow. The visiting side always used to enter the Sixth Form ground from the Field House Club. I recall that, when Jackson went in to bat, everybody stood, among them A. J. Webbe and A. C. MacLaren, who raised their right arms as if in a final valediction. Alas, Sir Stanley was yorked for 0.

Bad examples set by leading cricketers have their effect upon youngsters, who are always quick to ape their elders. Hence, maybe, the disappearance of the phrase once applied to a doubtful action: 'That's not cricket', virtually an essential part of the English language.

What a contrast with the folk I encountered when I went with the Hon. F. S. G. Calthorpe's M.C.C. team to the West Indies in 1925–26. The spirit of both players and spectators was remarkable and the crowds levelled far more criticism at their own cricketers than they did at us. Instead of having, as is sometimes the case nowadays, to avoid flying bottles, the deep fieldsmen were frequently offered a swig from a bottle of rum by an onlooker! I recall with glee one match in which the Hon. Lionel (later Lord) Tennyson was fielding at third man when a coloured woman of extremely ample proportions dashed on to the field and said to him: 'How would you like to be a fat old bitch like me?' Lionel's response was to give her a resounding kiss, to the cheers of the crowd.

From time to time the authorities have tinkered with the Laws without much beneficial result and, of all changes, that which shortened boundaries is the one I most dislike. I know it has been partially rescinded, but the very distant boundaries have virtually gone. It has proved specially discouraging to slow bowlers, for on quite a few grounds a batsman earns six runs from a stroke which formerly could well have resulted in a catch for a deep fieldsman.

I am also irked by the registration rule which permits players to flit from country to country like so many migrant swallows. The argument advanced in favour of this is that the players concerned would otherwise be lost to first-class cricket; but do we want to adopt in cricket the transfer system which results in the over-pricing of Association footballers? I am strongly against this, as I would have been, had I been alive at the time, at James Southerton, father of a former Editor of *Wisden*, appearing in one season for Sussex, Hampshire and Surrey. No, give me the rigid ruling of Yorkshire, who include in their ranks only players of Yorkshire birth.

I must mention, too, two other constant sources of irritation to me. One is the reluctance—or inability—of the vast majority of batsmen to use their feet, with the result that they are practically crease-bound. Then there is the questioning of umpires' decisions, both on and off the field, a custom in which some members of the Press, T.V. and Radio, also indulge much too frequently. Such a thing most assuredly was 'not done' in my day. We felt that the proviso in the Laws: 'if *in the opinion of the umpire*' forbade such actions, in addition to the fact that they did not coincide with our idea of sportsmanship.

The subject of pitches must not be overlooked. Far too much currently goes into the preparation of some of them, with the result that in normal circumstances they grossly favour the batsman. Conversely, they have for long imposed a heavy burden upon the bowler. Hence, instead of bowling at the stumps as once they did, bowlers have endeavoured to restore the balance by exploiting leg-theory, off-theory and 'bumpers'. I favour a return to more natural pitches, despite the argument that they would not stand up to the wear and tear of five-day Test matches—which in my view are too long and lead to slow non-chance-taking batting.

There is at present an acute shortage of highly specialised slip fieldsmen to add to the troubles of bowlers. Alec Bedser most ably set forth his views in an article on the bitter harvest reaped in Test matches. When I was at Cambridge, Braund had me out morning after morning practising catching for half an hour at a time, first, with the right hand and then with the left, until he made me, I was told, a first class slip—a fact with which I feel sure that G. O. Allen, an old Cambridge Blue and fast bowler and captain of Middlesex and England, would agree.

My time at the University was rightly termed 'The Golden Age of Fenner's.' During the first fortnight of the 1925 season the professional players engaged as coaches were L. C. Braund, E. Hendren, J. W. Hearne and A. S. Kennedy, all at the request of the current captain. What a fine job they did, especially Braund who, thanks to the generosity of my father, stayed on for the whole term. Picking the team for Lord's was no easy matter, not because of any shortage of talent, but because of a super-abundance of it, especially in batting. When the eleven was announced, I remember being asked by a distinguished cricket writer: 'Why on earth A. U. Payne when there is so much other talent available?' The answer was simple: Payne was the equal of any fieldsman in England and his presence was very much appreciated by the bowlers. This was really a classic case of a man being played for his fielding—a remark sometimes passed about a player who achieves little as a batsman and takes 'nought for plenty' as a bowler.

In N. B. Sherwell, I was able to call upon a splendid wicket-keeper who, like Strudwick, of Surrey and England fame, never 'blinded' his slips. Today the acrobatics of some wicket-keepers horrify me and I shudder to think what Braund would have said about them. After all, he was one of the world's best slips.

As regards K. S. Duleepsinhji, he was one of the greatest batsmen of all time. One writer of note on both cricket and Rugby football suggested to me that 'a young man from Cheltenham' was worth watching. What a masterly under-statement about this nephew of the legendary K. S. Ranjitsinhji! 'Duleep' or 'Mr. Smith' as Duleepsinhji was affectionately known in cricket circles, drew the crowds like honey attracts bees. The records speak for themselves, but they do not indicate his unfailing kindness and courtesy on and off the field. He went on to play 12 times for England and I cherish the story of him, when, appearing for the first time against Australia at Lord's, he hit 173. When at length he was caught in the deep field from a rather rash stroke, his uncle remarked: 'He always was a careless lad.' What a pity that ill-health, against which he had battled for years, foreshortened Duleep's cricket career. Incidentally, he was one of the first to acknowledge and praise the help and advice of Braund.

H. J. Enthoven was one of the best all-rounders of his day. We were together at Stanmore Park when the Rev. Vernon Royle, a Cambridge Blue in 1875 and 1876 and shortly afterwards an England player, was headmaster, and later at Harrow. What a friend and what a player was Enthoven. He scored hundreds in the 'Varsity matches of 1924 and 1925 and he performed the 'hat-trick' for Gentlemen v. Players. Incidentally even Denis Compton must be envious of his attempted run-outs!

R. J. O. Meyer, who gained a double first in classics and went on to become the highly successful headmaster of Millfield School, was a great swing bowler and a Jessopian bat at No. 10. To give us a good start to the innings were T. E. S. Francis, also a Rugby Blue and capped four times at football for England in 1926, and E. W. Dawson, who later performed with distinction for Leicestershire and England. L. G. Crawley, another excellent batsman and golfer, was also a magnificent fieldsman in the deep. I always liked the story of him in one University match when, fielding at third man, he stopped a cut from Jack Meyer's bowling and returned the ball to Ben Sherwell. Upon which a girl in the ladies' stand exclaimed: 'How clever—and with only one hand.'

The most lovable of all the members of my side was S. T. Jagger, an off-spinner subjected to much criticism by the Press. After we had drawn a match at Fenner's, I was having a drink with the reporter for *The Times* and he said to me very audibly in the near presence of Sam Jagger: 'I cannot understand why you persist in playing Jagger.' The only reply—but a pretty effective one—which I could make was: 'Please report in your paper that S. T. Jagger has been awarded his Blue.' The gift was justified by later events and made Jagger's career. Finally there was R. G. H. Lowe, a fast-medium bowler who, because Meyer and Enthoven nearly always opened, seldom received the chance to use the new ball. Lowe never uttered the least complaint about this and he was a staunch competitor.

I recall that when F. R. Brown was at The Leys School in 1925, it was arranged that he should come to Fenner's and enjoy the benefit of some coaching. I remember so well Hendren and Braund saying of him: 'What a nice young man. With luck, he should make a name for himself in the game.' Cambridge, Surrey, Northamptonshire, England and M.C.C. can testify to the accuracy of that prognostication.

Several Newmarket trainers took a vast interest in University cricket in my time and, as honorary members, came over to watch us in action at Fenner's whenever possible. Among them were the famous Jarvis brothers—Willie, trainer for King George V; Basil, trainer of the Derby winner Papyrus, and Jack, who trained for Lord Rosebery, a great cricketer in his own right for over 40 years. The brothers regularly donated 100 guineas annually to the Club. There were also Noel Cannon and his brother, Boxer. On Sundays these trainers took visiting professionals to look over their stables and be entertained to lunch. That dour Yorkshire-man, Emmott Robinson, a persistent friend of the bookmakers, always regarded this trip as the best part of his county's fixture.

In 1925 a fixture was arranged at Fenner's between the University and the Tramps' C.C., membership of which comprised trainers and jockeys. Among the jockeys to turn out were Charles Elliott and Harry Wragg. A splendid crowd attended to see these idols of the turf. As usual, the trainers were most generous to the ground-staff, the head of whom was Dan Hayward, brother of the famous Tom, of Surrey and England, and to the gate-men. I believe that was the only match of this nature ever to be staged at Fenner's. Charities benefited handsomely from the game. Not only did the 'gate' go to them, but also the takings from the sale of beer, provided gratis by Dale's Brewery—no longer a separate entity—who specially brewed the audit ale for the Oxford and Cambridge boat race crews.

Another game that lingers in my memory took place a fortnight after the 1925 'Varsity match. The late Admiral Sir Stuart Bonham-Carter wrote to me asking if it would be possible for me to bring down a side to play the Royal Navy at Portsmouth, adding that we would be well entertained. This turned out to be the greatest under-statement since Nelson's time! My team all agreed with alacrity to make the trip, with the exception of R. G. H. Lowe, who could not play owing to a prior engagement. So the twelfth man, J. V. Hermon, later, alas, killed at Salerno while serving with the Grenadier Guards, completed our full complement. The match was a great success, cheered by many sober and inebriated matelots.

The Navy fielding was superb. Their side included C. A. Kershaw and W. J. A. Davies, the great England Rugby half-back pair, and K. A. ('Monkey') Sellar and in our team was Francis. It could be a record that never before or since have so many Rugby luminaries appeared together on the same cricket field. Captain Bonham-Carter, as he was then, made 39, the top score of his career, thanks largely to some benign and totally undeceptive overs by Duleep. This was a game played for the sheer love of the sport—a spirit which, I regret to say, is at present almost extinct.

Many people are under the impression that apartheid is a comparatively recent cult. This is not so. I am assured that his colour limited Ranjitsinhji's appearances in the 'Varsity match to one, in 1893. That is probably why 'Ranji' played so much of his cricket on Parker's Piece for sides with no University connection. The feeling of his colleagues is illustrated by the photograph of the great man which still occupies a place of honour in the pavilion at Parker's Piece.

In my own time, I recall vividly the occasion when my team, playing on tour, received an invitation to attend the 21st birthday party of the daughter of a local civic dignitary. The invitation stated explicitly that the function was 'for whites only'—clearly an indication that Duleep would not be welcome. It was declined without thanks. The verbal reply of the late A. W. Carr, a member of the opposing team, was an outstanding piece of unprintable oratory.

A CENTURY IN THE FIJI ISLANDS [1974]

BY PHILIP SNOW

Fijian cricket has always been the stuff of which the wildest dreams are made. Long before Philip Snow's revelation about slip fielders catching intrusive swallows, Sammy Woods had described a visit to the islands in 1910 in which he dropped into a game, took twenty-seven wickets in an innings, and dropped out again with the score standing at 175 for seventy-two wickets. Woods insisted that after boarding his boat his pursuers continued their hounding of him with spears and arrows. Philip Snow said of this episode that 'it probably owes something to literary invention'. In another context

Snow describes how in modern times Fijian sides endear themselves to everyone in the ground by 'singing in fine harmony to the crowds'.

Philip Snow (b. 1915) belongs to a family well known for its writing. His elder brother, E.E., served as Hon. Sec. of the Leicestershire County Club, 1957–59, and published a history of the county's cricket and also a prized work called Sir Julien Kahn's XI. *Philip, who was awarded an* MBE *for his work on the far-flung outposts of Empire, captained the Leicestershire 2nd eleven in 1936–37, before becoming Administrator of Fiji and the Western Pacific, a post he held until 1952. During that time he founded the Fiji Cricket Association, captained the Fijian side and represented the island at the Imperial Cricket Conference. On retirement he became bursar at Rugby School from 1952 to 1976. A third brother, C.P., also wrote books, although not on cricket.*

D IAMETRICALLY opposite England on the globe is Fiji, the farthest point to which cricket could penetrate. The Navy carried it 100 years ago. This sounds as though gunboats made Fiji British. Far from it, the chiefs asked Queen Victoria to take over Fiji. H.M.S. *Pearl*, on February 21, 1874, played the Archipelago's then capital, Levuka, losing heavily. It was the first match—just before the independent kingdom became a Colony.

England has seldom seen Royal cricketers. A midshipman on H.M.S. *Bacchante's* 1881 circumnavigation, Prince George (later King George V), played against Levuka. His score significantly is not remembered. Next day he was demoted to *Bacchante*'s 2nd XI against H.M.S. *Cleopatra*; the Press reported that 'his score did not greatly affect the total'. When the Prince of Wales visited Levuka in 1970 for Fiji's Independence, he was shown the ground so little productive of regal runs: the Press described him as not unamused.

Levuka had been preoccupied with commerce. With the British Administration's establishment there was incentive to contemplate British culture (not overmuch thought was given to this in a South Seas port, its public houses cluttering up the tiny beach) and recreation. Fijians saw Europeans playing: they soon wanted to participate. Hon. Jocelyn Amherst (Harrow XI) and Sir Edward Wallington (Sherborne XI and Wiltshire, an Oxford Blue, coach of an England captain in Lionel Tennyson, and latterly Queen Mary's Treasurer), both of them Aides-de-Camp to Sir William des Voeux, Governor 1878–86, encouraged them.

Quick-footed, exceptionally muscular, piercingly sharp of eye, their *forte* has been to hit everything as hard and often as possible, to catch with maximum *élan*, to bowl as swiftly as arms allow single-mindedly at the centre stump, to throw with utmost verve. Their throwing and bowling accuracy were evolutions from their spear throwing, the speed and directness of which meant the difference between life and death in their cannibal wars. Their dress—shirt and *sulu* (knee-length, side-split skirt)—

contrasting with bronze, rugged, cheerful faces, their sinewy, bulging calves, bootlessness, provide a spectacle unique in the cricket world, seen by only two countries, New Zealand and Australia. The larger the crowd, the greater the panache, the radiation of zest. Fijians reserve briskness of tempo for their games as a contrast to their everyday existence.

For organising Fijians, European administrators have been essential. Sir Basil Thomson (later Governor of Dartmoor and Head of Scotland Yard) and A. B. Joske (later Brewster) of Polish origin (whose widow survives at 101 in Bath), had to resist Fijian attempts to overlay the game's laws with tribal ideas for improving them, such as the crack bowler after an over resuming promptly at the other end and chiefs' inclinations to leave fielding to commoners.

J. S. Udal, Attorney-General 1890–1900, who had played for M.C.C. (invited to go with W.G. Grace's 1873 team to Australia, he declined as he was qualifying for the Bar) and, like Wallington, for Dorset and the West of England, was influential enough to have an excellent ground made at Albert Park in the new capital, Suva. J. McC. Blackham's 1893 Australian team for England was prevented by a measles outbreak on their ship from playing Suva.

Udal, at 43 still useful, decided in 1895 to take a team the 1,000 miles to New Zealand. It consisted of six other Europeans (Sir William Allardyce, selected, could not go—he had played against Lillywhite's All England XI for the North of Scotland) and six Fijian chiefs. Ratu (Chief) Wilikonisoni Tuivanuavou bowled with distinct speed and success. J. C. Collins carried his bat for a century—only one of 16 occasions in New Zealand's history. Playing against the leading New Zealand exponents (F. Wilding, the world's outstanding tennis player, made their only century), Fiji won 4, drew 2, lost 2.

In 1905, *en route* to England, Australia, including V.T. Trumper, R., A. Duff, C. Hill, M. A. Noble, W. W. Armstrong, F. Laver and A. Cotter, met Fiji who, batting 18 (including H. S. de Maus, New Zealand's best all-rounder a decade earlier) scored 91 to Australia's 212. Trumper, feeling unwell, hit the biggest six made on Albert Park.

Greatly daring, Mbau Island (no larger than Lord's in acreage, with a male adult population of 60) in 1908 toured Australia, 2,000 miles away. Pre-eminent as players were its two highest chiefs, both grandsons of King Ebenezer Thakombau (the only King before Cession)—Ratu Penaia Kandavulevu and his cousin, Ratu Pope E. S. Thakombau, acknowledged in Australia as a State standard. Winning 5, drawing 16, losing 5 (opponents including New South Wales, Queensland, South Australia and Victoria), Fijians' intrinsic skill needs no further underlining. It was sufficient inducement for S. E. Gregory's 1912 team from England to Australia (including C. Kellaway and E. R. Mayne) and Australia's 1913 team to Canada under A. Diamond (including C. G. Macartney, W. Bardsley, J. N. Crawford, H. L. Collins and A. A. Mailey) to play in the Islands. As the opposition was only Suva (not Fiji and including merely one

Fijian), not unexpectedly they were comfortably beaten. Austin Diamond, New South Wales' leading batsman and second in Australia's 1907 averages, had worked in Fiji for the Sugar Company.

In parenthesis, just months before the First World War and his own death, Rupert Brooke, a steady slow bowler in the Rugby XI, reported: 'I played cricket! The Fijians play a good deal, very wildly and without great regard for the rules, but they have good eyes.'

Those 1912–13 visits to Fiji have been followed by only one more match by any country's fully representative team—the West Indies in 1955. V. Y. Richardson's team to Canada (including D. G. Bradman, S. J. McCabe, Mailey, L. O'B. Fleetwood-Smith and A. F. Kippax) and D. R. Jardine's 1933 team returning from Australia were to have played in Suva had it not rained torrentially. Sitting next to Bradman in 1953 at a lunch for his birthday in a Lord's box, I was told by Sir Donald that he recalled the fastest Fijian bowler (Turanga) asking if he might feel his biceps and, on doing so, letting the interpreter know that he could not credit Bradman's reputation as the world's best batsman.

In 1924, a New Zealand team including J. S. Hiddleston, arguably then that country's best current batsman, made the first tour of Fiji, playing two matches against Fiji—not representative since the only Fijians encountered were Mbau. With such omissions Fiji, not unnaturally, lost easily. 5 wins, 3 draws, no losses (but a fright given them by Mbau) conveys a misleading result for the New Zealand side.

Another New Zealand team, the Maorilanders, captained by H. B. Massey, a Test player, made a similar tour in 1936. Two matches against Fiji were played—1 lost, 1 won. Five Fijians were included to approach true representation: in one match the only hundred to date against a team touring Fiji was the achievement of Ratu Sir Edward Thakombau, great-grandson of King Thakombau, son of King George II of Tonga, now Fiji's Deputy Prime Minister, who had played for Auckland.

In 1938, when appointed to Fiji, I was astonished to find Europeans and part-Europeans playing separately from Fijians and Indians. This anomaly I determined to alter as soon as I could. In 1939, when elected Secretary of the Suva Cricket Club I had this European organisation changed to the Suva Cricket Association, so constituting the first multi-racial sporting organisation of any kind in Fiji. Immediately, the most cosmopolitan side, the Central Medical School, which I was asked to coach, captained by an American Samoan and containing three Tongans, two British Samoans, one Rotuman, three Gilbertese, an Ellice Islander, two Solomon Islanders and five Fijians (the team's fastest bowler, Ratu Sir Kamisese Mara, played for Otago and became Fiji's Prime Minister on Independence 30 years later) defeated everyone.

Sir Julien Cahn only had to see the Fijians for a few minutes in 1939, before negotiating with me for an English tour. This was frustrated by the War, and then his death.

In this War, New Zealanders were in Fiji in quantity waiting to push back the Japanese and playing cricket meanwhile. P. E. Whitelaw, joint holder of the world's third wicket record, and N. Gallichan, the Test match slow left-hand bowler, achieved little; D. S. Wilson, who played in Tests on his return, and C. C. Burke, who toured Australia and England, were more successful. The New Zealand Forces, including Burke, were heavily defeated by a weakened Fiji Representative Team in 1942 (which included for the first time an Indian in top-level Fijian cricket). Amenayasi Turanga, who had politely doubted Bradman's prowess, took six for 16 in the first innings. Of Voce's build, he had his fast, left-hander's bounce aimed at the batsman's shoulders. A gold-miner, he was accidentally electrocuted a fortnight later. One of the half-dozen best Fijians of all time, he was a ferocious hitter, once scoring 106 in twenty-eight minutes on a concrete pitch.

In 1946, with the backing of the leading chief, Ratu Sir Lala Sukuna, I was able to found the Fiji Cricket Association. Now fully representative Fiji teams could be established and Districts, whose Associations I had set up between 1940 and 1946, guided into regular competition.

The immediate result of the Fiji Association's foundation was organis-ation of a tour of New Zealand in 1948, the first truly representative Fijian one (and the second of any kind to go there in 53 years). Although there had been tests of ability against New Zealanders in Fiji conditions, Fijian prospects overseas were a risky estimate: I recall my cold feet when interviewed on deck as to our chances by the New Zealand Press arriving at dawn with Auckland's metropolitan skyline so daunting for us straight from the bush.

Starting on the right feet (mostly bare: there were 11 Fijians, with six Europeans and part-Europeans), we played all the first-class Provinces and leading Test players, W. A. Hadlee, W. M. Wallace, B. Sutcliffe, G. O. Rabone and many who were to extend England in Tests immediately afterwards. In three-day matches against the first-class Provinces Fiji won 2 and lost 3 (2 very narrowly). In the two-day matches Fiji won 4, drew 7, lost 0, and lost a one-day match. H. J. Apted, a left-hander with W. Watson's elegance, the youngest at 23, scored nearly 1,000 runs in 22 innings with an average of 46. Ilikena Lasarusa Talembulamainavaleniveivakambulai-mainakulalakembalau (mercifully for New Zealand and his tremend-ously-in-demand autograph, known as I. L. Bula), exceeded 1,000 runs with soaring straight drives of real majesty, and M. J. Fenn, bowling slow inswingers with only one offside fielder, took 100 wickets in 700 overs—remarkable performances.

Viliame Mataika, with arm-touching-ear action, bowled Tate-like whipbacks to help us defeat Wellington early in the tour, but never played after his stretched-out bare foot had been jammed by a somnabulist traveller in a train corridor door. Ratu Sir George Thakombau, great grandson of King Thakombau, son of Ratu Pope Thakombau and now Fiji's first Governor-General since Independence, who was my Vice-captain, had a bare toe broken by a yorker half-way through the tour: it was fortunate that Ratu Sir Edward Thakombau was able to join us then on return from Oxford. Ratu Sir Kamisese Mara was in mid-course at Oxford where injury deprived him of a Blue. His father once hit me for the highest six I have ever seen—vanishing into the sky to descend vertically into a 70-foot coconut palm's crown.

When I left Fiji in 1952, New Zealand was pressing for a repetition of the 1948 tour. Fijians, supreme guerilla fighters volunteering for the Malayan campaign, included Petero Kumbunavanua, reserve wicket-keeper in my 1948 New Zealand touring team. Selected with two other Fijians and Ratu Sir Edward Thakombau to play for Negri Sembilan State against Perak in 1952, Petero added to cricket's rare ornithological connection. Fielding at square leg and disturbed by swallows swooping on flies, he snatched one from the air and put it in his *sulu* pocket.

In 1954 P. T. Raddock (5 ft high, he had been my 1948 wicket-keeper) with Ratu Mara, 6 ft 5 ins. high as Vice-captain, took to New Zealand the next team—9 Fijians, 6 Europeans and part-Europeans. They won 1, lost 3 three-day matches, won 5, lost 3 two-day matches, and won the two one-day matches. The 1948 team's performance promised first-class status for this team before the tour began. W. W. Apted, brother of H. J. Apted (who also had a good tour), was the outstanding batsman, finishing 4th in New Zealand averages. Bula, so evocative of Gimblett, joined the select list of those with 8 sixes in an innings when scoring 102 v Canterbury. But during this tour, unlike the 1948 tour, all the leading New Zealand players were absent (touring South Africa).

A singular accomplishment was the defeat in 1956 by Suva (not Fiji) of the West Indies captained by D. Atkinson and including J. D. Goddard, G. St. A. Sobers, S. Ramadhin and A. L. Valentine. Suva's captain, Ratu Mara, opened the bowling. He told me, with the self-deprecatory touch which Fijians have in common with Europeans, that after about 30 runs had been scored quickly off him he had had a blinding flash of insight and took himself off. His replacement and the other opening bowler dismissed West Indies for 63, when to pass Suva's 91 had seemed easy.

In 1959 a modest tour was made to New South Wales Country Districts. Only one team of calibre was met: a New South Wales XI, including R. Benaud (captain), K. R. Miller, N. C. O'Neill and A. K. Davidson, was defeated in a one-day match, the Fijian fielding delighting the Sydney ground. Representing no advance on the 1908 tour by Mbau, the tour was marked by the first overseas selection of a Fiji Indian. Indians outnumber Fijians and are more prepared to take on administration than Fijians but have far to go to attain Fijians' playing standards.

Two further tours of New Zealand followed, one in 1961–62 containing 10 Fijians and 5 Europeans and part-Europeans. Astonishingly, no three-day matches were played. Nine two-day matches were lost, 8 won, 3 drawn; one one-day match lost, 1 drawn. The second, in 1967–68, managed by Josua Rambukawangga, Fiji's High Commissioner to the United Kingdom (a useful Mbauan), consisted of 11 Fijians, 3 Europeans and part-Europeans, and 2 Indians. It also played no three-day matches, won 4, lost 7 and drew 2 two-day matches, and won all 8 one-day matches.

H. J. Apted and Bula have been omnipresent in every tour since the War. Walter Hadlee considered Bula's inclusion (within the Rules as Fiji was not then playing first-class cricket and its players were therefore eligible to play for the nearest Test-playing country) for New Zealand's 1949 tour of England. After consulting me, Hadlee thought that Bula's modest knowledge of English might have led to homesickness in a long tour far away from home.

Bula holds Fiji's highest score, 246, beating the 214 not out and 196 in a fortnight of a remarkable all-rounder, Viliame Tuinaceva Longavatu who should have been seen overseas (he took 9 for 0 in 1.4 overs in 1933 in a high-grade match. I took his son, Isoa Longavatu, to New Zealand as the team's fast bowler; he had taken 10 wickets for 8 in 1941—the best of Fiji's seven instances of 10 wickets in an innings.). The most remarkable bowling feat in Fiji's history was at Lomaloma in the Lau Archipelago (half-way between Fiji and the Kingdom of Tonga): Saiasi Vuanisokiki took 8 wickets for 0 in an 8-ball over against H.M.S. *Leith*. A fast left-hander in Turanga's class, he would have been taken by me to New Zealand in 1948 but for an injury.

As remarkable in its way, more recently, has been 40 off 7 balls in an 8-ball over in a top-standard match scored by Nathanieli Uluiviti who had played for Auckland.

Fiji's cricket centenary, which is adding a rare connection of the game with philately by three stamps marking the event, runs parallel to a near-century of British Administration from the Islands' Cession in 1874. Independence in 1970, with Fiji becoming a Dominion in the Commonwealth, was a gentle evolution from that auspicious start of the Archipelago having been given to Queen Victoria, contrasting with the usual 19th century process of colonization by conquest.

New Zealand cricket judges who have seen all Fijian sides rank the 1948 team as the best. Each team has given enjoyment to every part of New Zealand, but it has become recognised that the Fijian standard, if measured only by the lower category of opponents in subsequent tours, has not been maintained for three principal reasons. Firstly, Fijians of high standing who have been on tours, for example, Ratu Mara and the two Ratu Thakombaus, respectively Prime Minister, Deputy Prime Minister and Governor-General, have had their time heavily taken up under a preoccupation as never before, contrasted with their predecessors as high chiefs able to give time to coaching.

Secondly, Fiji's success at Rugby Football on tours beyond New Zealand and Australia to Wales, England and France have diverted attention from cricket. Thirdly, there has been insufficient progress in Fiji's improvement and, with a population doubled since 1948, increase of grounds. Beautiful and bad are not the right requisites for playing areas. Albert Park, Suva, so picturesque with its vivid colour captured in the painting in the Imperial Gallery at Lord's, is muddied-up by football and hockey, by every kind of event and festival, the huge crowds squelching the grass out by its roots in the deluges that Fiji keeps for main happenings. Like other cricket grounds in Fiji it is not, and cannot be, enclosed: income is not gained from private generosity. No sport, even football, with its undemanding outlay on equipment, can advance that way.

Other factors contribute to an uphill struggle: (1) Cricket is expensive for a country where, outside the half-dozen towns, villages are mere clusters of houses with roofs and walls of thatch shaped like haystacks: equipment is always scarce. (2) A serious obstacle lies in the distances between the 100 inhabited islands. (3) Then there is the division of island pitches between matting on either grass or concrete. (4) Coaching is a quintessential requirement. So much talent waits to be steered delicately by a discerning eye—a coach without flair could extinguish the Fijian flame.

A fifth reason for Fiji's diminishing performances against New Zealand was recently explained to me by Bevan Congdon, the New Zealand captain, as being due to a sudden marked improvement in New Zealand standards.

In 1965 when the Imperial Cricket Conference became the International Cricket Conference, Fiji was the first country, with Ceylon and U.S. of America, to be admitted to the company of the Test-playing countries. England may yet see a Fiji side. One was arranged to come here in 1959 to play the Duke of Norfolk's XI, M.C.C. at Lord's and various Counties when it became apparent that Fiji's standard had suddenly slipped and local confidence declined: postponement was considered judicious. Little but a revival of coaching is needed to restore Fiji to its first-class standard. A World Cup, particularly if on a one-day basis to which Fijians are well suited, could see them participating after not too long.

THE GLORIOUS UNCERTAINTY [1974]

BY ROWLAND RYDER

Students of Wisden *will know that every few years a game turns up which defies the logical processes. Either through a quirk of the weather, or a sudden irruption of individual genius, or a freakish combination of perverse circumstances, a contest turns back on itself to produce a result which, an hour or two before, had not seemed within the bounds of possibility. Because every one of these cases makes enthralling reading, Rowland Ryder's 'The Glorious Uncertainty' is a delightful addition to the* Wisden *stock. Its only serious fault is its brevity. Had it been twice as long it might have embraced the 1911 match at Hove between Sussex and Notts in which a tail-ender called Edwin Boaler Alletson lived like a god for a brief hour after lunch. Or England against Australia at Old Trafford, July 1956, when Jim Laker carelessly omitted to take one of the twenty Australian wickets to fall and was obliged to console himself with the other nineteen. And what might have been most fascinating of all, Ireland versus the West Indies at Londonderry, July 1969, when the hosts bowled out the visitors for twenty-six runs and went on to score a comically comfortable victory. As the almanack for that year comments, 'Ireland's performance deserves a permanent record.'*

Among the myriad delights of cricket, not least is the glorious uncertainty of the game. Nothing is certain in cricket except its uncertainty. It is not likely that a batsman will hit every ball of an over for six; that a last wicket stand will add three hundred runs to the score; that a wicket-keeper will take off his pads and do the hat trick: none of these things are anything more than remotely possible, yet all of them have happened; and improbable events, their duration in time varying from a split second to a long drawn out week, interesting, exhilarating, sometimes unbearably exciting, are happening every year that cricket is played.

A match can be transformed by an inspired spell of bowling or by a splendid innings. It can be transformed by a single ball; an electrifying catch; a sudden run out; a drive to the boundary can mark a side's turning point from defence to attack and thence to victory; a stand of mammoth potential can be broken by an unexpected full toss. How often has the weather taken sides—a brief shower; a sea mist; a gust of wind; sunshine after rain? A captain's intuition; a new ball; a crumbling wicket; changing a bat; even a drinks interval or the arrival of The King: these are some of the ingredients that can fashion unexpected victory or defeat.

In the ensuing paragraphs an attempt is made to describe five of the most remarkable matches in the history of the game; all of them, in their respective ways, illustrative of the glorious uncertainty of cricket; beginning with the Test Match, in 1882, when Australia defeated England for the first time, and concluding with Durham's victory against Yorkshire in the Gillette Cup competition of 1973.

ENGLAND V. AUSTRALIA, 1882

On August 29, 1882, Australia beat England for the first time, winning the match by seven runs. The Australians, who were captained by W. L. Murdoch, numbered only thirteen in their touring side; they had a strenuous tour involving thirty-eight matches, and extending from mid-May until the end of September. This Test Match, at Kennington Oval, was their thirtieth game.

Australia were all out for 63 in their first innings, only Murdoch,

Blackham and Garrett reaching double figures; R. G. Barlow taking five for 19 runs in 31 4-ball overs. England, with a fine batting array that included 'W.G.', Hornby, Barlow and George Ulyett—indeed, only Peate, the Yorkshire slow bowler, had no pretensions to batsmanship—did little better. They were all out for 101, Ulyett making 26 and Spofforth taking seven for 46.

Australia's second innings started on a high note, the deficit of 38 was cleared by H.H. Massie and A.C. Bannerman. Massie was a vigorous but scientific hitter; in 1882, an eight-year-old English boy named Gilbert Jessop would certainly have heard of his exploits. In the first match of the tour, against Oxford University, Massie had scored 206 out of 265 while he was at the wicket; now, with the stonewalling Bannerman as partner, he scored 55 out of 66 in less than an hour. After this, Peate (four for 40) came into his own, and the innings closed for 122, leaving England with 85 to win.

Grace and Hornby made a confident start; then at 15 Spofforth bowled Hornby and Barlow with successive balls. Grace now had George Ulyett as a partner. They saw the 50 up: with 35 to win and eight wickets to fall, it was surely all over bar the shouting.

Frederick Robert Spofforth, twenty-eight years old, six feet three, devastating, sinuous and tireless, thought otherwise. He was called 'The Demon', because, said Lord Darnley, of 'the terrifying aspect of his final bound at the wicket when delivering the ball'. 'Variation is everything' was his own maxim—variation of flight and pace and break back, skilfully disguised by his flailing arms at the moment of delivery. His speed was of varying grades of fast medium; about once an over he sent down a ball that was tremendously fast.

At 51 Spofforth had Ulyett caught at the wicket, then Grace was out for 32, and England were 53 for four. Lucas and Lyttleton were now in, Lucas stonewalling, Lyttelton trying, unsuccessfully, to force the pace. The score reached 65 for four—20 to win. Twelve maiden overs were bowled (48 balls), followed by a piece of deliberate misfielding, so that Spofforth could attack Lyttelton. After four more maidens Spofforth bowled Lyttelton; the score was 66 for five. Lucas hit a four, but Spofforth had Steel caught and bowled; then he bowled Maurice Read. At 75 Lucas played on to an extra fast ball from Spofforth. Barnes failed. Peate came in last, with England wanting 10 to win. A blind swipe for two; another blind swipe, this time Peate was clean bowled, and Australia had won. Studd, at the other end, had not received a ball. Spofforth had taken seven for 44: the spectators carried him shoulder-high off the field, knowing perhaps that they would never see such bowling again.

This Test Match was the subject of the famous 'obituary' of English cricket, in the *Sporting Times*; Sir Neville Cardus has written one of his most evocative essays about the match, which also inspired John Masefield, when Poet Laureate, to celebrate in verse the triumph of the Australians.

ENGLAND V. AUSTRALIA, 1902

The fifth Test Match, at Kennington Oval, in 1902, resulted in a victory for England by one wicket. Australia had won two and drawn two of the previous Tests—they won the fourth Test by three runs. Had the teams come to the Oval with the series level, the fifth Test Match of 1902 might well have been remembered as the greatest Test Match ever played: as it was, it produced an unforgettable encounter, the climax mounting to almost unendurable excitement during the last two hours of England's innings.

Australia batted first and scored 324. Then came the rain; the rest of the game was played on a difficult wicket. England did well to score 183 in their first innings, narrowly avoiding the follow-on. When Australia batted again Trumper was brilliantly run out by Jessop for two. They did not recover from this disaster, and on a tricky wicket they took three hours to score 121 all out, Lockwood taking five for 45, and England were left with 263 to win.

The stage was set for an exciting finish. The wicket was still difficult; A. C. MacLaren, L. C. H. Palairet and J. T. Tyldesley were all bowled by Saunders, and three wickets were down for 10. Half the side were out for 48 when G. L. Jessop went in to bat, and played what has been described as 'the greatest innings in the history of cricket'.

'He walked in to bat with a big cap on his small head,'—C. B. Fry wrote of Jessop*—'peak well over his nimble eyes, at a fast pace and with no fears . . . he fled out to drive like an amateur thunderbolt projected by Jove after too much nectar . . . he spreadeagled any bowler in ten minutes, however good, unless the stars were against him.'

The stars were with Gilbert Jessop on Wednesday, August 13, 1902. With F. S. Jackson, who had gone in third wicket down, he put on 109 runs in sixty-five minutes, when Jackson was out for 49. Then George Hirst was his partner for about ten minutes, during which 30 runs were added. When Jessop was out, caught at short leg, he had scored 104 out of 139, in seventy-five minutes, having hit 'a five in the slips' and seventeen fours. George Hirst himself wrote of this occasion: 'It was a great treat to me, watching their bowlers' faces change with wonder and consternation in their efforts to try and block his shots by changing the field . . . It could not be done.'

With Jessop out, the score was 187 for seven: Lockwood stayed until 214; Lilley helped Hirst take the score to 248, when he was caught at deep mid-off. Wilfred Rhodes was last man in, and England needed 15 runs for victory. There is an apocryphal story of George Hirst saying 'We'll get them in singles, Wilfred.' Actually the partnership realised thirteen singles and a two. With the scores level, says *Wisden*, 'Rhodes sent a ball from Trumble between the bowler and mid-on, and England won the match by one wicket.' Hugh Trumble, the fast-medium bowler from Victoria, with

---

* G. L. Jessop by C. J. Britton. Cornish Brothers Ltd. (1935).

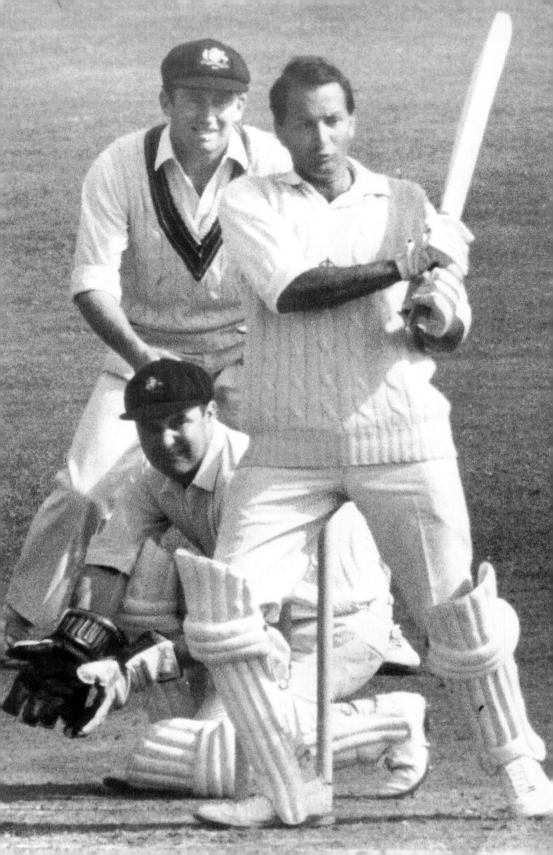

Previous page: The gentle D'Oliveira, whose enviable temperament somehow enabled him to retain his dignity while all about him were losing theirs

Right: Arthur Gilligan, the evangelical cricketer, who believed, contrary to the prevailing evidence, that God was in his heaven and all was right with the world, especially if Maurice Tate happened to be on song

Below: Gloucestershire, 1877. W.G. captained the side, with E.M. as secretary–treasurer. Whenever a Grace "benefit" seemed desirable, E.M. would double the admission fee. Billy Midwinter, beneficiary of the Grace patronage, stands in the back row, second from the right, a picture of innocence. Who says the camera never lies?

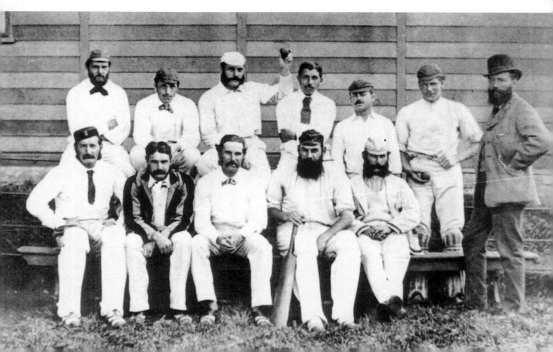

Above left: Sir Compton Mackenzie, who published 43 novels, 26 volumes of history and biography, six of essays and criticism, ten of autobiography, two of poetry, plus one play and 14 children's books, making him one of the tiny elite of literary gentlemen to score a century

Above right: Andrew Sandham, who, in his long association with Jack Hobbs, played the most tuneful of second fiddles. One of a tiny elite to score a treble century for England in a Test match, he very nearly made a hundred in old age, but died finally in his nineties

Opposite page: O Captain, my Captain! The most prodigious all-rounder in history performs a fox-trot of some punctilio with the most cerebral of skippers

Left: Ken Barrington in the familiar act of accumulating runs, while wicketkeeper Barry Jarman and his captain Richie Benaud follow the flight of the ball

Below: Graeme Pollock, the great lefthander who virtually never was. Politics did for his statistics but not his reputation

Right: There could be no more telling proof of the eminence of this young man than the fact that while the brand name appears seven times, the name of the hero using the product needs no mention at all

Below right: Was it all worth it? The hotels, the roads, the constant shift of locale, all for no more than a vicarious link with the sport on the grass? Of course it was. John Arlott is the man ever to make himself into two poets – the formal, written one and the impromptu speaking artist. At his last Test as a commentator, at Lord's, 1980, he sits with Keith Miller alongside, seeing other fields, other cricketers, probably Maurice Tate and Philip Mead

Opposite above: George Headley, who loved cricket and the drumming of Chick Webb, although not necessarily in that order of precedence. Arthur Wood and Walter Hammond watch as the ball flies over the hills and far away in the England–West Indies Test at the Oval, 1939 – the last Test ever to be played in England before the outbreak of war

Opposite below: Most mercurial of cricketers, and an all-rounder of comprehensive brilliance in the broadest sense. Fast bowler, big hitter, a genius in the field, a lawyer, peer of the realm, and at last cabinet minister. The much-loved Learie Constantine

Overleaf: Sir George Oswald Allen, Eton, Cambridge, Middlesex, the Gentlemen and England, known to the rest of us as Gubby, embodiment of the English cricket Establishment, a man who literally dedicated his life to the well-being of cricket. But he was born in Sydney. What would Lord Harris have said?

BRYLCREEM

for confident grooming

Men who hit the headlines know that smartness counts — and count on Brylcreem for perfect grooming. Brylcreem works in two ways — (1) It grooms without gumming, giving life and lustre to the hair. (2) The pure natural oils in Brylcreem are emulsified into a rich cream which, with massage, has a valuable tonic effect, preventing dry hair and dandruff. Brylcreem comes in tubs 1/8, 2/6 and 4/6, or handy tubes 2/6.

BRYLCREEM — the perfect hairdressing

31 overs in the first innings and 33.5 in the second, had bowled unchanged for Australia throughout the match.

WARWICKSHIRE V. HAMPSHIRE, 1922

Hampshire's defeat of Warwickshire by 155 runs, at Edgbaston, in June, 1922, was probably the most astonishing match in the history of the County Championship. Warwickshire won the toss, batted first, and, on a good wicket, were out for 223, scored at four runs an over; Newman having the unusual figures of four for 70 in 12.3 overs. F. R. Santall made 84 and the Hon. F. S. G. Calthorpe 70. When the last Warwickshire wicket fell, the general impression was that a good batting wicket had been wasted.

Then came the shocks. In fifty-three balls Howell and Calthorpe dismissed Hampshire for 15, their analyses were as follows:

	Overs	Maidens	Runs	Wickets
Howell............	4.5	2	7	6
Calthorpe........	4	3	4	4

The entire Hampshire innings occupied forty minutes, fifteen of which were taken up with the procession of batsmen walking to and from the wicket. Eight of the team were out for a duck. Philip Mead, going in No. 4, made 6 not out; the Hon. Lionel Tennyson was second highest scorer with 4. This was surely the most amazing achievement by opening bowlers in county cricket. Warwickshire themselves had been skittled out for 16 in 62 balls by Blythe and Woolley at Tonbridge in 1913; in 1901 Yorkshire got rid of Nottinghamshire for 13 in 15.5 overs, and in 1907 Dennett (eight for 9) and Jessop, opening the bowling for Gloucestershire, dismissed Northants for 12 in 11.3 overs, the smallest total ever made in first-class cricket, but on all these occasions the bowlers were helped by the pitch: Howell and Calthorpe were bowling on a batsman's wicket, as they found to their cost the next day.

Hampshire, following on, were 186 for six, and it seemed as likely as not that they would have to acknowledge defeat by an innings. Then things went wrong for Warwickshire. Perhaps they relaxed the pressure: if they did, they certainly paid the price. George Brown and W. R. Shirley added 85 for the seventh wicket, then, after A. S. McIntyre had failed, Brown and W. H. Livsey, the wicket-keeper, took the score to 451, before Brown was out for 172 in four and three-quarter hours. A last wicket stand by Livsey and Boyes added 70, Hampshire making 521 and Livsey 110 not out—his other thirty-six visits to the crease in 1922 brought him a total of 181 runs. Warwickshire, requiring 314 to win, never looked like getting the runs, and although 'Tiger' Smith, W. G. Quaife and Calthorpe offered resistance, the innings closed for 158.

This, above all, was George Brown's match. All-rounder extraordinary, a tall, humorous, kindly man of fine physique, left-hand batsman, fast-medium right arm bowler, wicket-keeper seven times for England, he will be remembered above all for his intrepid 172 that turned total defeat into impossible victory. A famed scorecard of the match was George Brown's most treasured possession in his home at Winchester. He always averred that Hampshire should have been out for 7 and not 15, as, in the general excitement of the collapse, Harry Howell bowled a ball that went for four byes when 'Tiger' Smith was unsighted; and Lionel Tennyson was missed off his solitary scoring stroke.

AUSTRALIA V. WEST INDIES, 1960

The first Test Match between Australia and the West Indies at Brisbane, on December 9–14, 1960, was, of course, an 8-ball over affair. It was a match that ended in a tie, and it was the last seven balls of the game that raised it to epic greatness. In a feature article for *Wisden* (1961), E. M. Wellings, who saw the game, wrote 'It was the Greatest Test Match, the Greatest Cricket Match and surely the Greatest Game ever played with a ball.'

The West Indies batted first and made 453 (Davidson five for 135); Australia replied with 505, Norman O'Neill making 181. In their second innings the West Indies scored 284 (Davidson six for 87), leaving Australia 233 to win in 310 minutes. Their last wicket fell with scores level, to the seventh ball of what was in any case the last over of the match. Such is the bare outline of the story.

Australia made a sorry start to their second innings, their target 233. Two wickets were down for 7. The fifth wicket fell at 57: Wesley Hall had sent back Simpson, Harvey, O'Neill and Favell. Six for 92; then Benaud and Davidson, the last of the established batsmen, actually took Australia to within seven runs of victory. 'They brought off some sterling strokes,' wrote E. M. Wellings, 'among which Davidson's hook off a head-high bumper from Hall stands out as a vivid memory. And they ran like whippets.' Now with the score 226 for six, seven to win, four wickets to fall, Solomon ran out Davidson from twenty-five yards and with one stump to aim at. When Wesley Hall began the last over, Australia needed six to win with three wickets to fall.

Grout was hit on the leg by the first ball, and he and Benaud ran a single. Benaud, 52, and going strong, now had the bowling: five to win. Off the second ball, a bouncer, he attempted a hook—and was caught at the wicket. Meckiff came in and played the third ball back to the bowler. Off the fourth ball Grout and Meckiff ran a bye: four to win. Hall bowled his fifth ball; Grout skied it, half a dozen West Indians converged, Hall got his hands to the ball but dropped it. The batsmen scampered a single. Three balls to go; two wickets to fall; three runs to win. Meckiff hit the sixth delivery towards the square leg boundary. He and Grout ran two and raced for a third, as Hunte threw in fiercely and accurately from near the boundary; Grout flung himself over the crease—too late. The scores were now level: there were two balls to go, and Kline was last man in. Hall bowled his seventh delivery, Kline played it towards square leg—and Solomon. It was Solomon who, a few minutes previously, had run out Davidson. It was Solomon now, as the batsman ran desperately for the precious single that would give them victory, who broke the wicket and tied the match before Meckiff could make his ground.

This match at Brisbane is the only Test Match to have ended in a tie, although a dozen or more have been very close things. Both sides at different stages of the game could have elected to play safe and to be satisfied with a draw, both sides preferred to stake everything and go for an outright victory. In the event both sides were successful: this was a victory for cricket.

YORKSHIRE V. DURHAM, 1973

Forward to 1973. The last ten years have seen the streamlining of the County Championship and the trend towards one-day cricket in the inauguration of the Gillette Cup (1963), the John Player League (1969) and the Benson and Hedges Cup (1972). The Gillette Cup is a knock-out competition for the seventeen First-Class Counties and the five leading Minor Counties from the previous season. Matches are of one innings a side, limited to sixty overs; no bowler to bowl more than twelve overs. Under this system Minor Counties come into conflict with First-Class County sides, hence the exciting possibility that a David might overcome a Goliath. In 1973 this possibility became astonishing reality.

On Saturday, June 30, 1973, Durham played Yorkshire at Harrogate. Yorkshire won the toss and batted first on a good wicket. Boycott and Lumb opened the batting against the bowling of Stuart Wilkinson and Alan Old, the England rugger player and brother of Chris Old, the England cricketer, who was playing for the other side!

When the score was 18, the fast, wiry, thirty-three year old Stuart Wilkinson bowled the ball that decided the match. He bowled Boycott neck and crop with a superb delivery that pitched on a length, came quickly off the pitch, and knocked back the middle stump. Boycott himself was quick to pay tribute to this splendid piece of bowling. The loss of Boycott clearly affected Yorkshire's morale. Lumb and Sharpe were soon out, and at 49, Lander, the Durham captain, took the wickets of Hampshire and Hutton with successive balls. Only Johnson resisted to any purpose; he scored 44 before being out to Greensword, the ex-Leicestershire player, who also had Bairstow l.b.w. when the latter seemed about to cut loose. Yorkshire's sorry start was retrieved to the extent that the hundred went up with six wickets down; but they were all out for 135 in 58.4 overs. Brian Lander took five for 15 in 11.3 overs. Yorkshire had failed against good medium-paced bowling, supported by splendid fielding.

Before the match started the Durham team were hoping to put up a good performance, and, if possible, to give Yorkshire a run for their money. That was the ceiling of their aspirations before opposing a team that included five England players. Now, with their opponents dismissed so cheaply, there was a feeling of confidence in the Durham dressing room— 136 was not too difficult a target, and the wicket was good.

Inglis and Atkinson gave their side an excellent start, putting on 58 for the first wicket. Four wickets were down for 96; and Yorkshire were still in the hunt; but Greensword was obdurate as sheet anchor, and the Yorkshire challenge died away. Riddell lived dangerously, hitting Nicholson for two 4's in succession, then the latter bowled him for 15. Durham were nearly home now. Greensword (35 not out) and Soakell stayed together until the end, Durham, 138 for five, winning by five wickets, with 8.3 overs to spare. Cyril Washbrook adjudged Brian Lander *Man of the Match*.

'The impossible has happened at last' said the *Sunday Times*, the following day, and the *Observer* described Durham's victory as 'A result more improbable than Sunderland's defeat of Leeds United in the F.A. Cup final.'

There was no fluke about Durham's victory: they dominated the match all day. What was astonishing was not the *way* that they won, but, rather, the *fact* that they won; that a side consisting largely of part-time cricketers, however talented, should outplay for nearly six hours the most illustrious First-Class County of them all.

NOTE BY THE EDITOR [1975]

As if picking up Arlott's cue, the editor that year also involved himself, if indirectly, in the all-rounder debate. The cricket world at the time was debating the rectitude of Lillee and Thomson, neither of whom was averse to the intimidatory bouncer. In an attempt to give the debate some sort of historical perspective, Mr. Preston quoted a familiar tale, possibly because he was otherwise at a loss for words to fulfil his brief. Nobody complained, because it is an excellent story, which not only lays to rest a fondly cherished myth, but explains how that myth was born. It is also interesting to hear how the perpetrator of the most notorious bouncer before the days of Bodyline was eventually coached into mending his ways, and how his handshake was almost as damaging as his beamers.

THROUGH W.G.'S BEARD

E RNEST Jones came to England with the Australian teams of 1896, 1899 and 1902 and legend has it that he sent a bouncer through W.G. Grace's beard. Sir Stanley Jackson, the Cambridge and England captain and Yorkshire player, who appeared in the match concerned and in many games with Jones, reckoned he was the best fast bowler of his time. In *Wisden* 1944, Jackson, who took part in the first match Jones played in this country for the Australians against Lord Sheffield's XI at Sheffield Park, Sussex, in 1896, said, 'In his early days of the tour he was very wild in his delivery, probably because the team came straight off the ship to the match and were short of practice. Jones gave the impression that his main effort was to show his immense pace.

'I went in first,' continued Jackson, 'with W.G. and we had to dance about a bit. One ball from Jones hit W.G. under the arm, and later in the innings another went head high past him and over Kel'y's head to the boundary. That was the ball about which the 'Beard Story' originated.

'I can see W.G. now. He threw his head back, which caused his beard to stick out. Down the pitch went W.G., stroking his beard, to Harry Trott (the Australian captain) and said, 'Here, what is all this?' And Trott said, 'Steady, Jonah.' To which Jones made the famous remark: 'Sorry, Doctor, she slipped.' I do not think the ball actually touched W.G.'s beard. The story was told afterwards, and I believe I was responsible. When I was out and returned to the pavilion, I said, 'Did you see that one go through W.G.'s beard?' The ball was bouncing and only Ranji seemed to like it.

'The pace that Jones was bowling impressed me because in the second innings when I had made about 10, I had the misfortune to stop one with my ribs, but with the assistance of W. A. J. West, the umpire, who rubbed me, I was able to continue my innings. When I went to London I had a good deal of pain and my father sent for the doctor, who said, 'It's cracked horizontally.' He strapped me up and I did not play for three weeks. Within a month of Sheffield Park I faced Jones at Lord's in the MCC match, and he came up to me and said, 'I am terribly sorry,' and he clasped my hand in a vice-like grip that left me wondering which was the more painful—my hand or broken ribs. Following these early incidents, Trott took Jones in charge and changed him into a very fine bowler. He made him shorten his run and taught him the value of length and control and Jones developed a beautiful action.'

BUYING BACK ONE'S PAST [1975]

BY JOHN I. MARDER

(PAST PRESIDENT, USA CRICKET ASSOCIATION)

The unexpected bonus to be found in the 1975 edition was located neither in Prince Philip's introductory essay, 'The Pleasures of Cricket' nor in Henry Blofeld's account of life as a touring journalist, which closes with the startling analogy between the Taj Mahal and the spin bowling of Bisham Bedi. The surprise packet turns out to be a contribution from John Marder, who had served in the unlikely capacity of President of the United States Cricket Association. Nottingham born, Marder went to Boston University to complete his education, stayed on, and did much good work in reviving interest in cricket. His two most tangible successes were his formation in 1961 of the Association whose first president he became, and his coup two years later in reviving the oldest Test fixture in all history, between the United States and Canada. He wrote often for assorted sporting publications, served as Wisden's *American correspondent, and, in 1975, took advantage of one minor but entrancing omission from the bibliography of writing about* Wisden.

In retrospect it is astonishing that not until as late in the day as 1975 did any writer take advantage of the embarrassment of riches lying in the files in the form of commercial advertisements. Having settled on this theme, Mr. Marder rejoices in the deflationary landscape of the past, but although his essay breaks rich new ground, it is no more than a preliminary sketch for the comprehensive review of the subject which will one day be written. The essence of the advertisements lay less in the plugs for bats and balls and ancillary goods, than in the oblique insights into the life of a gentleman provided by those advertisements which Mr. Marder has overlooked. Who, browsing through past Wisdens, could fail to be moved by the sesquipedalian excesses of Pears Soap, which claimed in the 1911 edition 'never to have been equalled for purity, saponaceous quality, emollience, and those complexion-beautifying properties which made it the World's Top Scorer in Toilet Soaps'; or by the instructions offered in the 1906 almanack by A. J. White, Hatters of Jermyn Street, for measuring the head: 'Cut piece of card or sticks for length and breadth, as shown in dotted line'; or the great coup of that same year, a Pears advertisement in the form of a full-page cartoon by Phil May; or the announcement four years later by the makers of Oatine Shaving Cream that 'the condition of a man's face after shaving depends on his razor'; or the extraordinary testimony of Tom Richardson in the same edition, to the effect that having suffered simultaneously from insomnia, melancholia, depression, shortage of breath and rheumatism, he suddenly found the complete cure for all these ailments in an elixir called Dr. Williams' Pink Pills, 2s 9d a box.

Steadily the volume as well as the range of the business increases. By 1914 Wisden was carrying a whole page on the delights to be found at the First Avenue Hotel, which claimed something called 'real comfort', closeness to places of interest, quiet bedrooms and proximity to the Tube; only the omission of its address detracted from the efficacy of the entry. The edition of the following year, that tragic contradiction, a wartime almanack dealing with the affairs of a lost peace, devoted its inside cover to an invitation to readers to attend Nevill's Turkish Baths in Northumberland Avenue, where 'the decoration of the bath rooms is tasteful, the shampooers capable and efficient, and the air heated by a scientific apparatus of considerable repute'. By 1926, the range of advertisers was dizzying, from the Canadian Pacific Railway and the Boy's Own Paper—'See that your *boy is brought up on the B.O.P.—as* you *were'—to Amplion, the Loud Speaker Supreme, the Daily Mirror, the Charing Cross Turkish Baths and the Shaftesbury Homes and Arethusa Training Ship. None of these items, nor any others, is touched on by Mr. Marder, but he deserves credit for having first drawn to the attention of readers an element of the almanack hardly acknowledged before.*

IT was Oscar Wilde who once said, 'No man is rich enough to buy back his past.' It may have seemed that way to the inimitable Oscar, but one can always make a backward safari through time in the pages of *Wisden*. The late A. A. Thomson used to say that if he were marooned on a desert island, he would like to have the 1903 *Wisden* with him so that he could fight the battles of the 1902 Tests again. Rowland Ryder in the 1965 *Wisden* evoked the pleasure that thousands of cricket enthusiasts get out of re-living old matches and looking up the careers of bygone players. I had a friend, Karl Auty of Chicago, who kept his *Wisdens* in his bedroom. If he couldn't sleep, he would roll out the rather uniquely designed bookshelf which fitted right under his bed and pick out an interesting year to browse over. *Wisden* has mirrored the cricket world accurately since 1864 and it has unconsciously brought back another world through its advertising pages—the everyday world, where it was once possible to live very well on five pounds a week.

For the first fourteen years of its long life, the Almanack didn't accept any advertising from other firms. It was deemed sufficient in those Victorian days to list discreetly on the back pages of *Wisden*, a 'List of Articles Stocked'. *Wisden* in those days was one of several annuals fighting for public recognition. It was quite sufficient that if any cricketing gentleman needed any supplies, he could consult the 'List' and make his wants known by a visit to the establishment.

The 1867 *Wisden* advertised a rather ingenious mechanical bowler—a Catapulta, which I believe was invented by Felix, the Kent cricketer. It was not until a few years later that a price was appended to the display. The mechanical bowler cost twelve guineas, which was rather expensive, compared with the annual fees paid to a ground bowler at the time.

Advertising in the mid Victorian era, was deemed rather vulgar and there was an upper class aversion to 'persons in trade'. Advertising agents were probably placed in a social niche slightly lower than a circus advance man. They were probably deemed rather a nuisance, advertising being regarded as 'hawking one's wares', and not having anything like the prestige acquired in this century. The first few advertisements in the Almanack were from other cricket outfitters, which was only to be expected—and from patent medicines! These remedies were stated to be almost miraculous in their healing powers. Epilepsy, boils, sore legs, dysentery—even cancerous ulcers, were cured only by application of these magic elixirs. They were described as 'pleasant tasting' too—all this for 2/6d a box! These wonder cures were of no value whatever to poor Fred Grace, who died in 1880 of congestion of the lungs, brought on, it was said, by sleeping in a damp bed. Such carelessness in regard to health and such carelessness in the attribution of magical cures to patent medicines, is typical of a credulous age. The motto of the day was 'Caveat Emptor'—let the buyer beware.

In 1881 an American President was assassinated and the first Boer War began. In some ways the world news showed a curious affinity to our own day. From a sportsman's point of view, games were much less expensive than they are today. A complete cricket outfit could be bought for £2–10–0 and many famous clubs started with just such gear. Top quality bats were 21/- and balls were no problem—they were 3/- per dozen! *Wisden* seemed to be rather broad minded with their advertisers—a Mr. J. D. Bartlett advertised that his premises contained 'the largest stock of bats in the world', rather an ambitious claim, but no one seems to have challenged him.

Competition appears to have been fierce among batmakers. Cobbett's advertised that 'some evilly disposed persons are stamping our name on common and inferior goods' which seems to give the lie to the oft believed myth that Victorians were a more sporting lot than their successors! Cobbett's warned that their bats carried a registered trademark and no Cobbett bat was genuine without it. There were no fair trade laws or any consumer protection laws in those days. Cricketers couldn't be sure of the quality they were getting. Perhaps the vogue for bats with the signature of a famous cricketer dates from this period. Lawn tennis was invented in the seventies and became popular very quickly. Advertisements of the period show ladies playing in the long sweeping dresses of the period, buttoned high at the throat. One wonders how they got enough freedom of action even to play the game, no matter how innocuous it was in those days. *Wisden* offered tennis 'bats' for 25/-. Fifty-one years later a similar racquet cost 67/-. Tennis nets cost 40/- complete with poles and balls were 8/6 a dozen.

There were many sporting newspapers during this period. After reading their advertisements one realizes the inroads that television and radio have made to our reading habits. It was a slower and pleasanter world. The *Sporting Clipper* carried the latest racing information for the venturesome punter and announced that its Saturday edition, at the unheard of price of twopence, was on the streets before the morning trains left for the neighbouring courses. One could also read *The Sportsman, Sporting Life, Bell's Life Daily* and the *Cricket and Football Times*. This was advertised at 10/- per annum and was said to have been written 'by gentlemen'. This brings to mind the fact that sport was dominated in those days by public schoolboys who founded the great soccer clubs of to-day, started the Rugby Union and administered the M.C.C.

Charles Spencer & Co. advertised a 'Pangymnasticon' which was a practical home gymnasium for ten guineas. It was claimed that this outfit would greatly promote physical health. Seventy years later the successors to the firm were advertising a slip catch trainer which perhaps had more appeal for clubs suffering from a lack of good fieldsmen. Echoes of sporting days in Scotland and on the Yorkshire moors are brought to mind by the advertisement of E. M. Reilly & Co. who sold wild fowl guns for ten guineas and gamekeepers' guns for £6–10–0d. First-class amateurs were always tempted after the Twelfth of August by invitations to join shooting parties and it would be a keen cricketer indeed who could resist the temptations of grouse shooting and agreeable feminine companionship.

Wisden soon carried advertising for cricket literature—the first books announced were later volumes of *Scores & Biographies* and Box's *English Game of Cricket*. There were not too many books published about the game, but Fred Gale's books were always available and there were summaries of the Oxford v. Cambridge match to 1876 which were popular. Until the twenties, there was a modest annual list of cricket books which later developed into a flood. P. F. Warner turned out a book or two on his overseas tours but 'tour books' did not reach real popularity until after the First World War. In 1925, *Wisden* carried annoucements of M. A. Noble's book, *The Game's the Thing* and of A. C. MacLaren's study of the batting of Jack Hobbs, *The Perfect Batsman*. Both were priced at 7/6. Tobacco advertisements came in during the eighties and it was still fashionable to advertise snuff. Virginia cigarettes were popular, one advertised brand being the 'President Arthur' variety. It was doubtful if President Chester A. Arthur of the United States had authorized the use of his name.

Wisden committed one of its rare boners in 1884 when the Calendar was headed 1844. Perhaps the editor was buying back his past! The Royal Bicycle and Tricycle Agency advertised light carriages for one or two horses. This mode of transport was termed 'most luxurious' and it certainly was. Motor drawn traffic was non-existent and English roads had not been improved too much since the eighteenth century. In fact they had not been improved since the stage coaches had ceased in the forties. Roads were almost chronically in disrepair. It took the twentieth century with its avalanche of motor cars to bring about an improvement in highways. Adventurous spirits could mount a 'penny farthing' and attain a speed of 20 miles an hour but at the risk of their necks! By 1891 the 'ordinaries' as they were termed, had disappeared from the road. Their place was taken by the 'safety' models that we have known ever since. Something of a cycling craze took place in the nineties and Sugg advertised bicycles for thirteen guineas.

E. Hawkins & Company of Brighton took many pictures of cricketers, most of them strategically posted near a potted palm or defending an obviously staged wicket. In 1886–87 Shaw and Shrewsbury took out an England team to Australia. Before 1903 these tours were arranged on a speculative basis and this team played at Bowral on January 23 and 24, 1887. Twenty-one years later, one of Australia's greatest batsmen was to be born there! Towards the end of the tour the Englishmen indulged in rather a novel match—both English and Australian players collaborating in a match between Smokers and Non-smokers. The Non-smokers batted first and Arthur Shrewsbury and W. Bruce of Australia put on 196 for the first wicket—this against Brigge, Palmer, Boyle and Lohmann. The Non-smokers showed that they did not miss a puff now and again by rolling up 803 for nine wickets. Quick to take advantage of this, the largest innings on record thus far in a first-class match, Messrs Hawkins offered pictures of the two elevens. The Smokers were proudly brandishing their cigars and pipes. The firm also advertised pictures of the Australians of 1886, taken in the field at an exposure of 1/20 sec., then deemed to be a record.

The nineties were heralded by an announcement that the International Fur Store would sell a 'good fur-lined overcoat' for £10–0–0. The accompanying cut could have been used in later days to portray a capitalist—top hat, rolled fur collar and all!

Frank Bryan, who are still advertising in *Wisden*, announced that their batting gloves in future would have a protective covering for the thumb.

Bryan would probably like to have buckskin leg guards for sale in the current year of grace, for 6/6d a pair. Serviceable cricket boots were 10/6d and sweaters were 4/6d. Cricket caps were 1/- each, with a few pennies extra for a monogram!

As the Victorian era drew to its close, there were slight evidences in *Wisden*. The obituaries refer to deaths in South Africa. One of the more prominent cricketers to lose his life was F. W. Milligan of Yorkshire. Some famous cricketers were at the front, but the war did not seriously interrupt the placid flow of life in England. Prices did not move upward, there was no inflation as in our more precarious days.

John Piggott could still advertise a lounge suit for 45/- and an overcoat for 12/6. One can be sure that these coats were not fur lined! Squash was a popular game and rackets were advertised at 17/6. Frank Sugg, the Derbyshire and Lancashire batsman, advertised extensively for some years. His trade slogan was 'The Reasonable, Practical Man' and his prices sound almost incredible seventy-five years later. Running pumps were 4/6d and track suits were 1/11d. Good football boots were advertised at 9/6d a pair and batting gloves were 8/6d. Cricket entered into a Golden Age in the early part of the twentieth century. Every county had its personality and W. G., as the acknowledged 'Champion' was emperor of a kingdom. This was the era of Jackson, Fry and MacLaren, Jessop, Trumper and Warner. South Africa became a cricketing power with her quartette of googly bowlers and the West Indies sent two teams to England. One could foresee their future greatness. Even Philadelphia were welcome tourists, the first and only American team to play first-class cricket. It was an exciting period for the game and the advertising in the Almanack reflected the opulence of the times.

All sorts of bats were on the market. A specially selected one would cost about 25/- and you could choose from Wisden, Gradidge, Abel, Tyldesley, Dark, Surridge and Ayres bats and many others. Wisden 'Crown' cricket balls were 5/- each and leg guards, real buckskin, had advanced to 9/9d. Famous players gave their autographs to bats almost absent mindedly and in one issue of *Wisden*, C. B. Fry gave his blessing to 'Imperial Drivers', 'Stuart Surridge' and 'J. T. Tyldesley' bats. His name on any product in the period before the First World War was eagerly sought. He was not only one of the best batsmen in England, he was also a first-class rugby player for Blackheath and played left back for Southampton when they reached the Final of the F.A. Cup. He was the Editor of *C. B. Fry's Magazine*, which also advertised in *Wisden*. It was billed as 'bringing a breezy cheerfulness to English homes'. C. B. Fry gave the stamp of his own personality far beyond those times. In 1919 he was seriously proposed as King of Albania. What a monarch he would have made! There is little doubt that the Albanians would have been playing Test cricket by now instead of being part of the Chinese bloc!

The ordinary cricket ground had used horse drawn mowers for many years. There was a time indeed when the Oval turf was cropped by having sheep graze on the ground. The Staten Island C.C. of New York are reputed to own the grazing rights to the Oval, garnered during an exciting poker game in the 1870s, but they have not seriously requested Surrey to use their services.

It was an accepted legend in many grounds that the horses would know when the last batsman had taken his place at the crease. At Trent Bridge, when Fred Morley came in to bat for Nottinghamshire, it was said that the horse would sidle over to the mower, ready for his job! Cricketing legend died when the mowers were motorized. Ransome's had advertised horse-drawn mowers for £32–0–0. By 1909 the same firm proclaimed proudly that they had sold nearly 200 motor drawn mowers. The Automobile Age, for better or worse, was upon us. In 1903 Lord's School of Physical Culture, possibly taking advantage of a more famous 'Lord's', was advertising physical culture courses by mail. It was an era of biceps flexing. Whiteley's advertised 'Two British Records, Foster's 287, and our Flexten home exerciser for 17/6d'.

Bicycles had declined in price from ten years previously. They were advertised for eight guineas each, although motor cycles were beginning to be popular. Club secretaries may have groused when they brought grass seed at a pound a bushel, little realizing the troubles of their successors. They could console themselves by smoking 'Alliance' tobacco at 5d an ounce. It was advertised as 'the most exquisite blending of the finest tobaccos'. Steel razors were 7/6d with ivory handles but many cricketers were beginning to use the new safety razors. Beards and moustaches were going out of style. By 1910 most cricketers looked very youthful and were cleanshaven, a style which persisted into our day. In the 1906 *Wisden*, a Mr. T. N. W. took a half page advertisement to announce that he had a complete run of *Wisden* for sale. One hopes that he got a good price for his set.

During the First World War, organized cricket stopped after the season of 1914. *Wisden* shrank in size but it continued to appear, a symbol of hope for more normal times—sooner or later, the 'Rolls of Honour' were fearsome but the 1916 edition carried the obituaries of A. E. Stoddart, Victor Trumper and the 'Champion' himself—W. G. Grace, dead at 67. He had seemed immortal to most cricketers. Even the enemy announced that his death was due to an air raid, which was not true.

Although first-class cricket was finished, the game was still played and other sports equipment was also advertised. Prices were little changed for the first year or two. Golf clubs were advertised at 6/6d, either woods or irons, and golf balls were 15/- a dozen. By 1918 post war inflation was beginning. Golf clubs were 8/6d and by 1919 prices really started to climb.

That year saw an experiment. County matches were restricted to two days. The trial lasted for only one year. Until one-day cricket made its debut in 1963, the first-class game was to know little change. Bats had advanced to 32/- and balls were double their pre-war price. The twenties saw matters slowly returning to normal. In fact, cricket enjoyed some of its greatest seasons with Hobbs enjoying a new career, closely followed by George Gunn, Mead, Hendren, Hearne and Frank Woolley. Wilfred

Rhodes was still wheeling them over for Yorkshire and he was a playing link with the Golden Age.

Charles Pugh Ltd. advertised a motor mower for thirty guineas which would cut 1,000 square yards in twenty minutes. Cricket sweaters were now 23/6d and the latest model Humber motor cycle cost £55.

The Thirties were more troublesome times. An obituary in *Wisden* gave a hint of the disorders in the world, E. R. Sheepshanks of the Eton XI, who died in the Spanish Civil War. Shortage of money was chronic and *Wisden* broke new ground when a moneylender advertised his services—loans of fifty pounds and upward! With the start of the Second World War, *Wisden* again shrank in size. The wonder was that it appeared at all. The continuity of almost a hundred years was not lost. Late in 1940 the firm's factory was destroyed by enemy action but work on the Almanack went on. The article on 'Public school cricket' was destroyed in the raid, the author had also suffered the loss of his notes at another place during the same raid. It was impossible to get another article ready in time for publication. Advertising came to the rescue. Four pages appeared between pp 185 and 188 of the 1941 *Wisden* instead of the article on the schools. Edwards Ltd. had advertised for many years but wartime restrictions made it impossible for the firm to supply their nets. They continued to advertise as usual although they had nothing to sell! Their display showed a cricket ball with the announcement, 'A net regret—government regulations prevent Edwards from supplying nets for this'!

The forties were characterized by a flood of 'Brylcreem' advertisements featuring Denis Compton, particularly after his fine season in 1947. His face not only appeared in *Wisden*, but on Tube posters and on billboards all over the country.

Cricket schools had advertised in *Wisden* since 1928, one of the first being the Faulkner School and now Alf Gover's East Hill School became prominent. The advent of sponsored cricket inevitably led to advertisements by Gillette, Rothman, Esso, Prudential, Haig and John Player, all of whom have done so much to popularize present day cricket.

The advertising in *Wisden* for the past hundred and eleven years is evocative of the times in which we and our fathers have lived. There is a ticket to 'buy back one's past' implicit in the Almanack. A browse through the advertising pages brings memories of days far different from our own.

Wisden has seen the transition of cricket from a country pastime to a world wide sport. Amateurs have now disappeared from county cricket and one-day cricket is with us. Test cricket will inevitably widen and include some countries not yet in the charmed circle. I think particularly of Sri Lanka who will no doubt merit Test status shortly.

As we 'buy back our past' we look forward to *Wisden* of 2001!

THE WILLING WORKHORSES OF FIRST-CLASS CRICKET [1975]

BY BASIL EASTERBROOK

It was in 1975 that Basil Easterbrook had a priceless brainwave. He would write about players not generally deemed to be worth writing about. The upshot was an excellent display of character study, shot through with humour and perception. It was also the first, and surely the last, piece of writing in Wisden *to invoke the unholy trinity of God, Winston Churchill and Frank Sinatra. It also added to the stockpot of good cricket jokes by preserving once and for all the story of how Bob White's name brought about a misunderstanding in the sporting prints. The essay ends with an extraordinary effusion which carries Mr. Easterbrook perilously close to the evangelical excesses of Mr. Ryder earlier in the decade. Under the circumstances it is excusable that he should have omitted the name of the cricketer responsible for the sermon.*

> *'To do my best with bat and ball*
> *From twelve o'clock till evenfall.*
> *Maintain a length, avoid a blob*
> *Is what I call an English job.'*

THE passing of half a century or more since these simple lines were penned has not affected their truth or their tribute to all those who will never be selected for the Five Cricketers of The Year section of this Almanack. Should anyone find any incipient jingoism in the last line let me hasten to add you can substitute Australian, West Indian, Pakistani or any other country except that it will not scan anything like so well as the word English.

Bob White will never be a great player but he is typical of those willing workhorses without whom there could be no county cricket. He is not the bubbling, extrovert type of Cockney but he is, like all his kind, armoured against the hard knocks life hands out so lavishly. For all but a handful of cricketers the one opportunity to come their way for any real material reward for their skills is a benefit. Most players can expect one after ten years' service with a first-class county, a few fortunates get one in less but for others like Robert Arthur White, the Nottinghamshire beneficiary in 1974, circumstances make the waiting period seem an endless affair.

'It took me twenty-one years from the time I started, but I'm lucky in as much as at least I did get a benefit. Some players and good ones never do,' says Bob, known to his friends and peers as 'Knocker' for a reason no one seems aware of. 'I can assure you it's not because I owe anyone money.'

He was born in Fulham nearly thirty-nine years ago, the son of an engineering worker and he went straight from Chiswick Grammar School to join the Lord's ground staff in 1953. He did not make his debut for Middlesex until five years later and in between Bob says, 'I would like a £1, even at present value, for every evening from five to seven I spent bowling in the nets to M.C.C. members. It was all part of the day's work for a groundstaff dogsbody but it helped me to develop as an off-break bowler as well as a left-hand bat so I'm not complaining.'

He progressed steadily with Middlesex and won his cap in 1963 when he made 1,355 runs; then he dropped out through injury and when he recovered there was no place in the team for him. Nottinghamshire came along in 1966, took him on special registration and were satisfied enough with the bargain to award him a cap the same year.

'A man came up to me once and said, "You are the fellow I saw on TV at Southampton take three hours making 35." What he failed to say was that Notts were 22 for five when I came to the wicket.' White is always likely to encounter this kind of situation in the ranks of such an unpredictable outfit as Nottinghamshire. Against Surrey at The Oval in 1967 he joined Mike Smedley with the scoreboard showing Notts 66 for six. When they were parted their stand of 204 represented what is still the record seventh wicket partnership for Nottinghamshire and White's not out 116 is his best score. In nineteen years of county cricket Bob has made around 10,000 runs including five centuries, picked up over 400 wickets and held about 150 catches.

He did not bowl seriously until he joined Nottinghamshire and those who have seen him are immediately struck by the similarity of his action to Fred Titmus. If you watch White you have seen Titmus. 'Yes, but only up to the moment of letting the ball go. There is a slight difference you'll agree in that Fred has taken about 2,200 more wickets than I have,' says a rueful 'Knocker'. White, who obviously could not expect to bowl for Middlesex with a world class off spinner like Titmus in the side, says he is not conscious of being a dead ringer for the man who played in 49 Tests for England, lost four toes in a boating accident in the West Indies, came back to bowl as well as ever and was dramatically recalled to the international scene for M.C.C.'s tour of Australia and New Zealand last winter.

'He is such a great bowler and I saw so much of him at close range that I suppose my subconscious mind decided I should bowl like him.' Derbyshire must have thought they had encountered Titmus at Ilkeston in 1971 when Knocker dismissed seven of their batsmen for 41 runs. White would like to stay in cricket and fancies exchanging the white flannels of the player for the white coat of the umpire when his active career comes to a close. Not long after he joined Nottinghamshire he was playing in a match when an approaching storm darkened the sky over Trent Bridge. The cricket writer of a local evening paper sent over the time honoured line for the stop press—'Bad light stopped play'. The female telephonist was new to the job and unfamiliar with cricket terms and the message reached a somewhat intrigued sub-editor as 'Bob White stopped play'. 'I've often brought play to a standstill with my batting but I was not guilty on this occasion,' cracks this likeable Londoner now permanently settled in the Midlands, a man clearly never lost for an answer.

Since I took my first tentative steps in cricket writing in 1939 I must have produced copy, adequate or indifferent, on most of the great players of my own time and the past, but if they have my unqualified admiration, my heart is with those who soldier on year in, year out with little reward beyond their own virtue. I write about the Bob Whites and Len Hills of the game because I have affection for them. The perceptive will recognise a fellow feeling no doubt.

There are those who believe in the osmosis of the spirit, that is to say, the qualities of someone admired being passed on to another human being. When Leonard Winston Hill was born in the little rustic Monmouthshire town of Caerleon some three miles from Newport in the spring of 1942, Hitler was holding down some 400 million people and Nazi Germany was at the peak of its bid for world domination. The hope that they would eventually fail centred around the personality of one English statesman— Churchill. Mr. Hill, the caretaker of Caerleon's local secondary school, and his wife chose their son's second name from the Prime Minister and Len has certainly shown the same determination and stickability as Churchill. He was awarded his county cap by Glamorgan on August 20 last year after scoring 90 in the incredible defeat of Hampshire, the champions, at Cardiff, a defeat which denied them retaining the title in 1974. What was remarkable about the award was that it came more than ten years after Hill had made his first-class début. Until 1974 his best score was 80 against Oxford University in The Parks in 1970 and the most games he had played in succession in any one season came to six.

The reason was simple. Len Hill was from 1963 to the spring of last year a professional footballer with Newport County and Swansea City. As inside forward or wing half—I am too old and unregenerate to employ terms like striker or midfield man—he played in well over 400 League and Cup matches scoring 73 goals. He was never free to join Glamorgan until early May and by mid-July he had to report back for soccer training. Halfway through his last season Len realised he was no longer enjoying his football and being the man he is, could not carry on just for the money. He decided that at 32 he might have five or perhaps ten years of good cricket in him and for the first time, in 1974, he put in a full season. Glamorgan in a period of transition after losing such stars as Don Shepherd, Peter Walker, Ossie Wheatley, Tony Lewis and others in a short span of years were as delighted with Hill's decision as he is himself.

He has all the best Welsh qualities – courage, loyalty, and the quiet fire that burns inwardly. His devotion to sport and his talent for it were born from sadness and compassion, two more words known to all Welshmen. When he was ten Len's father died in 1952 and his brother Royston, 14 years his senior became father as well as brother to the small, defenceless boy.

'He used to take me everywhere—to watch Glamorgan's home games and soccer and rugby in Cardiff and Newport. For years from the age of ten onwards he used to bowl to me in the backyard of our home. He was a good village cricketer and I tried harder for him than I ever would for any coach.'

Len attended the school where his father had been caretaker and when the time came for him to leave, his brother apprenticed him in electrical engineering. He never liked it and he will never return to it but like that other Winston the word 'quit' was not in his vocabulary. Rather than fail his brother he served the whole five years of his apprenticeship.

He goes into the 1975 season yet to make a century. He reached 96 against Gloucestershire at Swansea early last June 'but the last man got himself out so I shrugged and said to myself "Back to the drawing board, Len, mate." '

He is determined to be a good batsman over the course of the next few years. 'I'm learning all the time, even now. One of the things I find I still have to work at is self discipline. I tend to move about trying to get into line behind the ball too quickly, anticipating where the bowler is going to put the ball instead of keeping still until he has delivered.'

Len believes a man should know his depth and stay in it. 'I'll try and stay in cricket and for a bloke like me that means something like groundsman or umpire. I'm sorry I've no anecdotes, no exciting adventures. I must be the worst subject you've ever had.' As a matter of fact, Len, I'd say you were one of the best, in every sense. As long as our society can throw up characters like Leonard Winston Hill, the late arrival who was named after one of the great men of history, maybe there's just a chance it might survive.

There is no game to compare with cricket when it comes to honouring its hacks. They know they can never attain comparative wealth. M.C.C. tours are as far away as Mars but these are the men who don't opt out. They are paid to play, but their joy in belonging and the fun they get out of five months in every year means as much to them as the money.

'You cannot get closer to the real heart of Devon than a name like mine. Why, there was even one of my tribe on the old grey mare with Uncle Tom Cobley in the song "Widdicombe Fair".'

Jack Davey was 30 last September, a six footer with a sense of humour as lively as his left-arm fast medium seam bowling. Sharing the new ball with a world famous cricketer like Mike Procter is something Jack regards as both an exciting privilege and a help. 'The batsmen are so mentally apprehensive about how to deal with Mike they don't bother about the swede basher at the other end and often I manage to flatten a couple of them in consequence.' This, like so many of Big Jack's remarks was made lightly but it is no less than the simple truth. When Gloucestershire won the Gillette Cup in 1973 the two new ball bowlers collected 18 wickets in the competition, eight falling to Procter but ten to Davey.

Davey was born at Tavistock, the son of an auctioneer's clerk who in his spare time served the town's cricket club as player and secretary for nearly thirty years. Dad made occasional appearances as an off-break bowler for

Devonshire in the Minor Counties competition, so Jack, which is his baptismal name, grew up with the game in his blood and surrounded by its trappings. To the surprise of his father he bowled and batted 'the wrong way round'. Like Sinatra, Jack did things his way and received no coaching until he joined Gloucestershire. At Tavistock Grammar School and in his early club cricket Jack aspired to be a slow left-arm spinner. One day Milton Abbot, the village he played for, found themselves short of a seam bowler. Jack, a stripling not yet fifteen, was given the new ball and told to do the best he could with it. 'I'm not going to boast about what I did to the opposition that afternoon. Just let's say I have never bowled slow again.'

On leaving school Jack served and completed a five-year apprenticeship as a compositor on the *Tavistock Gazette*. He has a highly skilled trade at his finger tips but Jack thinks it unlikely he will return to it. 'How can I ever go back to an indoor job? I'm like a Dartmoor pony. I've smelt the summer turf and felt it under my feet, I've travelled and got the taste for it.' When he is forced to stop playing, Jack fancies a business of his own, but he is aware of the uncertainties of the time and he might continue as a lorry driver which is how he has spent the past two winters after obtaining a Heavy Goods Vehicle licence. He found he preferred driving around Wales and the South West to earlier winters working as a representative for a carpet firm in Bristol, the city where the Davey's have made their home. His wife, Melora, is also a Devonian. She comes from Princetown, the little village like a Klondike settlement after the gold rush had ended, whose only excuse for existence is the penitentiary at the top of its main street known all over the world—Dartmoor.

As Gloucestershire conquered Glamorgan, Surrey, Essex, Worcestershire and finally Sussex to win the Gillette Cup in 1973 no one in cricket knew that Davey was kept going by pain killing injections in both knees. He has since had an operation for the removal of lumps of fat under both knee caps. Looking at Jack's long, lean frame one could not imagine a more improbable complaint.

In terms of figures his best bowling was the six wickets for 95 he took against Notts at Gloucester in 1967, but the piece of bowling he is prouder of is conceding only 22 runs in 11 overs against Lancashire in the famous Gillette semi-final at Old Trafford that finished at five minutes to nine 'when a motorist driving without side lights on would have been pinched.' He also cherishes a Benson and Hedges semi-final at Leeds against Yorkshire when he gave away only 6 runs in nine overs, seven of which were maidens 'with Boycott at one end'.

His top score in eight years on first-class fields is the 37 not out he took off the Indian tourists at the old Wagon Works ground, Gloucester, last summer. Until then he could never get past 17. He made 17 against Lancashire and Leicestershire at Cheltenham both in 1967 but it was the 17 not out he made on the last day of the 1973 season which he regards as his supreme moment with the bat. When he came in Gloucestershire were 210 for nine, needing another 57 to beat Glamorgan. 'I never thought we had a price when I walked out but when they did not get my wicket quickly I decided to try to keep it going for "Mort" at the other end.'

John Mortimore took command and made the winning hit which also gave him a not out half-century, his only one of the season, but Davey, a Crown Prince of No. 11s, dealt with 94 balls. If that was his moment of delight his most embarrassing was splitting his flannels while fielding at third man before a big crowd at Romford 'spectacularly and with a noise I thought they must have heard all round the ground'.

We have a Londoner who made good in the Midlands as an all-rounder, a batsman to represent Wales and a bowler from the far West. Perhaps in conclusion we might look at a fine young cricketer from the North East. At 24 years of age Peter Willey had shown enough character, skill and fortitude to shrug off two cartilage operations both to his right knee, to finish second in the Northamptonshire batting averages in 1973 and make his first centuries in the county championship.

Sitting opposite me in the committee room at Northampton, this young man from County Durham tapped his right leg and said, 'If I could chop this off and get a new one I'd be the happiest person in the world. I've never wanted anything from life except to be a cricketer and now I'm saddled with this which means I can kiss goodbye to my ambition of being a real all-rounder. But life isn't obliging is it? Everyone has problems. You keep hearing of wealthy men all over the world who get themselves or their children kidnapped. I would not change places with them for all their money. I shall just have to make the best of this right leg of mine and I don't believe it will stop me making it as a batsman.'

Willey was born in the small town of Sedgefield, about which he remembers nothing, the family moving to the nearby city of Durham when he was a baby, and then on to Seaham Harbour. His father, a gas fitter, was a club cricketer who in Peter's words 'shoved a bat in my hands as soon as I could walk'. This sowed the seed that was to lead Master Willey straight from school to the ground staff at Northampton. His first cricket memories are of working on the scoreboard at Durham. At fourteen, he played for Seaham Harbour's third team, at fifteen he was in their first team and in 1966, aged sixteen and five months, he made his debut for Northamptonshire at Fenner's against Cambridge University. Willey was sent in to face the first ball of the match which bowled him. Peter decided he could only improve on a start like that and in the second innings he took 78 off the Cambridge attack. Northamptonshire nursed him carefully until in 1970 he scored 923 runs. They gave him his cap the following summer.

Peter told a master called Douglas Ferguson at Seaham Harbour Secondary Modern that he wanted to play cricket for a living. What he did not know at the time was that Mr. Ferguson was a talent scout for Northamptonshire, who had sent many boys from the North East down for a trial with the Midland County. Ferguson passed on a favourable report and Northamptonshire wasted no time.

Willey is a self made player. 'I am essentially an eye player. I like to hit the ball and as long as I'm middling it I'm happy. I believe it does not matter how you score runs as long as you get them. Coaching is all right up to a point, perhaps the point where it eliminates the bad faults, but it never makes a bad player into a good one. You either have a talent for a thing or you haven't.'

He celebrated the award of his cap in 1971 with his maiden century, 158 not out against Oxford University in The Parks. Then came the first cartilage operation which caused him to miss half the 1972 season. The next winter he was asked to go to South Africa with D. H. Robins' side. In the first game in January 1973 he injured the knee again playing against Eastern Province. That meant another operation and the missing of the first six weeks of another English season. Willey is good North Eastern stock, tough spiritually as well as physically. Instead of moping he waited all over again to show what he could do. When his patience was finally rewarded Willey made nearly 800 runs in 23 visits to the crease including 156 not out versus Essex and 105 off Kent. Tall and upright, he also had undeniable usefulness as a seamer before his knee trouble, as his five for 14 against Middlesex at Lord's in 1970 proved convincingly.

Willey played football for Durham County schoolboys and had trials for Sunderland and Northampton Town as a right back. 'Nothing came of them and after a short spell in local soccer in Northampton I packed the game in altogether. Even when I was trying to get taken on at Roker Park and later by the Cobblers, I knew I was a man who preferred the sun to mud.' He describes himself as a front foot batsman best on the off side, with the cover drive his favourite stroke. While confident that his knee will see him through if he sticks to batting he is aware of the possibilities of living under something of a threat. Peter treated me to that slow, attractive smile which those who come from Geordie country seem favoured with – 'When I have to give up, whether it is soon or late, I'd like to work at an outside job. Coach or groundsman would do me a treat.'

You can never tell about people. They can surprise you – and humble you. Last winter a young county cricketer invited me to his home for dinner. He was proud of his wife, her cooking and their home with every justification. During the course of that peaceful haven of an evening he took me on a conducted tour of the house. I had always thought of him as a good companion, a bit of a prankster but not much given to books or philosophic thinking. I was about to turn and leave the main bedroom with the appropriate word of approval at the decor when my eyes caught some lines of beautifully worked script attached to the inside of the door. Seeing my interest he said with an unsuspected diffidence, 'It's what I've tried to base my life on. It was found in a church I believe in Baltimore and dates back to 1692. Copy it down if you wish but if you publish it anywhere please don't associate my name as its source. The lads would laugh me out of every dressing room in England in 1975.'

I don't for one moment believe they would but I would be worse than a churl not to respect his plea for anonymity. I did copy it and I offer it here without comment –

'Go placidly amid the noise and haste and remember what peace there may be in silence. As far as possible without surrender be on good terms with all persons. Speak your truth quietly and clearly; and listen to others, even the dull and the ignorant; they too have their story. Avoid loud and aggressive persons, they are vexations to the spirit. If you compare yourself with others, you may become vain and bitter; for always there will be greater or lesser persons than yourself. Enjoy your achievements as well as your plans. Keep interested in your own career, however humble; it is a real possession in changing fortunes of time. Exercise caution in your business affairs; for the world is full of trickery. But let this not blind you to what virtue there is; many persons strive for high ideals; and everywhere life is full of heroism. Be yourself. Especially, do not feign affection. Neither be cynical about love; for in the face of all aridity and disenchantment it is perennial as the grass. Take kindly the counsel of the years, gracefully surendering the things of youth. Nurture strength of spirit to shield you in sudden misfortune. But do not distress yourself with imaginings. Many fears are born of fatigue and loneliness. Beyond a wholesome discipline, be gentle with yourself. You are a child of the universe, no less than the trees and the stars; you have a right to be here. And whether or not it is clear to you, no doubt the universe is unfolding as it should. Therefore be at peace with God, whatever you conceive Him to be, and whatever your labours and aspirations, in the noisy confusion of life keep peace with your soul. With all its sham, drudgery and broken dreams, it is still a beautiful world. Be careful. Strive to be happy.'

THE GREATEST CENTENARY
OF THEM ALL! [1976]

Australia v. England

BY GORDON ROSS

Even as the first copies of the 1977 almanack were appearing in the bookshops, the cricket world was marvelling over the great game between England and Australia to mark the centenary of Test matches between the two countries. At the time the anniversary arrived, the balance of power between the rivals was tilted generously in favour of Australia, but in the event the English side fought tenaciously right down to the fall of the final wicket and was eventually defeated only by a slender margin. But all considerations of form and performance were eclipsed by the stupefying coincidence which attended the climax of the match. In the inaugural match at Melbourne in 1877, the home team had won by 45 runs. A century later in the return match on the same ground the home team won. By 45 runs.

The memorable feature of Gordon Ross's excellent account of the first Test is the passage involving Edward Pooley, the Surrey wicket-keeper whose peccadillos are known only vaguely to the modern public, which has a foggy impression of him as a player who cheated for money. The true account does much to exonerate Pooley who emerges from Alfred Shaw's quoted recollection, not as a criminal but as a fairly sharp Cockney customer. The details of his chicanery, verging on, yet far short of cheating, make comic reading, although it does seem that he was one of those unfortunate men who never quite put his affairs in order. Pooley died in the Lambeth Infirmary in the middle of the 1907 season in his seventieth year, and Wisden, *in publishing his obituary, dropped dark hints as to his unregenerate character without actually supplying any details. Presumably Pooley continued to gamble and to drink hard to the end of his life, which prompted his obituarist to write:*

> Of the faults of private character that marred Pooley's career and were the cause of poverty in which he spent the later years of his life there is no need to speak. He was in many ways his own enemy, but even to the last he had a geniality and a sense of humour that to a certain extent condoned his weaknesses.

What Ross's essay hardly hints at is the degree of hardship attending the travels of the tourists in that 1877 tour. Alfred Shaw gave a hair-raising account of a journey in New Zealand. Due to play the Eighteen of Canterbury on the following Monday, Shaw and his men set out from Greymouth only to find that the bridge they were scheduled to cross had been destroyed by floods. They were ferried across the water instead. On landing at Hokitika they entered their coaches and began to drive to Christchurch. Passing through Otira Gorge in stygian darkness, they found the forge flooded, and in attempting to plod on, saw their horses swept up by the current. At last, after almost drowning and only just managing to drag the horses from the water, the cricketers walked on until they arrived at a sort of roadman's shelter, where they found a roaring blaze but no dry clothes. So they stripped off before the flames and waited until their clothes were dry. Next morning they set off again, but had to return to the shack when the path to Christchurch was found to be blocked by a landslide. By Saturday night there was no food left on the premises, so one of the locals killed a sheep and the cricketers baked bread cakes. On Sunday morning the tourists set off once more for Christchurch, arriving there at eleven-thirty; the match was due to start at twelve-thirty. Shaw swore that 'we could with the greatest difficulty keep our eyes open as we stood on the field'. They won the match by 24 runs, a victory which Shaw said 'rather disturbed local opinions'.

Ross touches on the episode, but a full account had been quoted by John Arlott in a 1953 publication called Cricket. *Both the account of Pooley's misfortunes and the trials of the travellers deserve to be known in full by all students of cricket history.*

ON March 15, 1977, a few weeks before the first copies of *Wisden, 1977,* are on the bookstalls, the greatest event in cricket history will be celebrated—the one hundredth anniversary of the first Australia v. England Test match, which began in Melbourne on March 15, 1877, the start of rivalry which has become a piece of history, and has survived the ravages of one war after another, to stand the passage of time unchallenged in national affection. The green caps of Australia (even the actual cap seems different in physical shape from any other cricketing cap!) have had a special magic about them; tradition has not tarnished a golden image; the cricket has mellowed through the years; it has lost nothing of its bouquet.

The England party touring Australia in 1877 were not the first to go there. They were, in fact, the fourth. It is generally accepted by historians that the first overseas cricket tour from England was in 1859, when a strong team under the captaincy of George Parr, sailed from Liverpool for Quebec on September 7. Financially the trip was a success, the players clearing £90 each, free of all expenses, not to mention the gifts that were bestowed upon them. News of this excursion was not long in reaching Australia. A Melbourne catering firm, Spiers and Pond, enterprisingly, sent a representative to England in the summer of 1861, and he, Mr. Mallam, approached H. H. Stephenson of Surrey with a request that he would collect a team and go to Australia with an idea of pioneering cricket of international standard in that country.

STEPHENSON'S TEAM IN 1861

The terms arranged for the cricketers was £150 each and full expenses; in 1861 this represented handsome reward. A number of leading cricketers of the day lacked the adventurous spirit and declined to make the trip, but twelve did, and so shaped cricket's destiny. They were: H. H. Stephenson (captain), G. Bennett, W. Caffyn, G. Griffith, T. Hearne, R. Iddison, W. Mortlock, W. Mudie, C. Lawrence, T. Sewell, E. Stephenson and G. Wells. The tour opened in Melbourne on New Year's Day, 1862 when, it is said, twenty-five thousand people paid half-a-crown each for admission. Spiers and Pond are alleged to have made a very handsome profit from their venture; all the more surprising that it took another hundred years for sponsorship to play a major role in cricket.

Stephenson's cricketers had arduous journeys to endure. They travelled to their second match in Australia, a distance of over two hundred miles, in a coach drawn by six greys—all to play a collection of gentlemen curiously titled 'The Ovens'. The Ovens were bowled out for 20 and 53, and when at the end of the scheduled contest, Griffith played a single-wicket match against eleven of them, all eleven suffered the extreme indignity of failing to score. To cap it all, when having to bowl Griffith out for nought in order to tie the match, The Ovens bowlers sent down two wides. This may have been a slightly Gilbertian cricket match, but it mattered little in the overall context of the tour. The players brought home with them such glowing reports of their treatment in Australia that no difficulty was found in raising the next side to go in the winter of 1863–64. This time George Parr was the captain and the rest of his party was G. Anderson, J. Caesar, W. Caffyn, R. Carpenter, A. Clarke, E. M. Grace, T. Hayward, J. Jackson, T. Lockyer, G. Tarrant, R. C. Tinley.

PARR'S TOUR OF 1863–64

The *Melbourne Age*, on April 25, 1864, wrote:

'Parr's Eleven, one and all, proved themselves good men and true, and during their stay of four months in the colonies they have shown themselves worthy of their reputation. Much has been said about the comparative merits of the two Elevens which have visited Australia; but there cannot be a doubt in all unprejudiced minds, that the Eleven now leaving these shores is greatly superior to anything the colonists have before seen in point of cricketing excellence. The previous Eleven showed nothing equal to the wicket-keeping of Lockyer, the batting of Hayward and Carpenter, or the bowling of Jackson, Tarrant and Tinley, and it is more than probable that the Eleven which first visited Australia would now find their match in a Victorian Twenty-Two. The visit of this Eleven will be productive of much benefit to colonial cricketers, if for no other cause by its having led to the retention of Caffyn, the best all-round man among them; and with the aid of such a coach, Victoria will doubtless in future inter-colonial matches take her proper position.'

History has not recorded why it was, in view of the fact that this tour was so obviously a success, that ten years elapsed before another English side set foot in Australia. These tours were privately arranged so that it first needed an invitation to be issued, and then it was a question of whether or not the financial arrangements were suitable to all parties. It seems that this was sometimes the stumbling block—and may have been the reason for a decade going by without a tour. It appears that an offer was made to W. G. Grace (then aged twenty-four) in the summer of 1872, but the inducement was not of a sufficiently tempting character, and the idea was abandoned, but in the spring of 1873 another offer came direct from the Melbourne Cricket Club to Mr. Grace to bring out a team of his own selection, and the proposal met with considerable favour. Circumstances, we are told, tended to cripple the Captain in his task of forming a Twelve. Emmett was unable, and Alfred Shaw unwilling. Pooley was in disgrace, Pinder in domestic disarrangements, and Hill, at hand if wanted, but not required. Amateurs, as is their wont, promised, and no doubt intended, to fulfil their promise, but failed at the crisis, or Messrs. Hornby and Bird might have been in the party. The final composition was nine from the South and only three from the North—W. G. Grace (captain), F. H. Boult, J. A. Bush, W. R. Gilbert, G. F. Grace, A. Greenwood, R. Humphrey, H. Jupp, James Lillywhite, M. McIntyre, W. Oscroft and James Southerton.

The team played fifteen matches; they won ten, lost three and two were drawn, which on the face of it would appear to be a reasonably successful tour, but one or two remarks made by members of the touring party gave a hint that all was not well at times. One of them wrote: 'We left our country, as we fondly hoped, for our country's good. We came back to some extent wiser, if not sadder men.' He went on: 'Whatever shortcomings there were during the tour might have been remedied with a little conciliation on both sides, and the want of an occasional concession from one leader or the other did much to magnify a mere scratch into an open sore.'

W. G. GRACE CAPTAIN IN 1873–74

The tour began on Boxing Day, 1873, twelve days after the P and O Steamship *Mirzahpore* had landed the party in Australia. Mr. Grace disappointed his team sadly. He was not given to, or fond of, losing the toss, but he did on this occasion, and the Eighteen of Victoria took the bat to win by an innings and 21 runs. Australian cricket had, apparently, been under-rated. The second time the touring team met Victoria the latter had been suitably handicapped and their numbers reduced to Fifteen; this time the tourists won by seven wickets. For the third encounter Victoria were restored to their full complement of eighteen; the match was drawn. The general feeling was that cricket in Australia had improved wonderfully and was still improving; some very useful cricketers had been seen. Whatever undercurrents may have flowed beneath the surface, and although this was by no means the best side that England could have found, the trip seems to have done inestimable good for Australian cricket. The players were able to sharpen their claws ready for the next visit by a side from England, a side that was to make history.

And so to the winter of 1876–77. On Thursday, September 21, 1876 twelve English professional cricketers left Southampton for Adelaide in the P and O steamer *Poonah*. James Lillywhite of Sussex was the captain, Southerton of Surrey his first mate. Yorkshire sent five representatives— Ulyett, Hill, Emmett, Andrew Greenwood, and Armitage—Notts two— Alfred Shaw and Selby—while Surrey also furnished Jupp and Pooley— and the remaining player was Charlwood of Sussex. Even so, this was still not the absolute best that could be found. In bowling they were undeniably strong with Alfred Shaw, Hill, Emmett, Southerton, Lillywhite and Ulyett, and their fielding was rated very highly. It was considered that, in Pooley, the side had the best wicket-keeper of the day, but it was generally felt that they might have been considerably strengthened in batting, and Daft, Lockwood and Shrewsbury might conceivably have taken the places of Southerton, Armitage and Charlwood, but any chosen party by any set of selectors is always open to question when alternative suggestions are bandied about. The party arrived at King George's Sound on November 2; they played their first match on the 17th.

THE HISTORIC 1876–77 TOUR BEGINS

Alfred Shaw was one of the players whom W. G. Grace had invited on his tour, but Shaw had declined. The conditions offered for Grace's tour to the professional members were £150, and second class passage, travelling and hotel expenses, the latter item being fixed, where possible, at 7s 6d a day. Shaw declined the offer because he objected to the second class proviso. For the 1876 trip the terms were £150 and first-class passage. It was Shaw who began the tour in dramatic fashion against South Australia in Adelaide when Eleven played Twenty-Two. His analysis was 226 balls, 46 maidens, 12 runs, 14 wickets. England (as they were billed throughout the tour) scored 153, the Twenty-Two South Australians could muster only 54 and 53. The wicket was sandy and broke up early. The Australians had not yet learned the subtleties of wicket preparation; they were afraid to use the roller for fear that it would bruise and kill the grass. In later years, this Adelaide wicket became as firm as concrete and as smooth as a sheet of glass. The credit for this transformation was largely due to Jesse Hide, the old Sussex player, who obtained some clay off the mountains nearby and worked it into the soil at a remarkable expenditure of time, trouble and elbow grease!

From the overwhelming success in Adelaide, England were brought down to earth at Sydney by Fifteen of New South Wales—England 122 and 97. New South Wales 81 and 151 for twelve, to win by two wickets. Shaw once again had impressive figures—376 balls, 68 maidens, 53 runs, 8 wickets. England were shattered by Evans and Spofforth—they took 16 of the England wickets between them. What are usually termed Country matches followed against Twenty-Two of Newcastle and Twenty-Two of Goulburn.

The fifth match of the tour, however, was rather different; it was against Fifteen of Victoria at Melbourne. It began on Boxing Day. England were beaten, despite the continued magnificence of Shaw. This time he took 12 for 74, but Victoria's bowlers, Midwinter and Allen, were the prime architects of a victory by 31 runs. Yet this match had once been threatened with legal proceedings. Originally, two teams had been announced to make a tour that winter from England. One was projected by Mr. G. F. Grace; the other was Lillywhite's. The Grace tour fell through, but the commodious Melbourne Ground had been engaged by Grace's agent. Lillywhite's agent had arranged for the East Melbourne enclosure, and the East Melbourne club went to considerable expense in preparing for the visit. When Grace withdrew his project, Lillywhite decided to play on the Melbourne Ground. This intensely annoyed the people of East Melbourne and threats of legal proceedings, heated newspaper controversies, and general unpleasantness resulted. Finally, the dispute was settled by the East Melbourne Club accepting Lillywhite's offer of £230, with free admission to their members, numbering 500, to the tourists' matches in Melbourne.

The ecstasy at the success of the Victoria Fifteen erased all memories of rancour and bitterness. After two more country matches England faced the return match with Fifteen of New South Wales at Sydney—and total humiliation. They were bowled out for 35, of which Charlwood was run out for 20. The scores of the remaining ten were: 0, 1, 0, 0, 1, 2, 2, 7, 0, 2. The bowlers?—precisely the same two—Spofforth and Evans, and they did it again in the second innings, having ravaged the first six batsmen for a paltry 18 runs, when they were thwarted by Armitage (38) and Shaw (30), and an England total of 104 resulted. The Fifteen scored 124 and 17 for one wicket to win by 13 wickets.

THE POOLEY STORY

A return game was played immediately, starting the next day, by which time the handicapper had been at work and England met New South Wales at level weights, each side having eleven players, England this time having incomparably the better of it. Ulyett hit 94, and England scored 270. New South Wales were bowled out for 82, and were 140 for six in their second innings when the match ended, Shaw once again being head and shoulders England's most successful bowler – he took eight for 54. On this note the first part of the Australian tour ended and the England team left for New Zealand. Not many historians could tell you off the cuff the results of any of the matches in New Zealand, but all of them will mention, as if it were a legend – the story of Pooley, and the trouble he got into. A number of versions have been given of the incident; age has a habit of over-colouring events; what is a little exaggeration here and there in the course of a hundred years!—but we must take note of what Alfred Shaw said; after all, he was there.

Here is Shaw's account of the proceedings:

'*It cannot be considered surprising that in quarters where betting was rampant, as was the case in Australia at this time, some of the members of our team, who needed very small encouragement to back their opinions and statements at any time, should be led to participate in enterprises they had better have eschewed. One of these enterprises had most unpleasant consequences to one member of the team and it led to the side being deprived of his services for the last few weeks of the tour. The victim was Ed Pooley. We were playing at Christchurch against Eighteen of Canterbury on February 26, 27, and 28, 1877. In a discussion as to the prospects of the match that occurred in an hotel bar at night, Pooley offered to take £1 to 1 shilling that he named the individual score of every member of the local team. It is a trick familiar to cricketers, and in the old days of matches against local eighteens and twenty-twos it not infrequently worked off against the unwary. The bet being accepted Pooley named a duck as the score of each batsman on the local side. A fair proportion of ducks was recorded and Pooley claimed £1 each for them, while prepared to pay a shilling for the other scores. The man with whom the bet had been made said it was a catch bet on Pooley's part, and he declined to pay. The man's name was Ralph Donkin. His refusal to pay led to a scene of disorder, and brought Pooley's services with the team to an unpleasant end.*

'*We had to go next to Otago and at the close of the match there Pooley was arrested on a charge of 'having at Christchurch maliciously injured property above the value of £5, and also of assaulting Donkin'. For the assault he had £5 and costs to pay. In the other charge he had as partner in trouble Alf Bramall, a supernumerary attached to our team. The two were committed for trial, bail being allowed for £100, with two sureties of £50 each. We never saw Pooley again during that tour. He and his companion were tried before the Supreme Court at Christchurch on April 6th, and found not guilty. The local public thought he had been hardly used in having been taken away from the team. They subscribed £50 for division between Pooley and Bramall, and in addition they presented Pooley with a gold ring. The old Surrey wicket-keeper had to make the journey back to England alone.'*

Pooley's experience was only one of the trials the team faced during their stay in New Zealand, which was financially a failure; stories live of a most frightening experience in Otira Gorge, when what should have been a shallow ford was a rising torrent of water and the coach came to grief in mid-stream. The four horses were dead beat and fell down in the water and the players leapt off the coach up to their waists in rushing water to free the horses. They had to walk on, wearied and exhausted, and with saturated clothing, to find shelter for the night. The hotels were described as being of the crudest and most trying character. But from a purely cricket point of view affairs were reasonably happy. The side was in New Zealand from the first match in Auckland on January 29 until the final game at Invercargill ending on March 8. Eight matches were played against combinations of Twenty-Two and Eighteen, England winning six and drawing two. And so back to Australia for the eighteenth match of the tour—and England v. Australia—Eleven each side—and the First Test Match!

THE FIRST TEST—MARCH 15, 1877

It was warm and sunny in Melbourne on March 15, 1877, when Charles Bannerman took guard and prepared to receive the first ball from Alfred Shaw in what has come to be universally regarded as the first Test Match. Bannerman did not commit his name to history purely because he scored the first run in a Test Match—he happened to make 165. Whether or not contemporary historians will fall out over the question of this being the first recognised Test match is quite immaterial; what cannot be disputed is that both sides were very much below full strength. W. G. Grace was missing to begin with. These early Australian tours were, as said earlier, organised by private individuals, and until M.C.C. took over the management of official touring teams in 1903–4, the sides were never fully representative. But the same can be said of Australia. In spite of being the home side they had considerable difficulty in their selection. Evans, Allen and Spofforth (three bowlers who had caused the England players some problems) all declined to play, the latter stating categorically that the absence of Murdoch to keep wicket was his reason for refusing to take part.

Bannerman's was a truly remarkable performance. He scored 165 before retiring hurt after receiving a blow on the hand; the next highest score by an Australian was 18—and this by Garrett, the number nine. Due to Bannerman's superhuman effort, Australia reached a total of 245; a collection was taken to mark Bannerman's feat and it raised one pound a run. England were 49 runs short of Australia's first innings total. Jupp, who opened, hit 63, Charlwood scored 36, and Hill, coming in at number nine, scored an unbeaten 35. England were all out for 196, but they swiftly struck back. Shaw and Ulyett, who had had a comparatively quiet time in the first innings, bowled magnificently, and the Australian innings was soon in some disarray from which it was never able completely to recover. Shaw (5) and Ulyett (4) had taken the first nine wickets to fall, until James Lillywhite bowled the last man in. Australia were all out for 104; England thus needed 154 to win and were favourites to get them, but they were shattered by the bowling of Kendall, who had taken only one wicket in the first innings; this time he took seven, to finish with an aggregate of eight for 109. England's first four batsman totalled 79 between them; the other seven contributed only 24—there were 5 extras.

Australia had won by 45 runs. There was great jubilation but also a few uncomplimentary remarks addressed to the England cricketers. *The Australasian* wrote that this was the weakest side by a long way that had ever played in the Colonies, notwithstanding the presence among them of Shaw, who was termed the premier bowler of England. It added: 'If Ulyett, Emmett and Hill are fair specimens of the best fast bowling in England, all we can say is, either they have not been in their proper form in this Colony or British bowling has sadly deteriorated.' *Scores and Biographies* had this to say: 'The defeat of England must candidly be attributed to fatigue, owing principally to the distance they had to travel each match, to sickness, and to high living. England were never fresh in any of their engagements, and, of course, had not near their best Eleven.' But what were the facts? Well, the party had landed from its New Zealand trip only the day before the match began. The date had been fixed to allow a few days after landing, but the ship was delayed *en voyage*, and the accommodation had been so poor that some of the party had been obliged to sleep on deck. They were in no shape for a serious game of cricket, least of all Armitage, who had something of a nightmare match. In bowling to Bannerman, he tossed one ball wide over the batsman's head—a delivery that brought forth the remark that the Australians could not reach Armitage's bowling with a clothes prop! The next ball he rolled along the ground; worse still, Armitage dropped Bannerman at mid-off, off Shaw, before he had reached double figures. All in all, for the players of England it was an unhappy match. And it was the first time that an Australian side confined to eleven players had defeated any eleven from England.

THE SECOND TEST

So nettled were the English party that they were anxious to arrange another match on level terms (eleven players each side) and this was done. On Saturday, March 31, 1877 and the Monday, Tuesday and Wednesday following, England met the Combined Australians on the Melbourne Ground. This time, Mr. Spofforth sank his differences, and was in the Australian team, and with his presence in their side the local public predicted a second victory. But England won by four wickets, due principally to the splendid batting of George Ulyett, who scored 52, in the first innings and 63 in the next. This time the Australian public accused

England of 'kidding' in the first match in order to obtain another game and another gate. On a previous occasion when Spofforth and Evans had bowled the side out for 35, and in the next innings Armitage scored 38, a critic asked: 'how can they be playing square, when they make only 35 one day between all of them, and on another day one man makes more than the whole of the team put together?'

Australia again won the toss, but their early batsmen wilted in the face of a fine piece of fast bowling by Hill, who took the first four wickets to fall, including the valuable prize of Bannerman, who had been strongly backed by the great gambling community to score a lot more runs; Hill bowled him for 19. Midwinter was top scorer for Australia with 31 and Australia were all out for 122. Spofforth, it will be remembered, had refused to play in the first match because Murdoch was not chosen to keep wicket. Spofforth, apparently, held the view that only Murdoch was able to take his bowling effectively. It seems that Blackham lost little time in proving to Spofforth how wrong he was. In Spofforth's third over, a fast delivery lifted, and Blackham, standing up, stumped Shaw brilliantly. As Kendall had previously bowled Jupp for a duck, England were 4 for two and remarks were already being made about the poor quality of the English side in derisory terms.

Throughout cricket's long and enduring history, the inherent steel-like toughness of Yorkshiremen has driven back many a foe in adversity. Yorkshire cricket is taught in a hard school, but like a golden thread it has entwined all the classical ages of cricket. Here, at Melbourne, on this March day in 1877 Yorkshire won a match for England. The scores of the five Yorkshiremen were: 49, 52, 48, 49 and 21. The scores of the other six players from Surrey, Notts and Sussex were: 0, 1, 14, 7, 2, 0. Greenwood (49), Ulyett (52), Emmett (48), Hill (49) and Armitage (21) carried England to a score of 261 and a lead of 139. The demon Spofforth had taken three for 67.

Australia batted consistently right down the card in their second innings, Gregory, the captain and number ten, scoring 43, the top score. England's attempt to score the 121 required for victory began calamitously. They were 9 for three and half the side were out for 76, but Ulyett stood in the breach once again with a magnificent 63. Hill struck the winning blow. England were home by four wickets, but even this victory did not alter the view of the Australian public that this was a weak England side, certainly the weakest of the four who had toured Australia.

They had a very high regard for the batting capabilities of Ulyett—and well they might have done—and they thought there were one or two average batsmen, but they rated Kendall ahead of any of the England fast bowlers. 'We would counsel whoever may enter into future speculations for importing an England XI', advised one writer, 'to bear in mind the great improvement of colonial cricket, and not to imagine that anything will do for Australia.'

Only one more match of this long tour remained—against Twenty-Two of South Australia; a low scoring game was left drawn with Ulyett making another fifty. So ended a tour which had begun on November 16 in Adelaide and had continued through Sydney, Newcastle, Goulburn, Melbourne, Ballarat, Geelong, Auckland, Wellington, Taranaki, Nelson, Greymouth, Christchurch, Invercargill, Otago, Melbourne, Sandhurst, Ballarat, Aratat, and back to Adelaide, ending on April 16. In view of the conditions of travel this was an immense undertaking.

THE FUTURE

What the tour had shown was that there had been a tremendous improvement in the standards of Australian cricket. Alfred Shaw wrote at the time: 'Cricket education is of a much higher type in the Colonies now; so high, in fact, that I am afraid they are the masters and we the pupils.' So even a century ago we were prepared to acknowledge Australian mastery on the cricket field!

The Australians themselves had not been too sure of their own prowess until they won the match on level terms in Melbourne. Prior to this, Lillywhite and Shaw had done their best to persuade the Australians to undertake a tour of England, and had even offered to accept the financial responsibility, so sure were they that the tour would be a success; the Australians had demurred, but their victory at Melbourne brought about a change of heart, and an immediate tour was planned, as an Australian enterprise, in a financial sense.

It was only a year later that the first Australian visit was paid to England. That tour is another story. What should not be forgotten is the part played by these early heroes; their adventurous spirit in the first place, and the hazards of a tour such as was undertaken a hundred years ago. Here is a quotation from the diaries of one of them:

> *'Jupp was suffering martyrdom from rheumatism, sciatica or something of the kind, and became so helpless from pains in the hips and loins that he could not walk or even get out of his berth without assistance. Selby and Shaw were as miserable from cold as two men could be. Hill appeared to be sickening for the measles or something of that kind, Ulyett said he wished himself in Sheffield, never to be tempted to go to sea again. In fact, all the party had an acute attack of the doldrums.'*

What they endured laid the foundation stone of one of the greatest sporting institutions the world has known. Alfred Shaw wrote at the conclusion of the tour: 'Let it not be forgotten that cricket has played a most important part in this happy concord', and the two events which marked its origin were the matches that James Lillywhite and his men played in March and April A.D. 1877 at Melbourne.

It is unlikely we *shall* ever forget—any of us.

THE FIRST TEST MATCH

LILLYWHITE'S TEAM V. VICTORIA AND N.S.W.

At Melbourne, Thursday, Friday, Saturday, March 15, 16, 17, 1877.
Australia won by 45 runs.

Victoria and New South Wales

C. Bannerman (*N.S.W.*) retired hurt	165	— b Ulyett	4
N. Thompson (*N.S.W.*) b Hill	1	— c Emmett b Shaw	7
T. Horan (*Victoria*) c Hill b Shaw	12	— c Selby b Ulyett	20
*D. W. Gregory (*N.S.W.*) run out	1	— b Shaw	3
B. B. Cooper (*Victoria*) b Southerton	15	— b Shaw	3
W. E. Midwinter (*Victoria*) c Ulyett b Southerton	5	— c Southerton b Ulyett	17
E. J. Gregory (*N.S.W.*) c Greenwood b Lillywhite	0	— c Emmett b Ulyett	11
†J. M. Blackham (*Victoria*) b Southerton	17	— lbw b Shaw	6
T. W. Garrett (*N.S.W.*) not out	18	— c Emmett b Shaw	0
T. Kendall (*Victoria*) c Southerton b Shaw	3	— not out	17
J. Hodges (*Victoria*) b Shaw	0	— b Lillywhite	8
B 4. 1-b 2, w 2	8	B 5, 1-b 3	8

1/2 2/40 3/41 4/118   245   1/7 2/27 3/31   104
5/142 6/143 7/197 8/242 9/245   4/31 5/35 6/58 7/71
                               8/75 9/75

Bowling: *First Innings*—Shaw 55.3–34–51–3; Hill 23–10–42–1; Ulyett 25–12–36–0; Southerton 37–11–61–3; Armitage 3–0–15–0; Lillywhite 14–5–19–1; Emmett 12–7–13–0. *Second Innings*—Shaw 34–16–38–5; Hill 14–6–18–0; Ulyett 19–7–39–4; Lillywhite 1–0–1–1.

James Lillywhite's Team

†H. Jupp (*Surrey*) lbw b Garrett	63	— lbw b Midwinter	4
†J. Selby (*Notts.*) c Cooper b Hodges	7	— c Horan b Hodges	38
H. Charlwood (*Sussex*) c Blackham b Midwinter	36	— b Kendall	13
G. Ulyett (*Yorkshire*) lbw b Thompson	10	— b Kendall	24
A. Greenwood (*Yorkshire*) c E. J. Gregory b Midwinter	1	— c Midwinter b Kendall	5
T. Armitage (*Yorkshire*) c Blackham b Midwinter	9	— c Blackham b Kendall	3
A. Shaw (*Notts.*) b Midwinter	10	— st Blackham b Kendall	2
T. Emmett (*Yorkshire*) b. Midwinter	8	— b Kendall	9
A. Hill (*Yorkshire*) not out	35	— c Thompson b Kendall	0
*James Lillywhite (*Sussex*) c and b Kendall	10	— b Hodges	4
J. Southerton (*Surrey*) c Cooper b Garrett	6	— not out	1
L-b 1	1	B 4, 1-b 1	5

1/23 2/79 3/98 4/109   196   1/0 2/7 3/20 4/22   108
5/121 6/135 7/145 8/145 9/168   5/62 6/68 7/92 8/93 9/100

Bowling: *First Innings*–Hodges 9–0–27–1; Garrett 18.1–10–22–2; Kendall 38–16–54–1; Midwinter 54–21–78–5; Thompson 17–10–14–1. *Second Innings*– Hodges 7–5–7–2; Garrett 2–0–9–0; Kendall 33.1–12–55–7; Midwinter 19–7–23–1; D. W. Gregory 5–1–9–0.

Umpires: Curtis Reid and B. Terry

THE SECOND TEST MATCH

LILLYWHITE'S TEAM V. VICTORIA AND N.S.W.

At Melbourne, March 31, April 2, 3, 4, 1877. England won by four wickets.

Victoria and New South Wales

N. Thompson (*N.S.W.*) lbw b Hill	18	— b Lillywhite	41
C. Bannerman (*N.S.W.*) b Hill	19	— c Jupp b Ulyett	30
*J. M. Blackham (*Victoria*) c Lillywhite b Hill	5	— lbw b Southerton	26
T. W. Garrett (*N.S.W.*) b Hill	12	— c Jupp b Lillywhite	18
T. J. D. Kelly (*Victoria*) b Ulyett	10	— b Southerton	35
W. Midwinter (*Victoria*) c Emmett b Lillywhite	31	— c Greenwood b Lillywhite	12
F. R. Spofforth (*N.S.W.*) b Ulyett	0	— b Hill	17
W. L. Murdoch (*N.S.W.*) run out	3	— c Shaw b Southerton	8
T. Kendall (*Victoria*) b Lillywhite	7	— b Southerton	12
*D. W. Gregory (*N.S.W.*) not out	1	— c Ulyett b Lillywhite	43
J. Hodges (*Victoria*) run out	2	— not out	0
B 8, 1-b 5, w 1	14	B 10, 1-b 7	17

1/29 2/29 3/50 4/60   122   1/88 2/112 3/135   259
5/96 6/104 7/108 8/114 9/119   4/169 5/169 6/196 7/203
                             8/221 9/259

Bowling: *First Innings*–Shaw 42–27–30–0; Lillywhite 29–17–36–2; Hill 27–12–27–4; Ulyett 14.1–6–15–2. *Second Innings*–Shaw 32–19–27–0; Lillywhite 41–15–70–4; Hill 21–9–43–1; Ulyett 19–9–33–1; Emmett 13–6–23–0; Southerton 28.1–13–46–4.

James Lillywhite's Team

*H. Jupp (*Surrey*) b Kendall	0	— b Kendall	1
A. Shaw (*Notts.*) st Blackham b Spofforth	1	— not out	0
A. Greenwood (*Yorkshire*) b Hodges	49	— c Murdoch b Hodges	22
H. Charlwood (*Sussex*) c Kelly b Kendall	14	— b Kendall	0
J. Selby (*Notts.*) b Kendall	7	— b Spofforth	2
G. Ulyett (*Yorkshire*) b Spofforth	52	— c Spofforth b Hodges	63
T. Emmett (*Yorkshire*) c Kendall b Spofforth	48	— b Midwinter	8
A. Hill (*Yorkshire*) run out	49	— not out	17
T. Armitage (*Yorkshire*) c Thompson b Midwinter	21		
*James Lillywhite (*Sussex*) not out	2		
J. Southerton (*Surrey*) c Thompson b Kendall	0		
B 5, 1-b 12, n-b 1	18		
		B 8, 1-b 1	9

1/0 2/4 3/55 4/72   261   1/2 2/8   (6 wkts.) 122
5/88 6/162 7/196 8/255 9/259   3/9 4/54 5/76 6/112

Bowling: *First Innings*–Kendall 52.2–21–82–4; Spofforth 29–6–67–3; Midwinter 21–8–30–1; Hodges 12–2–37–1; Garrett 5–2–10–0; Thompson 11–6–17–0. *Second Innings*– Kendall 17–7–24–2; Spofforth 15–3–44–1; Midwinter 13.1–6–25–1; Hodges 6–2–13–2; Garrett 1–0–7–0.

Umpires: B. Terry and S. Cosstick.

This is the first time *Wisden* has printed the full scores of these two famous matches.

F. R. FOSTER—A PRINCE OF THE GOLDEN AGE [1976]

BY ROWLAND RYDER

Rowland Ryder's tribute to the great Warwickshire all-rounder Frank Foster is curiously incomplete, making no reference to the two most dramatic facts of all. Foster's brilliant career was over by the time he was twenty-five, but Ryder surprisingly avoids the question of why. During the Great War Foster was lamed in a motor-cycle accident and was never able to bowl again. Long after he retired he was approached by the then England captain, Douglas Jardine, to explain his methods in the triumphant tour of 1911–12. Foster had used six leg-side fieldsmen and banged them into the batsman's ribs, for which reason he is sometimes nominated as the unwitting begeter of the Bodyline crisis of 1932–33. But Foster had always maintained a perfect length and never made bodily attacks on the batsman. Later he wrote:

> Jardine came to me and he asked me for my leg-side placings. I gave them to him. Had I known to what purpose they would be put in Australia, I would never have given them.

As to his brilliance in Australia in 1911–12, thereby hangs a tale. In 1921, in the first post-war visit to England of an Australian touring side, the host country was so outclassed that the Tests were barely contests at all, and it is not hard to understand why. One of their great bowlers, Colin Blythe, had died in Flanders. Their two star batsmen, Jack Hobbs and J. W. Hearne, were too ill to play. Foster was too lame ever to play the first-class game again.

But it was in the bowling department that England, decimated by Gregory, Macdonald and Mailey, were most woefully outclassed, a fact which raises an extremely vexed question, one which nobody has ever attempted to answer, and very few even to acknowledge, in the seventy years which have passed since. In 1911–12, a total of 95 Australian Test wickets fell, of which Foster and Barnes between them took 66. Of Foster's fate we know. But what of his partner? In 1921 Barnes was still the best bowler in the world. At the age of 48, he was a year younger than Wilfred Rhodes would be five years later when recalled to the national side. Yet no record exists, no faint hint, no scrap of evidence, no wisp of rumour, that anybody ever considered inviting Barnes to return to the England colours. Pelham Warner, displaying his familar mastery of the art of telling lies through the deployment of half-truths, wrote in defence of the selectors that 'S. F. Barnes had retired from first-class cricket.' Not a word about second-class cricket.

After the war, the minatory Barnes, bitterly laughing to scorn the Establishmentarian claptrap about playing up and playing the game, turned his back on first-class cricket once and for all, preferring the lesser labours and higher pay of the leagues and the comfortable backwaters of the minor counties. In his twenty seasons with Staffordshire he took 1432 wickets for eight runs each; in thirty-eight summers in the leagues he took another 3741 at under seven runs each. As late as 1928 the West Indian tourists nominated him as the best bowler they had encountered. In 1934, in his sixty-second year, he took 86 wickets for Staffordshire at less than eleven runs each. By the time the 1921 Australians arrived, Barnes had already mastered the delivery which so many of his predecessors had dreamed about, the fast leg-break. Yet the selectors, who comprised R. H. Spooner and two others who had never played Test cricket, John Daniell and H. K. Foster, never thought to send for him.

The explanation can only be that those responsible for the selection of England sides feared Barnes so much that they decided that ignominious defeat was infinitely preferable to reliance on this cussed man. Cardus wrote of him: 'He was the living image in flannels of the "Spirit of Denial"'; Patrick Morrah says of him: 'He was not remarkable for joie de vivre. He was dour, intense, unsmiling, quick to take offence.' Even MacLaren, who first plucked him from obscurity to place him centre-stage in world cricket, soon came to question his own wisdom. On the voyage out to Australia, passengers were warned that high seas put all lives at risk, at which, MacLaren, seeking for crumbs of comfort, murmured: 'If we do go down, the bugger Barnes will go down with us.' The most vivid testimony of all comes from the Staffordshire cricketer who played alongside Barnes but is better remembered as the editor of Punch. Bernard Hollowood quotes his own father, who played in the same side as Barnes, to the effect that 'he was as mean as they come'. Hollowood Junior goes on:

> His colleagues admired his skills, but were terrified of incurring his displeasure and found games with him a sore trial. So there was no great outcry when the selectors omitted the name of Barnes from their national elevens. I suspect that on these occasions—and they were numerous—all the more easy-going Players and most of the Gentlemen breathed a sigh of relief. I was frankly afraid of Barnes, afraid of his scowling displeasure, his ferocious glare, his crippling silences and his humiliating verbal scorn, and I played with him and against him only when he was beginning to mellow! 'There's only one captain of a side', he used to say, 'when I'm bowling—me!'

What Hollowood is saying is that grown men went in such fear of Barnes that they would rather lose matches than have anything to do with him. Or to put it another way, in Barnes England possessed the one cricketer in the world capable of putting the Australian face out of countenance. And chose to ignore him. It is interesting to speculate on whether the history of the 1921 series might have been different had Frank Foster been one of the selectors. Probably not. The spurning of Barnes was by no means the only blunder of the selectors. Mead was passed over until the series was lost, and E. W. Swanton sighs for George Gunn, 'whose total omission seems at this distance to have been an almost incredible piece of folly'. Surely, as the calamitous 1921 series unfolded, a suspicion of a smile softened if only for a moment the features of Sydney Barnes. And surely also the tourists must have gone to bed each night shaking with laughter.

F R. FOSTER was one of the most astonishing performers ever to have . played the game of cricket. His career lasted from 1908 until 1914; it was all over when he was twenty-five. A dashing personality, an inspiring captain with tremendous flair, a brilliant all-rounder, his enthusiastic verve set the cricketing world ablaze. At the age of twenty-two he had accepted the captaincy of a sadly struggling Warwickshire eleven and led them to victory after victory. After that, he went to Australia, and with Sydney Barnes, shattered the Australian batting. 'Before he was twenty-four' wrote P. F. Warner, 'he had done enough to earn everlasting fame in the history of cricket.'

Frank Rowbotham Foster was born on January 31, 1889, in Small Heath, Birmingham. He was of Lincolnshire descent, and was not related to the famous Foster family of Worcestershire. He attended what was then Solihull Grammar School, where he played his earliest cricket, and later played for Hall Green, gaining a reputation as a fastish left-arm bowler.

He got his first chance for Warwickshire in June 1908, playing against Derbyshire at Derby. He made an impressive start as a bowler, taking six wickets in the match for 52 runs. Warwickshire's next match was against Surrey, and the nineteen-year-old Frank Foster celebrated his first visit to London by capturing the wickets of Jack Hobbs and Tom Hayward. He played altogether five games in 1908, finishing with twenty-three wickets for seventeen runs each.

By 1909 he had become an established member of the side, under the captaincy of A. C. S. Glover; he played in seventeen matches, taking 48 wickets at 26 runs a wicket and scoring 530 runs for an average of 24; against the Australians he had the satisfaction of clean bowling Victor Trumper for 1. 'F. R. Foster, one of the most promising all round cricketers in the county' ran the Warwickshire report in *Wisden*, 'did admirable service with bat and ball . . . and he took more wickets than anyone except Santall.' It was suggested that he might have been still more effective but for sacrificing accuracy of pitch to a higher rate of speed—a tactful way of saying that he sometimes tried to bowl too fast! Like a good many left arm bowlers, he was a right-hand batsman, and he was already showing signs that he believed in keeping the scorers occupied.

Warwickshire had a poor season in 1910. A. C. S. Glover had resigned the captaincy and his official successor, H. J. Goodwin, could play in only half the matches. That season Foster came into his own as a bowler, taking a hundred wickets for the first time. For Warwickshire he took 91 wickets at 22 runs each, and in three games for the Gentlemen against the Players he took altogether 17 wickets for 242 runs, his victims including Hobbs, Hayward, J. T. Tyldesley (twice) and Rhodes (twice). The Warwickshire report in *Wisden* described Foster as 'a long way the most brilliant all-round man in the county'.

It seemed likely that 1911 would be even more disastrous for Warwickshire than 1910, especially as H. J. Goodwin was no longer available. Who then, should be the new captain? In desperation the committee offered the job to F. R. Foster, who like a batsman trying to run himself out, answered 'Yes', 'No', and finally, 'Yes' again.

Warwickshire's first match in the long dry summer of 1911 was against Surrey, and they lost by an innings early in the second day. It was this disaster which caused Foster, who had not played in the Surrey match, to change his mind and accept the captaincy.

Victories immediately followed, against Lancashire, Leicestershire and Sussex. Against Lancashire Foster showed uncanny flair by introducing the young Jack Parsons (now the Rev. Canon J. H. Parsons)—a promising batsman but hardly a first-class bowler—into the attack. The object was to capture J. T. Tyldesley's wicket. The move succeeded brilliantly. Parsons got Tyldesley caught behind and was then taken off. In Warwickshire's seventh match, against Derbyshire at Blackwell, Derbyshire needed 40 to win with five wickets to fall. At this point Foster took off Warwickshire's opening bowler Frank Field and put on A. B. Crawford—'a casual member of the side, a tall, bumpy fast bowler', as Foster described him. Crawford took two wickets and Warwickshire won by 14 runs.

By the end of June, Warwickshire had played eight matches, having won four and lost four. This was not bad going, but they were well down the Championship table and it is doubtful if, at this juncture, Foster himself had any serious hopes of winning the Championship. A new system of scoring had been introduced: there were five points for a win, three for a win on first innings and one point to the side behind, drawn matches with no decision on the first innings were not counted. As the sixteen counties competing in the 1911 Championship played varying numbers of matches, positions in the table were worked out on percentages.

During the remainder of the season Warwickshire, playing like a revitalised side, and responding superbly to the leadership of their twenty-two-year-old captain, won nine of their twelve remaining matches, and they very nearly won two of the three drawn games. In doing all this they picked up fifty-four points out of sixty.

July was heralded with an innings victory against Hampshire; next Warwickshire had much the better of a draw against Surrey, Foster scoring a chanceless 200 in three hours. Victories followed against Northamptonshire, Sussex and Gloucestershire. Foster scored 98 in an hour and a half against Northamptonshire, and took five for 25 in their second innings; he made 65 and took five for 52 against Sussex; in a seven wicket win against Gloucestershire he took five for 76 and three for 59; he also scored 56 and 87.

In their fourteenth Championship match Warwickshire completely outclassed Yorkshire at Harrogate. Set 257 to win Yorkshire collapsed before the bowling of Field and Foster, and were all out for 58. It is recorded that during this innings, one of the Yorkshire batsmen walked out without an appeal being made, saying that he had had enough. Foster made 60 in forty minutes and 101 in an hour and three-quarters. As a fast scorer he seems to rank second only to Jessop; his big innings were generally scored at 60 or more runs an hour.

There was a drawn game at Southampton, and then the crowds flocked to Edgbaston for the Bank Holiday match against Worcestershire. Nineteen thousand enthusiasts saw Foster score 85 in ninety minutes on the first day, and then later take four of the five wickets that fell before stumps were drawn. Worcestershire however, narrowly escaped defeat.

Next came a win against Derbyshire. Foster made 70 in as many minutes in the second innings, after which he took six for 37 in Derbyshire's total of 180. Lancashire were beaten by an innings—Foster scored 98 in a hundred minutes—and Leicestershire were defeated in two days at Hinckley.

The last match, against Northamptonshire, has passed into Warwickshire folklore. In order to win the Championship Warwickshire had to win the match. 'Are you going to beat 'em, Mr. Foster?' shouted a spectator, as the team left New Street station, Birmingham. 'Beat 'em? We'll paralyse 'em!' he is reported to have called back.

Northamptonshire won the toss, but were all out before lunch for 73, Foster taking five for 18 in 13.2 overs. At the end of the second day, Northamptonshire with seven wickets down, needed 71 to avoid an innings defeat. Foster recounted that on that night, most of the Warwickshire team were too excited to go to bed at all. Foster himself tried to get to bed at 4 a.m., but was quickly roused to play a game of 'Farmer's Glory', and he adds that the sun was shining when the team left the card table for the breakfast table. Northamptonshire lost their last three wickets in thirty-five minutes, and Warwickshire returned in triumph to New Street, where a joyous crowd awaited them. *Punch* celebrated the occasion with a full page cartoon, captioned 'Two Gentlemen of Warwickshire' depicting William Shakespeare shaking hands with a beflannelled Frank Foster. 'Tell Kent from me she hath lost' says Foster, and Shakespeare replies 'Warwick, thou art worthy'.

Warwickshire's success was indeed a splendid achievement; not since the Championship had expanded in 1895 with the introduction of new counties, had any team outside the Big Six—Kent, Lancashire, Middlesex, Nottinghamshire, Surrey and Yorkshire—won the Championship. Foster himself had played an enormous part in his county's success. Not only had his leadership revitalised the side; he was top of both batting and bowling averages, scoring 1,383 runs for an average of 44.61, and taking 116 wickets for an average of 19 runs a wicket. Foster himself, summing up Warwickshire's success in his memoirs* had this to say: 'The very hot season, the dry and fast wickets, the "keeping" of "Tiger" Smith, the will to win, the absurd changes of bowling, the friendship between the committee and myself, the advice of R. V. Ryder, the wickets prepared by Bates our groundsman, the friendliness of all spectators, the encouragement from the crowd, the help of the new ball and the help of Frank Field at Harrogate plus the help of Fate at Northampton made Warwickshire the Champion County for the season of 1911'.

* Cricketing Memories, by Frank Foster, London Publishing Co.

Wisden chose him as one of the Five Cricketers of the Year for the 1912 issue, the others being Phil Mead, Herbert Strudwick, Jack Hearne and Warwickshire's own Septimus Kinneir. 'Not since W. G. Grace in the early days of the Gloucestershire eleven' said *Wisden* in the Warwickshire report, 'has so young a captain been such a match-winning force on a county side. Foster was always getting runs, always taking wickets and over and above all this, he proved himself a truly inspiring leader.'

Frank Foster was naturally chosen to tour Australia at the end of the season; and his bowling partnership with Sydney Barnes proved the most important factor in England winning the Ashes. The M.C.C. team was to have been led by P. F. Warner, but, after scoring 151 in the first match, against South Australia, he became ill, and took no further part in the tour, J. W. H. T. Douglas deputising as captain. Foster opened the tour with centuries against South Australia and Victoria. He also acquired the reputation of being the best-dressed man in the team, inspiring an Australian rhymester to write:

> *'The flannel pants of Foster cost*
> *A guinea clear a pair.'*

In five Test matches Foster's performances as a batsman were creditable without being remarkable, his scores being 56, 21, 9, 71, 50, 15, 4–226 runs for an average of 32.28, his 71 being a most un-Fosterlike innings lasting nearly three hours.

It was as a bowler that he excelled himself. His greatest performance was perhaps in the third Test match. Australia in their first innings, batting on a perfect wicket, were all out for 133. 'Foster was in his deadliest form' wrote *Wisden*. 'He began by bowling eleven overs, six maidens for eight runs and one wicket and finished up with the remarkable average of five wickets for 36.'

His final analysis read:

Overs	Maidens	Runs	Wickets
26	9	36	5

His five victims were Kelleway, Hordern, Armstrong, Clem Hill and Minnett. The left-handed Clem Hill was out first ball, stumped by 'Tiger' Smith off Foster's bowling, while attempting a glide. P. F. Warner has described this planned piece of stumping as 'one of the technical masterpieces of the game'. 'Tiger' Smith himself, who 'kept' to Foster's bowling through much of the latter's career, and who recalls so vividly this Test match series, claims that Clem Hill should have been given out 'stumped Smith, bowled Foster 0' in his second innings, and that he was out by about twelve inches. However, the umpire thought otherwise, and Clem Hill went on to make 98. England won this match by seven wickets and the series by four matches to one.

Foster took five for 92 in the second innings of the first Test, six for 91 in the second innings of the second Test, four for 77 and three for 38 in the fourth Test, and four for 43 in 30.1 overs in the second innnings of the fifth

Test. The final figures of the Foster—Barnes combination for the five Test matches make interesting reading:

	Overs	Maidens	Runs	Wickets	Average	
Foster	275.5	58	692	32	21.62	
Barnes	297	64	778	34	22.88	

1912 was the year of the rain-ridden Triangular Tournament, involving England, Australia and South Africa, each country playing three Test matches against the other two, so that each country played six matches in all. Foster played in all six Tests for England. He did great things in the first Test match against South Africa, taking five for 16 in the first innings—all clean bowled, and three for 54 in the second. In general however, the pitches were too slow for him, and a third full season without a rest must have taken its toll. For Warwickshire he scored 600 runs for an average of 19.61, but considering the slow pitches, did surprisingly well with his bowling, taking 85 wickets at 16 runs a wicket.

In 1913 he was clearly not himself, and had to rest for three matches. He scored 782 runs for Warwickshire, including a century against Hampshire, but his ninety-one wickets—again on the hard fast pitches that he loved— cost over 24 runs a wicket.

In 1914, Frank Foster was back on top form. He scored 1,396 runs for an average of thirty-five, and took 117 wickets for a little over eighteen runs a wicket; his bowling figures, in fact, were slightly better than they were in 1911. Against Worcestershire, at Dudley, Foster played the innings of his life, scoring 305 not out in four hours and twenty minutes; during the course of this innings a stand of 166 with 'Tiger' Smith, who made 42, lasted seventy minutes.

The last game that Foster ever played for Warwickshire was against Surrey at Edgbaston on August 27, 28 and 29. He opened the innings, both as a batsman and as a bowler, scoring 81—'a delightful innings' says *Wisden*—and 7; taking four for 24 and five for 48 in a Warwickshire victory against a fine Surrey side. Eight of Foster's nine victims were clean bowled.

It is difficult to assess F. R. Foster in terms of cricketing greatness, owing to the comparative brevity of his career. It is chiefly as a bowler that he will be remembered; second as a dynamic captain, third, as a batsman. This at least can be said: as a bowler he went through an Australian tour with Sydney Barnes at his zenith, and wicket for wicket, proved himself his equal; as a captain, he evoked comparison with the young W. G. Grace; as an attacking batsman he was not far short of Jessop.

How did Foster bowl? This is what he wrote himself: 'I took a short eight-yard run, holding the ball always in my left hand with 'seam up' and I always delivered the ball from the very edge of the bowling crease.' Foster also felt very strongly that no left-hander should ever attempt to bowl over the wicket.

This is how P. F. Warner describes Foster's action. 'Bowling left-hand round the wicket with a high delivery—he was six feet tall—his action was the personification of ease. A few short steps, a graceful skip, an apparently medium-paced ball through the air, but doubling its speed as it touched the ground, he kept an exceptional length.' He did in fact once bowl two consecutive maiden overs to Jessop!

And a wicket-keeper's eye view—'I remember the first time I "kept" to him' wrote Herbert Strudwick. 'It was at Lord's in an England v. The Rest match. Seymour (Kent) was batting. The first ball Mr. Foster bowled appeared to be well on the leg side. Seymour shaped to play it to leg and I moved that way, but, believe me, we were both surprised when the ball flashed over the off stump, and when it went for four byes I thought I was in for a good afternoon.'

Foster bowled at the leg stump, and he certainly hit the wickets pretty frequently. In 1911 74 of his 116 victims were clean bowled and 10 were l.b.w.—a left-hander bowling at the edge of the crease could hardly expect more. Foster would seem to have developed his leg theory bowling during the Australian tour; in certain respects he did what Larwood was doing in Australia twenty-one years later; if Foster's thirty-two wickets, for an average of 21.62, were obtained at a slightly higher cost than Larwood's thirty-three wickets at 19.51, perhaps, all in all, Foster had a greater team to bowl against.

In his field placing for the Tests in Australia, Foster had a mid-off, cover and deep third man; wicket-keeper, long leg, a semi-circle of four close in leg side fielders (two in front of the wicket and two behind) and a mid-on. Foster's fourth, 'death trap' fieldsmen, as he called them, were George Gunn, Frank Woolley, Bill Hitch and Wilfred Rhodes: they took nine catches off his bowling in the Tests.

As a right-handed batsman he was stylish, vigorous and attacking, though *Wisden* says that his bat was not quite straight and that he took too many risks. An unfortunate motor-cycle accident in 1915 terminated his cricket career. His book of cricketing memories was published in 1930. Frank Foster died in 1958.

He was above all, a joyous cricketer, who played the game with splendid verve. During the wonderful summer of his achievement that lasted from May 1911 until March 1912, he was probably without equal on the cricket field. The photograph of him in the pavilion at Edgbaston, shows him at the wicket, modestly confident, cap set just so, bat upraised, left leg forward, prepared to meet all comers with a smile: F. R. Foster—Warwickshire and England.

TALES OF W.G. GRACE [1977]

James Gilman Recalls the Past

BY JACK ARLIDGE

Whether or not the two legal squabbles of the year will ever find their way into history, there is no question that history itself was on show in the interview with a gentleman so ancient that he remembered opening the

batting with W. G. Grace. Much less is known of Grace off the field of play
than posterity would prefer, so it is a pity that the recollections of a
nonagenarian turn out to be so familiar. Yet we are fortunate to have the
interview at all, which, to judge from the editorial introductory note, was
conducted under the very shadow of death. And it is somehow reassuring to
know the precise location of the Incident of the Collapsing Cab.

Major James Gilman gave this interview for Wisden *a few weeks before*
he died in hospital on September 14, 1976, aged 97. Gilman was elected to
M.C.C. in 1900 and there are only two older surviving members, C. H. B.
Fletcher and E. C. Wigan, elected in 1899.

THE legendary Dr. W. G. Grace strode across the dressing room and said
to a solemn faced young man: 'I'm taking you in with me to open the
innings,' and thus began a phase in the sporting life of James Gilman
which he was able to recapture in thrilling detail until his death at the age of
97 late last summer.

'It was during the reign of Queen Victoria, with the Boer War being
fought, in June, 1900' he recalled. 'I had been asked by Dr. Grace to report
to the old Crystal Palace where London County were to play the West
Indians, who were making their first tour of this country.

'I was sitting in that dressing room, with famous players all round me,
and the first time Grace spoke to me he asked: 'Are you nervous?', and his
eyes twinkled when I replied 'I'm terrified, Sir'. He then went out to toss
for innings, and it was when he came back that he told me to get padded up
and open with him. It was a kind and very shrewd move, because he could
see I'd have been reduced to a jelly if I'd had to wait to bat. It was typical of
W.G.—his bark was worse than his bite.'

Reluctant to talk about himself, still conscious of the commanding
presence of Grace in those days, Major Gilman glossed over the fact that
he made 63 and helped Grace to put on 136, and chuckled to remember
that his famous partner was out shortly after lunch for 71.

'This wasn't at all surprising' he said. 'The "Old Man" was very keen on
the catering and we had a sumptuous lunch, with hock and claret on the
table. He had a real whack of the roast, followed by a big lump of cheese.
He also tackled his whisky and seltzer, which was always his drink.

'A player named Constantine played for the West Indies, Sir Learie's
father. They were easily beaten but Grace, in that rather squeaky voice of
his, told us that he felt sure they would be very good one day. He was an
astute judge of play and players.'

Major Gilman, who lived at Shoreham-by-Sea in Sussex, watched the
Sussex matches at the nearby County Ground in Hove right up to the time
of his death, with Arthur Gilligan calling for him as he motored over from
his Pulborough home. Gilman was always being asked if Grace was the
autocrat of popular legend. Did he impose an iron will on players and
umpires alike? Was he a cheat?

Insisting that 'autocratic' was the wrong word, Major Gilman emphasised: 'He would certainly stand no nonsense. He just could not abide a non-trier in the field or slackness of any sort. I remember he caught me arriving late once and said: 'You won't be coming in with me, Gilman, you'll bat number eleven.' When all was going well he called us by our Christian names, but if he was blowing hot and cold then it was by our surnames.

'Yes, he could be awkward and fiery at times, rather frightening, come to think of it, but he was basically a kind and quite considerate man. In some matches he often felt—and quite rightly too—that the crowd had come to see him play and if he suspected a decision was a bad one he would get very angry.

'He was not very happy in a match at Derby that same season of 1900 when the home side caught us on a gluepot. A slow bowler named Hulme had the "Old Man" leg-before in the first innings—for 2 and Bestwick in the second for 0, also leg-before. I was batting at the other end so had a seat in the stalls, so to speak, to observe his reaction. The first decision did not seem a good one. Grace stalked off to the dressing room and when I went back there soon afterwards, there was a rare old rumpus. Grace had one leg out of his flannels and kept saying: 'I won't be cheated out, I've a good mind to go home.' We tried to calm him down and a whisky and seltzer came to the rescue. But the real hero was that same umpire who gave him out again!'

The awe and esteem in which Grace was held is clear, and emphasised by Major Gilman's story of the time when he was ordered to get a horse drawn cab and travel with him through London.

'Imagine my terror when the cab floor suddenly collapsed, and left us standing in the middle of Piccadilly! Grace's face was a study, but the extraordinary thing was that nobody laughed or even sniggered. There were murmurs of concern, a raising of hats by the men, sympathetic looks from the women. A dreadful moment . . .'

How did Grace compare with the great players since his day? Major Gilman who played for Cambridge University, Middlesex and Northumberland as well as London County, and was an all-round sportsman of considerable skill and ability, felt convinced the Doctor would have been an outstanding player in any age.

'He might not have the shots of Bradman nor the flowing strokes of Hammond, but he had a shot for every ball. W.G. was an orthodox batsman whether driving, pulling or cutting. No "shouldering arms" to a ball for him. He went out for his shots, and my old friend Herbert Strudwick, of Surrey and England, who used to live just round the corner from me at Shoreham-by-Sea, always maintained that he was a very easy batsman to keep wicket to. He rarely missed a ball! "Struddy" rated him as one of the greatest bats he ever saw.'

As a bowler, Grace did not turn the ball very much, Major Gilman remembered, but relied on length and flight. If he wasn't batting he liked to be bowling. He had amazing stamina, even in his fifties, for he was fifty-two in that match against the West Indians, and Gilman a stripling of twenty.

The wickets of those days were 'not too bad', but Grace might have found run-getting a little easier on modern pitches. He would certainly have become a sporting millionaire had he been playing today for, as his old opening partner recalled with a smile, 'He did not do too badly as an amateur.'

Major Gilman had vivid memories of other titans of cricket history. 'Ranji' was a brilliant batsman, elegant and composed, skilfully caressing strokes round to leg and Gilbert Jessop, contrary to many reports of his play, was never a slogger and it was not his driving which impressed most, but his magnificent square-cutting. 'I have never seen the ball cut with such power and precision.'

Major Gilman followed cricket very closely and his clarity of mind and expression was remarkable. He was a kindly critic who found much to admire in present-day cricket, and his opinions were eagerly sought as he watched play from his corner seat in the committee room at the Hove County Ground, in front of which his ashes were buried, on the pitch where Grace played for Gloucestershire against Sussex in the first match ever staged there, in 1872.

His epitaph for W.G. was: 'He had a great sense of mischief, but a twinkle in the eye' . . .

R. L. Arrowsmith writes: James Gilman, was the oldest living cricket Blue and probably the oldest first-class cricketer of any standing and the last man to open the batting in an important match with W. G. Grace. This he did for London County against the West Indians at the Crystal Palace in 1900: the match was not first-class and was the first-ever played by the West Indians in England. Gilman's share of a first-wicket stand of 136 was 63. He had been in the XI at St Paul's, but it was undoubtedly the experience of playing constantly in the next few years for London County with W. G. that made him into a good enough player to get his blue at Cambridge in 1902, his fourth year. His record for the University was not outstanding, but he fully justified his selection at Lord's. Set 272 to get in the fourth innings, Cambridge were 197 for 5 when Gilman came in to join that great batsman, S. H. Day, and they hit off the runs between them, Gilman's share being 37. He had played a few times for Middlesex in 1900 and 1901 but his first-class career ended when after 1904 London County confined themselves to club cricket. Later he played for Northumberland. He had been first-string for Cambridge in the half and had also represented them in the mile. In the last years of his life he was a constant spectator at Hove. His death leaves C. A. L. Payne, the Oxford Blue of 1906 and 1907, who has lived for many years in Vancouver, as the oldest surviving Blue.

OVER 100 YEARS OF
SCARBOROUGH FESTIVAL [1977]

BY J. M. KILBURN

Fluttering brightly across the gulf between country house cricket and the first-class game, the English Cricket Festival was a unique Victorian creation which surprisingly continues to maintain a tenuous hold on the summer itinerary. The idea that a town might for a few days each season become one huge cricket congregation was highly attractive to our great-grandparents, a generation for the most part free of the enticements of continental travel. That the Festival was essentially a Gentlemanly affair is shown by the extent to which the local grandees underwrote the expenses and dominated the social aspects of the occasion. Indeed, these extra-cricketing events were so intrinsic a part of the whole that more than a century ago Wisden was waxing eloquent on aspects of the festival at Canterbury which had marginally less than nothing to do with organised team games:

> The two county balls were crowdedly patronised by the beauty, rank and fashion of the county. The great concomitant of cricket in the Canterbury week, 'The Old Stagers' Theatricals', were 'blazes of triumphs'. (1874)

> There was pleasantly played military music on the ground each afternoon, and the usual theatricals of county balls in the city each night. (1875)

> The two County Balls appear to have been as numerously attended by the fair maids, matrons and magnates of the county as heretofor; and 'The Old Stagers' drew to the little theatre as large, lighthearted, laughing audience as they ever attracted since the theatricals of the O.S. were first played in the old theatre in 1842. (1876)

These dithyrambs reached their zenith in reports of the festival of 1881, when, in an account of a match between I Zingari and Gentlemen of England, the almanack broke new ground:

> The Old Stagers met with great success, the programme being 'The Charming Woman', 'Out of Light', 'Tit for Tat', 'A Thumping Legacy', and 'Hester's Mystery'. Lord Harris's absence was feelingly alluded to in the original epilogue. On Wednesday and Thursday the usual balls took place at the Freemasons' Hall, where dancing was kept up with great zeal.

As so it went on down the century, this charming fusion of late cuts and late nights, of dallying at the crease and dalliance behind the fronded embrasures of the nearest accessible conservatory.

None of the other festivals quite matched the splendour of Canterbury, but Scarborough has certainly proved as durable. J. M. Kilburn's all too brief account makes no mention of one of the more notorious tall stories connected with the festival and its most famous founding father, C. I. Thornton, one of the hardest hitters of a ball of his day. During one match, Thornton smashed a six into a thoroughfare adjoining the ground called Trafalgar Square. When later recounting the story to a young lady of sketchy intelligence, he was asked whether he had been playing at Lord's or the Oval at the time. The Old Stagers have long since vanished into the wings, and the only historic moment to have occurred at a festival in the years since was at Hastings in 1947 when Denis Compton, playing for South of England against the South Africans, hit his seventeenth century of the season, breaking the record of sixteen set by Jack Hobbs in 1925. Scarborough too has its claim to fame, of a rather more lugubrious nature. On the eve of the 1938 festival, Albert William Shelton, devoted functionary of the Nottingham County Cricket Club, and author of a history of Trent Bridge published in Wisden *in 1938 (see* The Wisden Papers, *1888–1946), was packing his bags in preparation for his customary visit to the Scarborough Festival when, overcome either by exertion or anticipation, he collapsed and died.*

L IKE SO many institutions of sturdy growth and long life, the Scarborough Cricket Festival derived from seed casually scattered on fertile ground. In the mid-19th century Scarborough found fashion in its spa waters, attracting visitors not only from the Yorkshire hinterland but also from London and its expanding environs. Some of the younger members of the holiday families were cricketers and sought scope for their interest by improvising teams to play against local clubs. They discovered a ready response and enjoyable cricket.

In 1871 a special occasion was designed. The Visitors arranged a two-day match against a team raised by the first Earl of Londesborough. The moving spirit among the Visitors was Charles Inglis Thornton, a London timber merchant renowned in cricket as a powerful batsman for Cambridge University, Kent, Middlesex and M.C.C. Lord Londesborough was an eager patron of sport, with a particular devotion to cricket, and his estate included a Scarborough residence.

Lord Londesborough undertook the presentation of the match. He staged it in the recreation field on Castle Hill, inviting public attendance without charge and providing marquees and enclosures for his personal guests. For his team he engaged leading Yorkshire professionals. Thornton captained the Visitors, who included two of the famous Walkers of Southgate. The game was played in showery weather on September 11 and 12 and was left drawn, but with every indication of public appeal.

It stirred fires of ambition in Robert Baker, secretary of the young Scarborough Cricket Club and himself a player of first-class standard and experience. In 1875 he persuaded Lord Londesborough and Thornton to promote another match, Yorkshire v. M.C.C., on Castle Hill and in the following year the same organisers presented nine days of September cricket to found the Festival.

After two years the Festival—or Carnival as it was commonly called—

was brought down from the windswept and inconvenient Castle Hill to the transformed ground of the Scarborough club, adjoining North Marine Road. There Baker's resolution and energy had turned a meadow into a comparative magnificence. From a rough, steeply-sloping field Scarborough constructed a splendid setting for cricket. An enclosing wall was built, the playing area was levelled to leave a terraced embankment on the seaward side, a wooden pavilion was put up and tenancy was exchanged for freehold ownership.

These undertakings involved heavy expenditure, but the cricket club found accommodating supporters. Patrons and donors carried the Festival first to possibility and then through years of establishment to an independent prosperity. Help given was in finance, hospitality and influence. Lord Londesborough opened his house to playing guests, Thornton assured prominent cricketers that the Scarborough experience was not to be missed, administrative enterprise created attractive fixtures including Australian representation.

Private patronage nurtured the Festival but the ultimate development depended on public favour. The Festival grew in strength and reputation because it was wanted by cricketers and cricket followers. It gave good value for gate money.

All the great players appeared in their turn and most of them left a memory of characteristic achievement. Thornton, the mighty hitter, hit the mightiest of sixes over bordering four-storey houses. W. G. Grace made centuries for the Gentlemen against the Players and for South v. North. Bannerman and Spofforth illustrated Australian power in batting and bowling. In the 'Golden Age' the Festival knew golden hours in innings by Ranjitsinhji, Jessop and Jackson and in 1899 a young bowler named Wildred Rhodes took nine wickets for 24 runs against the Australians.

Festival prestige grew with the passing years and Festival structure was strengthened when W. W. Leadbeater became the Scarborough secretary and a Festival character. Leadbeater was a cripple who struggled through a lifetime of disability that creased deep lines into his face and made him sometimes sharp of tongue, but he was a man of careful judgement, high principle and firm friendships.

He held office from 1898 to 1930 and raised the Festival to self-sufficiency, though the background of willing patronage remained available. He instituted the 'London Committee' which, through Lord Harris, Lord Hawke and H. D. G. Leveson Gower, ensured the assembly of players when Thornton grew old. Leadbeater's management brought pitch-covering into Festival custom and innumerable ground improvements were initiated and supervised by him. His efficient organisation gave the Festival first place in its sphere of cricket.

The Great War broke the sequence of Festivals but revival was immediate in 1919 and from then until the second interruption Scarborough was at its most profitable and prestigious. Players, professional and amateur, welcomed invitations; spectators from all parts of the country arranged co-incidental holidays; an express train, the Scarborough

Flier, ran with crowded carriages from King's Cross.

The match programme was not sacrosanct but it had a prevailing pattern of Yorkshire v. M.C.C., Gentlemen v. Players and the touring team of the season against a side under the banner of Lord Londesborough, C. I. Thornton or H. D. G. Leveson Gower. The cricket was recognised as first-class, it was undertaken seriously and specific contrivance was acceptable only if it would give general benefit. A follow-on, for example, would not be enforced at the risk of an early third-day ending, but the element of contest had to be preserved. An individual requiring a few runs or a few wickets for some personal record would be offered opportunity but not a manifest gift of the wanted wickets or runs. Play could be relaxed but it had to preserve reality. In the phrase of a Festival historian of the period, Scarborough offered 'first-class cricket on holiday'.

The holiday atmosphere was created in the background of luncheon tents and fluttering flags and a brass band. Players indulged themselves in multi-coloured caps and extravagant strokes, but custom demanded that the caps represent genuine membership of such organisations as Free Foresters, Cambridge Crusaders, Oxford Authentics and that the unusual strokes be of practical intent. The aim and the invariable achievement was pride in performance.

The Festival gained repute not only through its customs but also through association with players who served long and well. In the early 1920s A. P. F. Chapman won high regard for wonderful fielding in the covers, J. B. Hobbs for unselfish displays of his own batting at its best and J. W. H. T. Douglas became 'popularly unpopular' for dour batting that reflected his cricketing character in seeking to save losing causes. The 1930s were the decade of R. E. S. Wyatt, who was willing to bat or bowl all day and every day if necessary and of Pat Hendren who came to Festival after Festival with a smile and a practical joke and played some magnificent innings.

After the Second World War the Festival hurried back into activity and announced its return with one spectacular hit for six. C. G. Pepper, playing for the Australian Services, matched Thornton's huge straight drive of 59 years earlier over the Trafalgar Square housetops. For a few seasons of nostalgia the Festival thrived on trappings and beliefs of an era departed, but it could not evade a changing outlook on cricket and on social pattern.

There were misconceptions of Festival purpose on the field. Paying spectators were subjected to the spectacle of a fast bowler presenting slow leg-breaks. The desirable element of challenge was conspicuously absent in some of the bowling, fielding and captaincy. In one unworthy year batsmen were given their first run by connivance and legitimate appeals were forsworn. Batting and bowling figures lost meaning in a context of the first-class. A few spectators were perhaps amused, but the majority were not and cricket writers with the Festival future at heart composed firm reproof.

The lesson was quickly learned. The Festival pulled itself away from the brink of the farcical, but an older following had been disturbed and a new one was not easily promoted in changing circumstances. The family seaside holiday was giving way to the lure of the motor-car and of continental expedition. Playing resources diminished as amateurs disappeared and professionals were committed elsewhere. Australian touring teams shortened their programme in England and left before September. T.N. Pearce, who succeeded Leveson Gower in management responsibilities, found a harassing task in trying to present attractive players and fixtures. The Festival began to lose both glamour and practicality.

The chosen road to survival involved a change of format and of financial foundation. Commercial sponsorship was accepted, one-day matches were introduced and a week was substituted for nine days. Whether or not future prosperity has been assured remains for decision, but crowds have certainly been attracted to the Fenner Trophy tournament, the band still plays, the flags still fly and September cricket at Scarborough is still an enviable experience. The Festival goes optimistically into a second century of existence.

G.O. ALLEN—MR. CRICKET [1977]

BY IAN PEEBLES
(England, Middlesex, Scotland and Oxford University)

The first time I ever used Fleet Street as a device to follow the fortunes of an England tour was in the winter of 1936–37, when G. O. Allen's underdogs sailed away to do battle with Bradman and very nearly won, much to the stupefaction of all. Some idea of how fiercely partisan emotions rose to the surface of national life is conveyed by my recollection of the adult street urchins in the St. Marylebone of my childhood talking admiringly of how 'good old Gubby' was dishing the Aussies. When at last Bradman turned the tables it was generally agreed that the captain and his men had fought a brave fight, which was certainly true. But it was the age of Bradman, which meant that no visitors had much of a prospect on Australian wickets. But because of that tour, Allen became for a while an authentic folk hero.

The self-confessed eulogy of Allen by Ian Peebles which appeared in the 1977 almanack came from a man who shared most of Allen's tribal aspects: University, the City, Middlesex, all in the gathering dusk of Amateurism, which meant, for both the writer and his subject, a career in the labyrinthine purlieus of Leadenhall Street. Both men forfeited much of their playing career to the demands of the City, but both found the time to captain Middlesex and to play for England. So it is not surprising that the Peebles essay is uncritical. In his autobiography there appears a photograph of the christening of his son. The two men flanking the parents are Allen and E. W. Swanton. Swanton later became Allen's biographer. Peebles and Swanton shared a flat in bachelor days. In their differing ways, all three contributed a great deal to the game, and all three remained loyal to certain precepts which are as much social as sporting. For this reason, I feel the impulse to add a few observations of my own on the vexed question of snobbery and the class system.

When I, a hobbledehoy from the back streets near Lord's, spoke for the first time at one of M.C.C.'s winter suppers, Peebles did all he could to make me feel at ease. At a subsequent supper Allen did the same, being especially solicitous when it came to passing the roast potatoes. I had come prepared to speechify about cricket literature, but during the dessert Allen said something to me which caused me to amend my plans. He seemed genuinely intrigued by the depth of my commitment to the game, and asked me the why and wherefore. So I decided to use my speech to tell him, and the rest of the congregation. I began with my grandfather, an illiterate teenaged émigré who arrived from Russia in the back streets of St. Pancras in the summer when Dr. Grace scored 839 runs in three innings. By the time my father and his brothers arrived, between the end of the century and the outbreak of the Great War, my grandfather was still insulated from what H. G. Wells once defined as the jolly coarsenesses of English life, while the sons grew up streetwise and sportsmad. By the time I was following the fortunes of Allen's tourists, one of my uncles, famed locally as a centre forward and fast bowler, and now happily absorbed in the intricate mathematical gravities of a street bookmaking career, was paying out threepence a time to any of my contemporaries able to survive three of his underarm leg-breaks. My father would deliver me to the gates of Lord's in the days when he considered me too irresponsible to reach them unaided. I was witness to the deeds of Alex James and Jim Smith and Tommy Farr long before I was into double figures.

The question which intrigued Allen, and which I was unable to answer, was 'How?' But I do recall suggesting to him that games of all kinds were so much in the air as our disastrous century proceeded that to become acquainted with, say, the moral obliquities of Bosanquet, or the issue of Charlie Napier's sine die suspension from the Football League, or the horizontal tendencies of Jack Doyle, was literally unavoidable. I told the meeting of a newsagent's shop not ten minutes walk from Lord's, which had been run by a family much like my grandfather's. In the years leading to the Second World War, five of us would dash each teatime from our elementary school round the corner, stop short outside the shop, and, with trembling inky hands, take down the afternoon editions from the paper- rack to see how our team were doing, confident in the knowledge that one of us was the proprietor's son. We had one English grandparent among the five of us, yet between us also we spoke with a passion bordering on open warfare, for the fortunes of Kent, Middlesex, Surrey, Gloucestershire and Yorkshire. The routine was abruptly ended soon afterwards when both the corner shop and the elementary school were blown away by mental defectives in bombing planes. I hope Sir George, as he later became, believed the story, because every word of it was true.

I was too tactful that night to make any reference to our first encounter. He could never have remembered it, but I could never forget. In 1944 the Nursery nets were opened to the youth of the district. Bizarre though it may sound, the authorities had decided to make a gesture towards the improvement of cricketing techniques among the Great Unwashed, which meant that I, as a member of a youth club lodged in Ford Madox Brown's old home in Fitzroy Square, became a beneficiary of their largesse. For a few sunlit double summertime evenings, before the doodlebugs upset all calculations, we came along and played as best we could. On one of these evenings, Mr. Allen, flannelled and buckskin-booted, approached the nets with a friend, and stood there contemplating aghast the noisy solecisms of our play. I heard him turn to his companion and ask in genuine horror, 'Who let this crowd in here?' Yes, I thought to myself, if we too had attended Eton College and been coached by George Hirst, no doubt we could have made a better fist of it. I left the ground that evening outraged that the hero of Brisbane, 1936 should have changed into the villain of St. John's Wood, 1944.

When M.C.C. was about to celebrate its bicentenary, I was invited to participate in a one-hour programme for B.B.C. television, telling the history and function of the club, of which I was now a member. My selection as writer-narrator might have seemed perverse to some, including me, but I was given a whisper that an approving nod in my direction had come from Swanton. Known behind his back as the Bishop, and rumoured to be the sort of snob who would cut an earl because he was not a duke, Swanton had always gone out of his magisterial way to extend a friendly hand. In any case, I doubt the ability of any man to be unreasonable in these things when married, as Swanton is, to an outstanding amateur jazz pianist.

In the course of filming the Lord's programme, I found myself conducting a conversation with Allen in his home, backing on to the ground. The sting of the moment in the nets had long since faded, mitigated, perhaps, by those roast potatoes, and I found myself taking a liking to the man which was tinged with sadness. A series of hip operations had left him dependent on a pair of walking sticks, and he was pained by the realisation that the advent of the Test and County Cricket Board threatened the independence of his beloved club. Times had changed radically, and cricket too, since the days when he was studying under Professor Hirst, and all the while we talked, I had the sensation of lingering in a time-warp. What I could not quite bring myself to say was how much I now admired him for having stood out against the iniquities of Douglas Jardine's captaincy. He spoke in passing of his defiance of his captain on that calamitous tour, describing his threat to Jardine that if not left alone he would tell it the way it was. He ended with the recollection that on returning home in the spring of 1933, it was to discover that nobody at Lord's had any faint idea of what had been going on in Australia. When he told them, the club secretary refused to speak to him for the next two years.

And yet, on the subject of Jardine, which is to say, on the subject of sanity and sportsmanship, his generation still closes ranks whenever it sniffs a challenge. Peebles had once taken me to task in print for suggesting that Jardine might not have made the ideal ambassador, and later, when in a history of cricket butchered to make a publisher's holiday, I repeated my contempt for Jardine, Swanton was among those who assumed from my attitude that I was throwing stones indiscriminately at all chaps in coloured caps. This assumption disappointed me. It is true that I had once asked in print which was the more horrific fate, to be marooned on a desert island with Lord Harris or to be rescued from it by Lord Hawke; but the truth of the matter is that the degree to which a man ain't never bin lernt to talk proper is of less consequence than his perceptions about conduct. I have used the Allen essay as the pretext for recording these thoughts because, in my own brief dealings with them, neither Peebles nor Allen nor Swanton ever gave any indication that they considered themselves to be finer fellows than me.

IN September 1976 George Oswald Browning Allen ('Gubby' to the entire cricket world) retired as Treasurer of the M.C.C., an office he had held for twelve years. At that point he could well claim to have achieved a wider experience of the practicalities of the game of cricket than any predecessor for, in the course of a remarkable career, no man can have held so many different cricket appointments. As a player, selector and administrator, he had seen at first hand every aspect of the game with the possible exceptions of umpiring and scoring. His immediate background has always been Lord's for, besides his prominence in M.C.C. affairs he has been a great power in his own club, Middlesex; but his sphere of action has extended to the widest boundaries of the cricket playing countries.

With the M.C.C. at the centre of all cricket matters, a position it has retained in a changing world, the club has been well served by a succession of competent and devoted men without material reward, and often in the face of sharp and, occasionally, ill-informed criticism. Two names immediately come to mind as men of Lord's who, by their outstanding talents as players and administrators, are pre-eminent in the present century. They are Lord Harris and Sir Pelham Warner. Few contemporaries would dispute the addition of Gubby Allen's name to complete an illustrious trio. If this should at first sight appear to be an unduly bold claim the reader will, I hope, bear with this brief account of his qualifications and achievements and be convinced of its justice.

Each was very different in method and personality and, whilst it is not the object of this article to make profitless comparisons, it may be said that, as a great all rounder, Allen had the wider experience to bring to technical problems than the other two as batsmen pure and simple. It is also arguable that his career spanned a period of greater change and controversy (notwithstanding the bodyline rumpus) than that of any previous administrator.

Allen was born in Sydney on July 31, 1902 and came to this country when six years old. At Summerfields Preparatory School he captained the XI before going on to Eton, where his cricket career came under the influence of two remarkable men, C. M. ('Father') Wells, and George Hirst. In 1919 an injury to his back prevented him from bowling, but he made his first appearance against Harrow at Lord's as an opening batsman. It was an inauspicious start, for he was run out in the first over of the match without having received a ball, an event which King George the Fifth arrived just too late to witness. His second innings was much more successful, and he carried his bat for 69 out of a total of 143. In the next season *Wisden* remarked on his beautiful action, but the trouble with his back became so persistent that he almost abandoned his bowling altogether. Fortunately he was dissuaded from this by George Hirst. That shrewd man having bidden him to tea in his house on Agar's Plough told him that he had two invaluable qualities which only nature could bestow on a fast bowler— rhythm and the ability to make the ball hurry from the pitch. Encouraged by one he so greatly admired, Allen persevered and, not without some painful moments, overcame his affliction. In 1921 he played a couple of matches for Middlesex, 'But' as the chronicler records 'gave no warning of the great things he was to do in the future.'

Two fruitful years at Cambridge brought sharply contrasting fortunes in the University Match. When Oxford were completely routed in 1922 he took nine wickets for 78 runs. When, in the following year, the pattern of events was diametrically reversed, he played under protest that he was unfit, the truth of which was confirmed at an early stage in the game and he took but little part in it. This setback had its compensations for, almost as a last resort, he sought the services of a Mr. Blake, a famous chiropractor of the day. The treatment was efficacious and, although always rather prone to strains, he was thenceforward free from back trouble.

Allen was picked for the Gentlemen at Lord's in 1925 but it was not until late in the decade that he fulfilled his early promise for, as a hard working business man, the time he could devote to cricket was strictly limited. 1929 brought resounding success when he took all ten wickets for 40 against Lancashire, the reigning Champions, on a beautiful Lord's pitch. As one of the fielders, I can testify that it was a superb piece of fast bowling against a strong batting side and it remains a ground record for county matches. Later in the season he made 155 against Surrey at The Oval, adding 319 for the second wicket with Lee and underlining his emergence as an all-rounder of international calibre. This was realised the following year when he was picked for the Lord's Test Match. In the absence of an injured Larwood, he was called upon to lead the English attack against one of the most formidable Australian batting sides of all time, just when a perfect lifeless wicket had reached its most quiescent stage. The result will be remembered as the record score for any match at Lord's of 728 for six wickets and, for Allen, 34 barren overs for 115 runs. Undaunted, he made 57 in the second innings, helping Percy Chapman to add 125 for the sixth wicket, so saving his side from total ignominy. He did not play again in that series but, the following year, had a very good season and made a century against New Zealand at Lord's. To maintain a good balance he later took five wickets in the Oval Test for 14 runs.

Allen's playing career reached its zenith when he visited his native land with Douglas Jardine's M.C.C. side of 1932/3. Playing in all five Test Matches, he bowled magnificently, batted respectably and proved himself a first-class close fielder. As praiseworthy as his success on the field was his fibre in resisting the strong pressure his captain brought to bear on him to bowl to the packed leg side or bodyline field of which he strongly disapproved. When this practically amounted to an ultimatum he remained unmoved and Jardine, recognising a spirit as firm as his own, gracefully withdrew his insistence. Allen, for his part, continued to give his captain unwavering, loyal support for the duration of the tour.

On his return Allen was again immersed in a busy City life but reappeared to play in two Tests against Australia in 1934. He batted adequately but, still suffering from the after effects of a hernia operation, he did not repeat his bowling success of the previous series. At Old Trafford, in an effort to avoid a gigantic pit dug by O'Reilly and others, he bowled an eventful opening over of thirteen balls which included four no-balls, three wides, and two very catchable chances.

By the mid-thirties Allen was clearly the best qualified cricketer to lead England and he was duly appointed captain in 1936 for the series against India. He proved himself a most competent leader and additionally did well himself, taking 20 wickets cheaply in the defeat of India by two matches to nil, the other being a draw, a pleasant prelude to the sterner task of taking the side to Australia in the autumn. When the time came for his departure English hopes did not run very high, for Australia had regained the Ashes and looked well qualified to retain them under Bradman's captaincy. England on the other hand had several problems of selection. There was naturally great difficulty in finding an opening batsman to replace Sutcliffe and, with Larwood out of the running, there was some question if Voce was eligible and if so, whether he would accept the invitation. The latter was solved by Allen in a personal interview with Voce which ensured a powerful opening attack, but the rest of the bowling looked somewhat uncertain in Australian conditions.

All cricketers are familiar with the splendid performance of this underrated team. Led by what *Wisden* described as the 'herculean' exertions of its captain it outplayed the Australians in the first two Tests despite a plague of injuries. Had fortune not deserted it might well have won the crucial third match, the result of which was eventually determined by the weather. There was much controversy about the timing of Allen's declaration when his side was caught on an unplayable pitch and some thought that had it been earlier he might have won. But the situation was rather more complicated than it appeared to be and, as one observer reasonably remarked, the captain could scarcely be expected to have second sight besides being a weather prophet. He himself can put up a very good case for the decision he made in the circumstances. From then on fortune favoured Australia as Bradman won the next two tosses, making three in a row, all of which with the run of the weather, was a powerful advantage. No losing captain has ever been more warmly applauded than Allen, whose lead had brought so much credit to the venture.

There remains one lighter but pleasing glimpse of the exhausted captain making his return to England via America. Aubrey Smith persuaded him to take the field in Hollywood, stationing himself at first slip. There, in his seventy-fourth year, he took what his guest described as a 'blinding' catch, to the vast joy of the whole company.

Allen played no cricket in 1937 but was active again in 1938. His claims to lead England against Australia in that year must have been very strong in ordinary circumstances, but Hammond had turned amateur and also had a powerful lobby. The selectors finally preferred Hammond, who drew the series with Australia and defeated South Africa, but proved a very much less effective captain in Australia later on. This did not end Allen's career as an international cricketer, for in 1947/8 he took an M.C.C. side composed of young and promising cricketers to the West Indies and, aged 45, held his own with the youthful opposition and led his own side with skill and consideration.

Two last memories of that beautiful action and lively pitch which *Wisden* and George Hirst had remarked long since come to mind. In August 1946 Allen played for Middlesex against Yorkshire at Sheffield and took five wickets for 26. In the evening whilst he was relaxing his aching limbs in a hot bath his captain, Walter Robins, went down to the hotel bar where he got talking to a stranger who had been to Bramall Lane. 'I've really seen summat today,' said this good man. 'A young fast bowler named Allen.' His voice rose with his enthusiasm. 'If he doesn't play for England in two years time' he said, 'I'll eat my blooming hat.' Unfortunately the stranger had to leave just before the appearance of the youthful prodigy.

The other recollection also comes from Yorkshire where we played together in a club match on Allen's fiftieth birthday. A very good wicket-keeper, just half his age, had never seen him bowl so, when the veteran was persuaded to have an over, stood boldly up to the stumps. From this vantage point he saw one ball beat the bat and his glove before either had made a gesture. The next he took still on the rise at a respectful twelve yards back. Later he batted for some time with the bowler, who celebrated his anniversary by making a hundred.

Allen was introduced to the management side of cricket when he joined the Middlesex Committee in 1931. This he was persuaded to do by Sir Pelham Warner, as good a judge of a potential administrator as he was of a player. He immediately revealed his talents in this direction, bringing to the task a sound business intelligence, much practical knowledge, and the strength of personality to advance and sustain his views in all circumstances. He was thus well versed in the details of cricket affairs and committee work when elected in 1935 to the M.C.C. Committee, on which he found himself ten years junior to the next youngest member. The following year he was to gain his first experience of selection as the appointed captain of the team he was about to take to Australia.

In common with the rest of his generation Allen found his business and sporting activities abruptly halted in 1939. As a good citizen he had joined the City of London Yeomanry two years previously, so had some training in Ack Ack gunnery when he was attached for a period to the R.A.F. At his own request he went on a bombing mission over Germany to see things at first hand, a brave gesture, for the lot of the unfledged observer must have been a trying one. Later his organising abilities led to his transfer to the War Office.

The war over, he returned to his activities on the political and administrative side of cricket. His impact was immediate and was to be the foundation of a remarkable career in the course of which he was to initiate and sponsor measures affecting every aspect of the game. It was in the early fifties that, returning one evening from the country, he paused to watch a game of cricket on Putney Common. The players were all of mature years and their standards abysmal. The scene made a strong impression on Allen, and he returned to Lord's convinced that any coaching scheme must start with the young at the very roots of the game. Always a champion of the young, he went straight to the main committee and threw his whole considerable weight behind the project. The result was the Youth Cricket Enquiry and from it sprang the Youth Cricket Association with all its benefits for the less privileged cricketers of England. Allen furthered the scheme by co-operating with H. S. Altham in the production of the M.C.C. Coaching Book, which remains the standard work on the subject.

Nor was Allen forgetful of his own contemporaries and predecessors, for it was on his initiative that the M.C.C. in 1949 introduced twenty-six of England's greatest professionals in their retirement as Honorary Life Members. So the ordinary members were honoured and delighted to have as their fellows such heroes as Jack Hobbs, Sydney Barnes, George Hirst, George Gunn and many other illustrious figures. The privilege has since been extended to overseas players and is regularly augmented by retiring players of distinction.

Allen became Chairman of the Selectors in 1955, and held the position for seven years. Of all deliberations and decisions in the cricket world those of the selector are the most controversial for, with so many permutations available, there is always a mass of unsought advice and alternative theory on offer, some not very well informed, some downright peculiar. The Chairman has to bear the brunt of this guidance and censure so that few have escaped unscathed. Allen was more widely accepted than most, for several good reasons. He was manifestly devoted to his task, he had great practical knowledge of his subject, was a shrewd judge of a player and his temperament, and was just and courageous in all his decisions. His policy of going for class rather than statistics was bold and justified by results. When, in 1956, this entailed the recall of older players such as Sheppard, Washbrook and Compton it was successful in every case, so much so that, on Washbrook's triumphant reappearance at Leeds an admiring spectator was heard to say 'Yon Gooby Allen—has he ever tried walking ont water?' And (if I may be allowed a happy personal memory of the same occasion) I recall that, as we left the ground in his car, there was cheering and acclamation. A previous selector, Walter Robins, spoke up from the back of the car, 'It was a bit different in 1948,' he said. 'Then we waited until it was dark, and slipped out of the side gate.'

From 1956 until he became President in 1963 he was Chairman of the

M.C.C. Cricket Committee, at that time the most influential body in existence where the laws of the game were concerned. As concurrently he was Chairman of the Selectors and Chairman of the Umpires Committee he was as dominating a figure in domestic and international circles as the popular title of 'Mr Cricket' would imply. In retrospect he believes that no man ought to hold both of the first two positions at the same time as it tends to vest too much power in one pair of hands.

In his case he was able to exert this power to advantage in one very important instance. When the epidemic of 'throwing' or unfair bowling had reached a dangerous level, it was his ability to arouse and enlist the support of all parties, not least the Australians, which led directly to its suppression. It was undoubtedly the weight of hostile opinion eventually marshalled which quelled this evil, for, by the time a committee had been formed to clarify the law the battle had been won and, in any case, the findings of the Committee did not meet with universal acceptance.

In May 1963, Allen was nominated by the reigning President, Lord Nugent, to be his successor, which meant that he would officiate in the 150th anniversary year of the present ground. It was also the year of an Australian Test Match series, which added a pleasing sentimental note to his appointment. Being so long conversant with every detail of his duties he carried them out with all the grace and efficiency which colleagues and members had come to expect of him.

In 1964, Lord Cobham found that with the weight of his public duties he could no longer devote as much time to the affairs of the M.C.C. and so retired as its treasurer. Allen was the obvious successor and took over as soon as his Presidency had ended, thus continuing a distinguished line, the post-war Treasurers being the tenth Viscount Cobham, H. S. Altham, and the eleventh Viscount Cobham. The powers of the Treasurer were greatly expanded during the tenure of Lord Harris, a powerful figure and brilliant administrator, and has since been the key position of the whole organisation, the success or otherwise of which depends largely on the judgement and competence of the reigning official. He may be likened to a Permanent Secretary of State, an *ex officio* member of every committee, and responsible for their organisation and co-ordination. The financial affairs of the Club, although a wide and complex field in themselves, comprise not more than half of his manifold activities. Allen's span saw a huge spate of business, part of which involved the demolition of the Old Tavern and the large building programme in the South West corner of the ground.

In addition to these many duties Allen was usually the M.C.C., or British, representative to any cricket conference of importance, not by virtue of his office, but because for many years he had been recognised as the best qualified man for the job. All in all this meant that, from his appointment as Chairman of the Selectors in 1955 until his retirement as Treasurer twenty-one years later, it had been a period of intense activity at the very centre of cricket affairs. As early as 1962 he was awarded the C.B.E. in the New Year Honours List 'For services to cricket'.

In April 1976 he presented his last budget speech to the Annual General

Meeting. On this occasion he ranged rather more widely than the customary financial statement, surveying briefly the events during his stewardship. Particularly he spoke of his regret that he had failed to convince the authorities in this country and overseas, of the evils of the alteration to the L.B.W. law introduced in 1935. In his own words: 'In his infancy and to his everlasting shame', he had supported it at the meeting, but very soon recognised many of the undesirable results arising from it which, he was now more than ever convinced, had led to a number of flaws in the modern game. He will receive much support in his judgement, not least from many who also thought it a good measure at the time of its introduction.

Even the relatively brief chronicle of his achievements in the realm of cricket leaves little space for a view of the man himself through the eyes of a friend, nor of his extremely active life in the City and in other pursuits such as squash and golf, in both of which he was a very competent performer.

As may be imagined, his circle of friends is considerable and his number of acquaintances vast. It may be surmised, again correctly, that one who has achieved so much is a strong personality. To some extent he has the autocratic strain of the man who gets things done and is occasionally impatient of rival strategists. But if in the countless situations with which he has dealt he has encountered numerous opponents the number of his enemies is singularly few, for he has that quality which, when he gets his way causes the defeated to smile, if sometimes wryly. This springs from an unaffected honesty which is not unconnected with another disarming trait. I have referred to his interest in the young. One might also remark on an instinctive consideration for the weak and the obscure whom he treats with an unfailing courtesy, not always accorded to pompous contemporaries.

I have declared my interest in writing as an old friend. Another, hearing that I was to do this piece, laughingly said that it would be a eulogy, to which I replied 'Why not?' Having chronicled all these deeds and achievements and reflected on their author I think it was an appropriate answer.

THE CRICKET RHYMESTER [1977]

BY BASIL EASTERBROOK

One of the most demanding of all challenges to the reader, whether concerned with cricket or with politics, with romance or with religion, is to try to follow the debate through the sensibilities of those who lived and loved in another time. Today the idea of a cricketing versifier, plying for hire with his jingles among the crowds at a first-class cricket match, is somehow too bizarre to contemplate. Were he to try his luck at the average county game he would be lucky to sell six copies to the sadly shrunken, quiescent congregation. If it were a great occasion, a one-day final perhaps, or the Saturday of a Test match, he might see his effusions scattered by drunks, or be escorted from the ground for breaching the regulations of the Ministry of Employment or the National Union of Journalists. And suppose he were fortunate enough to persuade a few folk to read what he had written, then derisive laughter would crackle unkindly in the air.

Albert Craig was a Victorian. As Basil Easterbrook reminds us in his affectionate tribute, it was a world in which a recital of 'Gunga Din' or a rendering of 'Come into the Garden, Maud' was accepted by many as the very apex of popular art. Already the masses were thronging to the Music Hall, there to enjoy the flattering experience of having their own emotions and prejudices flung back at them in the form of doggerel pieces like 'We Don't Want to Fight, but by Jingo if We Do', 'The Man Who Broke the Bank at Monte Carlo' and 'My Old Dutch'. Patriotism, Money and Sex, the unholy trinity of human longing, all expressed in terms naive enough to reach an unsophisticated audience. Only in such an unworldly world could a man write of his sporting idols what Albert Craig wrote of Bobby Abel, or Jack Hobbs, or Tom Hayward, and then sell the result to the crowds at a penny a time. He was the sporting equivalent of that other al fresco journeyman, the busker who dispensed his modest art before the theatre queues, an amateur raised by necessity to a sort of quaint professionalism, and ironically to win an audience much larger than the Poet Laureate's.

In disclosing the crudity of Craig's technique, Easterbrook gambles on our charitable instincts and wins. No more dramatic proof of the way the world has changed could anyone ever hope to find than the anecdote describing how Craig quelled a riot at a football match. Study what Craig said to the crowd and try to imagine the same sentiments addressed to the terraces a century later. We digest those childlike sentiments, we smile a smile of condescension and wonder whatever happened to Craig's world. It sank into the mud of Flanders a few years after his death, but it is a pretty thought that the Prince of Wales should have considered Craig important enough to write to him. Patriotism and Fair Play, Honesty and Good Sportsmanship, these were the counters of Craig's morality, discredited counters whose efficacy it never occurred to him or his readers to question.

We don't have rhymesters at cricket matches any more. Instead we are obliged to make do with the graffiti on lavatory walls. The loss, I should say, is ours; but it was a happy thought of Mr. Easterbrook's to preserve the man and a little of his work, a noble deed on the part of Wisden to publish it, this tribute to a self-appointed 'Captain of the Spectators' who once wrote:

> For though of football for five months I've sung,
> I'm mighty glad now spring has sprung.

This humble poetaster stands somewhere between the bathos of Alfred Austin and the inspired lunacy of William McGonagal. The role he played in the history of cricket may have been peripheral, but sometimes it is out on the periphery that we find the vital clues to the spirit of an age.

At the turn of the century, Albert Craig was universally known in cricket as 'The Surrey Poet'. The man himself never used that description, signing his verses simply 'A.C. Cricket Rhymester'. He was a phenomenon of his time as in their different ways were W. G. Grace, Sir Donald Bradman and Sir Neville Cardus. Craig was once heard to observe that poet was a word reserved for a Wordsworth, a Byron or a Keats. He knew his limitations and he was a good psychologist into the bargain as the following anecdote indicates. He went down to Canterbury Week in the 1890s and as he walked round the ground selling his verses he said 'I know that any fool among you could write a better poem than this, but I defy anyone else, however intelligent, to sell it at 2d a copy.' This was greeted with roars of laughter and the tuppences flowed in merrily.

There would be meat on the table for several days to come at the Craig home in Mayflower Road, Clapham. He had a wife and children who outlived him and this was how he supported them—by writing verses at cricket and football grounds all over the country, having them run off by the printer and persuading enough spectators to buy them to save him from returning to his native Yorkshire, where he was born towards the end of 1849.

The only picture of his personality that I managed to come across was in an ancient letter to the *Daily Telegraph* by Professor F. J. Cole, who wrote: 'His education must have been very indifferent, and to the end of his life the letter H always beat him. He had a great command of humour and invective, and his little serio-comic lectures were always skilfully adapted to the section of the crowd he happened to be addressing. He could silence the knocker, and the member of the crowd who attempted to score off him always had the laugh turned against himself.'

There were so many pitfalls waiting for Craig, for was not cricket even then studded with 'obbs, 'itches, 'earnes and 'arrises? But Albert was quick and lively and when he got himself a job as a clerk in the post office in the Bradford area he soon made a name for himself for an undoubted gift for topical verse. Today it would have done nothing for him except possibly earn him the tag of a pest to be avoided or squashed or in some way humiliated according to personal inclination, but Albert lived in times when the singing of 'Come into the Garden Maud' or the reciting of 'Gunga Din' represented the epitome in spontaneous entertainment.

Encouraged by the enthusiastic reception of his ditties by his fellow Tykes, never the most demonstrative of human beings, young Craig sought permission from the Yorkshire County Cricket Club to sell verses at Park Avenue during a visit by Gloucestershire. Permission obtained, Albert went to the match and wrote one piece on George Ullyett and another on Fred Grace, brother of W.G. In two hours he sold a thousand. In those two hours he had made what it would have taken him two months to earn as a clerk. As Albert Craig trudged home in a happy daze, his every pocket bursting with coins of the realm that jingled as eloquently for him as Bow Bells did for Dick Whittington, Albert muttered 'Post Office be boogered'.

It was not long before he was on the train to London—but he was canny enough to buy a return ticket. Shortly before his death in his 60th year in 1909 Albert Craig produced from his wallet a faded square of cardboard, tatty round the edges. It was the return half which he had never needed to use.

Craig's activities after throwing up his job in the Post Office and going to London were by no means confined to The Oval. He followed Surrey, Australia and South Africa about the country and favoured both Kent and Sussex with his presence. At both cricket and football Craig saw himself as the captain of the crowd and the real measure of his achievement was, I suppose, that he got himself accepted. Just how great has been the change in public attitudes can be seen in this tale involving a Cup tie between Chelsea and Northampton in 1908. The crowd became incensed at a decision by the referee and at the end attempted to invade the pitch. Craig stood, a lone figure, and shouted, 'Boys, do nothing tonight that you will regret tomorrow. I have been your captain for twenty-six years, so take my advice and go home.' Today, he would have been Kung-fued the length of the King's Road but seventy years ago it was possible for a man like Craig to get the mob to do as he asked. The club sent him an official letter of thanks for saving its good name.

Craig's verses have no power to communicate with anyone living in the second half of the 20th century. The only way to approach them is in the way the audience attires itself for a visit to the Palace of Varieties at Leeds. There must be a conscious effort to project oneself into the spirit of the age. To have a peep at Albert Craig and the people we were a lifetime ago, we can only be our own chairman bringing our mental gavel into play whenever our laughter tends to be heading for contempt or mild nausea. We are dealing with history, not fiction, and let us not lose sight of the fact that Albert Craig had the regard of the mighty as well as the masses.

When he lay in bed gasping away the last nine weeks of his life with an abscess on the lung a letter was delivered at his home in Mayflower Road. It came from Marlborough House and it read: 'Dear Sir—The Prince of Wales much regrets to hear that you have been seriously indisposed. His Royal Highness desires me to express his earnest hope that your health may be restored and that your friends may soon be able to welcome you back to The Oval. Yours faithfully, Arthur Bigge.'

When Craig let it be known that his intention if he recovered was to convalesce at Bournemouth at his sister-in-law's and there write his autobiography, Lord Hawke, most famous of Yorkshire captains, expressed a wish to finance him in the undertaking. Craig died on July 8, 1909. Just three years earlier he had composed 18 lines which was probably the first major public tribute paid to Sir John Berry Hobbs.

Craig headed the broadsheet 'Young Jack Hobbs to the Rescue' after he had made 162 not out against Worcestershire at The Oval in July, 1906. The lines ran:

> *Joy reigns supreme amongst the Surrey throng,*
> *Patrons break out in one triumphant song;*
> *Young Hobbs we loved as hero of today,*

Gaily he steers along his conquering way;
The modest youth has but one end and aim,
To conquer, or if dying, to die game;
Why marvel that the lad adorns his side,
Has he not had a Hayward as his guide?
And has he not well learnt the lessons taught,
By one experienced—as all youngsters ought?
Mark you his triumph will not make him vain,
Still greater heights the lad will yet attain;
Surrey can trust him in the deadliest strife,
He treads the pathway of a sober life;
That path is safe Jack, never leave the track,
Which feels the happiest, Hayward or young Jack?
How glad are we the well earn'd praise to sing,
Of one who came from Surrey's '2nd string'.

How little the passing of twenty years had changed his style can be judged by a five verse epic Albert published in early August 1886 after Kent had beaten the Australians by ten wickets at Canterbury. He offered it modestly as a 'First Prize Rhyme on the Game of Cricket' and addressed it to the Kent captain, Lord Harris.

Proud of your men my lord! we do not wonder,
Your arduous task has been most nobly done.
'Twas not the outcome of some serious blunder,
Right valiantly the fight was fought—and won.
You left your friendly rivals far behind;
'Tis not your first achievement of the kind.

Your brilliant deed was but a repetition
Or former triumphs 'gainst Colonial teams
You were, my lord, in extra fine condition—
Kent did their duty; so at least, it seems,
'Twas no mere fluke—on conquering you were bent;
You did it by ten wickets; bravo! Kent.

Your conquest was to us a source of gladness;
'Twas at The Oval we received the news;
The welcome telegram assuaged our sadness;
To cheer on neighbours we could not refuse.
Just like old Surrey; by your pluck and skill
You prove what men can do, if they've the will.

We know your Lordship's ardent love for cricket;
We honour and admire your fervent zeal.
We've often seen you guard with care your wicket;
A settled confidence in you we feel.
All lovers of the game your fame have heard;
With cricketers, your name's a household word.

Well done, Old Kent! three hearty cheers we'll give you
The 'Cornstalks' have a thing or two to learn.
A grand reception Surrey longs to give you,
Well done friend Wootton! Frank and Alec Hearne.
Let good old Canterbury raise a shout
For George Hearne's splendid fifty three—not out.

When Queen Victoria completed 60 years on the throne it was left to Albert Craig to mark the occasion on behalf of cricket with four verses entitled 'Loyal Hearts at the Tonbridge Cricket Week!' Before launching into rhyme A. C. wrote 'At lovely Tonbridge, at Headingley, in the Surrey–Yorkshire match and at our other centres of county cricket, the two elevens, from the centre of the ground, joined heartily in 'God Save the Queen', thousands of spectators unitedly joining in the grand old Anthem followed by prolonged cheers for Her Majesty.' Then he was straight into his stride and as always there was not a single line or word to which anyone could take the slightest exception.

High and lovely, great and small,
Men and Maidens, one and all,
British born—on foreign strands—
Foreign friends from foreign lands,
Even children praises bring,
Seem to make Heaven's arches ring,
With a song, brimful of fervour,
Bless Our Queen—great God preserve her.

Loyal hearts assembled here,
Hold their gracious Sovereign dear,
One united voice we raise,
May Heaven lengthen out her days.
Cricket patrons, what say ye?
Shall we show our loyalty?
Gladly join in hearty fervour—
Bless Our Queen, great God preserve her.

From the fields of fruitful Kent,
Every heart's best wish is sent,
York and Surrey, too, agree:
Send the same from Headingley.
Middlesex prove quite as true
and the Philadelphians, too—
Greet our Sovereign Queen with fervour,
May high Heaven this day preserve her.

From the illustrious western shire,
Comes a friendly welcome wire
From our grand old chieftain, Grace—
Noblest, of a noble race,

From The Oval—classic ground;
Friends of cricket shout with fervour—
Bless Our Queen, high Heaven preserve her.

I have unearthed other examples of the work of the Cricket Rhymester and the things that inspired him. They lie on my desk as I write. 'An Honoured Name' is the title of one, written on the occasion of Tom Hayward reaching his 2,000 runs in the 1904 season. 'Kent Full of Hope for the Future' says another souvenir of the summer of 1904 when Seymour made a century in each innings against Worcestershire in the first week of June at Maidstone. 'Sensational Score by Our Charlie' was to mark the achievement in July 1897 of Baldwin taking 234 off the Kent attack at The Oval which began

Most hearty plaudits seemed to rend the air
You might have heard it at Trafalgar Square.

The August Bank Holiday clash of Surrey and Nottinghamshire at The Oval in 1907 conjured a 52 line epic from the Rhymester's pen and if I reveal the opening stanza was 'Darling Old Oval, once again we meet, One clan to triumph, one to bear defeat' I am certain you'll agree with my decision to withhold the remaining 50 lines from you. The broadsheet was topped with 'Respectfully dedicated to Lord Dalmeny, Surrey's popular Chieftain'. He really was a fearful old forelock tugger was A.C.

Unlike many who have written on the subject of cricket in more modern times, Albert was never likely to get caught going out on a limb, as his concluding lines on the Surrey v. Kent match in August 1887 give convincing proof.

Kent, good old Kent, means victory, but it will not be so.
If Surrey fail to win the match, 'twill finish in a draw.

The Times in September 1955 reproduced Craig's verses in full of this match and thought fit to add an explanatory note which ended 'The prophecy (or prejudice) contained in the last line above was justified, for Kent, after gaining a first innings lead of 120, were held to a draw.'

'Hail' to this team, 'Welcome' to that one, 'Esteemed', 'Honoured', 'Illustrious'—these were the stock in trade words of Albert Craig. Not for him the exposé, the dressing room row, the attack on the selectors. He was always conscious of that return half to Bradford in a corner of his wallet. A.C. was the forerunner of the public relations officer and there was a good bit of the agent in him as well. He was never averse to slipping in an advertisement or two on his broadsheets. For example to the conclusion of his welcome to Sherwell's 1907 South Africans in 24 lines of doggerel, Craig informs us 'The finest Toffies yet produced are those made by the famous cricketer George Hirst. Ask your wholesaler at once for his goods, or write direct to Hirst's Yorkshire Toffee Co. Ltd., Ashbrow Works, Huddersfield'. Alongside was an invitation to make the acquaintance of Mr. Frank Matthews, bone setter, of Melcombe Place, Dorset Square, if you were suffering from nervous disorders or all forms of lameness 'supposed to be incurable'. A.C.'s unfailing supporter on nearly all his broadsheets was C. Savage's Dining Rooms at 414 Kennington Road.

Here hot joints were at your disposal between 12 and 2 and again in the evening between 8 and 10, with sandwiches cut to order and special quotations for breakfast if you wanted to stake an early claim for a particular seat at a particular match at The Oval.

After MacLaren had made his 424 for Lancashire against Somerset at Taunton in July 1895, still the greatest individual score made in England after more than 80 years, F. H. Ayres, who were one of the biggest sports outfitters at the time, prevailed upon the autocratic Archie to advertise their product. On the back of a Craig broadsheet in type so small as to need a magnifying glass is a letter '4 Oxford Terrace, Old Trafford, Manchester, Aug. 6, 1895. Sir—I have often been asked during the last few days what was the bat I made my runs with against Somerset and I think it is only fair to write and tell you that it was one of your own make. For driving power yours are not to be beaten. Yours truly, A. C. MacLaren'.

As both lived close to The Oval that was the mainspring of their lives it was perhaps not surprising that Albert Craig's closest friend in a game which both accepted and showed affection for him should be Bobby Abel. A.C. made a special effort in 1895 for 'The Guvnor' as Abel was known to his contemporaries. This was the year he took his benefit against Yorkshire in August and Albert went into print as soon as Abel became the first 'to follow in the footsteps of our monarch Dr. Grace' in reaching 1,000 runs in June. The title of the poem was 'Good Lad Bob'—well, what else? A.C. did show a touch of genius though when he reserved the only mention of the coming benefit to a single reminder after the poem with the words attached—'Try and bear the date in mind'. The broadsheet was well backed by advertisers and I enjoyed this paragraph, which stated: 'Dr. W. G. Grace informs us that most of his big scores have been secured off a bat manufactured by Mr. F. H. Ayres. Mr. Ayres ascends in the estimation of cricketers, to the position in which his lawn tennis balls have long ago placed him in the eyes of lawn tennis players.'

The friendship between Craig and Abel endured and the Surrey batsman made himself responsible for the funeral arrangements 14 years later. We have seen something of Craig as a rhymester and crowd leader and now it is perhaps time we glanced briefly at his unceasing efforts to turn an honest coin in the role of prose writer and statistician. He wrote a series of vignettes published on stiff paper 6½ inches across, 5 inches high which could be conveniently folded down the centre. The front carried a daguerreotype photograph of the player and A.C. distributed his favours among the printers he employed—The All England Athletic Publishing Company, 29 Paternoster Square; Wright & Co, 23 Paternoster Square; Cricket Press, 25 Temple Chambers.

If he had a certain talent for producing rhyming verses his prose was notable only for a complete absence of style or originality. I offer without comment a 200 word thumb nail sketch he sold for a penny a copy on the Australian J. J. Lyons who came with Blackham's side in 1893.

> 'When Lyons, the mighty hitter, was bowled—for nothing—the first ball of the match (said 'English Sports' on a memorable occasion), he grew hot under the collar, and vowed revenge. That was why he banged the English bowling for 149 in the second innings of that contest—which was (needless to remind cricket lovers, because they will probably never forget it), M.C.C. v. Australia. Lyons was born at Gawler, South Australia and celebrated his 30th birthday on the 21st May. He was always a fast scorer, and once upon a time he made 158 runs in just over an hour, 32 coming from one over. There were four sixes and an eight, all run out, while the remaining ball of the over he spared. Jack made his début in important cricket in 1885 and was first seen on English fields in 1888. Bearing some of his past achievements in mind, to say nothing of his position in the average tables of the present Australian team, we feel fairly safe in opining that no Colonial batsman can lay on the wood with more power than the big six footer. In addition, he has some good bowling performances associated with his name.'

Albert was, too, a shameless old name dropper, as for example when he began his sketch of the Nottingham born, Surrey fast bowler, William Lockwood—'My friend the Prince, who of course is Kumar Shri Ranjit-sinhji, when recalling his entry into first-class cricket etc. etc.' A.C. in one sentence could encapsulate a player's all-round skill by stating that as a manipulator of the leather he had come to stay while at times he was a more than useful wielder of the willow. He was in top form the day in 1897 he immortalised Tom Richardson in print—the verbal portrait growing from the following opening lines—'Unlike George Lohmann, this crack fast bowler is a Surreyite by birth, which is a superior characteristic to all "qualifying Fakements" so frequently resorted to. On 11th August 1870, the year remarkable for the conclusion of the Franco-German War, Tom Richardson disturbed the quiet serenity of Byfleet by the initial usage of his lungs. Since acquiring the knowledge of how to use a cricket ball, he has disturbed a great number of wickets.' Those who waited with their pennies at the high port were going to get value for them.

After Plum Warner's team had won the series 3–2 in Australia in 1904 A.C. felt obliged to write an open letter to 'The Recoverer of The Ashes'. He complimented Warner on his intelligence, tact, good fellowship and force of example but he could not resist the observation—'To meet you in frock coat and silk hat one would never think that you could score many runs. How deceptive are appearances!' A little further on Albert added with his unfailing magnanimity: 'Still you have done wonderfully well, and I should not be at all surprised to see the championship find a resting place this season with Middlesex.' A.C.'s judgement was at fault there for the title was not to return to Lord's until 1920–11 years after his death.

Just once did Albert Craig wish to do something beyond his daily verse accounts of the cricket or his pen pictures that all helped to keep that return ticket to Yorkshire in his wallet. He called the poem 'One of the Noble Brigade' but I believe it could have been equally well dubbed 'Self Portrait'.

When I was a bit of a youngster, I cared for nothing at all;
I've missed my meals a hundred times for an hour with bat and ball:
Age didn't improve me either, if anything I grew worse,
Our parson, a bit of a terror, vowed cricket would be my curse.

He dubbed me most awfully stupid, I didn't care what he said,
When he offered me books as prizes, I yearned for wickets instead.
He declared my deep love for cricket would be my besetting sin,
But in trying to knock it out of me he hammered it further in.
When I told him to mind his own business, and I would attend to mine.
So I thought the affair was ended, each went his separate way,
He hurried away to his preaching, and I hurried off to my play.

And just gave my mind to the business, to prove 'twas no idle dream
And mark you I soon was acknowledged and placed in the county team.
I never disgraced 'em either, so long as I wielded the bat,
I was honest in all my actions, I always feel proud of that.

My mother had taught me my lessons and I managed to learn them well
Ah! bless her, in duty's pathway she prayed that I might excel,
Ah! lads, it's a downright pity when we live to be ashamed
Ashamed of our dear old parents whenever we hear them named.

I remember one County fixture, a regular grand affair,
Holiday folk in their thousands with the rank and file were there,
Our five best batsmen had fallen most lucklessly in the fray,
And our score was a modest thirty, not a man had made a stay.

I was seventh to take up the willow, but wasn't a bit depressed,
A score of admirers whispered—'take courage and do thy best',
I felt nerved while the great assembly were cheering me all the while
Still I ran up my century grandly in fine and brilliant style.

I was carried to the pavilion and heartily feted there,
For we lowered their colours nobly with fifty five runs to spare.
The crowd gathered round the entrance, from every point they came.
And there wasn't a man among them but said that I'd won the game.

In front of me stood a veteran with white and silvery hair
Accompanied by his daughter, a lady young and fair;
My friend, he exclaimed, forgive me since I was so harsh to you.
I've learnt that a lover of cricket may be a true gentleman too.

'Twas the parson I knew in my childhood, he stood there as real as life
Since then we're akin through marriage, his daughter is now my wife.
One word of advice and I've finished, for I've taken a lengthy spell
Guard your wickets and watch the ball lads, but guard your actions as
*   well.*

No, that was not quite the reality of the Surrey Poet's life but as sure as the Resurrection it was its essence. Craig was entitled to his moment as Walter Mitty. If we are to use the word Poet, and in fairness remember Craig himself signed his work with the word 'Rhymester', there could never be a place for him in any anthology of cricket poetry. For John Arlott, for Alan Ross, for Norman Gale, for Francis Thompson, for Siegfried Sassoon, for Norman Nicholson, for twenty more—yes, any place, any time. For Albert Craig, a wink, a nod, a nudge and finally a shake of the head, a shrug of the shoulders inevitably evoked by a man who defies being placed. I look at a picture of him for the last time as he walked across The Oval, his left arm cradling a bundle of broadsheets fresh from the printer, his waistcoat open against the heat of the summer day. He was not badly dressed, nor was he ill favoured in looks and physique and he smiles back at me with a smile that could easily have made a friend out of me.

Certainly the picture is not that of either a knave or a weakling and that return railway ticket that never left his possession for a generation of time proves that he was no fool. If his prose was Grub Street at its worst time and his poetry not a major gift, he was not lacking in talent completely. I thought the final verses gave him at least a nodding acquaintance with Robert Service. My opinion in this matter is unimportant. Albert Craig's achievement and his meed of immortality rest with his capacity for escaping the drab routine life into which he had been born. If cricket looks back a lifetime and grins at the recollection of a gamin I think it can also spare him a tip of the cap. Any romantic who survives against the odds for even a spell is deserving of that.

THREE STUDIES IN GREATNESS [1978]

BY BASIL EASTERBROOK

It was in 1978 that Basil Easterbrook, evidently without a grand design for a full essay, hit on the useful dodge of building one up by forming a triptych of three shorter pieces. If the form was eccentric, some of the content was priceless, for Easterbrook was careful to select as his three subjects men whose careers, though strikingly successful, had not been described in detail before. Astill, Turnbull and J. C. White typify the kind of past giant whose career we think we know all about but do not. Turnbull's heroics must have been familiar to many readers of the 1977 almanack, but in examining Astill and White, Mr. Easterbrook was returning to the amplitudes of life before the Great War. Having read the three pieces we became enriched by at least two fragments of knowledge, that in his youth Astill suffered a curious debility of the cricketing will, for which the cure turned out to be four years of fighting in the war; and that Jack White would advise young aspiring slow bowlers not to spin the ball too much. One detail not included in the sketch but lovingly recorded in the autobiography of R. C. Robertson-Glasgow is that White was not especially interested in other ball games, much preferred cards and was 'one of the best poker players in Somerset'. Easterbrook's triple fugue worked so well that he was to return to it, as we shall see.

WILLIAM EWART ASTIL
(Leicestershire)

A man's destiny unfolds in strange ways for which there are no possible explanations, the story of Ewart Astill being a good example. He was born at Ratby in Leicestershire on St. David's Day, 1890, the son of a star player in the local village cricket team. No cricket was played at the school Astill attended but the game was in his blood and it was soon realised at Ratby that he was going to be a better player than his father. Leicestershire took him on their staff when he was 15 in 1905 after some remarkable performances in a local Sunday School League. His promise was such that at 16 the county gave him a solitary taste of first-class cricket.

It was against Hampshire at Southampton towards the end of August and the stripling bowled 32 overs in the match, took three wickets for 76 runs and batting No. 10 made 12 not out in one innings and a duck in the other. Leicestershire lost the match by six wickets but they did not take the field without Astill once in the next four seasons. Twice in those four seasons he headed the bowling averages and once he was second. He could bowl either off spin or leg breaks, varying them between slow and medium pace and at the start of the 1911 season had a countrywide reputation of being a bowler of considerable skill and cunning.

And then it all began to go wrong for Ewart Astill just after his twenty-first birthday. After four years of being an ever present he was actually dropped. He got back into the side in 1912 and did just enough to justify himself but in 1913 had another poor season. The summer of 1914 was a personal disaster for Astill. He took just three wickets. He was washed up, through, due to be sacked at the end of the season and no one knew it better than Ewart. Then on August 4 the first World War began and Astill along with the rest of the youth of a tragic generation was swept into it. He served in the army with such distinction that he gained a commission—a considerable feat sixty years ago for a man who earned his living at sport in peace time.

Ewart's lack of success in cricket in the three seasons leading up to the war was a malaise of the mind and spirit rather than a loss of skill. He had come to the top too quickly, perhaps too easily and became jaded, with a consequent loss of concentration. In 1919, a season of two-day county cricket, Astill played only three innings. Then came 1920 and normal conditions for cricket and living were restored. The effect on Ewart Astill was little short of extraordinary. He seemed to realise that he had survived intact the war that had killed, maimed and broken millions of other men, that he had been spared to savour again the game and way of life that had made him well-known and admired a decade before. What then he took for granted Astill now found infinitely precious. His batting which had been very slow to ripen showed an improvement that was as vast as it was quick. Even *Wisden* felt obliged to say, 'Astill took, as it were, a new lease of life.' In 1920 he was fourth in the Leicestershire batting and second in bowling and in 1921, for the first time, accomplished the double. The ennui was gone and it never came back. Between the two world wars he and George Geary were to all intents and purposes Leicestershire. In all he was to do the double nine times and few players with as much work as Astill had thrust upon him retained their form so consistently for so long. *Wisden* honoured him in 1933 by making him one of their Five Cricketers of the Year and the notice included the following sentence:—

> '*It can be said with safety that day in and day out Astill, since the war, has been the best all-round player in the Leicestershire team and probably had he played for a county occupying a higher position in the Championship he would have achieved even greater distinction.*'

Apart from his unfailing reliability with the bat and ball Astill was frequently called upon to field in the slips, possibly because Leicestershire had no one as good in that responsible position as he was. He went on M.C.C. tours to the West Indies twice, to South Africa and India but it was as a county cricketer that he found his true forte. We all have our disappointments however successful, and Astill's was that he never played against Australia, his nine Tests being against South Africa (5) and West Indies (4), all abroad.

In seven years the only break Astill had from competitive cricket was the winter of 1928 and, fair and slight, his strength was never more than moderate. An extremely good amateur billiards player, he was once champion of the British Army of Occupation on the Rhine. He was immensely popular and when he gave up regular first-class cricket in 1938 he took on the role of county coach. Les Berry once told me, 'He was a good coach for he had a happy way of instructing and correcting faults.' Ewart played two final first-class matches in 1939, bowling 18 overs for one wicket and scoring 21 runs. A whispered farewell.

A few weeks later the 49-year-old Astill found himself donning officer's uniform again. Ahead of him lay a six years' stint of further military service throughout the Second World War. When that was behind him Astill took the appointment of cricket coach to Tonbridge School in 1946 but now over thirty years of non-stop activity and travel presented their account. His health began to fail and Ewart had to give up his post at Tonbridge. He could look back on career figures which will keep him for all time among the company of the great all-rounders—22,468 runs, 2,428 wickets and 402 catches. When he died in a Leicester hospital three weeks before his fifty-eighth birthday in February, 1948 I like to think they were a source of comfort to him in his last days.

MAURICE TURNBULL
(Cambridge University and Glamorgan)

Major Maurice Joseph Turnbull of the Welsh Guards was killed in action near Montchamp in Normandy on August 5, 1944 at the age of 38. During an attack his company got cut off and it became vital that a reconnaissance should be made. An officer of field rank is not expected to undertake that kind of job and he could have ordered a lieutenant or a sergeant to do it. But Turnbull jumped up and said, 'I'll go.' They were the last words he uttered. A concealed sniper shot him through the head, killing him instantly. Ironically the Germans were at their last gasp in Normandy. A few days later they were streaming out of France back towards their own frontier. One could understand J. C. Clay, that great father figure of Glamorgan cricket, writing of Turnbull's end in these words—'It exactly describes his leadership of Glamorgan in the days of peace and shows that in his greatest Test of all he did not alter his style but played his own game to the end.'

Turnbull was born at Cardiff on March 16, 1906, the son of a Yorkshireman who captained Wales at hockey for many winters. Maurice learned all his early cricket at the famous Roman Catholic public school, Downside, where he was five years in the eleven, in the last three of which he established a great reputation as a schoolboy batsman. In 1924 when 18 he made his début for Glamorgan at St. Helen's, Swansea, scoring 40 and 16 against Lancashire on a bowler's pitch, contributions which helped the Welsh team to a totally unexpected victory by 38 runs.

During his first season at Cambridge it was noticed that he was mainly an on side player with a tendency for the left wrist to be behind the handle. Missing his second summer at Fenner's because of a knee injury sustained at rugby, Turnbull went away quietly to work on the problem of his top hand and—to use his expression—changed himself into a fairly normal player. His leg-side play fell into desuetude and soon he was standing forth as a fine off-side stylist. His first century, 106 not out, was made for Glamorgan against Worcestershire at the old Arms Park ground at Cardiff. In 1929 as captain of Cambridge he scored three centuries and in the winter of 1929–30 went on the first tour of New Zealand under Harold Gilligan when four tests were played, a solitary victory being enough to give England the rubber.

Turnbull was on his way to sporting greatness. He was made captain and secretary of Glamorgan in 1930; he played cricket for England, rugby and hockey for Wales and added the squash rackets championship of South Wales to that formidable list of achievements. The 40 he made in his début for Glamorgan in 1924 was top score for the county as was the 156 he made against Leicestershire in his last match in 1939. By the time he was 33 Turnbull had scored 29 centuries, aggregated nearly 18,000 runs and held over 300 catches.

Wilf Wooller has said that in his opinion Turnbull was the best player of his generation who never captained England. The great John Clay was fascinating on the subject of Turnbull, for he had known him from the day he came to Cardiff in July, 1924 to have a net in readiness for his début the next day against Lancashire. 'He was so nervous and did so badly that he suggested it might be best if he stood down. Luckily for him and for Glamorgan I was able to talk him out of it with some nonsense about a bad dress rehearsal guaranteeing a successful first night. He stood up to Ted McDonald, Dick Tyldesley and Parkin at their best on a pitch favouring bowlers with a maturity worthy of one double his age.' Only a year later when Glamorgan were playing in London Turnbull showed the same confidence and maturity beyond his years when he sent for the forbidding-looking wine waiter of a large hotel and rebuked him on the quality of the claret. *Autres temps, autres moeurs.*

Not the least of Turnbull's achievements was that he was the first man to justify Glamorgan's elevation to first-class status in 1921. By 1929 they had already had the wooden spoon three times under no fewer than seven leaders. When Turnbull took over they were indeed a bedraggled flock without a shepherd. Turnbull linked Monmouthshire with Glamorgan, ran a Minor Counties side, improved the membership and by 1937 the improvement had advanced to a point where Glamorgan won 13 matches and finished seventh, in the top half of the Championship for the first time.

Turnbull not only launched a financial appeal and organised dances and functions in most remote villages of South Wales—he attended them personally. Clay said drily, 'If the figures were known, the number of miles he danced for Glamorgan might be favourably compared with the number of runs scored by some of the side!'

By 1939 Turnbull had converted a shambling, shamefaced bankrupt into a worthy and respected member of society, which could actually boast a credit balance at the bank of £1,000. Turnbull played in Tests, but he was never an accumulator, never made runs unnecessarily. He did not give a fig about raising his average. He was a d'Artagnan, always attacking the bowling, a member of a line of Corinthian sportsmen already doomed to die out. He was at his best when others were failing or when runs were needed against the clock like the 119 he scored at Swansea against Charlie Parker and Tom Goddard to see Glamorgan home against Gloucestershire with ten minutes to spare.

The Glamorgan professionals of the thirties described him as a grand boss to work for. One said of him, 'Maurice was a quiet captain. There was no fuss, no gesticulating, no shouting on the field. He never got rattled or irritable, and always continued to make you feel that, although the scoreboard said otherwise, you were really doing pretty well.' Clay paid him this tribute—'I always bowled much better for him than I ever did for myself or anybody else.' Turnbull scorned playing for safety, but often decisions of his which looked foolhardy at the time turned out to be extremely well calculated risks. As a fielder he was out of this world and began the Glamorgan tradition of being superb at short-leg. He was well read, appreciated good wine and co-operated with Maurice Allom in a couple of books. The Army's description of Turnbull was—'Quiet, confident, thinking always of his men.'

When Michael Carver published his book on the battle of El Alamein in 1962 he wrote a poignant final sentence—'As in all battles the dead and the wounded came chiefly from the bravest and the best.'

The terrible futile waste of war claimed Turnbull, a man who had been pencilled in for high rank in post-war cricket administration, certainly as a future Secretary of M.C.C., possibly as chairman of Test selectors. Nothing was beyond Turnbull's reach until that moment an unknown German with his eye to a telescopic sight took second pressure on the trigger of his marksman's rifle.

The news of his death came through while Glamorgan were fulfilling a wartime fixture at Cardiff, the scene of his very first century. The crowd rose unbidden and just stood there in the August sunshine in silence. Many must have seen in their imagination the well known figure out there on the field. After a decent interval the people sat down and play restarted. Glamorgan were carrying on. Maurice would have wanted that above everything.

J. C. WHITE
(Somerset)

John Cornish White, who died in the first week of the 1961 cricket season, having exactly completed three score years and ten, was one of the best left-arm slow bowlers of all time. From his first appearance in the Somerset side in 1909 when he was seventeen until he retired in 1937 he took over 2,350 wickets and only fourteen bowlers in cricket history have done better.

From 1921 to 1930 he played in 15 Tests for England and toured both Australia and South Africa. On the triumphant tour of 1928–29 when England beat Australia by 4–1 in the Test rubber he was vice-captain to Percy Chapman and never before or afterwards did he demonstrate his prowess or endurance to such effect. England won the first Test at Brisbane, which has been a postwar bogey ground for us, by the incredible margin of 675 runs. When sunshine followed rain in the night White took four prime Australian wickets for seven runs in less than seven overs. From the fourth Test at Adelaide England eventually emerged victors by 12 runs. In boiling heat White performed with an untiring skill matched by unflagging accuracy and endurance, sending down just on 125 overs and coaxing 13 wickets out of that shirt front pitch. They cost him 256 runs but on a batsman's paradise England got home by a whisker, thanks to White.

In the last Test Chapman was ill and White led England in a match which lasted eight days and was at that time the longest Test ever played. Weary and weakened England lost but as they had won the first four it was no sort of compensation to the Australians. Monty Noble, Australia's captain for most of the first decade of this century, said of White, 'One of the most tireless workers with muscle and brain that this or any other England team has ever possessed. On bad, worn and good wickets alike White was always able to call the tune and compel the batsman to dance to it. A truly capable, modest, unassuming sportsman, Jack White.'

Oddly enough no one in Britain ever called him Jack. He was known in the game and by the fans either as 'the Jasper' or 'Farmer'. He was in fact the son of a well-to-do cricket-loving farmer, being born at Holford near Taunton on February 19, 1891. Educated at Taunton School, he came under the influence of a former Somerset professional, E. J. Tyler, and said he learned much of what he knew about bowling from his coach and mentor, but as Tyler said, 'A coach can only do so much. Greatness of the kind J. C. White possessed comes from inside a man.'

At this point I must attempt to define what made 'Farmer' a world-class left arm spinner by any standards at any given period in cricket's development. He took 100 wickets or more in a season fourteen times and even modern heroes like Statham, Trueman, Don Shepherd, Laker, and Alec Bedser never accomplished that.

Where to start? Well, he obviously had the two greatest virtues of his kind—uncanny command of length and the ability to make the ball really spin. To these he added all the cunning and concentration of a nimble mind. If he got on a wicket that was 'doing a bit' he pitched the ball on the leg stump of a right hand batsman and made it go fizzing across him. He used sparingly a faster ball that was invariably deadly because he never varied his approach or run up to the bowling crease. On hard pitches giving him no help he concentrated his attack on flight, varied with a slight swerve or wobble in the air and a tempting slow ball well outside the off stump to which he imparted an extra degree of real finger spin. He had an armoury to exploit every possible combination of conditions.

If the wind helped him he could make the ball dip disconcertingly and he swerved it late. If the wind was against him he could still make the ball swerve but so superb was his control that he could lessen the swerve. 'You must guard against making the ball do too much' he used to warn young bowlers who sought his help and advice. He was blessed with an iron constitution that helped him to prolong his career until shortly before the Second World War. He remained economical to the end and his great haul of wickets cost him fewer than 19 runs each.

White was a regular in the Somerset side as early as 1913 and but for the First World War would probably have taken 3,000 wickets. By 1928 he was the Somerset captain and another aspect of his greatness then made itself apparent. He allowed his professional bowlers to pick the end they fancied, quite happy to operate at the other. 'Farmer' of course was so good that he could take wickets from the end no one else wanted.

He was a long way from being a mug with the bat. He scored over 12,000 runs and in 1929 and 1930 completed the double of 1,000 runs and 100 wickets in a season, although he always roared with laughter at any suggestion that he was an all-rounder. 'My ground fielding is shocking sometimes' he would say as justification for his mirth. It was not too bad when the ball was in the air, for he clung on to some 400 catches in his illustrious career. When England beat South Africa two-nil with three matches drawn in 1929 White was captain on three occasions. He once said to Gubby Allen 'I can't think why they keep calling on me to do the job. Don't they know we've all got straw in our hair down in Somerset?'

One side who knew differently was Worcestershire. In 1919 he took 16 of their wickets for 83 runs in a single day at Bath. Two years later at Worcester he took all ten wickets in an innings for 76.

By the time cricket was started up again after the Second World War the name J. C. White had no magic for the fans, but those inside the game would never forget him. For a time he served as an England selector and his counsel was always heard at Taunton with reverence. Fond of all forms of sport, he lost an eye in a shooting accident but his life was crowned in its final year when the county which had given him a chance at the age of 17 made him its President over half a century later.

THE PACKER CASE [1978]

BY GORDON ROSS

On May 11th, 1977, the Lancashire side arrived at the Hove ground to play a championship match against Sussex. The prospects were bleak. Leaden skies leaked rain down on to the town in a style which suggested that the sun might never shine again. The previous match, against the Australians, had been washed away after less than two hours' play. Patches of the ground were still under water, but during a brief lull in the downpour the players went through the motions before a virtually non-existent crowd. When the Sussex score had reached ten for no wicket the heavens reopened, the players ran for the pavilion and the representatives of the press, obliged to hang around just in case a miracle happened and it was possible to resume play, kicked their heels and killed time. The world was awash with water. Everyone awaited the official announcement that this travesty of a cricket match had finally been abandoned. Had anyone dared to suggest that this game would be remembered in history, there would have been jeers and demands for men in white coats to remove the lunatic.

But then, as the rain battered down, it was announced that the home captain, A. W. Greig, was holding a Press conference, a piece of news which baffled everyone except A. W. Greig, who, having spent the previous weeks undermining the structure of the first-class game, was perfectly well aware of the likely effect of the sensational revelations he was about to disclose. It appeared that the Sussex and England captain had for some time been recruiting volunteers for a piratical escapade destined to destroy utterly the balance of power in the cricket world. The plan was for a sizeable body of star players from all nations to renege on their obligations and go to work for an Australian mogul called Kerry Packer, who was offering the inducement of far higher salaries than most players had ever dreamed of. Sensing that the game was ripe for a bit of asset-stripping, Packer was taking advantage of the parlous financial condition of the average English professional, who was never paid according to his skills, and was paid not at all the moment the season was over. We have only to measure the financial rewards of the world's greatest cricketers against those of its star golfers and tennis players to see how ripe the game now was for the entrance of the entrepreneurs.

Greig was Packer's agent in England, moving stealthily around the counties under the umbrella of his England captaincy, persuading all sorts of famous men to opt for renegacy.

The irony was that the imbroglio was a purely Australian domestic affair, a fight between the Australian Board of Control and the Packer group for the right to transmit Test matches on television. In compiling an anthology of Wisdens of the period, I was obliged to assess the issues at stake, and as I can say no more now than I did then, I may as well scale the heights of self-idolatry and quote myself:

> The Packer affair embroiled the entire cricketing world. It bought up entire teams, it spanned the planet, it dismantled the structures of four cricketing continents, and when at last it was taken into an English court of law, it routed its opponents with a casual ease which dismayed some administrators and reduced others to a lick-spittle subservience which would once have seemed impossible. So far as English cricket was concerned, the fates were malignant indeed, because the Packer revolution was an Australian domestic argument which just happened to spill over into the embarrassed laps of Australia's cricketing opponents. Nor was the revolution about cricket, nor about the rights of players to move in a free market, nor about Trade Unionism, nor about Restraint of Trade. It was about Television, and the fact that the game could be turned on its head because of a fight between entrepreneurs looking for ratings is an indication of what had happened to the wandering garrison of English cricket now that the sanctuary of the castle of patronage no longer existed.

In his account of events leading to a recourse to law catastrophic for the English Establishment, Gordon Ross keeps a level head, reproaching nobody for disloyalty or avarice. Reactions outside the pages of the almanack were not so cool. Greig was dismissed by many as a Judas who had shamefully betrayed the very factions which had raised him to eminence. Packer was dismissed as a philistine, and his style of television coverage rightly derided as being infantile in several aspects. But nobody could deny either the effectiveness of Packer's campaign or the lightning speed at which it had been conducted. Realising that players alone were insufficient for his purposes, Packer also recruited umpires, commentators, and even scorers, including Irving Rosenwater. Some questions were never answered, for example how Richie Benaud contrived to manage Packer's matches while remaining persona grata at the BBC. But the most startling aspect is seen in retrospect to have been the patent unwillingness of the English to react against Packer. Incredible as it now seems, Greig, who held the notorious Press conference at the start of the season, was still England's captain at the end of it. There was one other development worth noting in the turbulent summer of 1977. The eventual loss of Greig to the England side was clearly serious, because of his stature as an authentic all-rounder. But in his last few games for England before opting for the circus ring, Greig played alongside a cricketer whose powers were so overwhelming that Greig was to be forgotten almost as soon as he departed. The cricketer's name was Ian Botham.

FIRST news of what was to become, virtually, 'The Packer Explosion', came from South Africa towards the end of April 1977 when South Africa's *Sunday Times* broke the news that four South African cricketers had signed lucrative contracts to play an eight-week series of matches throughout the world. It was said that when the team visited South Africa and played local teams it would have immeasurable benefits for the game there.

In the middle of May, *The Bulletin*, Australia's 97-year-old magazine owned by The Australian Consolidated Press Limited (Chairman, Kerry Packer) announced the completion of a huge sporting deal in which thirty-five top cricketers had been signed for three years to play specially arranged matches, beginning with a series of six five-day Test matches, six one-day games, and six three-day round robin tournaments in Australia in 1977-78. Prize money would be $100,000. The deal had been put together by JP Sports and Television Corporation Limited, proprietors of Channel 9 in Sydney (Chairman, Kerry Packer).

The thirty-five players signed up were:

Eighteen Australian and seventeen from Overseas, chosen by Ian Chappell and Tony Greig; I. M. Chappell (Captain), R. J. Bright, G. S. Chappell, I. C. Davis, R. Edwards, G. J. Gilmour, D. W. Hookes, D. K. Lillee, M. F. Malone, R. W. Marsh, R. B. McCosker, K. J. O'Keeffe, L. S. Pascoe, I. R. Redpath, R. D. Robinson, J. R. Thomson, M. H. N. Walker, K. D. Walters.

A. W. Greig (Captain), Asif Iqbal, E. J. Barlow, D. L. Hobson, M. A. Holding, Imran Khan, A. P. E. Knott, C. H. Lloyd, Majid Khan, Mushtaq Mohammad, R. G. Pollack, M. J. Procter, B. A. Richards, I. V. A. Richards, A. M. E. Roberts, J. A. Snow, D. L. Underwood.

G. Boycott was invited to take part in the scheme but declined. Richie Benaud and his Sports Consultancy Company were engaged in the management of the series. Many of the signings were carried out during the Centenary Test match in Melbourne, and the New Zealand-Australia series. Austin Robertson and John Kitto (Secretary and Attorney of the Television Corporation Group) flew to West Indies where West Indies were playing Pakistan, and then to Britain to finalise the arrangements with the English and South African players.

The Australian team was already in England. The Manager, Len Maddocks, was quoted as having said: 'I do not envisage the present development having a detrimental effect upon this tour. But if any of them play for a side contrary to the jurisdiction of the Australian Board, they will place their careers in jeopardy.'

On May 13 The Cricket Council issued a statement at the end of an emergency meeting to the effect that Greig was not to be considered as England's captain in the forthcoming series against Australia. The statement went on: 'His action has inevitably impaired the trust which existed between the cricket authorities and the Captain of the England side.' F. R. Brown, Chairman of the Council, added: 'The captaincy of the England team involves close liaison with the selectors in the management, selection and development of England players for the future and clearly Greig is unlikely to be able to do this as his stated intention is to be contracted elsewhere during the next three winters.'

On May 25 it was announced from Lord's that a special meeting of full and foundation members of the International Cricket Conference would be held at Lord's on June 14 to discuss the situation, and the next day the Test and County Cricket Board said that the selection committee should 'pick England sides this summer strictly on merit', which obviously meant that Greig, Knott and Underwood could play.

At the end of May, Packer arrived in England, and at a Press Conference, said: 'It is not a pirate series but a Super-Test Series. I have sent telegrams to all the cricketing bodies but they don't reply. I am willing to compromise but time is running out.' He referred to cricket as the easiest sport in the world to take over, as nobody had bothered to pay the players what they were worth.

At this point the only cricketing subject being discussed from the highest Committee Room in the land to the Saloon Bar of the tiniest inn, was 'Packer', and from all the multifarious points raised, one was likely to be proved the dominant factor in the end. In this age of extreme partisanship, had non-partisanship cricket any future? Does the world not want to see England beat Australia, or Arsenal beat Tottenham, or England beat Wales at Twickenham—or vice versa, according to particular loyalties? Could a collection of players, however great, stimulate public interest, when there was nothing on the end of it, except a considerable amount of money for the participants? The fact that tennis players and golfers are a constant attraction was irrelevant: they are individuals playing for no-one but themselves. And moreover, the whole crux of this matter was linked to big business—the business of television, and not so much to the furtherance of cricket or cricketers.

Mr. Packer, as Chairman of Channel 9 in Australia, was bitterly disappointed that an offer he had made to the Australian Board of Control for television rights for conventional Test cricket had not been given the due consideration which Mr. Packer felt the offer had merited. Out of this frustration, his scheme was born and nurtured. Meanwhile, unanimous agreement on their attitude to Packer's television 'circus' was reached at the emergency meeting of the International Cricket Conference on June 14, Mr. Packer, who left Heathrow that evening for the United States, was to be invited to discuss his plans with representatives of the I.C.C. at the earliest possible moment. This meeting was arranged for June 23, but negotiation was not found possible on one salient point—Mr. Packer demanded exclusive television rights from the Australian Board of Control from 1981 when their present contract with the Australian Broadcasting Commission ended. The I.C.C. representatives told him that it would be totally wrong in principle if this were taken as a condition of agreement.

The representatives of all the countries present were unanimous that no member country should be asked to submit to such a demand. The I.C.C.'s five conditions were:

1—Programmes and venues of the 'circus' to be acceptable to the home authority, and the length of programme not to exceed six weeks. Matches under home authority and the laws of cricket.

2—No player to participate without the permission of his home authority, who would not withhold it unreasonably.

3—No teams to be represented as national. That is, not Australia, possibly 'an Australian XI'.

4—Players contracted to Mr. Packer to be available for Tests, first-class fixtures and other home-authority sponsored matches.

5—The home authority must be able to honour all contractual commitments to existing sponsors and advertisers.

Afterwards, Packer said: 'I will take no steps at all to help anyone. It isn't 40 players, it's 51.' It seemed clear that his purpose in signing up the players was essentially as a bargaining weapon to help him to secure the exclusive television rights he so badly wanted. Names of other players to have joined Packer were being announced from day to day—D. L. Amiss, A. I. Kallicharran, C. L. King, B. D. Julien, C. G. Greenidge. At the crucial meeting at Lord's on July 26 the I.C.C. tabled three principal resolutions.

1—No player, who after Oct 1, 1977, has played or has made himself available to play in a match previously disapproved by the Conference, shall thereafter be eligible to play in any Test match without the express consent of the Conference, to be given only on the application of the governing body for cricket of his country.

2—Any match arranged or to be arranged by J.P. Sports (PTY) Ltd., Mr. Kerry Packer, Mr. Richie Benaud or associated companies or persons, to take place in Australia or elsewhere between Oct. 1, 1977 and March 31, 1979 is disapproved.

3—Matches are liable to be disapproved if so arranged as to have the probable result that invitations to play in such matches will conflict with invitations which have been or may be received to play in first-class matches.

Zaheer Abbas was yet another to defect from cricketing authority, making the known total at that time forty-one, except that it was announced that Jeff Thomson had withdrawn, as indeed had Kallicharran, according to Mr. David Lord, the Australian agent for them both. Packer swiftly answered this possible damage to his cause by setting out for England to talk to them. Lord, who also acted for Vivian Richards, said: 'I shall be offering them the same advice that I have given to Jeff. I am going to make it my job to see as many players as I can to try and persuade them to follow this example.'

Mr. Packer then announced that he would apply for an injunction and damages in the High Court against the International Cricket Conference and Test and County Cricket Board, and a similar action was to be started against Mr. David Lord, claiming that Mr. Lord had wrongfully induced players to break their contracts with the Company. A temporary injunction was granted against Lord, but the T.C.C.B. gave an undertaking that no Packer player would be banned until the Court hearing.

The meeting at Lord's on August 10 produced the following conditions:

The T.C.C.B.'s new sub-rules to meet the I.C.C. request concerning players who are members of the Packer group are:

1. No player who, after October 1, 1977, has played or made himself available to play in a match previously disapproved by the Conference shall thereafter be eligible to play in any Test match without the express consent of the Conference.

2. No county shall be entitled to play in any competitive county cricket match, any cricketer who is and remains precluded from playing in a Test match on the above grounds before the expiration of a period of two years immediately following the date of the last day of the last match previously disapproved by the I.C.C. in which he has played or made himself available to play.

This, of course, was subject to any High Court ruling which might follow. The name of Bob Woolmer was added to the list of Packer players. On Monday September 26 the High Court hearing began, and it lasted 31 days, the judgment, occupying 221 foolscap pages, took five and a half hours to deliver. Herewith are extracts from this massive document, summarised from *The Times*:

THE JUDGMENT

Mr. Justice Slade granted three English cricketers who had contracted to play for Mr. Kerry Packer's World Series Cricket Pty Ltd. declarations that all the changes of the rules of the International Cricket Conference and all their resolutions banning them from Test cricket are ultra vires and void as being in unreasonable restraint of trade. So, too, are the Test and County Cricket Board's proposed rules governing qualification and registration of cricketers in Test and competitive and county cricket.

His Lordship also granted similar declarations to World Series Cricket.

The three cricketers, the individual plaintiffs, were Mr. Tony Greig, Mr. John Snow and Mr. Michael Procter.

His Lordship said that as a result of the entry of World Series Cricket into cricket promotion, the International Cricket Conference in July, 1977, changed its rules in a manner which, if implemented, was likely effectively to disqualify any of the individual plaintiffs from playing in official international Test cricket for an indefinite time if he played in any cricket match organized by W.S.C. The T.C.C.B. proposed, subject to the court's decision, to change its rules in a manner which was likely to disqualify any of the plaintiffs from playing in English county cricket for at least several years if he played W.S.C. cricket.

In both actions the plaintiffs claimed that the new or proposed new rules would be legally invalid, and sought orders which would effectively prevent the I.C.C. and T.C.C.B. from implementing them. W.S.C. further claimed that those rules were or would be an unlawful inducement to a number of players who had entered into contracts to break them.

His Lordship considered that there were nine principal questions for ultimate decision.

(A) Are the contracts between W.S.C. and its players void?

(B) Has W.S.C. established that, as at August 3, and subject to any statutory immunity conferred by the 1974 Act, it has a good cause of action in tort against the I.C.C. based on inducement of breach of contract?

(C) Has W.S.C. established that as at August 3 and subject as aforesaid, it had a good cause of action in tort against the T.C.C.B. based on the same grounds?

(D) Subject to the provisions of the 1974 Act, are the new I.C.C. rules void as being in restraint of trade?

(E) Subject to aforesaid, are the proposed new T.C.C.B. rules void as being in restraint of trade?

(F) Is the I.C.C. an 'employers' association' within the 1974 Act?

(G) Is the I.C.C. an 'employers' association'?

(H) If either the I.C.C. or T.C.C.B. or both be 'employers' associations', does this itself bar any cause of action that would otherwise exist?

(I) In the light of the answers, what relief (if any) should be given to (i) the individual plaintiffs and (ii) W.S.C.

Summarizing the evidence, his Lordship commented that the evidence relating to the conditions under which cricketers worked, particularly in the United Kingdom, would have filled a book and would doubtless provide useful raw material for cricket historians of the future.

His Lordship could see the possible force of criticism directed against Mr. Greig, who, when he signed his contract with W.S.C. and recruited others to do so, had just completed a tour of Australia as captain of the England team, was still generally regarded as its captain and could have looked forward with reasonable confidence to his formal reappointment as such. There was obviously a case for saying that his responsibilities to the T.C.C.B. were of a rather special nature.

However, two points had to be borne in mind in regard to him and all the other United Kingdom players. (1) Neither the Cricket Council (the governing body of cricket in England recognized by the I.C.C.) nor the T.C.C.B. had themselves entered into any kind of commitment, legal or otherwise, ever to offer employment to any of those players again. (2) The players themselves had entered into no contractual commitment with the Cricket Council or the T.C.C.B. precluding them from playing cricket for a private promoter.

In conclusion his Lordship said that Mr. Michael Kempster, in his opening speech for the defendants, generously but correctly, acknowledged five positive beneficial effects which, on the evidence, had already been produced by the emergence of W.S.C. as a promoter of cricket. First it had offered the promise of much greater rewards for star cricketers. Indeed, it had gone farther—it had offered secure, regular, remunerative employment in cricket to more than 50 cricketers, in most cases for three English winter seasons, at a time when most of them would otherwise have no guarantee of regular employment in the game. Secondly, it had already stimulated new sponsors for traditional cricket. Thirdly, it had brought back to the game in Australia several talented players. Fourthly, it, or the group of companies of which it formed part, had initiated a useful coaching scheme for young players in New South Wales. Fifthly, it had increased public interest in the game.

For all those acknowledged benefits, the defendants had held the strong opinion that I.C.C.'s effective monopoly in the promotion of first-class cricket at international level had been good for the game and that the emergence of W.S.C. into the promotion field was bad for it. However, whether or not that opinion was correct had not been the question for the court. The question for decision had been whether the particular steps which the I.C.C. and the T.C.C.B. took to combat what they regarded as the threat from W.S.C. were legally justified. The long investigation had satisfied his Lordship that the positive demonstrable benefits that might be achieved by introducing the I.C.C. and T.C.C.B. bans and applying them to players who had already committed themselves to contracts with W.S.C. were at best somewhat speculative.

On the other hand there were demonstrable disadvantages if the bans were to be applied in that way. They would preclude the players concerned from entry into important fields of professional livelihood. They would subject them to the hardships and injustice of essentially retrospective legislation. They would deprive the public of any opportunity of seeing the players concerned playing in conventional cricket, either at Test or at English county level, for at least a number of years. By so depriving the public they would carry with them an appreciable risk of so depriving the public enthusiasm for conventional cricket and the receipts to be derived from it. Furthermore, the defendants by imposing the bans, in the form which they took and with the intentions which prompted them, acted without adequate regard to the fact that W.S.C. had contractual rights with the players concerned, which were entitled to the protection of the law. The defendants acted in good faith and in what they considered to be the best interests of cricket. That, however, was not enough to justify in law the course which they had taken.

Judgement was given for the plaintiffs in both actions with costs.

BEARING THE COSTS

It was estimated that the costs to the defendants were likely to be about £200,000, and whilst this sort of figure was a severe blow to any organisation—certainly to the game of cricket, there were three cardinal factors to be borne in mind in connection with the financial administration of Test and County Cricket in this country. First, since the International

Cricket Conference were co-defendants, it is assumed that they would bear some of the costs. Secondly, as a result of the Packer intervention, Cornhill moved in to sponsor Test cricket in England, a sum of one million pounds spread over five years was mentioned, and not, apparently, being far from the mark, and thirdly, the Test and County Cricket Board received £150,000 from Mr. Packer for the television rights for his Channel 9 coverage of the England v. Australia Test matches during the 1977 summer.

Whatever the net loss to the T.C.C.B., it would be spread over the various beneficiaries from the T.C.C.B.'s income for 1977 such as the seventeen first-class counties, the Minor Counties, Universities, and so on. Admittedly, the county budgets could not readily accommodate any deduction from their share, but overall the blow divided by at least twenty was brought down to more bearable proportions.

The defendants were given six weeks from the date of entering of the order to consider the possibility of an appeal. They no doubt took account of three important factors—the total lack of crowds at Packer's early matches in his series, and, although Packer brushed this aside as having no consequence because he was only interested in television reaction and ratings, one must take the ramifications of a lack of interest on the part of paying customers as being important. Secondly, that Australia beat a very good Indian side in three Tests without their Packer players, and thirdly that the England side held their own in Pakistan where both sides were without their Packer players. A good deal of water will have flowed under the bridge before a total clarification of all the implications, short, and long-term, is possible.

Early in February 1978, the International Cricket Conference and the T.C.C.B. decided not to appeal and agreed to share their burden of the costs.

JUDGE HITS CRICKET BAN FOR SIX [1978]

The Packer crisis and the legal flummery which followed in its wake was of course the dominant theme of the moment, but Ross's essay was by no means the most readable in the 1978 almanack. It was not even the most entertaining essay involving the antics of the British judiciary. Attached to the end of Ross's essay on Packer, like a tin can tied to a dog's tail, was the uplifting story of how a householder in a Durham village was rebuked by the law for attempting to illegalise cricket in the locality for no better reason than that it constituted a threat to life and limb. The judgment that the plaintiff might care to sell up and move elsewhere, that if, in effect, he did not like it he was free to lump it, deserves to be included as a footnote to the career of Mr. Justice Cocklecarrot. It was a callous, unfeeling and irrational piece of advice, and there can be no lover of cricket who could fail to applaud it.

A village cricket club on April 6, 1977 won the support of the Appeal Court in London to carry on playing—and hitting boundaries. By a 2–1 majority the court lifted a legal ban on the hitting of sixes into a neighbouring garden.

Lord Denning, Master of the Rolls, said that if Mr. John Miller, whose house adjoined Lintz Cricket Club, Burnopfield, Durham, did not like it, he should sell his house and move elsewhere.

'For over 70 years the game of cricket has been played on this ground to the great benefit of the community as a whole, and to the injury of none,' said the judge. The court allowed an appeal by the cricket club from a decision of Mr. Justice Reeve, in December 1976.

On an application by Mr. Miller and his wife, Brenda, the judge had banned cricket matches until adequate steps were taken to prevent balls being hit on to their property.

Lord Denning said Mr. Miller had bought the house four years ago in midsummer when the cricket season was at its height. He might have guessed that there was a risk that a hit for six might possibly land on his property.

If he found he did not like it he ought, when cricket was played, to sit on the other side of the house or in the front garden—or go out. Or take advantage of the offers the club had made of fitting unbreakable glass. 'Or, if he does not like that, he ought to sell his house and move elsewhere,' the judge said. 'I expect there are many who would gladly buy it in order to be near the cricket field and open space.

'At any rate, he ought not to be allowed to stop cricket from being played on this ground.'

Lord Denning asked: 'Does it suddenly become a nuisance because one of the neighbours chooses to build a house on the very edge of the ground—in such a position that it may well be struck by the ball on the rare occasion when there is a hit for six?

'To my mind the answer is plainly "No". The building of the house does not convert the playing of cricket into a nuisance, when it was not so before.'

Lord Denning said that if any damage was caused to the house or anyone in it, it was because of the position in which it was built. A private owner would be in much the same position as a farmer who previously put his cows in a field.

'He could not complain if a batsman hit a six out of the ground, and by a million to one chance it struck the cow, or even the farmer himself,' said Lord Denning.

'He would be in no better position than a spectator at Lord's or the Oval, or at a motor rally.'

Lord Denning said that if cricket was stopped on the ground, the cricket club might disappear.

'The young men will turn to other things instead of cricket. The whole village will be much the poorer. And all this because of a newcomer who has just bought a house next to the cricket ground.'

Disagreeing, Lord Justice Geoffrey Lane said there was no doubt that if cricket was played damage would be done to Mr. Miller's tiles or windows or both.

'So long as this situation exists it seems that damages cannot be said to provide an adequate form of relief.'

The judge said, however, that he would have postponed the operation of the injunction for 12 months to enable the club to look elsewhere for an alternative pitch.

Lord Justice Cumming-Bruce, agreed with Lord Denning.

Mr. Bob Jackson, chairman of the club, said: 'It was a victory not only for the club but for sport in general. A lot of clubs who might have found themselves in similar positions to us will breathe sighs of relief.'

Although in the last two years 109 sixes have been hit at the ground, Mr. Jackson stressed that only two of these had landed on the Millers' property. Other lofty clouts in the Millers' direction had been 'fielded' by the 14ft-high chain-link fence bordering their garden.

The club's legal costs have been underwritten by the National Cricket Association and the Test and County Cricket Board.

THE PACKER CASE [1979]

BY GORDON ROSS

The Packer case rolled on, into the law courts and out again, at which point the Test and County Cricket Board, having been badly burned by the judiciary, decided not to appeal. Some players still with an international future, particularly the two Kent stars Knott and Underwood, were seen to have ended their international careers, but the county, more intent on trophies than on moral rectitude, opened its arms. There was hardly a day on which rumour, denial and counter-rumour did not fill the pages of the sporting prints. Each Test-playing nation sought its own route to salvation, while Mr. Packer blithely continued to mix it even though patently the victor. Of individual cases, none smacks more of Mr. Justice Cocklecarrot than the contradictions of Jeff Thomson's predicament. In retrospect it is surprising that nobody announced his intention of turning the Thomson muddle into a musical comedy. Funded by Packer, naturally.

In the documentation of the Packer case in last year's Wisden *it was possible only at the last minute to add the words: 'Early in February, 1978, the International Cricket Conference and the T.C.C.B. decided not to appeal and agreed to share the burden of the costs.' The story, therefore, is taken up at the point of this decision, but in greater detail, as it was not possible to elaborate on the appeal decision at the time.*

IT was announced from Lord's on Thursday, February 2, 1978 that an appeal against the High Court ruling by Mr. Justice Slade the previous November in favour of Mr. Kerry Packer and some of his players would not be in the best interests of international cricket. Mr. Jack Bailey, secretary of the International Cricket Conference, said that once the delegates had agreed there should be no appeal—the first item on the agenda—all discussions that followed were in the light of the High Court judgment. No pressure could be brought to bear upon member countries about whom they should select to play; the I.C.C. could not make stipulations concerning this aspect. Mr. Bailey told a Press conference that, though it was felt that both the I.C.C. and the T.C.C.B. had reasonable grounds for appeal, there was no guarantee of success, and to appeal just for the sake of appeal would be churlish.

The selectors of individual countries will, as now, be responsible for making their own decisions and there may be different criteria used— consideration of the short-term or long-term requirements of that particular country.

As far as the T.C.C.B. were concerned, Peter Lush, the spokesman on their behalf, said that the selection by counties of World Series Cricket players was a matter for individual members; just as, in the case of the I.C.C., the T.C.C.B. was not in a position to make recommendations. At this moment, six England players were under contract to W.S.C.—Greig, who had just been relieved of the Sussex captaincy because of derogatory remarks made about Boycott—Amiss, Snow, Knott, Underwood and Woolmer. The I.C.C. meeting, which lasted two days, agreed that the costs of the High Court hearing would be divided between the I.C.C. and the T.C.C.B. The question of making contractual arrangements with players had been aired, but no collective decision was taken. If individual countries were approached by W.S.C., any discussion would have to be with the I.C.C. as a whole.

Meanwhile, W.S.C. were continuing to sign up players; or rumour had it that they were. On February 3 *The Sydney Sun* claimed that Sunil Gavaskar and Bisham Bedi were to be offered lucrative contracts for the next season, though Bedi said he knew of no such offer, and was loath to comment further until he did. On February 7 it was revealed that Greig and Sydney promoter David Lord had had lengthy discussions with a view to effecting a compromise between W.S.C. and the I.C.C., with a new international series, under the auspices of the I.C.C., to be played in addition to scheduled Test series. In what struck observers as a most curious finale to their discussions, it was stated that Greig had not signed the 'joint statement', because it did not constitute a perfectly true expression of his views. The Australian Board's view has never wavered from its original course; that if W.S.C. wished to re-open talks with the Board, it should do so through the I.C.C. in London. On this they stood firm.

In any event, a joint statement not signed by the second party hardly constituted the basis for serious discussion. On the same day, in England, a meeting of Kent's full committee decided to have back all their four Packer players should they wish to return. Hampshire announced at the same time that Greenidge, Richards, and Roberts would again be playing for them in the summer. Inevitably, all shades of opinion were being expressed. A letter to *The Times* from Surrey's chairman, Raman Subba Row, advocated a genuine discussion between the I.C.C. and the rival system; two days later, Oliver Popplewell, QC, in a letter to the same newspaper, stated that the authorities should stand firm and beware the siren song of compromise until such time as Kerry Packer notified them that players signed by him would be released for the whole of the England tour of Australia in 1978–79.

During these diverse expressions of opinion, the W.S.C. Packer matches were taking place in Australia to attendances considerably smaller than Packer would have hoped for. The exceptions were matches played in floodlight, which obviously had a novelty attraction and were well patronised. Before a crowd of 2,716 W.S.C. Australia prevented a run of three defeats at the hands of the W.S.C. World XI by winning by 41 runs. Comparative failure by Australia, in any sport, is something that appeals less to Australian crowds than to those in most other cricketing countries, and the Australian team's performance clearly could not have aided the Packer cause.

The true financial picture of this first series may not emerge for some time—if ever—but estimates put the loss in excess of £2,000,000; derived from an outlay of some three and a half million, with receipts from advertising revenue about a million, and gate receipts of a shade under half a million. Packer's comment was: 'We are still amateurs, but we are more professional than we were, and will become even more professional.'

It was said that the prize-money, worth $A201,500, had gone into a provident fund for three years, after which it would be paid out with interest. Still on the question of finance, it was apparently agreed, at a meeting between the Victorian Football League and Kerry Packer, that the mobile pitches at VFL Park would stay in place throughout the football season at an additional cost to W.S.C., who paid VFL $A850,000 for the use of the ground for three summers, with an original agreement to remove the pitches before the start of each football season.

When the dust was allowed to settle on this first adventure, followers of traditional cricket throughout the world had some comfort that this adventurer, Mr. Kerry Packer, had clearly not met with the resounding success for which he had hoped. On the other hand, any new enterprise is subject to teething troubles. Moreover, Mr. Packer's make-up is such that he was most unlikely to throw in the towel after a disastrous first round, and suffer a loss of pride as well as of money. In the end, of course, he may have to decide how much money he can afford to spend on pride. At a much later date a new managing director, Andrew Caro, emerged, clearly with the brief to make W.S.C. pay, and to fight what, at that stage, appeared to be a battle with authority.

In Australia, one factor in the whole affair had remained constant—the unwavering line pursued by the Australian Board. Any opinion suggesting that the Australian Board might have taken a more conciliatory view of this rather ugly menace thrust upon them, holds little water when it is accepted that the Board, even if somewhat reluctantly, were party to the working arrangement proposed at the I.C.C. meeting, which Packer turned down, out of hand. The Board knew well enough, after this, that they had a fight on their hands, and they prepared for the fray. Who could blame them? Australia's point of view was fairly and comprehensively put by Mr. E. W. Swanton, in an article in *The Cricketer* of May 1978 entitled 'Bob Parish pumps home the facts'. Mr. Parish, chairman of the Australian Cricket Board, was at great pains to point out, in a speech in his home state of Victoria, the enormous improvements in payments made to their players in recent years; long before Packer's arrival. The following is worth quoting:

'In 1974 the Board resolved that it would pay to the players the maximum it could afford after taking into consideration its overall responsibility to Australian cricket at all other levels. The Board has honoured the undertaking. In 1974–75, Test match payments were $A250 per Test. In 1975–76 this was increased to $A475 plus a bonus of $A400, a total of $A875 per Test. In 1976–77 the match fee was maintained at $A475 and a bonus of $A250 was paid, a total of $A725 per Test. In 1977–78 the match fee payment was $A800.

Sponsorship was introduced to cricket in the 1974–75 season. The Board decided that 30 per cent of the sponsorship should go to the players as prize-money. Sponsorship of first-class cricket in Australia by the Benson and Hedges Company has increased from the initial $A50,000 to a massive $A250,000 this season [1977–78] and $A350,000 next year. This season a total of $A175,000 was provided as prize-money for the five Tests against India and the Sheffield Shield matches. Each of the Tests carried a winner's prize of $A6,000 and a loser's prize of $A3,000. In addition to the prize-money there was a team sponsorship fee of $A802 per Test. This is provided by the Benson and Hedges Company from a team sponsorship arranged by the Board with the approval of the players in January 1977. So, for each of the Tests against India, Australian Test players received from the Board $A1,825 if the match was lost or $A2,102 if the match was won. Australia won three and lost two Tests this season. So a player who played in all five Tests received from the Board $A10,010. Sheffield Shield and Gillette Cup earnings would together total another $A4,000 to $A5,000, and add to this another $A7,000 for the West Indies tour and the total for the 1977–78 season would exceed $A20,000 (£12,000).'

Mr. Parish, with a touch of irony, substantiated the improvement in the lot of the Australian cricketer by quoting from a book recently published by Greg Chappell, in which the former captain of Australia wrote; 'Cricketers' rewards have increased dramatically in a comparatively short time. In a matter of just two seasons the base Test payment doubled from $A200 to $A400. Sizeable bonuses have been handed out at the end of the past two series, provident fund money has been increased, cash endorsements are flowing as never before, and the Test team is now sponsored for three years. It's hardly surprising that Australia leads the way in providing a far better deal for cricketers.'

Chappell's words seem to make a mockery of the well-worn cry that Establishments do little to improve the lot of the first-class cricketer. However, it is only fair to say that the advent of Packer was clearly instrumental in substantially improving the lot of the England Test player. Not, of course, from the purse of Mr. Packer, but in the way the surrounding controversy brought into the public gaze the fact that perhaps the England Test player was inadequately rewarded for his labours on behalf of his country. So in one way, Greig's cry that what he was doing was for the good of all cricketers, and not just the élite, had the ring of truth about it; but possibly not in the precise way that Greig had contemplated.

Just as Australia was firm, Pakistan, too, was doing its best to follow the hard-line. When the Board of Control for Cricket in Pakistan announced the names of about 30 players to attend the training camp in preparation for the tour of England, Majid, Imran, Mushtaq, and Zaheer were omitted. The Board stated they were prepared to consider the Packer players, provided they could guarantee their availability to play for Pakistan, not only on the tour of England but for all future commitments. This, they could not give; and there followed a raging controversy, the result of which was a meeting called on March 26 under the chairmanship of the Chief Martial Law Administrator and attended by former Pakistan captains, prominent cricket organisers, and representatives from every province. At the end of it, the Administrator ruled that Packer players would not be included in the Pakistan team. There, it seemed, the matter was closed, but shortly before the team was due to leave, rumours spread that Miandad, Haroon, and Sarfraz had signed Packer contracts. This was denied by the Board, but suspicion lingered on. In the end, the air was cleared when a Packer representative announced that neither Miandad nor Haroon had signed any form of contract, and Sarfraz, in due course, announced that neither had he. The poor showing of the Pakistan team, deprived of the Packer players, was later to generate some re-thinking.

West Indies, perhaps the most vulnerable of all I.C.C. members in the matter of cricket finance, was placed in an increasingly difficult position. The distance between the islands—1,200 miles, for instance, between Jamaica and Barbados—and multifarious other problems have made it an intense struggle for any treasurer of the West Indies Board to make ends meet; and a West Indies team that was virtually a second team would impair this rickety financial structure even more. It is not surprising, therefore, that West Indies had taken the most moderate line with Packer players. The Board were against the original I.C.C. ban, although subsequently voting for it in the interests of unity, and they decided to continue to play their Packer men, provided they made themselves available. Anyone with first hand knowledge of West Indies cricket will readily understand their thinking.

In the series beginning in the Caribbean in March, West Indies included the Packer players; Australia did not. As a result, West Indies won the first two Tests with some ease—by an innings and 106 runs, and by nine wickets. But just before the third Test, at Georgetown, Guyana, a balloon of sizeable dimensions went up. When the West Indies team was announced, three Packer players—Haynes and Austin, recently signed, and Deryck Murray, secretary of the West Indies Players Association—were dropped and replaced by non-Packer players. Clive Lloyd made an immediate protest and resigned as captain, although the Board stated they had not been officially informed by Lloyd of his decision. Lloyd then sought a meeting between the Board and the Packer players, but by the time the Board's president, Jeffrey Stollmeyer, arrived in Guyana, the Packer set had already written to the Board withdrawing from the Test; which was due to start the day after Stollmeyer's arrival.

The result was that West Indies took the field for the third Test with six players new to Test cricket. Williams joined the cricketing élite by scoring a century in his first Test, and Gomes, another of the original triumvirate, also scored a hundred in a huge second innings total of 439. This looked to have secured the match, but for the second time in a 1977–78 series Australia scored more than 300 in the fourth innings to win a Test; they had done so to win the second Test against India in Perth.

Australia's dramatic recovery provided the West Indies Board with another headache. A match had been narrowly lost; the presence of the Packer players in the West Indies side would almost certainly (as certain as a game of cricket can be) have produced a different result. The Board, understandably, had already announced that the Packer players would take no further part in the series because the players had been unable to give an assurance that they would be available for the tour of India and Sri Lanka.

The Board had set March 23 as the date for a decision from the players. Packer himself flew to Georgetown and held a Press conference. And in the grand manner he sent his jet aircraft to pick up former West Indies players who had problems in getting flights to a dinner party he gave at the Sandy Lane Hotel, Barbados, using his visit to put his case on television, and to win over his receptive audience. Events followed events and immeasurably widened the gulf between the Board and the Packer players. The West Indies Board, so far the only I.C.C. member to play their Packer men, were now realising they were on a collision course. There was precious little evidence that Packer was looking for an amicable compromise.

The international position at this moment was that Australia, England, and Pakistan were not playing Packer players, West Indies, though having done so, were now in line with the others; India, New Zealand and South Africa were not specifically concerned, though India and New Zealand could conceivably be in the future. South Africa, not playing Test cricket, would not.

An important factor was to affect the thinking of both the West Indies and Pakistan Boards; the opinion of cricket followers in both countries. Clearly, throughout the Caribbean, sympathy was with the Packer players;

or more precisely with West Indies always fielding the best available side in Test cricket. The same applied in Pakistan; if anything, feeling was heightened by the palpably poor performance of the Pakistan side in England. Attempts were made by Pakistan's supporters to make martyrs out of the discarded Packer players and ridicule the team, at a time when it needed firm support. Clearly, something had to be done, especially by the West Indies Board who faced the stark reality of a huge financial loss on the series with Australia; it was rumoured to be in the region of £100,000.

It was not so much a turn-about, therefore, as facing reality when the West Indies Board recommended that dialogue between the International Cricket Conference and World Series Cricket be re-opened at the earliest opportunity; and, if necessary, on the initiative of the I.C.C. The second resolution offered the Board's services to initiate such discussions. Meanwhile, W.S.C., which had named Deryck Murray as its Caribbean representative, was writing to the clubs responsible for the major grounds in West Indies, plus Antigua and St Lucia, to set up a West Indies v. Australia W.S.C. series in 1978–79. The West Indies Board were to have the enemy on their doorstep—if enemy they were to be—doing irreparable damage to the future of organised cricket in West Indies. It left the Board with virtually no option but to seek a peaceful solution.

World opinion and interest was now focussed on the International Cricket Conference meeting that was to begin at Lord's on Tuesday, July 25, and this was not without its dramatic overture. On the eve of proceedings, Mr. David Clark, president of M.C.C. and thus chairman of the I.C.C., resigned from the Kent County Cricket Club committee, on which he had served for 30 years, following Kent's decision to offer new contracts to the three W.S.C. players: Asif, Woolmer and Underwood. Mr. Clark's position, in the light of this decision, left him with no option but to resign, otherwise he could have been accused of double-dealing.

Kent's decision to make their policy known when they did was considered by many to have political implications; it was felt they were trying to influence I.C.C. thinking, and perhaps give the impression that all English counties felt the same way. There were also rumours that the players concerned were bringing pressure to bear on Kent during the week before the Benson and Hedges Cup final at Lord's; Kent were finalists and obviously would not want disruptions during the run-up to a final. The county had previously met legal requirements by offering contracts of only one year to Packer employees; Knott, being one of them, withdrew (for the time being at any rate) from first-class cricket. Among other aspects, it seems that Kent had not solicited the views of the Cricketers' Association, whose opinion, as a thoroughly responsible body, should have been sought.

It subsequently transpired that David Clark and Jack Bailey had, prior to the meeting, gone to the United States to hear the W.S.C. proposals for an amicable solution, both parties being particularly anxious that the meeting should be a matter of great secrecy. These proposals, given in detail below, are so ludicrous, as to evoke intense speculation as to what

W.S.C. hoped to achieve by them. Was it that Packer had no wish for an agreement, and was confident of his own future without any need to placate anyone in cricket? If he was looking for a middle-of-the-road settlement, then these absurd proposals would generate contempt rather than stimulate a mood of reconciliation and lead to sensible discussion. The Packer package was as follows:

W.S.C. ask for fully representative teams (to be selected by W.S.C.) to be available for W.S.C. matches on the following basis:

A—October–November: India, New Zealand and Pakistan to play a preliminary knockout competition in one of these countries to provide a winner to participate in the one-day internationals and 'super Test' series in Australia later in the season.

B—December 22–January 24: Australia, England, West Indies and Pakistan (or whoever may be the winners of the preliminary competition) and a World XI to play in a series of one-day internationals, avoiding actual dates of official Test matches in Australia.

C—February 2–March 12: Australia, England, West Indies and Pakistan (or whoever may be the winners of the preliminary competition) to play in a W.S.C. 'super Test' series. These teams, plus a World XI, would also play further one-day internationals.

D—Assuming Australia were the winners, for approximately three weeks in March–April, May–June, September–October and October–November, the winners of the W.S.C. 'super-Test' series to play in West Indies, England, India and Pakistan respectively.

The I.C.C. gave their reasons for finding these proposals totally unacceptable, though elaboration was hardly necessary. This was the dignified reply.

1—Any official tour to Australia would be disrupted by having to release some or all players for a number of days in December and January. The leading Australian players would also be unavailable for their domestic cricket in this period.

2—No official tours allowing free selection of teams could be arranged between member countries between mid-December and mid-March (the prime period in most countries) because of the necessity for national teams to remain intact while touring other countries.

3—It would be virtually impossible to arrange any worthwhile official tours prior to mid-December, bearing in mind the proposed W.S.C. commitments of India, New Zealand and Pakistan and the 'super Test' tour to Pakistan.

4—Official tours after mid-March are not feasible other than in West Indies (until late April) and in England (May until August). The W.S.C. programme would involve the 'super Test' champions visiting West Indies in March and April, and England in May and June.

Despite the two sides being poles apart, it was agreed that the dialogue should be continued and that W.S.C. be asked to reconsider their proposals. A sub-committee was to be set up to monitor all future developments. It had, in any case, been understood by both parties that no alteration to tours already arranged for the coming winter was possible. Andrew Caro, managing director of W.S.C., gave his version of events as showing the first real chink of light (some chink, and some light, a few would say!) and followed at a Press conference by calling the W.S.C. proposals a working document and giving a few nebulous alternative ideas.

Just what sort of a hand was W.S.C. playing? Did they hold all the honours or not? If they were contemptuous of organised cricket, and in no need of it, why bother to submit proposals? The plot deepens. One feasible explanation could be that Packer, like a good union official or shop steward, must put on a good front on behalf of his players and be seen to give them confidence in the future. Clearly, such terms as those outlined above would create the impression of negotiating from strength while, at the same time, playing for time. Packer would obviously want to know how W.S.C. matches fared in Australia with an official Australian v. England series going on. That would give him some guide as to the depth of his roots.

It was said in the early days that Packer resented the use of the word 'Circus' in relation to his cricket, which was to be series stuff at the highest level. Hardly the highest level in September when his stars went to New York and, as 'World All Stars', met an 'American All Stars' XI for a rather undistinguished trophy given by a Brooklyn sporting goods shop—and lost! Mr. Greig announced that he would be back in a year's time—and win. Perhaps with players like Greig, Sobers, Hookes, Majid Khan and Fredericks in the Packer contingent, it was better mileage to lose, so creating a big story. Who knows?

In the meantime, Pakistan, smarting from the very poor showing of their side in England, turned back to their Packer players. General K. M. Azhar, responsible for cricket in Pakistan, said: 'We do not have the schedule of the Packer series, but if there is no clash of fixtures and nothing in their [the Packer players'] contracts to stand in the way, then we should welcome them.' Five Pakistani players were then under contract to Packer—Imran Kahn, Majid Khan, Mushtaq Mohammad, Zaheer Abbas and Asif Iqbal.

It had already been rumoured that Richard Hadlee, who had improved his reputation in England in the summer of 1978, was not on the Packer list of potentials. It was said that Hadlee's involvement would be limited to a series of professional matches to be staged in New Zealand between November 2 and November 16, before W.S.C. opened their second Australian season. There was also talk that Geoff Howarth, the other New Zealander to play well against England, was a candidate. With Richard Hadlee's father, Walter Hadlee, chairman of the New Zealand Board, it was a ticklish situation for him, and one he would almost inevitably want to leave to the other members of his Board, hoping they could reach agreement without needing the chairman's casting vote.

In England, at the end of the summer, attention was focused on two players at the opposite ends of the earth; Dennis Amiss in Warwickshire and Jeff Thomson in Australia. Amiss was told by Warwickshire that, as a Packer player, he would not be retained by the county in 1979. Thomson, despite being under contract to the official Australian Cricket Board, signed a three-year contract with World Series Cricket. It was announced that the Board would be seeking legal advice.

To take Warwickshire first. The announcement that Amiss would not be retained caused a furore amongst Warwickshire members. Their view was: Why should Warwickshire deplete their ranks when Kent, who had just won the Championship, were retaining their Packer men, as were a few other counties. It seemed that Warwickshire cricket was spilt right down the middle, and it was no great surprise when a Special General Meeting was convened for Tuesday, September 26. The surprise was that at the request of Amiss himself, the meeting was called off. Why? There is a ready answer. It appears, almost for the first time since the Packer saga began, that the Cricketers' Association was able to play a substantial part in striving for peace.

They apparently advised Amiss that if, during the winter, talks between W.S.C. and the I.C.C. could establish some sort of peace, Warwickshire would obviously be happy to retain a player who had scored over 2,000 runs for them in the summer; especially as the player himself wanted to stay. If nothing was achieved, then Amiss could re-think the situation. In any event, the Cricketers' Association had one or two crucial resolutions to deal with at their next meeting, and they felt that these would be better kept on ice until the outcome of any talks during the winter.

It seemed that both the Cricketers' Association and some of the Packer players were anxious for W.S.C. and the I.C.C. to get together as soon as possible, to see if the framework of an agreement could be worked out. Warwickshire were alone in standing on principles, but their supporters' view that what is good for the goose is good for the gander is readily understandable. Dennis Amiss, at this point, emerged from the furore with honour, as did the Cricketers' Association.

Thomson's move, however, represented yet another twist in his topsy-turvy relationship with Packer. First he signed; then he withdrew on the advice of his agent, who was taken to court by Packer. Now, on the eve of an Ashes series, he had defected again in breach of another contract. The Australian Board were particularly unfortunate, because obviously Thomson was Australia's principal drawing-card in the series against England. Packer knew this well, and countered with a contract and a cheque book; in 1978, the two together seem to be a passport to anywhere.

Swiftly on the heels of Thomson's defection, the Australian Cricket Board issued the following statement:

'*It was announced last Friday, September 29 that World Series Cricket had entered into a three-year contract with Mr. Jeff Thomson despite its awareness that Mr. Thomson had agreed to play only in matches controlled by the Board and state associations during the 1978–79*

Australian season, and despite the publicity given to the fact that the Board had refused Mr. Thomson's request that he be released from his contractual obligations to the Board.

The Board would naturally have preferred to resolve this matter without resort to the courts and, in order that Mr. Thomson's contractual obligations to the Board should be respected, the Board sought an assurance from World Series Cricket that it would not select Mr. Thomson to play cricket in any of its teams until after the conclusion of the Australian cricket season on March 31, 1979. World Series Cricket has declined to give such an assurance.'

In the subsequent court action, Mr. Justice Kearney decided, after a twelve-day hearing, that Thomson, who has said he will never play Test cricket for Australia again, was bound by a contract he signed with the Australian Cricket Board earlier in the year. He could not, therefore, play for Packer until April. Judge Kearney said that some of Thomson's evidence before the court had been quite unreliable. He awarded costs against Thomson and World Series Cricket. Thomson replied by saying that he would probably spend the summer as a professional fisherman off the Queensland coast rather than play grade cricket; in the words of the famous Bing Crosby song—'Gone Fishin'.

Meantime, it was rumoured that the W.S.C. organisation was busy recruiting Indian players who were at that time on tour in Pakistan. Bedi, the captain, in particular was mentioned, as was Gavaskar, the opening batsman. It was also said that a prominent Pakistan cricketer close to the organisation was acting as the recruiting officer. No official confirmation was issued either way at the time.

So, amidst litigation, rumour, resignations and Press conferences, this long-drawn-out saga rolls relentlessly on, first in one direction, then another, as apparently it will continue to do for a long time to come.

THREE MORE STUDIES IN GREATNESS [1979]

BY BASIL EASTERBROOK

Meanwhile, as if in an attempt to reassure readers that cricket did still exist in a recognisable form, Basil Easterbrook repeated his ploy of 1978 by presenting a triple portrait of players whose biographical enchantments had perhaps been overlooked in recent years. Mr. Easterbrook's six sketches were so efficacious as to inspire a dream in which every first-class cricketer was given the same treatment, all as part of a Cricketing Dictionary of National Biography. This was never forthcoming, and the hungry student has to content himself with the two sets of three lives. In all three selections for 1979 there was an element of the bizarre which might have been looked for in the pages of the Hotspur *or the* Wizard *but hardly in* Wisden. *Tom Goddard's false start and his subsequent lonely regeneration in the nets at Lord's, Bill Copson's potential as a demon bowler which lay dormant till the General Strike of 1926 disclosed it, the decision of Kenneth Farnes to fly by night and the tragedy which swiftly followed, all three cases help to explain the fascination which the game holds for the diligent researcher.*

All three of Mr. Easterbrook's subject were famous men in my elementary schooldays and I can still savour my dismay when in 1936, thanks largely to Copson's bowling, Derbyshire interrupted the all-conquering Yorkshire side on its procession towards its umpteenth championship. But the greatest of the three seemed to be Farnes, who in 1938 was honoured by his selection for the John Player cigarette card series. There he was, elegant and gentle in his Cambridge colours, looking exactly like the young man Mr. Easterbrook so affectionately describes, interested in reading, writing and painting. When one morning, in the playground of a London school obsessed with football I read of his death, I remember wondering what Australia might do to us without Farnes when the time came. The answer can be found in the 1948 almanack.

TOM GODDARD
(Gloucestershire)

Long of face, each feature strong and clearly defined, a tall frame, capped by coal-black hair, and with a gravel voice, Thomas William John Goddard, one of the greatest off-break bowlers cricket has ever produced, looked every inch the fast bowler of imagination. That, in fact, was exactly what he was when he came into the game in 1922. For six years he persevered with this form of attack, but although in 1926 he took 68 wickets it was already apparent he was never going to be anything other than a second-rater.

Gloucestershire did not fire him; instead they offered him re-engagement at reduced terms, but Tom refused them. A brief and undistinguished first-class career seemed at its end, by no means an uncommon story. Goddard, however, was determined that his life lay in the game, and he took his 6ft 3in frame off to London where he got himself a job on the groundstaff at Lord's. It was not much for a man who had been on the county circuit for several seasons, but it gave him unlimited opportunities for the practice he wanted in order to change his style.

Tom had massive hands and had always been able to spin the ball. But Gloucestershire, able to call on Parker, Dennett, and Mills in the twenties, had been interested in Tom only as a pace bowler. Tom was soon spinning the ball in the Lord's nets to a remarkable degree and word eventually filtered back to B.H. Lyon, the Gloucestershire captain. Lyon came up to Lord's, and from a secluded vantage point, taking care Goddard was not aware of his presence, watched his failed fast bowler at work.

On the strength of a single observation Lyon urged the Gloucestershire authorities to take Goddard back on the staff as a spinner. What a return 1929 was, for Tom took 173 wickets at just over 15 runs each for the county and 184 in all. Bowling round the wicket with three and even four fieldsmen at short leg, Goddard was a problem for the best batsmen. He once bowled Pat Hendren at Bristol with a ball that pitched a full foot outside the off stump and hit the leg stump.

Those long, strong fingers, combined with suppleness of wrist, enabled him to turn the ball even on the plumbest of pitches. He was surrounded by colleagues willing and able to help him. Lyon gave him invaluable assistance with advice on field settings. Wally Hammond and Charlie Parker, all-time greats both of them, nursed him steadily along to maturity and an immortality equal to their own. Goddard learnt as he went along, discovering he could surprise a batsman with a little extra pace off the pitch. Then he discovered that his height made his flight steep and difficult to judge, and his skill in this aspect of his bowling blossomed.

Goddard and the slow left-armer Parker became the most feared spin twins in the Championship—the Laker and Lock of their day. He was unfortunate in that his peak coincided with a period when off-spinners were not fashionable in Test cricket, but he played eight times for England. He did the hat-trick six times in his career, only once less than the all-time record of seven by Doug Wright, the Kent wrist spinner.

The most famous of these was in a Test against South Africa at Johannesburg on Boxing Day, 1938. He held a return catch off Dudley Nourse, had the next batsman, Gordon, stumped, and then bowled Wade. In his only Test against Australia at Old Trafford in 1930 he took two for 49. His best bowling in a Test, also at Manchester, was in July 1937 when his six for 29 in New Zealand's second innings gave England victory by 130 runs. He played in another Test against New Zealand, and twice against West Indies in 1939, but he was robbed of a second chance against Australia, at Manchester in 1938, when rain prevented a ball being bowled in the match.

On no fewer than sixteen occasions Goddard took 100 or more wickets in a season and four times reached 200. His best year was 1937 when he had a haul of 248 wickets. Two years later, on his beloved Ashley Down ground at Bristol, Tom took seventeen wickets in a day against Kent—nine for 38 and eight for 68. Only Colin Blythe of Kent, killed in the First World War, and Hedley Verity of Yorkshire, killed in the Second, have performed this feat. In his great season in 1937, for which *Wisden* gave him its accolade by making him one of the Five Cricketers of the Year, Tom took all ten Worcestershire wickets in an innings for 113 at the Cheltenham Festival. He had taken six for 68 in the Worcestershire first innings! On seven occasions he picked up nine wickets in a single innings.

I asked him one rainy day at Chesterfield, towards the end of his career, which of all his memories he cherished most. He had no hesitation in picking the match at Bristol in which Gloucestershire tied with the formidable 1930 Australian side. He took three wickets in the space of five balls at one stage, and with the scores level after four innings dismissed the last Australian batsman, Hornibrook.

During the Second World War Goddard was commissioned in the RAF.

He came back to top-class cricket in 1946 and for five years went on adding to his mounting harvest of wickets. By now he was having bronchial trouble and on October 1, 1951, on his 51st birthday, Tom reluctantly announced his retirement. Throughout that winter he became obsessed with the magic figure of 3,000 victims—so tantalisingly close to his mighty grasp—and when the county were unable to find a replacement Tom came back to play thirteen Championship matches in 1952 and take a further 45 wickets. Finally, a bout of pneumonia laid him low and at his age, with his increasing chest problems, there was no question of his playing again. Consequently Tom Goddard had to give up, just 21 wickets short of becoming the fifth bowler in history to take 3,000 wickets. The four who have done so are Wilfred Rhodes 4,187, Tich Freeman 3,776, Charlie Parker 3,278, and J. T. Hearne 3,061.

Tom had two benefits; one in 1936, which brought him £2,097 and a second in 1948 which netted £3,355. Umpires and cricket writers of my vintage will never forget him sliding in to bowl, even less his appeals for lbw. He had the most menacing 'How's that?' in the business. Because of his health Tom made a clean break with cricket after 1952. He established a successful furniture shop in his native Gloucester and was fully active in it until a year before his death on May 22, 1966 at the age of 65.

WILLIAM HENRY COPSON
(Derbyshire)

The manner in which Bill Copson became a cricketer who reached county and Test level was so improbable that if a novelist or TV scriptwriter presented it to his public, any credibility he possessed would vanish in a flash.

He was born at Stonebroom, a small village near Alfreton in Derbyshire, on April 27, 1909, and throughout boyhood and adolescence showed not the slightest interest in cricket. There were no facilities at the village school he attended in Stonebroom and, when at 14 he became a miner at Morton Colliery near Chesterfield, his life seemed to be following an entirely predictable pattern for a youth in those parts and in those times.

The early summer of 1926 was to be his personal catalyst, for the General Strike, which lasted some ten days at the beginning of May, was to prove the making of him. Ten years later he was to be a cricketer of international renown. As the miners gathered at the local recreation ground, a series of games of cricket was organised and Copson, a lanky auburn-haired youth of 17, was urged to join in. 'I've never had a cricket ball in my hand in my life,' he demurred. 'No odds' replied one of his mates. 'It'll help pass the time any road.' Copson reflected for a moment and then said slowly, 'That's true. All right, I'll have a go.'

He watched for a bit, and then someone asked him if he fancied bowling an over. No one showed him what to do. He simply ran to the wicket in his own way and, like most youngsters, hurled the ball down as fast as he could. The ball pitched on a perfect length and wrecked the wicket before the startled batsman had time to offer a stroke. There was a burst of guffaws from players and watchers. Someone said, 'What a bloody fluke! Talk about beginner's luck.' Copson, whose long face rarely showed any emotion, stood gazing at what he had done and, although the choice of words is mine and not my old friend Bill's, it was undoubtedly a moment of revelation. He took the ball and went on bowling. He also went on pitching a good length and kept hitting the stumps.

To the end of his career in 1949, Bill could never tell you what he did and how he did it. He was a born fast bowler who in all probability would never have discovered the fact if there had been no General Strike. When the country went back to work Bill was given a place in the colliery second eleven for the rest of the season. A year later he was a valuable member of the first team. For four years Bill was content with playing for Morton, but in 1931 he joined the Clay Cross club in the Derbyshire League. 'They'll find you out now,' said one of his mates. He got it the wrong way round, for Bill found out the League players. Playing against Staveley he took all ten wickets for five runs. The secretary of Morton Colliery Cricket Club was a man called Fred Marsh, and after Bill's feat against Staveley he felt it was time to get in touch with the Derbyshire county authorities. They had him along to the Derby nets and liked what they saw.

Early in 1932 they gave him his début, and it could hardly have been a tougher one—Surrey at The Oval. Copson must have thought back to the day six years earlier when he first turned his arm over. In he ran to bowl his very first ball in top-class cricket and with it he bowled no less a batsman than Andy Sandham. He went on to dismiss Douglas Jardine, Tom Shepherd, and Percy Fender. Overnight the headline writers had a new name to play with. He took 46 wickets in his maiden season and in 1933 he progressed to 90 for just over 21 runs each. Despite trouble with his health in 1934, Copson collected 91 wickets at less than 18 a piece, and in 1935, although again forced to miss several matches, his 71 victims cost him only 16 each. With experience he was getting increasingly difficult to score off.

Derbyshire were delighted with their unexpected find, but they were concerned about his continued breakdowns and sent him to Skegness for a holiday. The club had him examined by all kinds of specialists, and finally it was discovered he was suffering from a strained sacroiliac joint at the lower extremity of the back. As part of the treatment to remedy this, Bill went into training with Chesterfield football club at Saltergate, and the value of the physical regimen he was put through was reflected in Derbyshire's winning the County Championship in 1936. Copson's bowling was the deciding factor without a doubt. He took 160 wickets for just over 13 runs each—140 of them in the Championship at 12.8. When Surrey came to Derby he had match figures of twelve for 52. Recognition came to him by his selection for the Players against the Gentlemen at Lord's, and for the North against the South in the Test trial. At the end of the season he was picked for the tour of Australia.

How do I remember the laconic ex-miner? His run up to the wicket was an easy affair and he seemed to hesitate fractionally before releasing the ball. He looked deceptively slow through the air, but he could make the ball swing and swerve either way very late and he also seemed to make the ball gather pace off the pitch. He either forced the batsman to make a hurried stroke or caught him totally unprepared. In his heyday he could bring the ball back so unexpectedly and so viciously that at times he was almost unplayable. Few men of pace in my lifetime have ever been able to extract so much out of an easy-paced, even lifeless, pitch.

Bill once made 43 at Blackpool, but he never made a 50 in his life. He had a streak of perversity in his makeup which made him take a somewhat twisted joy in the fact. I remember a day at Worthing in his final season when in an hilarious knock he took 28 off the Sussex attack and was dropped five times! He came in to a thunder of applause, for everyone loves a bowler who has briefly tried to be the Prince of Denmark, and he had gone through the pavilion gate before he realised he had not acknowledged it. Suddenly he loped back on to the field and raised his bat in salute. Naturally he was twitted about this in the dressing-room and I think it was the only time in his life Bill gave a sheepish grin. 'Well lads,' he said, 'I forgot the drill—you see, I'm a bit out of practice acknowledging applause for my batting.'

Bill did not walk, he trudged; possibly a legacy of his back trouble. On one occasion, watching him come up from third man to bowl, Denis Smith said, 'Bill, tha bloody walks like Groucho Marx.' 'Ay, and sometimes tha bats like him,' replied Bill, his features as immobile as Buster Keaton's.

With his late swerve and pace off the pitch Bill had many great days. Five for 33 and seven for 19 against Surrey, five for 38 and seven for 16 against Worcestershire. The season after he won the Championship for Derbyshire he took four wickets in four balls against Warwickshire at Derby, and his full analysis for the innings was 8.2–2–11–8. Seven of his victims fell to him in the course of 23 deliveries.

He went to Australia with Gubby Allen's M.C.C. team of 1936-37, and although he did not play in any of the Tests he headed the bowling averages for the tour. His three Test appearances were all in England. He took more than 100 wickets again in both 1938 and 1939, and in the latter season he forced himself into the England team against West Indies at Lord's, where he took five for 85 and four for 67. At Old Trafford his three wickets cost him only 33 runs.

Three times he performed the hat-trick, against Worcestershire and Warwickshire in 1937 and against Oxford University in 1939. From the time he developed back trouble, some said a legacy of working down the pit, he was never to know full health again, but the game he had not discovered until his early manhood was upon him was so infinitely precious to this undemonstrative man that he came back to it after the war. In 1947 he was called up for the last Test against South Africa and, although in his 39th year and well over the hill as a new-ball bowler, he made the Springboks pay for the indignity of hitting 112 runs off him by claiming three of their wickets.

When he was forced to quit in 1949, well past 40, he had in a comparatively short career of less than a dozen actual playing seasons taken 1,094 wickets at a cost of under 19 runs each. That is how good a bowler he was. It was a very real delight to me and to his countless friends and colleagues in the game when he reappeared in 1958 wearing the white coat of an umpire. His renewed association with big-time cricket lasted nine years, but his treacherous health forced him into early retirement at the end of the 1967 season. He died in his 63rd year on the day the 1971 season came to a close. The timing of his going, like the control of his length and the accuracy of his aim, was as one might have expected; immaculate.

KEN FARNES
(Essex)

At a time in cricket history when the need to find a genuine fast bowler has never been so acute, England's selectors must envy their predecessor 'Percy' Perrin in discovering Kenneth Farnes in the summer of 1930. Farnes, who was born at Leytonstone, had derived a love for the game early from his father, who was a prominent club cricketer. He was educated at the Royal Liberty School, Romford, and by the time Perrin first saw him at 19 he was 6ft 5in tall, had a fighting weight of 15st 6lb, and was perfectly proportioned. He measured out a run of only eleven paces but he picked up his stride immediately and had reached maximum pace at the moment of delivery. This, allied to the fact that he sent the ball down from over eight feet, made him an England bowler in three years.

His was an entirely natural talent married to exceptional physical endowment. He could make the ball rise sharply on a hard wicket, and to add extra nip to his bowling he perfected a downward flick of the wrist at the point of release. He held the ball in a loose grip with one finger on either side of the seam, and a natural body action enabled him to impart swerve and occasionally make the ball dip late or break back from the off.

In less than nine full seasons Farnes took 720 wickets. He was a fine close-to-the-wicket fielder and held many catches that would have been impossible for a man of less spectacular height. He was a born No. 11 as a batsman, but like every comedian with a secret desire to play Hamlet just once, Farnes yearned to make a century. Once at Taunton in 1936 he failed by just three runs to do so against Somerset. He and Wade, the wicket-keeper, put on 149 for the last Essex wicket in two hours, but Wade got out, leaving Farnes unbeaten on 97. Wade, realising that Farnes would probably never again come so close to a hundred, was inconsolable but Farnes treated the whole affair as a huge lark. He also took six wickets in the match, which Essex won by an innings and 66 runs.

Farnes, as might be expected, captained his school eleven and then joined the Gidea Park Club. It was in a match against the Essex Club and Ground side in 1930, in which Perrin played, that the man who is still revered as probably the best batsman that county has produced immediately spotted star quality in Farnes. Within a few weeks Perrin had talked Essex into playing the unknown youth in a Championship fixture against Gloucestershire at Chelmsford. Those were the days of Wally Hammond and Charlie Barnett, and Farnes's first match analysis in the big time was no wickets for 76 runs.

The next match on the Essex fixture card was against Kent, another formidable batting side, and some of the committee had misgivings about exposing Farnes to another experience which might shatter his confidence. Perrin said tersely, 'Play him', and he got his way. Farnes rewarded his judgement with five for 36 and thereafter his place was never in doubt. The following year he went up to Cambridge and was in the Light Blues side for three seasons. He turned out for Essex during vacations, and the county had to be satisfied with this situation, for after his University days he took a teaching appointment at Worksop College.

When Farnes joined Essex each July the county would start winning matches left, right, and centre. In 1934 his eleven wickets for 131 gave Essex their first win over Yorkshire since 1911, the year of Farnes's birth. That season he got his first Test call against Australia, and although England lost at Trent Bridge by 238 runs Farnes took five wickets in each innings.

The 1936 match between the Gentlemen and Players is still remembered by all who saw it for Farnes's bowling, regarded as the fastest seen at Lord's since the time of C. J. Kortright. In one deadly spell in the second innings Farnes clean-bowled Harold Gimblett, Hammond, and Joe Hardstaff—and in each case a stump went catapulting head high before falling at the feet of a quaking wicket-keeper standing twelve yards back. When he toured Australia the following winter, injuries restricted him to only two Tests, but he took six for 96 in an innings of 604 in the fifth Test. In 1938 he was at the pinnacle of form and fitness. He was England's leading wicket-taker against Bradman's side that successfully defended The Ashes, and he achieved the best match figures of his career at Clacton against Glamorgan—fifteen wickets for 113 runs. In the first innings of the Gents v. Players match he had another great triumph at Lord's, taking eight for 43. It was described as the finest bowling in this now-forgotten annual event since Arthur Fielder took all ten in the Gentlemen's first innings in 1906.

I once asked Hardstaff what it was like facing up to Farnes. 'He got such a degree of lift off a good length', he said, 'that he was terribly difficult to time.' However, Farnes too knew difficult periods, as in 1932 when he was no-balled 21 times in the University match and again when he was forced to miss the 1935 season through injury. In the first instance he showed the necessary self-discipline to correct quickly a faulty approach to the crease; in the second he showed the character to shrug off the disappointment. Farnes filled his life with good things—teaching, cricket, painting, music, reading, and writing, having one book published in 1940.

By that time England was fighting its battle for survival against Germany and Farnes, scorning the opportunities to land himself the cushy number he could have easily attained as a sporting celebrity, opted to fly in the RAF. He did his pilot's training successfully in Canada. When he returned to the United Kingdom, the Luftwaffe's day-time efforts had been bloodily repulsed and the need for the months ahead was for men who could fly at night. Pilot Officer Kenneth Farnes volunteered for conversion to what was an area still very much in its infancy. He had been training for less than a month when, on the night of October 20, 1941, three months past his 30th birthday, he misjudged his landing and died in the blazing wreckage of his crashed aeroplane.

Not the least of war's manifold tragedies is its tendency to take from us the best human material.

MY LIFE REPORTING CRICKET [1980]

BY ALEX BANNISTER

Of the army of scribes whose names were as familiar to readers as their physical appearance remained mysterious, Alex Bannister was among the most senior as well as among the most reliable. For a third of a century he travelled the earth in search of cricket, his by-line in the Daily Mail *becoming as familiar a feature of the landscape as the political leader or the gardening article. He had survived a world war, seen manners and morals slide to the parlous condition of the 1970s, and stayed in the game just long enough to be saddened by the compulsive totterings of the Packer fiasco. Understandably his farewell gesture is shot through with a sweet regret at the passing of the old days and the old ways. He gives a revealing if all too brief glimpse of shipboard life, notes the touching persistence of the game in the matter of imperial grandeur, ironically underlined elsewhere in the almanack by the editorial notes, which record the awarding to cricketers of the Order of the British Empire, and closes with an expression of pained disappointment at the apparent disregard of moral obligations in the Packer episode.*

The remark attributed to Sir Frank Worrell is a good example of Bannister's careful preservation of the apparently passing moment which speaks volumes. In this category is Alf Valentine's charming unworldliness, Fred Trueman's obstreperousness, the upsetting of tea on a royal trouser-leg symbolising the upsetting of the balance of power which brought it about, the case of the murdered chef, the whimsical way that one time in New Delhi William Makepeace Thackeray (of all people) came lumbering to the rescue. And there are delightful recollections of Fleet Street dementia involving aeroplanes, all-night vigils, and, most poetic of all, the old convention by which a cricket reporter would be shipped out to the last port of call for the visiting Australians, share the last days of the voyage with them, ferreting all the time for copy to cable back to E.C.4.

By one of those flukes which can sometimes tempt a man to believe in the deities, I happened to move into the Hertfordshire village where Bannister lived. Every now and then on Saturday mornings we would meet in the crowded High Street, each encumbered by shopping baskets, or we would cross paths when I was hurrying past his house to catch the London train. We would exchange a few words on the depressing condition of English cricket, and always I was left with the impression that he was not quite fulfilled in retirement. He spoke once or twice of work on a book, and on one occasion imparted another of his memorable quotes. It was to do with the regal reception for Bradman laid on by the Oval crowd in 1948 when he strode in to bat for the last time in a Test in England, a moving processional followed by his sensational dismissal by Eric Hollies for nought. Alex told me that he had asked Bradman how such a thing could have happened to which Bradman is said to have replied, 'It's hard to see the ball when your eyes are full of tears.'

It was not long after that exchange that I became aware one morning that I had not bumped into Alex for some weeks. I have never seen him since, and assume that the family must have sold the house and gone to live somewhere else. I was sorry to lose his occasional acquaintanceship, for he was the only professional cricket reporter I ever knew, the only one whose words I had once read with bated breath, with whom I have struck up an odd sort of friendship, an unspoken alliance against the tiresome world of shopping baskets and family chores.

WHEN I joined the *Daily Mail* from the Press Association (the news agency dubbed the 'University of Fleet Street') 33 years ago, cricket had not yet been sucked into the vortex of world politics and High Court action. And if there was such a thing as player power, it was represented by the deeds of Denis Compton, Len Hutton, Alec Bedser, Bill Edrich and others on the field of play.

The one-day game was not conceived, nor was even a twinkle in the eyes of the legislators; overseas tours were long, comparatively leisurely and crammed with stuffy receptions; grounds were full in the post-war sporting boom; and there was still a division between amateur and professional. Indeed, until the abolition of the thin distinction in 1963, it was still possible to hear, as I did at Lord's, this pre-match announcement: 'In the match card, for F. J. Titmus please read Titmus F. J.'

At Adelaide in 1950, invitations to temporary membership of a club were extended only to the four amateurs and to those of the press who were members of MCC. It was politely declined. On board ship, the amateurs were put at a separate dining table, but the whole party travelled first-class and in style—unlike the modern trial of endurance of the jumbo jet.

Domestically the season consisted of Tests, matches with the tourists, the County Championship, prestige fixtures like Gentlemen v. Players, Oxford v. Cambridge, and the festivals. Pride in the swiftly disintegrating Empire remained in titles. There was the *Imperial* Cricket Conference (now the International Cricket Conference), and as late as 1953 it was the *Imperial* Cricket Memorial Gallery (The Memorial Gallery and Library). Contact between the all-powerful M.C.C. and the working press was minimal. Selectors offered no public reasons for their decisions, and the list of secretaries read like a military gazette. The Advisory County Cricket Committee's annual meeting coincided with the University rugby match, and no-one was ever late to Twickenham for the kick-off.

Sir Don Bradman, who gave a new meaning to batting, was still leading his invincible Australians, and the West Indies were emerging as a potent force—though it was still predicted in some islands that all would collapse under a future black captain. In due course Sir Frank Worrell, a remarkable person as well as being a great cricketer, united the widely scattered and diverse cultures of the islands as no politician was able to do, before or since. His early death was a cruel blow to the entire cricket world, and I have pictured him as the perfect intermediary in the South African dispute. I remember the forthright R. W. V. Robins bluntly asking him if he ever found it a handicap to be black, especially when he was in England. Frankie's laughing response was: 'Only when I'm shaving.'

Twenty years passed before South Africa's racial laws blew up in cricket's face, and those attending the seemingly interminable meetings at Lord's in 1970 will never forget the ominous sight of the square behind barbed wire and under floodlights. With security guards and dogs in patrol, the ground assumed the grim appearance of a POW camp. After the 1968–69 tour of South Africa was cancelled, at the time I would have been leaving Heathrow I found myself interviewing an eleven year old at Aylesbury on why he wanted to play for Manchester United!

Pakistan, gaining full Test status in 1952, is one of the countries adamantly opposed to South Africa's re-entry. The new Muslim nation was so little known in the early years that, on an early tour there, a Commonwealth team's blazer carried the gilt-lettered word: PARKI-STAN. Yet within five years Pakistan had beaten England, Australia and West Indies. The victory at The Oval was a classic case of a team, previously outplayed, being taken too lightly. A much-changed side suddenly found themselves fighting a losing battle against Fazal Mahmood, a bowler of the Bedser type, on a pitch to suit him. Fazal was one of the best of his age and was a police traffic inspector. Years later, as a passenger in his jeep threading a miraculous path through a tangle of bullock carts, camel trains, cars, buses, rickshaws and wandering pedestrians, I asked him how he controlled his Karachi traffic. 'You have as much chance as bowling out Hutton without stumps in the ground,' he replied.

As the game might have been invented for their bubbling skills and vitalities, the rise of the West Indians was inevitable. In 1950, when they gained their first victory in England at Lord's, a very fine opening pair in Jeff Stollmeyer and Alan Rae preceded the might of the immortal Ws; Worrell, Clyde Walcott, then a wicket-keeper, and Everton Weekes. And the most experienced English batsman could not handle the novice spinners, Sonney Ramadhin and Alf Valentine.

When they arrived in England, the combined experience of 'those little pals of mine, Ramadhin and Valentine', as the calypso went, was two first-class matches. It was Jack Mercer, the former Glamorgan bowler, then coaching in Jamaica, who urged the selectors to send Valentine. Mercer used to tell Valentine to spin until the blood showed from his fingers. Nobody could pick Ramadhin, and Valentine spun like a top. All John

Goddard needed to do was put his slow bowlers on and they would do the rest. Valentine was charmingly vague. 'When is the England captain coming in?' he asked when he was bowling out England in the Trent Bridge Test. 'You dismissed him an hour ago,' he was told.

Another story I associate with Jack Mercer involved Freddie Trueman on the 1953–54 tour of the West Indies. MCC were playing at Spanish Town, not far from Kingston, at a sugar plantation. Across the entrance was strung a banner exhorting the employees on the virtue of WORK, OBEDIENCE, DISCIPLINE. Trueman, who was sharing a car with Mercer and myself, looked with disgust at the banner and exploded: 'I bloody well wouldn't work here!'

When West Indies won at Lord's, their supporters, singing and dancing, invaded an astonished Long Room, where I also saw an old member innocently bump into the Duke of Edinburgh, who had just opened the aforementioned Imperial Cricket Memorial Gallery. The Duke's tea spilled down the royal trousers, leaving a most unfortunate appearance. Perhaps it was just as well for his peace of mind that the member shuffled away blissfully ignorant of his gaffe.

Yet I doubt if the Duke was more taken aback than Jeff Thomson, the fire-eating Australian bowler, after his first over to Colin Cowdrey, who had just joined the England party in Australia in 1974. As England were down to twelve fit players, including two wicket-keepers, Colin was pressed into premature service, although he had been in the nets for only four days. You could almost hear the dreaded Thomson's ears flap back in expectation as Colin took the pallor of an English December to the wicket. His last Test innings had been three and a half years before, but the old touch was not lost, and at the end of the over the lamb blandly approached the lion and murmured: 'I don't think we have met—my name's Cowdrey.'

Cowdrey in Pakistan, 1969, Hutton in the West Indies, 1954, and Peter May in Australia, 1958–59, were captains on singularly difficult tours. The unsuspecting May, comfortably England's finest post-war batsman, found himself in the centre of bitter throwing and umpiring controversies, and Hutton and Cowdrey, from the start of their misadventures, must have thought they were being committed to tip-toe barefoot through fields of broken bottles. On many occasions in the West Indies and Pakistan I had anguished doubts after filing my story. The events of the day seemed so irrational as to be the child of an overheated imagination.

Hutton found the young Trueman a frightful handful, and rumour of the most bizarre nature on a variety of themes spread through the lovely Caribbean like an unchecked forest fire. Finally there was the episode of the flamboyant Honourable Alex Bustamente, Jamaica's Chief Minister. During the final Test, with his score at 205, Hutton entered the pavilion at tea hoping to snatch a shower and a cup of tea. He was no sooner in the room than an excited official burst in and stormed: 'This is the crowning insult.' It transpired that Mr Bustamente's hand had been one of the several thrust out to Hutton, who had replied to the shouted congratulations with 'Thank you'. The interval was spent sorting the matter out, and making it clear that had he but known Mr Bustamente had been there he would have stopped. Despite a stout denial from the Chief Minister that he had been 'insulted', the incident continued to be blown up out of all proportion.

More evidence that cricket was being dragged into the political maelstrom came in Pakistan. In retrospect, it is obvious that Cowdrey's tour should not have been attempted during a period of civil disorder. England arrived after a brief stay in Sri Lanka to find the itinerary changed, armed troops patrolling the streets, and a general picture of chaos and crisis. Far from bringing stability to the scene, as officialdom hoped, the Tests attracted student agitators and play was constantly interrupted. Both the local Board and British diplomatists shirked the responsibility of calling a halt to the wretched and dangerous situation. Cricket was used as a political shuttlecock.

Oddly the most peaceful Test was at Dacca, which was considered to be the flash-point, because the local students took over the policing of the match. On the eve of the match their leaders conducted a serio-comical press conference at which I wondered whether I should laugh or be scared. The only casualty proved to be Cowdrey, who had £30 pinched from his pocket as he walked the width of a pavement from the bus to the ground entrance.

In the end the mob won at Karachi, with the Test abandoned on the third morning after the most serious of several riots when England were 503 for seven. Colin Milburn had scored 137 in what sadly proved to be his last Test innings and Alan Knott was within 4 runs of his maiden century for England. The team left for home that night, and I wrote my eye-witness account, of the riot, at home with one half of a broken stump in front of me. It was safer there.

Milburn's career effectively ended with a motor accident as his genius had started in full bloom. He had spent the winter with Western Australia and flew to what was then the east wing of Pakistan as a reinforcement when Cowdrey's fitness was in doubt. The boys prepared a welcome for him. As he came down the plane steps they sang 'The green, green grass of home'. They also arranged for the coach to stop at a disreputable hotel, and filed out. Colin's jaw dropped, and just as he was prepared to make a bolt for home the players returned and took him to the team's head-quarters at the Inter-continental.

During a period when the side was confined to the hotel at Lahore, Roger Prideaux, then captain of Northamptonshire, slipped out to give a trial to a young student fast bowler. The nets at the Gymkhana were surrounded by barbed wire, and soldiers stood protectively by. The trialist was Sarfraz Nawaz, and it can be truthfully said that he lived up to his unconventional start.

I would not like to give the impression that all tours to Pakistan were fraught with danger. The early ones were not examples of feather-bedded luxury, but India and Pakistan can now offer comforts undreamed of at one period. At one of the less attractive centres Keith Fletcher switched on a large fan in the hope of getting rid of a colony of bats in the ceiling.

Immediately a rain of mutilated bats descended on the diners below. On another occasion an England team arrived at an up-country hotel to see a corpse under a white sheet being carried away. It was the chef, knifed in a kitchen quarrel.

No cricket education can be considered half complete without a tour of India, though admittedly it can be wearing at the time. One widely held fallacy there is that anyone remotely attached to the visiting team has access to a vast pool of complimentary tickets, and is willing, nay anxious, to discuss every aspect of the game anywhere at any time. I have found strangers in my hotel room—and in the most private area—who have called in for a chat. At New Delhi, my only relief was to lock myself in the bathroom, where the light was not visible from the outside, and read *Vanity Fair*, borrowed from Mike Brearley.

A Test at Calcutta is comparable to five days of the fervour of a Wembley international between England and Scotland with crowds of a comparable size. Before the 1977 match there was the astonishing sight of the grass on the pitch, such as it was, being scraped away with household scrubbing brushes.

Melbourne 1955 provided the mystery of the Damp Pitch . . . except that it wasn't really a mystery. Despite official denials at the time, there could be no doubt that there was an illegal watering on the rest day. On the Saturday evening cracks had begun to appear and the pitch was worn. On Monday, after a hot Sunday, the pitch and its surrounds were damp. The Melbourne newspaper *The Age* published a story that sprinklers had been used, but among the speculation which followed was a learned explanation that the cause was a subterranean river directly under the ground. If that was right, how remarkable that the effect should be confined to a tiny area in the middle of a vast ground. There was no sinister motive, however, and the error was accepted as a groundsman's inexperience. But an England victory spared Australia no end of embarrassment.

Godfrey Evans made one of his famous catches to dismiss Neil Harvey, and in the course of 12.3 eight-ball overs Frank Tyson, who in three Tests of the series was the fastest bowler I have ever seen, and Brian Statham won the match. Tyson had seven wickets in the innings and Statham two, and I remember Sir Don Bradman, in the lounge of the Windsor Hotel, making a special effort to tell Statham that England would not have won without his brilliant support.

Inevitably in the highly competitive field of Fleet Street, a long career brings its ups and downs. Memories are the most perishable of all commodities and one's standard is measured by the last story. I have had a few successes and some failures, but I regard my part in recruiting Bradman for the two home series with Australia in 1953, the coronation year, and 1956 as my greatest coup. It happened by chance.

When teams travelled by ship I used to join the Australians at their last port of call—Malta, Naples or maybe Marseilles—and file a daily story. One morning, while waiting in a queue outside a Purser's Office, two of the Australian players told me The Don would have enjoyed making the trip.

Normally I am opposed to player-writers as it can be a deception of the public and goes against my journalistic principles, but Bradman was an exception and capable of making a huge impact with his unique perception, judgement and reputation. I cabled my editor, who responded with enthusiasm and set the operation in motion.

The outcome was a dazzling success. It brought The Don, who wrote every word himself, congratulations in the fourth leader of *The Times*, and gave the newspaper a new status among the discerning public. Fully to appreciate The Don's insight and knowledge of the game it is necessary to be with him over a long period, and that was my privilege. I also understood the price he had paid for his unique fame, with incessant requests for autographs and hopeful conversations opening with, 'You must remember me, we stayed at the same hotel at Leicester in 1930.'

Later I had a different style of collaboration with Johnny Wardle when he was signed, in the teeth of intense competition, to reveal his troubles with Yorkshire exclusively to the *Daily Mail*. Nearing midnight I was awakened and told to go immediately to Wardle's home at Wakefield. I had two basic instructions: one, to make sure no other newspaper intervened; two, to produce three articles the next day.

After arousing the village taximan I went to King's Cross, where a rail voucher and the terms of agreement awaited me, and then on to Wakefield station to join two others in a hired car. We parked outside Wardle's home until the family came down for breakfast, and then whisked him to the paper's offices at Sheffield. Johnny was so upset by Yorkshire's decline, and what he thought the causes to be, that the articles were simple to write. The main target of his criticism was Ron Burnet, the captain, who had been appointed to instil discipline into the side.

In the afternoon, photographs were taken at the Grand Hotel—one of Johnny at a typewriter—and as we went into the foyer, to my embarrassment, we ran into Burnet. For my part I liked both Johnny and Ron, and I felt as if I had intruded into a family quarrel. It is always to Burnet's credit that he never held a grudge and rose above the sea of disputes with dignity. In fact, I did a signed piece for him when Yorkshire won the Championship at Hove.

If Wardle was at fault, it was that his passion for Yorkshire over-boiled. When he was sent to Australia with me on Peter May's tour I found him conscientious and intelligent, as well as fearless. He was particularly useful on a tour tormented by throwing controversies, for his technical know-how was outstanding.

Of several stunts I became involved in, the most amusing was with Richie Benaud's team. Again it was aboard ship. The day before the arrival of the Australians at Tilbury I had a shore-to-ship call from J. L. Manning, a particularly demanding Sports Editor, to arrange to assemble the players at starboard stern at 1.30 p.m. precisely. A *Daily Mail* plane would then take a photograph of them, and I was to give the exact position of the ship at 1.30 p.m.; repeat, exact position.

Benaud, as always obliging, agreed, but understandably the bridge said it was not possible to give the exact position several hours in advance. Mr. Manning was not to be put off within a nautical mile or two, and I lost some poundage running up the stairs to the radio room.

As the appointed time approached, the sea became choppy, there were rain squalls, and the overcoated cricketers became increasingly disenchanted with the project. 'If we had weather like this we'd give Australia back to the Abbos' said one through clenched teeth. Suddenly, to my relief, a plane appeared and circled three times at a drunken angle. The picture appearing on the breakfast tables the next morning was a little out of focus, but no reader was to know that at the moment of crisis the photographer was being violently sick!

With the sixties came the time of cricket's upheavals and changed attitudes. Cricket journalism moved into sterner and more specialised dimensions. Instant judgments had to be passed on the weightiest of subjects, often after long and complicated briefings. After the International Cricket Conference had tried to thrash out the complex question of throwing I was urged by my office: 'Can't you simplify it?' As generations of legislators had tried for almost a century to find the right wording I was not too ashamed to reply that it was beyond me.

I am inclined to think that if the same resolve was shown in curbing the menace of bumpers and intimidations as was applied to throwing problems, some of the recent insults to the fair name of the game would not have happened. Unfortunately an endemic weakness called self-interest and parochialism, which left the game so divided during the Packer struggle, takes over. The soft option of passing the buck to the hard-pressed umpires is seized upon avidly. There have been clearly defined regulations to stop excesses of bumpers, and I trust the experiment of the one-an-over restriction will have more success. The latest legislation represents the last chance to prevent cricket slipping into perpetual violence.

Bumpers, in fair numbers, are part of the game. Intimidation is not, and must be stamped out. One thought does occur to me: as the human frame is now infinitely bigger and stronger, is 22 yards the right length of the pitch? When 22 yards was officially drafted into the 1744 Laws, the bowling was underarm!

So swift, complete and dramatic have been the changes in the last few years, both on the field and in administration, that it almost invites ridicule to pass comparisons. Some of the old chivalry and morality, which put cricket apart from other games, has ebbed away in the tide of awards and prizes, sponsorship in its many forms, and larger appearance money. There must be some concern that the benefits of the newly developing 'marketing' are not cornered by a small élite of privileged players. There is much to commend in the dedicated attitude of players who demand more say in their affairs. Fine! As long as it is remembered that they owe a responsibility to the game at large.

Crowds are different today, and the trend is towards instant cricket and instant results. It is possible there will be little place for five-day Tests in the future, particularly in an impatient country like Australia.

On playing standards I am sure the great players of the immediate past of the class of Bradman, Hutton, May, Arthur Morris, the Ws, Compton, Martin Donnelly, Dudley Nourse, Vijay Merchant, Alec Bedser, Fred Trueman and Co. would be just as effective today. All the so-called progress of negative bowling and field placing would not have stopped Bradman. He might have been slowed down—partly because of the decline in the over-rate—but he would still have scored a staggering number of runs.

Equally Viv Richards, Sunil Gavaskar, Geoff Boycott, Barry Richards, Clive Lloyd and the other modern batting giants would have found Bedser's cut and swing and the fast bowling of Ray Lindwall and Keith Miller just as difficult. The best all-rounders I have seen are Sir Gary Sobers, Miller and Mike Procter, and Ian Botham may aspire to that class.

The Packer affair was a supreme tragedy, particularly as it had its origins in an Australian commercial TV struggle. I know all the arguments, but the over-riding disappointment to me was that negotiations were going on in secret during the nostalgic Melbourne centenary Test match. To be able to do so suggested the players involved had no affiliation whatsoever with the spirit and sentiment of their distinguished predecessors.

C. W. ALCOCK [1980]

BY BASIL EASTERBROOK

An appreciation of Charles William Alcock, J.P. (1842–1907) was long overdue. If the claim of Sir Robert Ensor in the Oxford History of England *that 'the development of organised games on any reckoning may rank among England's leading contributions to world culture' has any credence at all, then the figure of Alcock looms as one of the most influential of all Victorians, sporting or otherwise. As the initiator of the first Test match between England and Australia in England, at the Oval in 1880, as the secretary of the Football Association from 1867 to 1896, as secretary of the Surrey County Club from 1872 until his death, he is revealed as a prime mover in the codification and administration of the two major sporting preoccupations of the English. In fact he achieved more than this, especially in the world of cricket; no researcher of the game could fail to acknowledge the huge debt he owes to Alcock for having created the magazine* Cricket, *which he edited from its inception in 1882 until the day he died.*

Basil Easterbrook's tribute was timely enough, but he omits to say that the reason why Alcock failed to find a place in the Harrow eleven was illness as much as incapacity. His Wisden *obituary tells us that he turned out occasionally for the Gentlemen of Essex, the Butterflies, Harrow Wanderers and Incogniti. Two other aspects of Alcock's career vital to any assessment of his place in the scheme of things are also absent from the Easterbrook essay: his prose style and his extraordinary escapades as a European cricketer. In referring to the notorious occasion when Alcock led France in a Test match against Germany, Easterbrook confesses a failure to have discovered any clarifications. In a priceless essay entitled 'Some Notes on Early Cricket Abroad', published in the* Cricketer *annual, 1922–23, F. S. Ashley-Cooper describes how Hamburg enjoyed the greatest cricketing episode in its history in 1865, when there was a Grand Cricket Week. Among the English worthies present during the week were James Round, one of the best amateur wicket-keepers of his day and for thirty-eight years a member of the House of Commons; the Reverend Stirling Cooksley Voules, of Marlborough, Oxford and the Gentlemen; and C. W. A. Alcock, who led England against Seventeen of Europe in two games, both won, and finally captained France, represented by the Paris C.C. against Germany. Having made top score for France, Alcock was presented publicly with a cricket bat, which he accepted with a speech of masterly ambiguity: 'It must have been made in France.'*

As to his literary style, Alcock was invited by the Illustrated Sporting and Dramatic News *to contribute an essay to its Diamond Jubilee edition of 1897. He wrote 'Cricket under Queen Victoria', closing with this touchingly Panglossian peroration:*

That cricket was never more popular than it is at the time is certain. The public interest was never keener; the game is played in the spirit of true sport, and on the whole the tone is good in all ways. The history of athletics cannot, indeed, show anything more gratifying from the standpoint of public interest or of public morality than the record of cricket during the Queen's reign.

It is pleasing to record that this well-meaning old boy with the chortling walrus moustache and the very best intentions was himself a worthy example of public morality. Ranjitsinhji remembered that when, as a young stranger to England, he accompanied his tutor to the Oval to watch Surrey play the Australians, it was Alcock who took the trouble to introduce the prince to the tourists.

IN the year that marks the centenary of Test cricket in England, it is only just that tribute be paid to the man who made it possible. It would be fair to say that without the work and diplomacy of Charles William Alcock, the historic first meeting between England and Australia on English soil at Kennington Oval on September 6, 7, 8, 1880 would not have taken place.

The team Lord Harris had taken to Australia in the winter of 1878–79, when the only Test played ended in victory for the Australians, became involved in events which for the first, but by no means last, time seriously affected the friendly relations existing between cricketers of the two countries. There was feeling on both sides of the world that the tour of England scheduled for 1880 should be deferred. Eventually the Australians decided to make the long voyage, but so late that most of England's leading sides had completed their county programme by the time James Lillywhite was authorised to make up a fixture list.

Derbyshire, Gloucestershire and Sussex were the only counties to give the Australians an official match. Two fixtures with Yorkshire were not under the auspices of the county club. It is unthinkable for the current generation of cricket lovers to consider an Australian tour without their appearance at Lord's, but W. L. Murdoch's team never trod the turf of Marylebone. Nor indeed was there any hope of them playing in the capital's other equally famous cricket enclosure, The Oval, until Alcock gently urged the Surrey authorities to suggest a match against a team representing England, to mark season's end.

There were still two problems to overcome—the consent of Lord Harris and the finding of a suitable date. The 'Mr Cricket' of his day gave immediate and hearty approval, but the date was a trickier business. The only suitable days were September 6, 7, 8 and on those days the Australians were scheduled to play Sussex at Hove. The task of sweet-talking the Sussex committee was given to Alcock, then in his ninth year as Secretary of Surrey.

Alcock, in the modern idiom, had a lot going for him. A shade under six feet and weighing 13st 6lb, he was a clear-eyed, facially handsome man with an impressive moustache. Moreover, he had been educated at Harrow. And a hundred years ago that, again to revert to a contemporary phrase, gave him the inside track. Even so, he also needed tact, charm and diplomacy. He prudently went down to Canterbury during cricket week to ensure Lord Harris was not merely an assentor but an ally. The fateful meeting which gave birth to Test cricket in England was held in the pavilion at Hove, presided over by the Earl of Sheffield, President of the Sussex County Cricket Club. Alcock and Lord Harris were given a sympathetic hearing, and Sussex agreed to put back the dates of their match with the tourists until later in September.

So on September 6, for the very first time, Australia met England at Kennington. Alcock, a prolific writer on cricket, permitted himself the comment: 'In the eternal fitness of things, too, the game was in every way worthy of a historic occasion.' I am struck by the phrase 'eternal fitness of things' for this tends to show itself again and again in the story of mankind.

The Graces of Gloucestershire, W.G. and E.M., opened the innings for England with a stand of 91, and a new dimension had been added to cricket in the land which had given birth to the game. Australia took the field severely handicapped because they were without their legendary fast bowler Spofforth, who had injured a finger in a match at Scarborough. This put the onus on bowling out England on a perfect pitch on two medium-pacers, Palmer and Boyle, and they were not up to it. They bowled 114 overs in England's first innings but had only one wicket for 187 between them. In England's second innings, when they were the only two bowlers called on, Palmer took three for 35 and Boyle two for 21, but by then the issue had been long resolved.

We have only to recall England's 5–1 victory in the 1978–79 series in

Previous page: Jim Laker airborne as the spring, tightened to the required tension, is about to uncoil. In a moment the feet will return to earth, the arm wheel over, the ball fizz away from the fingers into an arc yet to be fathomed by the batsman

Above: Two young men striding out of the pavilion of Time and Space into the record books. No pairing since Gilbert and Sullivan, or possibly Wooster and Jeeves, had given so much pleasure to so many

Right: Not quite Boswell and Dr. Johnson, but at any rate the biographer and his subject. Seen here in the garden at Lord's are E.W. Swanton, for many years a magisterial summer-up of the day's play on radio, and G.O. Allen, who lived just beyond the wall in the background

Left: A sunset touch as Michael Brearley takes the field for the last time in the most curious of first-class careers. A varsity wicketkeeper who captained Middlesex and England with an all-powerful intellectual command, he remains a vivid example of the old saying that 'what do they know of cricket who only cricket know'. Not only has Brearley devoted his latter years to the rehabilitation of those in need of psychiatric help, but he plays the clarinet, always a sure sign of a gentleman

Below left: Not since Dumas Père's Man in the Iron Mask has any public figure appeared before his audience so absurdly accoutred. This could be anyone. In fact it is Graeme Hick protecting his profile from the Middlesex bowling at Lord's, 1988

Below right: Messrs Kerry Packer and Tony Greig contributing to the continual welfare of the English legal profession. It has never been revealed what, if anything, Greig was carrying in the brief case

The Centenary Test group at Lord's:

1.F.J.Bryant (Australian Cricket Board) 2.T.C.J.Caldwell (ACB) 3.L.V.Maddocks 4.A.N.Connolly 5.M.H.N.Walker 6.A.E.Moss
7.P.E.Richardson 8.C.R.Ingamells (ACB) 9.K.R.Stackpole 10.R.A.L.Massie 11.R.B.Simpson 12.R.T.Simpson 13.W.M.Lawry
14.A.Turner 15.R.Tattersall 16.R.A.Gaunt 17.M.J.McInnes (ACB) 18.A.W.Walsh (ACB) 19.J.W.Gleeson 20.A.C.Smith 21.G.B.Hole
22.D.L. Richards (ACB) 23.D.A.Allen 24.R.M.Prideaux 25.H.W.H.Rigg (ACB) 26.R.Subba Row 27.T.R.Veivers 28.F.J.Titmus
29.F.W.C.Bennett (ACB) 30.K.D.Mackay 31.T.W.Cartwright 32.R.Edwards 33.J.T.Murray 34.W.Watson 35.R.M.Cowper
36.C.S.Serjeant 37.J.S.E.Price 38.M.J.K.Smith 39.J.M.Parks 40.C.C.McDonald 41.B.L.D'Oliveira 42.A.S.M.Oakman 43.J.A.Flavell
44.J.A.Ledward (ACB) 45.L.J.Coldwell 46.R.Benaud 47.I.R.Redpath 48.G.R.A.Langley 49.P.H.Edmonds 50.G.A.R.Lock
51.F.E.Rumsey 52.J.H.de Courcy 53.K.V.Andrew 54.R.B.McCosker 55.H.B.Taber 56.J.H.Hampshire 57.F.M.Misson
58.T.W.Graveney 59.A.K.Davidson 60.K.D.Walters 61.G.D.McKenzie 62.P.J.Loader 63.E.W.Freeman 64.G.D.Watson
65.G.E.Corling 66.A.J.W.McIntyre 67.D.B.Close 68.G.J.Gilmour 69.I.M.Chappell 70.F.H.Tyson 71.R.Illingworth 72.D.J.Colley
73.J.B.Statham 74.K.Taylor 75.P.H.Parfitt 76.R.Appleyard 77.P.J.Sharpe 78.C.G.Howard (MCC) 79.I.J.Jones 80.E.R.Dexter
81.A.R.Barnes (ACB) 82.I.D.Craig 83.C.S.Elliott (TCCB) 84.V.J.W.M.Lawrence (MCC) 85.K.F.Barrington 86.J.H.Wardle
87.W.E.Bowes 88.J.G.Dewes 89.A.G.Chipperfield 90.C.J.Barnett 91.T.G.Evans 92.E.W.Clark 93.J.A.Young 94.W.Voce 95.J.C.Laker
96.Sir L.Hutton 97.E.R.H.Toshack 98.E.L.McCormick 99.W.A.Johnston 100.K.E.Rigg 101.A.R.Morris 102.D.T.Ring 103.F.R.Brown
104.S.J.E.Loxton 105.K.R.Miller 106.D.V.P.Wright 107.A.V.Bedser 108.K.Cranston 109.M.G.Waite 110.C.Washbrook
111.C.L.Badcock 112.N.W.D.Yardley 113.A.L.Hassett 114.H.E.Dollery 115.W.A.Brown 116.J.T.Ikin 117.L.G.James (MCC)
118.W.E.Hollies 119.J.A.Bailey (MCC secretary) 120.A.R.Border 121.J.Dyson 122.G.Dymock 123.R.J.Bright 124.B.M.Laird
125.G.M.Wood 126.G.N.Yallop 127.K.J.Hughes 128.R.W.Marsh 129.L.S.Pascoe 130.J.R.Thomson 131.A.A.Mallett 132.D.K.Lillee
133.P.M.Lush (TCCB) 134.J.R.Stephenson (MCC) 135.D.B.Carr (TCCB secretary) 136.D.J.Constant (umpire) 137.P.Willey
138.J.Emburey 139.C.W.J.Athey 140.R.D.Jackman 141.D.L.Bairstow 142.M.W.Gatting 143.C.M.Old 144.M.Hendrick 145.G.Boycott
146.G.A.Gooch 147.D.I.Gower 148.H.D.Bird (umpire) 149.W.J.O'Reilly 150.L.S.Darling 151.E.L.a'Beckett 152.W.H.Ponsford
153.A.Sandham 154.R.C.Steele (ACB) 155.P.B.H.May 156.G.S.Chappell 157.S.C.Griffith (MCC president) 158.I.T.Botham
159.R.J.Parish (ACB chairman) 160.F.G.Mann (TCCB chairman) 161.H.S.T.L.Hendry 162.G.O.B.Allen 163.R.E.S.Wyatt
164.P.G.H.Fender

Australia against a team without Lillee, Thomson, Walker, the two Chappells and Marsh to realise just what it meant to go into that first Test at The Oval without a bowler who, a hundred years on, is still instantly recognised by the nickname 'Demon'. Oddly enough, Spofforth in 1880 bore a slight resemblance to Dennis Lillee.

In the first week of January 1879, Australia had defeated Lord Harris' England side by ten wickets at Melbourne, but the second Test was cancelled after a riot had ruined the English touring side's match against New South Wales at Sydney. The needle had been forged and it has never been pin-cushioned. Whether that be good or bad must remain a matter for opinion, but it has certainly contributed to giving the England v. Australia series a very special sporting cachet. More than 40,000 spectators paid to see the first two days of the 1880 Test and the supply of scorecards ran out. Spectators besieged the printer's box, presenting envelopes and leaves out of notebooks to ensure a copy of the official record.

The road to an English victory was surely paved in the first innings. After E. M. Grace had gone for 36, the second wicket did not fall until 211, with A. P. Lucas of Surrey scoring 55 in partnership with W.G. There were no failures among the first eight batsmen. W. Barnes of Nottinghamshire contributed 28, Lord Harris of Kent 52, F. Penn of Kent 23, A. G. Steel of Lancashire 42 and Hon. A. Lyttelton of Middlesex 11. Towering over all was W. G. Grace with 152—England's first Test century. By the close on the first day England were 410 for eight. There was a light fall of rain during the evening, and though some said it did not affect the pitch, the Australians said it did. At this remove there can be no profit in discussing it. In all honesty a contemporary writer can deal only with facts, and these were sombre indeed for Australia. England's last two wickets scratched about for twenty minutes of so adding 10 runs before the innings was ended at 420. By lunch Australia were 126 for nine, with no chance of avoiding the follow-on.

Fred Grace, the third member of the immortal Gloucestershire family, was to go down in history as the only Englishman in the match to bag a pair, but he took two splendid catches, the second of which, at long-on, dismissed the mighty Bonnor, a Colossus among men. The ball was in the air interminably and Fred Grace declared his heart stopped; he had to wait for so long. It was a grimly prophetic choice of words. Two weeks later he was dead, having neglected a chill suffered as the result of a railway journey.

Boyle and Moule added 23 for the last wicket after lunch, but W. G. Grace brought Australia's first innings to a close at 149, and going in again 271 behind they were quickly in desperate trouble at 14 for three. In their compendium of Test cricket covering the years 1877 to 1968, Ralph Barker and Irving Rosenwater ended their account of the second Test at Melbourne in April 1877 by quoting an Australian writer as follows: 'We would counsel whoever may enter into future speculations for importing an England XI to bear in mind the great improvement of colonial cricket, and not to imagine that anything will do for Australia.' *Nil satis nisi optimum*, indeed! On that September 7, 1880, Billy Murdoch was going to begin a tradition that, whatever the state of the scoreboard, there is always the danger of the Aussie who comes good.

There was no way the little Australian captain could turn a losing situation into a possible platform from which a bid for victory could be launched, but he could still make the Poms sweat; and how he did. His was a captain's innings in every sense. A nineteen-year-old called McDonnell gave him real assistance in a fourth-wicket partnership of 83, but at the close of play on the second day Australia were 170 for six, still seemingly booked for an inevitable innings defeat. Bonnor disappointed for the second time, being bowled by Steel at 181 on the final morning, and Palmer gave the same bowler a return catch at 187. Alexander, the tour manager and a useful player with both bat and ball, came in to make 33 out of 52 for the ninth wicket, during which association Murdoch, 79 overnight, reached three figures. Australia's last wicket then astonishingly proved to be the most productive of the innings with 88 runs, which obliged England to go to the wicket a second time to make 57 runs for victory. Moule hit 34 before being bowled by Barnes, leaving Murdoch unbeaten with 153, one run more than W.G. had made in building England's winning 420. Australia were all out for 327 in the second over after lunch and, with the rest of the day to complete the formalities, England followed a fashion that long persisted in first-class cricket in such circumstances; namely taking liberties with the batting order. Nothing could have been better calculated to raise Aussie danders. When they saw Lyttelton and Fred Grace come out to open the innings, they reacted as if it was an insult. Palmer bowled both of them and had Lucas caught at the wicket. Barnes was caught at mid-on off Boyle, who bowled E. M. Grace second ball. Half the side were out for 31, and had Spofforth been available who can tell how it would have ended? But now from the pavilion came a figure ample even in youth. Lord Harris had decided it was time to end the nonsense and W. G. Grace, of course, did not fail him. With Penn well set, the necessary 26 runs were gathered in and England won the first of all the home Test matches by five wickets.

Which brings us back to Charles Alcock, who quite literally was an extraordinary man. We have seen how he made the first Test match possible, and this, alone would have ensured him his place with the immortals. But for Alcock it was the kind of thing he would throw off as all in a day's work. Nor was he being studiedly modest, striking the Englishman's pose of deliberate understatement. Consider the facts of his life and you cannot come to any other conclusion.

In the official history of the FA Cup, written by the former and most distinguished Association football correspondent of *The Times*, Geoffrey Green, we are informed on the first page that 'The origin of the Cup is to be found in the background of the man who founded it. The moving spirit was C. W. Alcock, secretary of the Football Association from 1870 to 1895. He had also been a member of the Forest Club which played near and was named after Epping Forest, and from which sprang the famous Wanderers Football Club. Alcock had been educated at Harrow School, had taken

ENGLAND v AUSTRALIA, 1880

England

E. M. Grace c Alexander b Bannerman	36	— b Boyle	0
W. G. Grace b Palmer	152	— not out	9
A. P. Lucas b Bannerman	55	— c Blackham b Palmer	2
W. Barnes b Alexander	28	— c Moule b Boyle	5
*Lord Harris c Bonnor b Alexander	52		
F. Penn b Bannerman	23	— not out	27
A. G. Steel c Boyle b Moule	42		
†Hon. A. Lyttleton not out	11	— b Palmer	13
G. F. Grace c Bannerman b Moule	0	— b Palmer	0
A. Shaw b Moule	0		
F. Morley run out	2		
B 8, l-b 11	19	N-b 1	1

1/9 2/211 3/269 4/281 5/322   420
6/404 7/410 8/410 9/413

      1/2 2/10   (5 wkts) 57
      3/22 4/31 5/31

Bowling: *First Innings*—Boyle 44–17–71–0; Palmer 70–27–116–1; Alexander 32–10–69–2; Bannerman 50–12–111–3; McDonnell 2–0–11–0; Moule 12.3–4–23–3. *Second Innings*—Boyle 17–7–21–2; Palmer 16.3–5–35–3.

Australia

A. C. Bannerman b Morley	32	— c Lucas b Shaw	8
*W. L. Murdoch c Barnes b Steel	0	— not out	153
T. U. Groube b Steel	11	— c Shaw b Morley	0
P. S. McDonnell c Barnes b Morley	27	— lbw b W G. Grace	43
J. Slight c F. G. Grace b Morley	11	— c Harris b W. G. Grace	0
†J. McC. Blackham c and b Morley	0	— c E. M. Grace b Morley	19
G. J. Bonner c G. F. Grace b Shaw	2	— b Steel	16
H. F. Boyle not out	36	— run out	3
G. E. Palmer b Morley	6	— c and b Steel	4
G. Alexander c W. G. Grace b Steel	6	— c Shaw b Morley	33
W. H. Moule c Morley b W. G. Grace	6	— b Barnes	34
B 9, l-b 3	12	B 7, l-b 7	14

1/28 2/39 3/59 4/84 5/84   149   1/8 2/13 3/14 4/97 5/101   327
6/89 7/97 8/112 9/126   6/143 7/181 8/187 9/239

Bowling: *First innings*—Morley 32–9–56–5; Steel 29–9–58–3; Shaw 13–5–21–1; W.G. Grace 1.1–0–2–1. *Second innings*—Morley 61–30–90–3; Steel 31–6–73–2; Shaw 33–18–42–1; W.G. Grace 28–10–66–2; Barnes 8.3–3–17–1; Lucas 12–7–23–0; Penn 3–1–2–0.

Umpires: H. H. Stephenson and R. Thomas.

part in the Cock House competition, a system of house matches based on the knockout principle. His fellow members of the Football Association, too, had been at Public Schools, and they also understood and loved the tradition surrounding house matches . . . The FA Cup competition, in effect, was an adaptation on a national scale of what Alcock and his fellows had known at school, and it was no wonder then that Alcock found immediate support for his original proposal: 'That it is desirable that a Challenge Cup should be established. . . .'

Seven men, headed by Alcock, met in a small oak-panelled room at the *Sportsman* office on July 29, 1871, eight years after the foundation of the Football Association, Alcock's proposal was 'That it is desirable that a Challenge Cup should be established in connection with the Association, for which all clubs belonging to the Association should be invited to compete.' At a subsequent meeting on October 16 the rules were drafted, the entries received and, as Green puts it, 'history took a deep breath and prepared for the plunge'.

On March 16, 1872 the first Cup final was played at The Oval before a crowd which today would be the equivalent of a gathering at a Fourth Division match at Rochdale or Halifax on a wet Sunday in mid-December. Of the fifteen sides who entered, only two came from north of Hereford-shire and one of these, Donnington School, scratched in the second round because they could not raise the money to travel to Glasgow to play Queen's Park. Queen's Park themselves scratched from a replay after drawing their semi-final with Wanderers for the same reason in reverse. The final was Wanderers versus Royal Engineers and was decided by a goal to the Wanderers in the first quarter of an hour. The scorer's name was rendered as 'A. H. Chequer', but this stood for 'A Harrow Chequer'. The man's real name was Monty Betts. The captain of the first team to win the FA Cup was Charles William Alcock. Seven years earlier, he had captained England against Scotland. That match, too, was at The Oval and ended in a 2–2 draw.

Alcock had, at the time of the first FA Cup final, been Surrey's first paid secretary at an annual salary of £250 for three years and was responsible for The Oval being used for the final, for England's first home soccer internationals against Scotland and Wales, and for England's first home rugby internationals against Scotland in 1872 and Ireland in 1875.

Charles William Alcock was born to a life of privilege at Sunderland on December 2, 1842. He died at Brighton, not three months after his 64th birthday, on February 26, 1907.

All his working life had been vitally concentrated on a few square miles of London. As a cricketer he was described in a volume of his time as 'a steady bat, a fair change fast bowler and an excellent stop or long field'. He did not gain his place in the Harrow XI, but he played club cricket and once had the curious experience of captaining France in a match against Germany at Hamburg, although the writer of his obituary, noted in the *Wisden* of 1908, does not say how this came about. He became secretary of Surrey County Cricket Club on February 6, 1872, a position he held until the time of his death. He was a most voluminous writer on cricket and in 1882 founded *Cricket*, of which he was the editor from the first issue until the day of his death. For 29 years he contributed to James Lillywhite's *Cricket Annual* and was the chief writer of *Surrey Cricket, Its History and Associations*, published in 1902. After his success in arranging the first meeting of England and Australia in this country, which we are now celebrating, Alcock was handed the job of arranging fixture lists of touring teams in the closing period of the nineteenth century. For the last ten years of his life he was a vice-president of the Football Association.

In *The Way of All Flesh*, Samuel Butler wrote 'Youth is like spring, an over praised season.' I am old enough to understand that this can apply to many of us, but never, I suspect, to Charles Alcock. He could never have led a lotus-eating existence in an age when someone of his background was not expected to work; but after playing two great team games with no little distinction he devoted the whole of his life to promoting their growth so that they could be enjoyed by an ever-widening circle of people. As an English gentleman of a certain period in history he practised reticence in his opinions and actions. It had not become fashionable to give free rein to displays of emotionalism embracing everything from bedroom athletics to racism. There is, however, some evidence that he dreaded the thought of approaching retirement, for he once remarked to Ashley Cooper: 'I cannot visualise myself just sitting in the chimney corner.' I could be wrong, but I believe that at the end of the winter, with what in all probability would have been his last season as part of the pulse of cricket ahead of him, he quietly turned his face to the wall.

What is deeply ironic is that none of the games he did so much to expand has granted him the status he deserves. Sir Donald Bradman, Sir Leonard Hutton, Sir Stanley Matthews, Sir Stanley Rous—they have the titles and are the stuff of which folk-lore is made. Alcock has rested 73 years unsung, but thousands of young men who escaped the mine shaft, the factory bench, the humdrum office job, to earn their bread and motor cars playing cricket and football, have reason to bless his name. Those who read this appreciation can go away and trim their lamps and know that in the reading they have perhaps come close to the heart of things.

CRICKETANA—A 'BULL' MARKET [1981]

BY DAVID FRITH

(Editor of *Wisden Cricket Monthly*)

The ever so slightly demented reverence of cricket for the relics of its own past was, by the start of the 1980s, beginning to become big, or at any rate medium-sized, business. The sales room gradually became more willing to take their commissions at the auctioning of W. G. Grace's shirt studs, or a dinner plate embellished with scenes from Lord Hawke's moustache. In this burgeoning bull market no artefact advanced more spectacularly than Wisden itself, whose early editions had already taken on the patina of sacred medieval texts. When, not long after the end of the Second World War John Arlott went to his bank manager and negotiated overdraft facilities for the purchase of a complete set of Wisden, the sum involved was £19. In the year when David Frith published his review of the market, so piddling a sum as £19 would have been woefully insufficient to purchase almost any of the eighty-six volumes which the Arlott overdraft covered. Some of the editions of the 1880s, always scarce, were already beginning to fetch prices which smacked of manipulation by the professional dealers, and the time was not far distant when a price of more than a hundred pounds for a single volume was not considered prohibitive, especially by those with no sense of proportion.

But at least an ancient almanack may be perused. Frith's study discloses that in addition to books, there was a growing lust to possess other, less practicable fragments of the past, an ashtray, a scarf, a hat, a menu, a ball, a bail, a belt. Of course cricket is not at all unique in this regard. To render tangible a remote past is a common enough desire, which has feathered the nests of countless collectors of first editions, literary autographs and the like. Frith ends by wondering if the ceiling had not been reached, and mentions the possibility of a gentle falling away. On the contrary, prices have continued to rise, the sales rooms have continued to be crowded on cricket days, and no item of memorabilia, no matter how insignificant, seems too trivial to attract interest.

David Frith (b. 1937) is an Australian ex-Grade cricketer who made his home in England some years ago, much to the enrichment of the local journalistic scene. In addition to editing The Cricketer *from 1972 to 1978, and then creating and editing* Wisden's Monthly, *he has produced a stream of readable books, at least two of which,* The Golden Age of Cricket; 1890–1914 *and* Pageant of Cricket, *are indispensable. He is noted for his close interest in the deaths of cricketers, even down to the minutiae of their epitaphs. This interest may strike some as slightly morbid, except that the last days of men like Albert Trott, A. E. Stoddart, Arthur Shrewsbury and others are an important part of cricket history.*

Not so very long ago, cricket books and ephemera were collected by enthusiasts for the pure, albeit competitive, joy of possession. The scene has changed. Public interest in cricket has risen since the early 1970s; the frailty of currency in times of economic inflation has persuaded people—not all necessarily cricket-lovers—that cricketana is a solid investment; and the obsessive nostalgia which dependably visits mankind in time of stress has done the rest.

The 'business' of collecting cricket material was brisk enough in the days when Leslie Gutteridge presided over his cavern of literary treasures, extraodinarily fairly priced, at Epworth's Bookshop in London's City Road. E. K. Brown of Liskeard, Cornwall, took the premier spot among dealers when Mr Gutteridge moved to Canada, and J. W. McKenzie and Martin Wood, of the younger breed, further answered and encouraged the growth in interest which accompanied cricket's latest ascendancy.

Yet it was the sudden concentrated awareness of London's auction rooms which triggered off the unprecedented boom. In September 1978, some of Phillips's estimates for over a hundred lots were doubled, even trebled. Unlike the notorious Cahn sale as Sotheby's in 1951, this was attended by a large gathering, and bidding was determined beyond mere doggedness. A. H. Burr's oil on canvas, *A Game of Cricket*, fetched top price at £7,500 (an almost identical work entitled *The Veteran Bowler* made £2,800 a year later); the charming *The Young Cricketers* (English school) £2,600; and lithographs after J. C. Anderson £50 or £60 apiece.

That these unique or rare and desirable lots should realise such high sums was no surprise. A first edition *Felix on the Bat* (1845) made £280, Denison's *Sketches of the Players* (1846) £180, and Sir Jeremiah Coleman's *The Noble Game of Cricket* (1941), one of a limited edition of 150, £460, establishing positively a new era of valuation. But when a bisque figure of W. G. Grace saw bidding escalate to £440 and a W.G. Century of Centuries Coalport plate raised £800, when a W.G. commemorative handkerchief made £850 and a signed photograph of the 1909 Australian touring team made £190, there was no doubting that cricket's stock market was in a state of excitement.

There came the inevitable reaction. Seven months later, at the same saleroom, when the most historically interesting item was a mid-eighteenth century bat (£550), an original Victorian cast-iron pub table with moulded portraits of W. G. Grace on the legs fetched £140, half the figure at the previous sale (only for values to be confounded again in December when, at Sotheby's, a modern reproduction was sold for £180); a W.G. handkerchief made £220—still an astonishing price, yet little more than a quarter of that at the earlier sale—and another handkerchief, The Australian Cricketers 1882, made £340. While prints and paintings, ancient and modern, fetched substantial sums, there were signs that things were settling down.

Whatever the oscillations in price in the areas of silver, art and ephemera, books held steady, with *Wisden Cricketers' Almanacks* the gold bullion. A run of 97 *Wisdens* from 1864 to 1969, lacking nine pre-1900, took bidding to £4,200. This transaction was topped a year later when Sir Pelham Warner's *Wisdens* (1864–1963) were bought for £7,800. Even the auctioneer gulped as bidding reached this unexpected peak. It should be remembered, too, that 11½ per cent had to be added as buyer's premium plus VAT.

The salesrooms now filled each time a cricket auction was staged in London, for media interest had increased public awareness. It also caused one buyer to realise too late that, having confessed to a radio audience of millions that he had paid £60 for eight coloured lithographs of the 1882 Australians, he could hardly expect to conceal the fact from his wife.

Postcards, medallions, tankards and pots, salvers, magic lantern slides: they came out of the bureaux and down from the attics and found their current values according to demand. The dealers, armed with sizable budgets, proved almost unbeatable when they set their sights on books, and there were suspicions that the market was being cornered, a depressing prospect for budding collectors. But by May 1980, a W.G. handkerchief—admittedly perhaps less pristine than others—had slipped to £65, and a large white marble figure of a boy with a bat, which had sold for £2,000 twenty months before, was knocked down, or conceivably bought back, at £750.

Wisdens and 'Graceiana' continued to be the most appealing hall-marks. Even an 1894 telegram from W.G. to his mother was so highly regarded as to fetch £90.

The occasional hidden gem slipped through. Alerted at the preview, a West Country buyer paid little for a darkened bat which, it transpired, bore a lengthy inscription and signature by Arthur Shrewsbury. But the feeling persisted: that prices were getting out of hand, that the frenzy for possession would create a vacuum in its wake. Absurdities such as the pair of prints (1977) which went for £16, though still available from the publisher for £5, guaranteed this backlash.

'Spy' cartoons and Chevallier Tayler chromolithographs came through in profusion; menus, signed photos, scorecards; 'Plum' Warner's England blazer and a dozen caps, one of them his renowned Harlequin 'lid'. 'Spy's' original watercolour of Tom Hayward sold for £300, while Frank Reynolds drawings went for £50 or so per pair. A stevengraph of W.G. made £300, and in the book department Ranji's *Jubilee Book*, the signed, limited edition, made £110. *The Laws of Cricket*, revised at the Star & Garter, Pall Mall, in 1774 proved a prize catch, and made £500 to a Northern collector. The silver cigar-box presented to Wally Hammond by the 1928–29 M.C.C. team went for £270. A delightful little eighteenth century Bilston patch-box, decorated with a view of a match at Sevenoaks in 1782, fetched £1,250.

By now, Phillips's sales were being scheduled several times annually, and taking two or three hours to conduct. With the scope now so broad and the hammer prices having levelled slightly, there was potentially plenty for everybody, particularly among the lesser rarities. The queue at the collection counter was long. Over £30,000 changed hands at Phillips's sale of May 1980, and £18,000 in September—when a daguerreotype of a cricketer, after being dropped to the floor accidentally, made £55. Other desirable items were A. P. F. Chapman's four photo albums (£180) and a copy of *Biers & Fairfax Australian Cricketer's Guide* for 1856–57 (£240). Spasmodically, well-known names appeared in the commodity descriptions: formerly the property of Jack Hobbs . . . Arthur Fielder . . . J. R. Mason . . . author Eric Parker . . . and, by a circuitous route, John Arlott.

In the spring of 1980, Sussex County Cricket Club, severely financially embarrassed, took their cue and mounted an auction at Hove of purportedly duplicate cricketana from the club's library and museum. Some £10,000 was raised: a late eighteenth/early nineteenth century oil of Kent v Sussex, Malling (surely no duplicate) made £1,650; Tony Greig's 'Last' Sussex bat £200 and a boxful of his ties £22; two small Felix watercolours brought £300.

Next, Worcestershire pulled in almost £5,000 at the end of the season, auctioning donated objects which included the Benson and Hedges Gold Award medallion withheld when Somerset captain Brian Rose declared, rendering the match void. Someone thought highly enough of this oddity to pay £300. The ball used for the seventeen deliveries in that doomed match made, with arithmetical neatness, £17. Peter May's England cap fetched £38, Basil D'Oliveira's £33, and David Sheppard's Sussex cap £15. These will not have gone unnoticed by county beneficiaries of the future.

The last major sale of 1980, Sotheby's at Gleneagles, saw a most special heirloom change hands when a five-piece silver tea service presented to Mrs. W. L. Murdoch by Prince Ranjitsinhji was offered to the public. With its evocative associations it seemed reasonably priced at £450 when the auctioneer's hammer descended.

The comfort for all genuine cricket-lovers whose purses have not stretched to the heavier demands comes in the knowledge that while so many people care about the preservation of the game's tangible heritage, it will remain protected. In an ideal world all worthwhile exhibits, to say nothing of a copy of every cricket book ever published, would be on permanent view to the nation and its overseas visitors, rather than scattered in private collections. But while the temptations exists to sell soon after buying, at least a kind of availability persists, given the funds. And for the poorer spectator there is at least the chance to examine the goods at auction previews before attending the sale and watching the tight-jawed purchasers in fervent competition.

Will values hold? If inflation continues to subside and if the boom in cricket's grip on the public's imagination runs into a recession, as predicted by the jeremiahs, then probably not. But the delight in handling a book first held by an *aficionado* a hundred years ago, or of placing an Edwardian Test cricketer's cap upon one's head, will never cease momentarily to paralyse an addict with ecstasy.

FIFTY YEARS ON [1981]

BY G. O. ALLEN

The prime requisite of attaining magisterial status is to outlive all one's contemporaries, and this sad state of grace descended on George Oswald Allen when in 1978 Frank Woolley was dismissed for ninety one in the incongruities of Halifax, Nova Scotia. Too many of Allen's teammates in the 1930 Lord's Test had died without remotely approaching the durability of Woolley's generation, several of whom lived to become nonagenarians, including Rhodes, Barnes, Strudwick, Sandham and Fender. Allen's opponents at Lord's in June 1930 proved to be more resolute. When the 1981 almanack appeared, Messrs Ponsford, Bradman and Oldfield were still sufficiently animate to read it, and of the rest, Tim Wall had only just died, while Clarrie Grimmett's passing was so close to the publication of 'Fifty Years On' that his obituary appeared in the same edition as the essay. Allen was to live on, through the 1980s, to within a few weeks of the new decade, by which time he had been knighted for services to cricket.

One of the most dedicated students of the game, and always a perceptive judge of talent, Allen's comparative assessment of cricketers displays all his acuity, from the sarcastic dismissal of the latterday fast bowler's amble back to his mark as a succession of 'country strolls', to the relentless deployment of statistics to show to what shocking extent the modern professional, by deliberately slowing down the pace of the proceedings, has been thieving from the paying spectator. Allen is, of course perfectly correct in his assumption that the match in which he made his Test debut against Australia was richer in players of class than their successors fifty years on. Allen's teammates that day included Hobbs, Woolley, Hammond, Duleep-sinhji and Tate; among his opponents were Bradman, Ponsford, McCabe, Oldfield and Grimmett. Well might the survivors of Allen's generation mourn the death of the past.

THE Test match against Australia at Lord's in 1930 was my first. Now, 50 years later, presumably because I am, sadly, the only surviving member of that England team, I have been asked to record my impressions of, and draw some comparisons between, that match and the Centenary Test match against Australia at Lord's last summer.

That the former was one of the great games in cricket history and the latter was not was due partly to chance. For one thing, the weather in 1930 was perfect. So, though on the slow side, was the pitch, which had been specially prepared, this being the first ever four-day Test match at Lord's. In 1980 it rained often enough on the first three days to have confounded even the 1930 sides from providing as much entertainment and fine cricket as I believe they did half a century ago. To that extent, Chappell and Botham and their two sides were up against it from the start. On the other hand, I am sure that in 1930, in conditions similar to those on the Saturday of the Centenary Test match, play would have started much earlier than it did. In fact, looking back to the thirties, when pitches were uncovered and there was much less covering generally, I think that play was often started too soon; but surely the pendulum has now swung too far in the opposite direction.

It must seem incredible to many who play and watch the game today that England could have made 425 in the first innings of a four-day match, as they did at Lord's in 1930, and yet have lost. In reply, Australia scored 729 for six declared. In the last two hours forty minutes on the second day, Australia went from 162 for one to 404 for two—255 runs, that is, in 160 minutes, of which Bradman made 155. At the start of the last day England, in their second innings, were 98 for two, still 206 behind with Hobbs and Woolley out, and it needed a great innings of 121 in two and a half hours by Chapman to save his side from an innings defeat. In the end Australia, losing three wickets (including that of Bradman) for 22 runs, had a minor crisis to surmount before winning with an hour to spare.

But this was the age of the batsman, the age before the lbw law was changed, and this was a batsman's match throughout. The pitch, for the reason I have mentioned, was easy-paced, and the bowlers, the leg-spinners and White excepted, were perhaps slightly below standard, Tate by then being a little over the top.

For England the outstanding innings were those of Chapman and Duleepsinhji, though Woolley's 41 in very quick time on the first morning was a gem. Duleepsinhji's 173 in his first Test match against Australia was one of the most graceful exhibitions of batting I have ever seen; he was a superb player of spinners as he proved on this occasion. Chapman's was a fine effort, particularly the second half of it, though he played and missed many times in his first fifty. I can vouch for this as I was in with him, and he should have been out before scoring. I can see it now: he failed to spot Grimmett's googly and hit a skier on the off side. Woodfull, Richardson and Ponsford all could have caught it easily, but at the last moment, no one having called, each left it to the other. Amidst much laughter and some apologies all Grimmett said was 'Never mind, I'll get him out next over.' When watching the Centenary match with Ponsford, I mentioned the incident to him. He remembered it well, but to our mutual enjoyment he was disinclined to admit to more than a minor share of the guilt.

For Australia, the first four, Woodfull, Ponsford, Bradman and Kippax, all played fine innings, each in his own rather different style: Woodfull with his short backlift, very sure but always looking for runs; Ponsford mainly on the back foot or up the wicket to the spinners and a superb timer of the ball; Kippax a very elegant stroke-player on both sides of the wicket—and then, of course, Bradman. The best comment on Bradman's innings is probably his own. When asked which was the best innings he ever played, he is on record as saying: 'My 254 at Lord's in 1930 because I never hit a ball anywhere other than I intended and I never lifted one off the ground until the stroke from which I was out.' Some believe he was unorthodox. Well, perhaps he was when he was really on the rampage, but in defence and when necessary, none was more correct. It was his early judgment of length, his quickness of foot and his ruthless concentration which made him the undoubted genius he was.

The Centenary Test match is a different story. As I have already said, conditions were unfavourable from the start. Even had M.C.C. acquired an additional cover, and before the match the captains and umpires had been requested by the authorities to be rather less stern in their judgement as to fitness for play, I doubt if it would have helped greatly as it is always difficult to make a game flow once it has been subject to frequent interruptions.

I hate saying it, but I do not think either looked a very good side. There were, of course, several high-class batsmen amongst them, and in Lillee certainly the best fast bowler in either match. Although perhaps not quite as fast as he was, his rhythm, his ability to move the ball and vary his pace, and his unbounded determination were a feature of the match.

For Australia, Wood played a sound first innings and Chappell two good though for him rather subdued innings. In form, with all his strokes going, Chappell must rank high amongst batsmen of our time. But in this match it was Hughes who caught the eye, at least mine. Of course he took some chances and had his moments of luck, particularly in the second innings, but he was reluctant to be dictated to, moved his feet well, and with a wholesome backlift was able and prepared to play all the strokes. After 50 years one's memory is hazy, but of one thing I am sure—his straight six off Old was unquestionably the best hit in either match, indeed possibly the most remarkable straight hit I have seen. To take two paces up the wicket to a fast-medium bowler of Old's class and hit a flat 'skimmer' on to the top of the Pavilion at Lord's takes some beating. Goodness only knows where it might have gone had he, to use a golfing term, taken a slightly more lofted club.

For England, the batting, with two exceptions, was below Test match standards, even after making allowances for the excellent fast attack of Lillee and Pascoe and the fact that the match took place late in the season after a difficult series against some relentless West Indian fast bowling. Boycott showed his undoubted class in two typically determined innings. Technically he is head and shoulders ahead of any other batsman in England, indeed his technique is so good it is surprising he does not tear the attack apart more often. Gower twice played some fine strokes and was beginning to look the batsman all Englishmen hope and believe he will be, only to get out to two bad shots. Unfortunately Gooch, who is now an extremely good opener and a powerful striker of the ball, failed in both innings.

So much for my impressions of the two matches; now for some comparisons. My first and foremost must be regarding the pace at which they were played, and the Centenary match is a fair example of how the game has slowed down over the span of years. I may have some regrets about the present-day game, but this is my one real criticism of it. Statistics are often boring and can be unjust, but in this instance I think they are interesting and revealing in that they provide some indication as to how much and why this state of affairs has come about.

In the 1930 match 1,601 runs were scored in 23 hours 10 minutes, that is at an average of 69 runs per hour, whereas in the Centenary match 1,023 were scored in 21 hours 7 minutes, an average of 48.4, per hour. A difference of 20 runs an hour is disturbing, to say the least; yet if one looks at the runs per 100 balls one finds very little between them, there being 53 runs in 1930 and 51.2 in 1980. If one then takes into account the importance nowadays attached by captains to containment and the present high standard of fielding, it is clear the batsmen must be exonerated.

And so, inevitably, to the over-rate. In 1930, 260 overs of pace and 245 of spin were bowled at an average of 21.50 an hour: in 1980, 210 overs of pace and 112 of spin were bowled at an average of 15.82 an hour. These figures for pace and spin suggest to me that it is not solely the predominance of fast bowling that is responsible for the loss of 5.68 overs an hour. The endless discussions between bowlers and captains, the frequent changes in field-placing—and the waiting for new batsmen to reach the crease before making some of them—waste part of the time. But it is the absurdly long runs-up of many of the fast bowlers, and even of some of the medium-paced bowlers, often coupled with a funereal walk back to their marks, that are the real cause of the trouble. For those who saw little or no cricket before World War Two, I can assure them one could count on the fingers of one hand the number of fast bowlers who ran more than 25 yards: nowadays one can count on the fingers of one hand those who do not—and some run 40 or 45 yards. Of course a few of these long-runners are a fine sight coming in, but please let us be spared their country strolls.

One last statistic, a sombre thought. In a 30-hour Test match, the loss of 5.68 overs and 20 runs an hour could mean the loss of as many as 170 overs and 600 runs. Put another way, the debit, in terms of the modern rate as compared with the old, is roughly two whole days' play.

The comparison between the number of paying customers and the takings for the two matches is illuminating: in 1930, 110,000 people paid £14,500 to watch the four-day match; in 1980, 84,938 over the five-day match paid £360,850 and had the weather been kinder that figure must have been in excess of £400,000. At the moment the situation is clearly very satisfactory, but might not the crunch come if the tempo is not increased, especially when the opposition is less glamorous?

As regards the fielding there can be no argument. In the 1930 match it was moderate. For England Hammond and Duleepsinhji were two fine 'slippers'; I still maintain that the former was the best I have ever seen. Chapman, who made magnificent catches to dismiss Bradman in both innings, was excellent anywhere, as was Robins. Hobbs, Hendren and Woolley, who had all been of the highest class, were by then getting on in years. For Australia only Bradman and Richardson really stood out. In the Centenary match the general standard was far superior, the ground fielding and throwing being superb. The catching was not put to the test, but knowing something of both sides I am certain it, too, would have been of the highest order. The 'sliding tackle' is a spectacular innovation. In the thirties, even if I had thought of it, I could barely have afforded the additional cleaning bills.

In addition to the tempo there was another fundamental difference between the two matches, namely the approach and tactics of the sides in the field. In 1930, with both teams relying heavily on a leg-spinner and slow left-armer, the theme was always likely to be attack. In the modern game, though rather less in evidence in the Centenary match, defensive field-placing, containment, call it what you will, plays an important rôle. Hence the attraction for the crowds lies more in the brilliance of the fielding and perhaps a fierce sense of conflict engendered by the menace of the fast bowling. It is not surprising that defensive tactics have crept into cricket—they are common to most sports today. No doubt more or earlier use of them might have been advantageous in the Thirties, but strange, even crazy, as it may seem now, I simply do not think that was the way either captains or players wanted to play their cricket.

I said earlier that I might have some regrets about the present-day game. Well, I do have one or two. I particularly regret the lack of variety, once one of the charms of cricket, and for much of this I blame, each in its own way, the change in the lbw law introduced way back in 1935 and the lack of pace in many of the pitches. The changes in the lbw law was designed to prevent 'padding-up'; it was also argued that it would help all types of bowlers equally and increase off-side play. In the event, apart from reducing the use of the pads to some extent, it has, in my opinion, done more harm than good. As it has helped disproportionally bowlers who bring the ball into the batsman, it has swung the game more towards the leg-side and has contributed in no small degree to the demise of both the leg-spinner and the slow left-armer. Then, with pitches getting slower and slower, containment was bound to become the order of the day. I, for one, do not blame the players, I simply pray for more variety. But how to restore it is the baffling question.

I regret, too, the predominance of the 'forward prod' to balls short of a length: that can certainly be blamed on the lbw law. It is safer forward. But excessive forward play must restrict the batsman's range, there being so many attractive and lucrative strokes to be found off the back foot.

And my last lament: I find the incessant noise on many big-match days thoroughly irksome. I welcome the enthusiasm, the cheering and the clapping, but the banging of cans and the endless alcoholic shouting is not for me.

But I have no wish to end these thoughts on a critical note. The game has undoubtedly changed in some respects, mainly in the last 25 years, but in saying this I am not suggesting that it is not in a healthy state; it is. Sadly, circumstances conspired against the Centenary match; yet it was a happy, nostalgic occasion, wherein old rivalries were recalled and old friendships renewed. There is, after all, nothing in cricket to compare with England v Australia, the oldest of all Test match fixtures.

RADIO REFLECTIONS [1981]

BY E. W. SWANTON

The retirement of John Arlott from commentating at the end of the 1980 season prompted one of his fellow-communicators to compile a brief history of cricket reporting on radio. At one time, with the rapid spread of the eczema of television, it had been assumed by the wiseacres of the industry, wrongly as it happened, that the audience for radio would dwindle away into insignificance. The contrary proved the case, in sport reporting as well as in other aspects of national life. By 1981, for all the technical ingenuity of the cameras, TV coverage was not to be compared with the consistent inspiration of 'Test Match Special' on the radio. The shrewd follower had long since realised that ideal coverage could be obtained by watching dumb pictures to the accompaniment of the radio commentary. Nor did it matter in the slightest if weather conditions should stop play. The talk went on regardless, always animated, discursive, reminiscent, sentiment and facetiousness masking deep scholarship. Indeed, when the team really got going it was often a case of Good Light Stopped Talk.

At the heart of this tiny republic of enlightenment was the rich Hampshire burr of John Arlott, the policeman-turned-poet whose mastery of improvised English was probably unmatched by any professional in Britain. He shared with Alistair Cooke the distinction of possessing the best-loved voice in radio, but Cooke's 'letters from America', peerless examples of the broadcasting art though they are, were carefully scripted. Arlott aspired to, and often attained, the same felicity with extemporised conversation prompted by a succession of complex actions. He began this remarkable career by reporting the matches of the Indian tourists in 1946, and within a few seasons had become a prized national possession. Blessed with a voice, a turn of phrase and a knack of compassionate humour which could quickly entrance even the non-cricketing public, Arlott became as much part of the English game as any of the cricketers. The day of his farewell Test commentary, at Lord's for the England–Australia centenary match, proved to be an extraordinary occasion, not so much for the cricket or for the gathering of dozens of legendary cricketers, as for the reaction of everyone in the ground to Arlott's impending departure. As he spoke his last lines of commentary: 'It's 69 for 2, nine runs off the over, 28 Boycott, 15 Gower—69 for 2, and after Trevor Bailey it'll be Christopher Martin-Jenkins,' listeners heard something unprecedented, loud clapping from inside the commentary box, followed by an announcement on the public address system that John had completed his last spell of commentary. The cricketers paused in their ballet to turn to the box and applaud, and the entire crowd joined them. I remember standing nearby, watching as John, in a broad-striped shirt suitably conspicuous for the occasion, left his post in the box and threaded his way out. People were standing and cheering all over the ground. When the game was over and John was about to present the Man of the Match award, the huge crowd standing on the grass awaiting his arrival on the balcony greeted him with a crashing ovation lasting several minutes. No cricketer had ever been received in this fashion. We all sensed that with John's retirement a period in the nation's social history was passing.

By modern standards John was young to have retired from a sedentary occupation. Or so I thought. He was only sixty-six, and Cardus was still exfloriating into his eighties. But it was not a sedentary job after all. On his farewell day at the cricket John bought me a cup of tea in the Press Room snack bar and told me of his physical weariness. The travelling from town to town, match to match, had finally exhausted him, and he intimated that perhaps his employers had not quite done all they might have to ease the ache of constant travel. I was dumbfounded at this. If the executives had had any sense at all, should they not have provided John with a Rolls and a chauffeur, a valet and a secretary to keep the honeyed words coming? But they had not, and now it was all over. When I asked him if he had planned his autobiography, he answered, 'For the first six months I think I'll sleep.' He *then added that he wasn't sure he would write one at all. But he did. It took ten years, but at last he published* Basingstoke Boy.

As Swanton tells in his resumé, there has been a succession of memorable broadcasters of the game. But none has attained the eminence of Arlott, who continues to stand, more than ten years after his departure from the game he loved so passionately, as a symbol of the friendly sound of cricket floating through the ether. As the last decade of this calamitous century opens, there is much talk of discontinuing the principle maintained by 'Test match Special' of the ball-by-ball commentary. Thatcherite Britain has been guilty of some of the worst acts of philistinism in our recent history, but can even it be so stupid as to dismantle one of the most proficient as well as one of the best-loved institutions of our lives? I suppose it would at least be consistent.

THE retirement of John Arlott, who over the course of the 35 summers since the end of the war has spread over the air more words about cricket than any other man has done, or perhaps is ever likely to do, is an appropriate time to look back to the beginnings of cricket broadcasting on Sound radio and attempt some sort of sketch of its development. The first of all cricket broadcasts concerned the first match of the first New Zealand tour to England in 1927, against Essex at the old county headquarters at Leyton. Plum Warner—and who more appropriate?—gave eye-witness accounts of each day's play, while later that summer the Rev. F. H. Gillingham, the well-known cricketing parson, was in action similarly at The Oval. The very first of all sporting broadcasts had been made at Twickenham by H. B. T. Wakelam only in January, 1927. Cricket, therefore, was early in the field.

History is somewhat misty regarding the first years, for a bomb played havoc with the pre-war archives of the BBC. It is clear enough, though, that cricket was not, for a while, rated very highly as entertainment by the hierarchy. Almost up to the outbreak of war, other games, wherein the action was faster, were given wider attention. Don Bradman's first visit to England in 1930 coincided with the first coverage of Test matches, but only to the extent of periodical reports: by M. K. Foster, youngest but one of the brotherhood of seven, on the first Test, by A. C. MacLaren on the second and third, and by Aubrey Faulkner on the fourth and fifth.

An interesting sidelight on these early experiments discloses that John Snagge, a BBC staff man from the earliest Savoy Hill days, was sent down to The Oval to help Faulkner, who was unwell. According to Snagge, and not surprisingly, he struggled a bit in an unfamiliar role. Yet on the strength of his performance he was chosen by Gerald Cock, the first head of outside Broadcasts, to cover the Boat Race the following year. Thus, fortuitously, he began surely the longest of all sporting assignments, for he broadcast every race from 1931 until his retirement from the job in 1980.

Thereafter things at first moved but slowly, MCC taking much longer to appreciate the evangelistic possibilities of radio than, for instance, the equally conservative Rugby Union. Hence the story of how Howard Marshall, who was to become the first professional cricket commentator, was required in the early 1930s to hustle from Lord's round the corner to a semi-basement room in Grove End Road, where he had to compete with extraneous noises including that of a child's piano lesson in a room above. However, by 1934 Marshall was at least installed inside the ground, even though he had to tell the world about Hedley Verity's famous rout of the 1934 Australians on a turning wicket from a window in the old Tavern at square leg.

Arlott, to whose researches for the BBC publication, *Armchair Cricket*, I must make due acknowledgment, recalls his youthful memories of Marshall's rich, unmistakable voice in paying tribute to him as the innovator, 'the first person to link the news-duty of the commentator with visual and human impressions'. There never was a deeper, more melli-fluous and attractive voice than Howard's, and when Seymour de Lotbinière became Director of Outside Broadcasts in 1935 the pair of them, along with Michael Standing, 'Lobby's' deputy and himself, like Marshall, a competent club cricketer, began to explore the possibilities of the running commentary.

In the later 1930s, county cricket began to be covered in this way in addition to the Test matches, this increased activity culminating in the England-West Indies series of 1939 which was broadcast, for the first time, in its entirety ball by ball. It was then that I joined Marshall and Standing to make a commentary team of three. This comprehensive arrangement, as I recall, put something of a strain on BBC resources. It was said to have been instigated by a BBC governor who, on a winter cruise in the Caribbean, had discovered the islanders' deep fervour for the game and promised them the full treatment.

I expect I was conceited enough to think that the decision may also have owed something to my having blazed the trail the preceding winter in South Africa, where I toured with Walter Hammond's MCC side. This was the first time cricket had been broadcast in South Africa. Nor had anyone previously gone out from England to broadcast cricket home. The first reward was, in the very first Test, to find myself with a hat-trick to describe; the second was to report the longest of all Test matches. It was Tom Goddard who woke up a few at home, dozing after their Christmas dinners, by achieving the second of only three Test hat-tricks by an Englishman in this century. As to that dreary ten-day marathon at Durban, I have a memento in the form of a letter from the BBC, saying that the great Corporation had been considering the question of some further remuneration, seeing that the match fee had been based on a duration of four days, and that they thought an extra payment of 25 guineas would be a fair arrangement. In case anyone should think this an odd computation, they pointed out that there had been no play on one of the days because of rain. Careful were the BBC in those days: my first post-war contracts offered match fees plus railway vouchers (first-class) plus expenses at the rate of one pound 'for each night necessarily spent away from home'.

But to less frivolous matters, and the great surge of interest in cricket after the war which broadcasting of all first-class cricket on a wide scale did so much to stimulate. Where hitherto cricket had strained to keep up in the broadcast race, now it set the pace. Rex Alston had abandoned school-mastering at Bedford in favour of the BBC, where his first-hand sporting experience of athletics, cricket and rugby football were at once utilised. In all three activities he was a key member of the broadcast team for twenty years or more. At first Alston, Standing and I formed the Test panel, and divided between ourselves—without benefit of scorer—the lengthy cover-age of many county matches as well as the Lord's classics of University Match and Gentlemen and Players.

There came, too, a fresh figure on the scene, a member of the BBC staff seconded to follow the 1946 Indian team, John Arlott. It is no stretching of the truth to compare the impact made on listeners by him with that which had been made by Neville Cardus of the *Manchester Guardian* ('Cricketer') on the cricket world a quarter of a century earlier.

With both, perhaps, the facts and the technicalities of the game sometimes ran second to the characters involved and the context of the occasion, the places and the people. John Arlott, his Hampshire tones distinctly lighter than in his later days, like Cardus, had imagination, keen powers of observation and not least the gift of words. There was an element of chance in the binding of both to cricket, Cardus being sent out for a summer's fresh air after illness, and Arlott having joined the BBC the previous year not on the sports staff but as a talks and poetry producer.

In the emergence of these two at moments when interest was booming anyway, Cardus after the first war, Arlott after the second, the game had two rare strokes of luck, for each man developed his own new following. Not least, each put across a wit and humour, which helped persuade readers and audiences that cricket was a game played by flesh-and-blood characters, to be savoured and enjoyed. For 35 years until his retirement at the end of last summer John kept at it, for much of the period doubling broadcasting and journalism. Having worked alongside him for most of that time, it is for me a pleasure to add, in cricket's official chronicle, this appreciation to the many others he has received.

Marshall pursued other interests after the war, and though sometimes to be heard on major occasions—notably from Westminster Abbey at the Coronation—he did no more cricket broadcasting. Yet the technique which he had evolved, with the ever-present advice of de Lotbinière, was aimed at by us all in our own individual ways. Howard's running commentary leading up to Len Hutton's breaking of Don Bradman's record score of 334, in The Oval Test of 1938, which is re-broadcast on nostalgic occasions, may seem a stately period-piece to some of the modern school, but most of them could profit by noting how scrupulously he observed the ground-rules.

The general picture of the occasion—the field, the weather, the crowd, the personalities and attitudes of the players, the position of the game, tactical appreciations and the options open to the captains—all these and maybe other aspects less immediate invite a wide variety of comment. By the time de Lotbinière gave his celebrated 'teach-in' to the foremost outside-broadcasters in 1951, all this was called 'associative material'. To a large degree it makes or mars the whole performance. Yet in cricket, as in all games, the focal point is the ball, and all must be subsidiary to the bowler's approach and delivery and the batsman's reaction to it. In other words, timing is all-important in commentary, and it is a cardinal sin to be late on the stroke. 'The golden pause' was, I believe, first commended as one of the many attributes of the late Henry Longhurst as a television commentator on golf ('If you've nothing to say, don't say it!'); but I have always thought it also applicable to the break of a couple of seconds or more immediately before the bowler's arm comes over in the last stride and the man at the 'mike', having drawn breath, reflects the speed of the ball and the nature of the stroke as he describes it all at an increased tempo to his listeners.

Nowadays, of course, the commentator of the moment has not only a statistician, perhaps Bill Frindall, on one side of him but one of the regular summarisers, Trevor Bailey, Fred Trueman or Tony Lewis maybe, on the other. If the ball bowled has had some dramatic effect, whether to the batsman's advantage or otherwise, the commentator will probably bring in one of these for his opinion, or the scorer will chip in with a relevant fact or two. Yet the man at the controls, so to speak, is still the commentator.

Marshall, as long ago as 1934, was the first man to use a scorer. At his request Lancashire lent him a young groundstaff cricketer named Arthur Wrigley for the England-Australia Test at Old Trafford—which, as England declared at 627 for nine, was a prescient move on his part. It was not, however, immediately followed up. Not until after the war (according to my memory and Michael Standing's) were scorers used, and then for a further while only for Test matches.

One important advantage the older generation of commentators had over those of today was the regular training and practice they received from broadcasting county cricket. What was then the major part of the over-all coverage of cricket gave the BBC in addition the chance of trying out new material. The modern instant reports, lasting a minute or two from county grounds, demand little knowledge of the game, and one wonders how the gaps will be filled when Brian Johnston, seemingly perennial and in his particular jovial way still a highly popular element in the team, eventually follows Arlott into retirement. Though others have made acceptable contributions—and Henry Blofeld chalked up a marked success in Australia—the only other notable addition among the younger generation who comes across as combining close knowledge of the game with facility of expression is Christopher Martin-Jenkins.

Many overseas broadcasters accompanying the touring teams have added flavour to the over-all performance, notably a succession of West Indians from Learie Constantine to the present explicit, conspicuously fair-minded Tony Cozier. But for both quality and length of service, Alan McGilvray's career at the microphone stands alone. To the listeners of every Test-playing country he stands for generous-minded, unbiased, factual common sense. At any crucial moment of an England–Australia

Test, the ideal recipe, for me, is to turn on the television picture, turn off the sound, and listen to Alan.

Naturally, as an old hand, one cocks a friendly yet critical ear to the Radio 3 Test programmes, and in the most important thing of all they earn surely very high marks. For they convey the feeling that they are enjoying what they are doing, and also, in so far as they conscientiously can, that this is a game played by men who, however great the financial rewards, have still for the most part some respect, diluted maybe in certain cases, for the traditional spirit of cricket. This being so, it is a valuable if tacit sanction that the cricketers know that, if they overstep the mark, commentators and critics in whom the public have confidence will not fail to say so. To this extent, apart from all else, the broadcasters fulfil an important function. It would be an evil day for cricket if its reporting over the air were to fall into prejudiced, over-sensational hands.

One feels now and then that there is so much free, uninhibited talk that one cannot see the wood for the trees, and also that we are getting a slight overdose of statistical material. But, comparing the present with the past, consider how much has to be said about so little. Thirty or forty years ago one had to describe 120 balls an hour, sometimes more. There was little time for reminiscence and chit-chat when Ramadhin and Valentine were spinning England into knots at Lord's in 1950. Nowadays, fast bowlers are allowed to wander back interminable distances, and the ration can be 72 balls an hour, sometimes even less. No wonder Bill Frindall—a formidable repository of fact as were his forerunners, Arthur Wrigley and Roy Webber—is an essential member of the team. Too much dressing-room jargon for the ordinary listener? On the whole, yes. And there is one perpetual irritant, the regular use of the utterly superfluous word 'on' before a score. This was never, until comparatively recently, part of the language of cricket. Yet on the whole, surely, the pleasure far outweighs the pain.

SOME THOUGHTS ABOUT MODERN CAPTAINCY [1982]

BY J. M. BREARLEY

To this day readers of the almanack who rush to the 1982 edition in the expectation of the reporting of legendary feats may be pardoned for feeling cheated as well as astonished by the omission. The previous season had been one of the most lurid ever known, a season in which English cricket, through the efforts of one man, had been raised to the heroic plane. No writer of fiction would dare offer an account of a Test series remotely as sensational as the truth of the 1981 battle for the Ashes. The feats of Ian Botham in winning three successive Tests virtually singlehanded appear doubly incredible when we take into account that after having won one match with the bat, he then won the next with the ball, and the one after with the bat once again. Without question the events of 1981 incorporated the greatest exhibition of virtuosity in the higher reaches of the game than cricket had ever known before. Yet, in choosing to publish an essay called 'A Great all-Rounder', Wisden selected as its hero quite a different man. Without wishing to question Mike Procter's wonderful all-round gifts, it seems either silly or spiteful not to have published a tribute to Botham in the 1982 edition. The oversight is especially surprising in view of the fact that the editor of the almanack had published in the pages of The Times, *on the morning after one of Botham's two superhuman innings, an essay wondering if this was not the greatest Test innings ever played.*

One of the great speculatory themes, then and since, has been to what extent Botham's apotheosis was linked to the captaincy of Michael Brearley. In the first two Tests Botham had performed so lamentably while serving as captain that he resigned his position just before being deposed. Brearley was recalled as captain, at which stage Botham, under the tutelage of his leader, turned the series on its head. Brearley will be remembered as one of the most astute captains the English ever produced, a thinking man whose later career in psychiatric medicine seems less outré in the light of his reflections on the art of captaincy.

I would not have been tempted back to cricket more than ten years ago without the allure of the captaincy of Middlesex: nor, I think, would I have continued to play without the stimulation of that job. At times, the thought of letting someone else deal with the hassles is attractive, but however good it would be for my soul to give up the reins, I doubt if I could do so willingly and still play. I think, therefore, that it is worth trying to describe the nature of captaincy, as its scope is remarkably wide.

The captain of a county cricket team is, all at once, managing director, union leader, and pit-face worker. He has almost total charge of the daily running of the concern; he is the main, if not the only, representative of the work-force in the boardroom (i.e. on the committee): and he has to field, bat and maybe bowl. He conducts the orchestra and he performs: perhaps on the front deck of the violins or as second tambourine. (It varies; I've been both.) Consequently it is hard to play God, to read the Riot Act about carelessness or incompetence, when one throws one's own wicket away or plays ineptly—if not today, tomorrow or yesterday. Any conscience on this score can inhibit one's own play: the captain oscillates between pawki-ness—being over-anxious about carelessness and, aware of the tendency to criticise others for slow-scoring, an inappropriate desperation for quick runs.

Social changes, together with the related changes in cricket's arrange-ments, have over the past fifteen or twenty years made the captain's job more, rather than less, difficult. Social hierarchies have become flatter: authority-figures are taken for granted less and criticised more. A leader has to *earn* the respect of the led. Doctors are sued more frequently for alleged incompetence: I await the day when a captain is sued for negligence by an injured close-fielder. The aristocratic tyrant has given way to the collaborative foreman, although some older players still yearn for the old-style discipline and for the voice accustomed to command. There are, moreover, county sides in which over half the players believe that they themselves should, or could, be captain. Twenty years ago, such ambitions would have been much more circumscribed. Envy, today, is less limited, and criticism from within the team less inhibited.

Similarly, criticism from outside is more vociferous. At Old Trafford in 1981, F. S. Trueman, broadcasting on the radio, was writing Bob Willis off in extreme terms: he did not know by what right Willis was drawing his money, he had never seen such inept bowling. (I wonder even whether Trueman had the decency to be abashed when Willis took three wickets in his next over.) And because current Test players are under far more scrutiny than ever before, the captain has to bear the brunt of it on behalf of his team. D. R. Jardine was able to toss up before the start of a Test, walk back into the dressing-room—where all seventeen members of the party would be dressed in whites, opening batsmen padded up—and pin the team-sheet on the wall. He felt no need to tell the players in advance, let alone the two British pressmen, one an expert on lawn tennis, who accompanied the team on its sensational journey around Australia. Harold Larwood told me that if any journalist had dared to ask Jardine if he was considering standing down from the side, Jardine would have punched him on the jaw.

Today's press are more demanding and inquisitive. They expect answers, 'quotes', and cooperation. Kim Hughes, speaking at a dinner shortly before last summer's final Test, agreed that his team had not batted well and deserved criticism. But, he went on, some of the things said about them were such that, 'if you were walking along the street and a fellow said that to you, if you had any go about you at all, you'd deck him!'

Last summer, I found an England team more embittered by the press than I'd ever known. Ian Botham refused to speak to them after his century at Leeds, and Willis was outspoken on television immediately after that match. I myself felt that rows were planted, cultivated and encouraged out of the most arid, unpromising soil by certain sections of the media. Of course there always has been some meanness in the relations between performer and critic, but the type of writing fostered by the modern craving for excitement and sensation puts today's public figures under a type of pressure unknown to their pre-war predecessors.

This same demand for excitement has, in addition, led to the revival, and proliferation, of one-day cricket, and this too has made a difference to captaincy. In all types of cricket there have been captains, perhaps a majority, who more or less work to rule, following whatever happens to be fashionable at the time. And it is especially tempting to think of the job along these lines in limited-overs matches. One county captain used to have decided, before every Sunday league game, exactly who would bowl each over. As usual, if he has a good side, the captain who follows a rigid pattern will achieve adequate results, but this approach is a pale shadow of proper captaincy.

It is, of course, essential to have some plan or outline of policy. But situations vary enormously throughout a game, and no simple formula can fit all contingencies. The ideal captain will have a feeling for the moment when a batsman has taken the measure of one of his bowlers. He will know which bowler is least likely to be heaved to the short boundary on the leg-side. He will keep some of his resources up his sleeve, but will know when to go all out for a wicket. He will gauge accurately when to stop worrying too much about saving singles and to concentrate on saving fours. In the midst of impending chaos he remains calm, juggles his bowlers sensibly, and manages to keep weak fielders out of the way. This applies in all forms of cricket: the captain remains responsible for assessing the proper balance between attack and defence. I felt that Tony Greig would switch too suddenly and dramatically from one to the other.

Cricket today is less courtly than it once was. Before limited-overs cricket, slips were, in a sense, compulsory. It would have been unsporting to put all one's fielders back; just as in the air battles of the First World War it was ungentlemanly to aim at the pilot. As Bradman has admitted, it would have taken him much longer to score his runs in the modern game, and not merely because of the decline in the over-rate. We live in an era of cost-effectiveness, though occasionally a giant like Botham transcends all calculation.

Although some subtleties of the game do disappear with limited-overs cricket, there are nevertheless many occasions for the exercise of tactical judgement. However, the crucial difference is not so much tactical as psychological. There are nowadays far more close games, crucial moments, hectic situations. Many more instant and pressured decisions have to be made. County cricket used to be incredibly sedate. There was the slow rhythm of the three-day matches, with close finishes rare. Play would be held up while aeroplanes passed overhead, or until barracking died down. Bowlers rarely posed a physical threat. Aggression was low-key.

Complaints that the standards of sportsmanship have declined since those balmy days are sometimes coupled with the suggestion that the causes of the decline are financial. Players are so interested in the money available that they will stoop to get it. I would argue that the changes are mainly mis-described and certainly wrongly explained.

Off the field, too, many county captains still have much power. We have been remarkably untouched by the tide of specialisation. We have the major say in selection: and the almost total say in how much, and how, the players are to practise. The only other official closely involved with the playing staff is the coach; but his domain is mainly the Second Eleven. Moreover he is often—in our case at least—the only scout. The captain is responsible for players getting from one match to the next, and deciding who takes his car and which players. He looks after day-to-day discipline, unless a case is bad enough to go before the committee, and is involved in questions of contract and salary.

Not surprisingly, the breadth of the traditional role is under attack, and now the cricket manager has arrived in county cricket. He can be a help to the captain, especially in taking away many irritating little jobs, and can contribute to the whole approach of the team. But whether his contribution is worth its cost, especially when so many clubs are short of money, I rather doubt. There are, moreover, ticklish questions of priority between captain and manager. Cricket is too complex and personal to be controlled at a distance: only the captain, in the middle with his bowlers and fielders, can sensitively react to the needs of the moment. The precise role of the manager needs, I suspect, revaluation in some quarters.

One peculiarity of cricket amongst games and sports is that, while each individual duel is between two protagonists, bowler and batsman, these individual contests take their meaning from the overall contest between two teams. It is the captain who is primarily responsible for the fusion of the individual and the group. He is, or should be, the leader. He must try to inculcate team-spirit—the identification of the individual with the interests of the whole group—without loss of personal flair or individual opportunity.

Sometimes the need is to rediscover the expectation of winning. Last summer, England had gone twelve Tests without a win. They were dropping as many catches as they were holding; the bowlers were looking, at times, slightly half-hearted. Spirits sagged if a fielding session yielded no tangible successes. Not long after, virtually the same team was catching everything, and bowling and fielding with a new vitality. This transformation, I hasten to add, was achieved almost entirely by inspiring individual performances. The fact remains that the main shortcoming in a team may well be that it has lost the taste—even the sniff—of success.

As in other areas of mutual activity, communication is vital. Both county staff and touring party are so small that most exchanges are face to face. The problems are immediate, practical, and personal. There is no separation between management (the captain) and work force. In industry, managers are concerned more with long-term plans and with outside organisations. They can easily be cut off from their fellow employees, both physically and by the nature of their job. Socially and culturally, too, there is often a chasm between managers and managed. On the cricket field a captain can and should be constantly in touch with the rest of the side. It was pointed out to me that I do some of this keeping in touch literally, especially with bowlers, with a hand on a player's arm or round his shoulders. I also have constant eye-contact with the fielders. This lets them know that I am aware of their efforts and feelings, that I'm satisfied or dissatisfied: and the habit of it enables me to move a fielder with a minimum of fuss.

The group is small enough to enable everyone to have a say on tactics and on the general running of the tour or of the team. A captain cannot always have six or seven players homing in on him on the field with advice at critical moments; autocracy is at times essential. But it is even more important to enable everyone to express opinions off the field, both informally and at team meetings.

At one such meeting in 1980, when Middlesex were playing below potential and there was a sense of insecurity in the side as a result of some team changes, one player said he had in the past felt a change in attitude towards him from the other players when he was dropped—as if he was no longer in quite the same sense one of them. This valid and perceptive point would have been much harder to get across had it come from an authority figure.

The spreading of the authority role is very important. In Australia. Bob Willis helped me, as vice-captain, by being prepared to take a tough line with players on occasion, to share the responsibility for an unpopular decision or a critical attitude. As in families, it is much better if those in charge are capable of saying both yes and no.

More broadly, the secret of motivation—easier to talk about than to achieve—is getting everyone to motivate each other and himself. In intense heat, say, and half-way through a second day in the field, bowlers need to be made to feel that the rest of the team fully value their efforts. As Rousseau said, individuals can identify not only with their personal good but with the common good.

One important asset in mutual motivation is humour, which can bring an outsider into the group, even as a butt. Through jokes, conflicts can sometimes be tactfully aired and defused. Pomposity is deflated. Humour softens the edge of authority. The enemy is rendered less dangerous by nicknames—Rodney Hogg quickly became known as Quentin, Road and Hedge after other noted hogs—and team-mates are helped to feel part of the group by names that are private to it or originated within it.

The success of a team depends to some extent on compatibility and happiness, but even more on respect. Without respect, humour becomes nasty and criticism carping. On tour, one common schism is between the party-goers and the stayers-in. To the former, the latter are no fun: and what is more they don't do their share of going to the functions that are not compulsory, but at which some representatives of the team should appear. Stayers-in see the others as frivolous and excluding. One of Greig's strengths as captain was being able to stand up for either side—having been very much a party-goer himself. If players respect each other, then different social tastes do no damage.

Any group of people tends to throw up the same types. I have already mentioned fun-lover and kill-joy. In addition, there are complainers and pacifiers, the punctual and the latecomers. There are humorists and fools. The roles that these individuals fall into may affect their performance adversely, and then the captain must try to modify the role if he can. For example, some people find that their only route to a sort of acceptance is to play the fool. No doubt a cricket field is not the only locus for their role; a poor self-image may have led them to take this way out since childhood. However, it may become prominent in their cricket, for professional cricketers are often very quick to spot a weakness and are quite ruthless at probing it. The group itself may well push such a man further into the court-jester's part.

We had such a player at Middlesex some time ago. At his previous county he had the reputation of being difficult to deal with and temperamental. His captain there was alleged to have said, when asked how overseas players fitted into the dressing-room, that he'd had no trouble with them, but that bloody 'Smith'! 'Smith' was a thorn in his flesh, and a figure of fun to the rest. On one occasion, 'Smith' felt that he should have been bowling and not the captain, so he allowed the ball to pass by his foot and hit the boundary board before lobbing it back in. We took him on because of his undoubted talent. Besides, I rather liked him. In our preseason practice matches, I noticed that when he bowled he tended to fall over, which provoked slightly stifled laughter, and that he presented himself as an appalling fielder, spindly and uncoordinated. This, too, provoked laughter, though I knew that we would all be irritated if it happened in competitive matches. He also made rather provocative and often odd remarks. I decided that we should not allow him to present himself as a fool, and that we should take him seriously from the start. Gradually, 'Smith' spent more time on his feet than on his knees: and his fielding improved remarkably. For a while all went well, until various difficulties intervened.

There are three separate domains of captaincy: the technical (or tactical), the psychological and the administrative. These areas overlap. There is no point in having brilliant tactical ideas if your bowlers think that, coming from you, they are bound to be hogwash, or if the members of the team are pulling in different directions. Similarly, players are unlikely to remain highly motivated if they find your tactics are stupid.

How well the captain carries out his administrative role also affects his other roles. He is likely to be the only representative of the players on the committee, so he has a responsibility to represent their views and, to an extent, to explain the response from the committee. A side is not likely to be well motivated if it feels that the committee has taken on or got rid of the wrong players: has grossly undervalued their services: or does not listen to their ideas. And though the captain is not the committee, he is partly responsible for good working relations between it and the playing staff.

One of the main pitfalls for a captain is an exaggeration of his own importance. He feels utterly elated when things go well, and devastated when they go badly. These swings in feeling occur along with the swings in the side's fortune, regardless of excellence or luck. Moreover, they ignore the fact that the captain's impact, though real, is limited. There are teams which would need an exceptionally bad captain to prevent them from winning, while others could be led by Napoleon and still be doomed.

The media do not encourage sanity in this area. One's own tendencies to both self-glorification and self-denigration are fanned by being hailed as a hero one day and chastised as a villain the next. This happens to any performer, but in cricket, whereas individual results are glaring, the captain's contribution is much harder to assess.

However modest the captain may appear to be, this exaggeration of one's own significance may reveal itself. He may feel more than reasonably depressed if the team has a bad day, and even if he himself has played well he may find it hard to be energetic and active. He may feel personally let down and correspondingly angry: even full of hate towards his players. Conversely, when all goes well, he loves the players and glows with pride.

KEN BARRINGTON—AN APPRECIATION [1982]

BY ROBIN MARLAR

There is something slightly odd about Robin Marlar's affectionate farewell to Ken Barrington, something smacking a little of the gentle art of the pussyfoot. The implication is that Barrington's sad and shocking death was caused by a heart attack, that the heart attack was the upshot of Barrington's pangs of guilt at having inadvertently injured the England opening batsman on the eve of a vital Test, and that this propensity to guilt was a by-product of a life for cricket too intensely lived. If this were true, why was Barrington invited to tour with the England team? Those who knew him and loved him were presumably those also who appointed him to an arduous job. Perhaps he should have been left to enjoy his retirement. If all this is in fact the case— and there is no reason to suspect that the writer is trying to mislead us—then Barrington's death can be put down to an excessive love of cricket.

I met him only once, in whimsical circumstances. It was in the Long Room at the Lord's Test of 1981, during the collapse of our batting. I stood at the threshold of the pavilion and watched Botham striding out to play a captain's innings against the enemy. Before I had had time to take my seat he was striding back again, disgusted with himself for having failed to score, all unaware that within a few days he would be rewriting the record books. As he clomped off to the dressing-room, like a giant trying to locate his castle, I fell into conversation with Harry Secombe, who was as puzzled as I was at the failure of our batsmen to do themselves justice. While we chatted, Barrington walked up to us, fresh with tidings from the England dressing-room. There was doom and destruction in the air up there, and Barrington, desperately willing to try anything in an attempt to raise the spirits of the young men under him, said to Secombe, 'For Chrissake, Harry, go up to the dressing-room and cheer the buggers up. They could use a laugh.' And off the two of them went, hopeful that a few minutes of buffoonery might change things.

Whether Secombe succeeded in his difficult mission I have no idea, but it certainly didn't work for Botham, who became one of the few England captains to bag a pair in a Test. In the end England fought an honourable draw, which suggests that perhaps if Barrington had mustered Charlie Chaplin and Groucho Marx to cheer the players we might have won. It is certain that had Barrington believed it would work, he would have tried it.

He would have tried anything, and it was that commitment which did for him at last.

THERE should be no need for reticence in anyone paying tribute to Ken Barrington. He died of a heart attack in his hotel room at the Holiday Inn in Barbados on March 14, 1981, Saturday night of the Barbados Test, while serving as assistant-manager on the England tour of the West Indies. As a player, as a friend, as a businessman and latterly as a leader of England's cricketers in the field, he was a man who always did what he could and, when the chips were on the table for all to see, one who could be relied upon to give of his best, his uttermost. The world and especially the cricketing world cannot ask for more. That is why Ken Barrington, master of the malaprop, the man who slept not like a log but 'like a lark', commanded such affection all over the world. His widow, Ann, accompanied him on some of his later trips, and it is good that Ann is still involved in the game through the Lord's Taverners, to whom Ken gave so much.

Yet reticence there is, and the hesitation is on his family's account in recalling the circumstances of Ken's tragically premature death at the age of 50. However, *Wisden* is a book of record, and historians sometimes find that its early pages tell the facts but less than the whole truth.

To my mind, the story of Ken's death is as heroic as so many of his innings. It came as a great shock in the spring of 1969 to learn that the chest pains which had led him to withdraw from a double-wicket competition in Melbourne had in fact been a heart attack. After due reflection, taking into account not only his family but the fact that, at 38, batting in Test matches, always Ken's particular forte, was not going to get easier, Ken Barrington retired. Immediately the cares of carrying England's rickety batting through the uncertain and far from satisfying Sixties slipped off his shoulders, like some leaden cloak. As he took to the village greens of charity cricket and to the golf courses where his game was good enough to be successfully competitive—and therefore a source of pleasure to a man who hated to be beaten—Ken Barrington's step seemed lighter and his nature in cricket enhanced. His admirers, both far and near, began to realise just how much private effort had gone into coping with 'chuckers' and bouncers, as well as the vagaries of form and the whims of selectors.

None the less, a heart attack is a warning, a red light that never joins with amber and turns to green. Although he had managed tours to India, Pakistan and New Zealand, and indeed had had the well-deserved honour of leading the England party at the Melbourne Centenary Test, nothing in his managerial career had tested him quite like this final West Indian ordeal. As a player he had not only plundered bowlers on the great Indian sub-continent but, the son of a soldier who might well in other times have done tours in India of a different nature, he established such a good-humoured relationship there that win or lose, come triumph or disaster, the pressures of touring were easily absorbed. In Australia, where the results mattered more, his role was that of coach, so that the burdens were shared first with Doug Insole and then with Alec Bedser.

He was playing that same familiar part in the West Indies. Ironically, he had not been one of the early selections, but as an old player scarred in earlier wars against Hall and Griffith, he knew better than most the perils that a new manager, Alan Smith, and an inexperienced captain, Ian Botham, were flying into as they took on the world champions with their fast bowling quartet in the increasingly stormy Caribbean. In Guyana the heavy and persistent rain meant that the practice sessions which were his charge were suspended. They had been difficult in smaller islands like Antigua and St Vincent in the early weeks of the tour. And then he had to take the team, badly defeated in the first Test and now with their morale increasingly affected by the start of the Jackman affair, as well as their collective lack of practice and form, to the one-day beating at Berbice, while Alan Smith began to play one of his best innings with the politicians. The events of those few days deeply disturbed Barrington. He was also worried about Ann's imminent arrival if the tour was to be cancelled.

But once the party arrived safely in Barbados he seemed to relax. My own last, long and treasured conversation with him was in the happy atmosphere of a Cunarder's bridge, a party in the harbour which he himself had organised. Whatever he felt, he was full of hope for the more distant future, his absolute faith in the ability of Botham and Gatting made more significant by the summer of '81. He knew there were gaps in the England side, but he was old enough in the ways of cricket to know that they are not easily filled.

It was a little thing, at least in the context of that global conversation, that piled all the pressure back on to this caring man. At fielding practice it was Barrington who hit the ball that split Gooch's hand. Gooch was due to bat that day, and in fact played better than anyone—as he told me, without too much discomfort. However, Ken took it badly, as he was bound to do, but it was the way in which he said to Bernard Thomas, 'I didn't mean to hurt him,' that in retrospect gave the party's medical superintendent the first indication that events were getting out of proportion, upsetting the nervous balance. It was that night, with the Barringtons ready for bed, that the attack struck Ken down. Ann Barrington summoned Bernard Thomas, who was next door, and he knew at once that the attack had been instantaneously fatal. Next morning, when the team stood in Ken's memory, there were many tears.

My own first encounter with Ken Barrington was in 1948 when I was a boy at Harrow. Tom Barling, the new school coach, brought over from The Oval, where he had not long ceased to play for Surrey, a young leg-spinner from Reading with a West Country burr in his voice. The intention was not only to give us practice against a type of bowling that Harrow were likely to meet in the match against Eton at Lord's but also to show us what a proper cricketer in the making looked like. We were both seventeen. From then on his career in cricket progressed with its ration of setbacks until he became a record-breaking Test batsman, proudest of all in his unique achievement of scoring a century on every Test ground in England and in every Test-playing country.

As *Wisden* is a chronicle and as this was a man who rated only the best, it is not inappropriate that the essay on him as one of the Five Cricketers of the Year in the 1960 edition should have been written by Norman Preston and the piece on his retirement by John Woodcock, Preston's successor as Editor, in the 1970 edition. It is appropriate, too, to add to those assessments of his playing ability his ever-maturing skill as a leg-spinner. No-one ever bowled more enthusiastically in the nets on tour than Barrington, and whether they realised it or not the England players who faced him were getting practice against a player who might have done the double in the 1930s, a decade less demanding at Test level than the 1960s.

It is with his career in cricket during the last ten years of his life that this eulogy is chiefly concerned. It was at Adelaide during the difficult Australian tour of 1974–75 that Barrington first began to believe that he had a contribution to make as a coach at the highest level. He was brought up in a generation which believed as an act of faith that once a cricketer had played at Test level he knew it all. How else could he have been selected? Furthermore, and this is still a more prevalent attitude than Barrington liked, a player who makes as much of a fetish about practising as Boycott is regarded as a freak. As one who had to work out his technique, to subordinate under a layer of discipline the stroke-making ability he had acquired in his early days, Barrington by the time he retired was a batsman who, if he never knew it all, was a scholar (as well as a gentleman) compared to the players he now saw trying to cope with Lillee and Thomson at their devastating best. More than once Barrington himself had had to change his approach both in style and mind, and so he was ideally suited to the task of developing younger talent and skills.

Not every captain appreciates the need for such a role: or knows how to put such available experience to its best use. Ironically, it was on his last tour that Barrington really came to fulfil himself in this the last, and to my mind, most difficult of his cricketing lives. By that time he had mastered the art of subordinating self and position without losing respect or the power to contribute. 'He would get me a cup of tea, suggest something which I'd reject probably because I was tired, but then I'd do it and usually it worked.' This was Ian Botham during his apprentice days as captain. To the generation that is coming to full maturity Ken Barrington had become as important as the maypole: something solid. He was the 'Colonel' around whom a team of cricketers could revolve while playing no part in the dance himself.

Like the maypole he was, too, a source of great happiness, with that rare gift of turning events into comic sketches as they happened. The rat hunt in the Ritz at Hyderabad is now part of cricketing legend. Some wretched rodent, unaware of the niceties of protocol, had eaten the shoulder out of the manager's England blazer in its search for nesting materials. By the time the 'Colonel's' army was assembled, the entire staff of the hotel and all its brushes and brooms were ready to go into action. The villain was struck but not apprehended, and after such a warning honour was seen to have been satisfied on all sides.

Now that he is gone, it is possible that the role he created and played may be forgotten through want of a successor. But Ken gave so much to cricket in the 1970s that he had left a few campaigners for the cause for the remainder of the 1980s. Even now as Gooch starts or finishes a drive or Gatting hooks, a memory of Barrington the batsman is stirred. For a coach there is no finer memorial than that. It is the man, though, that his contemporaries will miss; and for this one, at least, the hole that he began to dig on the Sixth Form Ground at Harrow more than thirty years ago is never going to be filled.

THE CAREER FIGURES OF
W. G. GRACE [1982]

BY MICHAEL FORDHAM

Cricket is the only game in the history of the world to have spawned a society dedicated not to the game but to the facts and figures of the game. It is as though the English political system were to breed an organised group which, caring nothing either for political theory or social morality, busied itself with the number of votes garnered over a specified period. As it happens there are such folk, and they are called candidates, but it seems altogether bizarre that cricket should have developed its own variation of the breed. Most men grow out of a schoolboy tendency to regard averages and analyses as being more interesting than strokes and spin, but the residue of those who never did outgrow the preoccupation finally brought about that solemn convocation, the Association of Cricket Statisticians. For the most part their burrowings are no more harmful than the labours of a family of moles who only rarely disfigure the lawn. Sometimes their presence actually becomes rather touching, as I discovered one evening a few years ago.

Not long after the opening of the splendid indoor cricket school in the Nursery at Lord's, I participated in a quiz for charity held in the new building. The two sides were M.C.C. and the A.C.S. It hardly needs saying that we were soundly beaten, or that the defeat could not detract one iota from my bliss at having represented M.C.C. in a sporting contest at last. It comes back to me that I began the evening determined to do or die in the cause, and that my mood changed abruptly when the question came up of who was run out for 99 playing for England against Australia at the Oval. When the correct answer was given by one of the statisticians as 'Betty Snowball', I experienced an abrupt shift of mood, reminiscent of one of those childhood refusals to enter into the spirit of things. The proceedings that night grew steadily worse, finally achieving red-nosed comedy, it seemed to me, when we were asked to name six one-eyed county cricketers. What was somehow risible was not the question but the ease with which the statisticians supplied the answer.

Amid this welter of grave inconsequentiality, I could find only one consolation, which was that if we were to descend to these levels, then perhaps my own small collection of arcana might be about to get an airing. This list of idiotic items includes:

Who was the only cricketer whose bride sported a monocle at the wedding ceremony?

Who is the only jazz recording artist to have served as President of M.C.C.?

Who returned match figures of three wickets for no runs without bowling a maiden?

When did the same county provide both captains in a Test match, in which the captain of the county played but not as captain?

Which county provided two England captains within a span of four months?

None of these questions came up during that contest at the school, but it is depressing to have to admit that had they done so, someone among the band of statisticians would have known the answers to be Percy Fender, Maurice Allom, Tom Hayward, Somerset and Middlesex. As to Tom Hayward's achievement of the apparently impossible, in a match for Surrey against Leicestershire in 1985, his figures were one for nought in 0.3 overs in the first innings and two for nought in 0.3 overs in the second. During a brief passage in the Oval Test against the West Indies at the Oval in 1981, the Somerset captain, Brian Rose, found himself playing under the captaincy of his county vice-captain, Botham , at the same time that the West Indians, depleted by an injury to Clive Lloyd, were led by another Somerset player, Vivian Richards. And I recall being misled as a child into believing that Middlesex had an agreement with the authorities to provide an endless succession of England captains, this misconception being sustained by the fact that on February 26th, 1937, G. O. Allen led England at Melbourne in the final Test, and that on June 26th of the same year R. W. V. Robins captained England in the first Test against New Zealand at Lord's.

All good comic stuff, but when in the 1982 almanack there appeared an essay stating the case for a radical amendment to the career of W. G. Grace, the A.C.S. seemed to me to have overstepped the bounds of comic propriety. Apparently none of the members was able to grasp the elementary proposition that once facts and figures have survived long enough to become sanctified by their own antiquity, there is no force on heaven or earth which can change them. Were the arrival at Hastings of William the Conqueror be proven to have occurred in 1065, the reaction would be that William was early, not that the date was wrong. In the same way, the fact of Grace's 126 centuries is written in stone, or at any rate in Wisden, and the foolish attempt of statisticians to preside over a revision on the feeble grounds that they were right and the rest of the world wrong is only further proof that the fanatic always runs the danger of keeping his ear so close to the ground that he cannot see the landscape.

The rebuttal to Michael Fordham's po-faced rejection of the magic figure of 126 could have been merely arithmetical, but Wisden's *editor is much to be praised for adding to his defence of tradition a seasoning of wit. He rightly reminds us of something none of the members of the Association of Cricket Statisticians had thought of, that were their demands to be met, the on-going consequences would be so terrible that a sort of domino effect might bring about the collapse of the entire infrastructure of cricket history. If Grace only scored 124 centuries, what of the euphoria of the hundredth hundred tributes and testimonials which swept England in the tail-end of the century? If the correct figure was 124, what of the day that Jack Hobbs broke what was thought to be the record at Taunton? If two of the Doctor's centuries were invalid, what of the career figures of all the other cricketers who participated, not only in those games, but in all the others of suspect pedigree? But Mr. Fordham, making no reference to the mare's nest before him, rested his case. Where it has remained ever since. I cannot help thinking of those scholars who count the words in the Bible as proof of their religiosity.*

Editor's Foreword

There follows an article by Michael Fordham, *Wisden*'s chief statistician since 1979, in which he gives his reasons, and those of the Association of Cricket Statisticians, for wanting to change, quite significantly, the career record of W. G. Grace. While acknowledging the amount of work done by Mr. Fordham and his fellow scrutineers, and though grateful for the pleasure they give us, I prefer to leave the great man's figures as they have been for as long as anyone cares to remember.

That they appeared in *Wisden* 1981, my first as editor, in their 'revised' form was because Mr. Fordham thought, mistakenly, that he had cleared them with me. In future, various books of reference, though not *Wisden*, will show 'W. G.' as having scored not 126 but 124 hundreds. To avoid confusion, the figures now claimed by the Association of Cricket Statisticians are to be found in footnotes on pages 180 and 200.

No amount of research could, to my mind, justify changing a record so honoured by time and custom. If wrong decisions are thought to have been made, they should be altered reasonably soon or left to stand. That one-day games played more than a century ago should have been termed first-class need not surprise us: there were no regulations in those days stipulating the minimum time for a first-class match. Then, as now, contemporary opinion was the best criterion.

So, in *Wisden* at any rate, 'W. G.'s 152 at Lord's, for the England team that had toured North America in 1872 against Fourteen Gentlemen of M.C.C. (with Rylott), survives, as does his 113 for Gloucestershire against Somerset at Clifton in 1879. To remove them, as the Association of Cricket Statisticians would have us do, would, I think, be presumptuous and sadly unromantic. The first of them, anyway, is referred to in *Wisden* 1874 as having been one of the Doctor's 'superb lot of *first-class* triple figure scores'.

Who, too, would wish to invalidate such historic occasions as 'W.G.'s' hundredth 100, the origin, as *Wisden* put it at the time, of a national testimonial taken up with enthusiasm 'in many places far beyond the limits of the United Kingdom', or the great match at Taunton when Jack Hobbs first equalled Grace's total of hundreds and then passed it? In recognition of Hobbs's feat, *Wisden* wrote how 'the match was rendered forever memorable by the triumph of Hobbs, who, playing innings of 101 and 101 not out, beat the "Grand Old Man's" record. Circumstances generally combined to invest the occasion with exceptional excitement. Tremendous cheering greeted the accomplishment of the feat: indeed so pronounced was the enthusiasm that the progress of the game was delayed while at the end of the over all players in the field shook hands with Hobbs and the Surrey captain brought out a drink for the hero, who raised his glass high and bowed to the crowd before partaking of the refreshment!' Far be it from me to say that that might as well never have happened—John Woodcock.

Some surprise was caused last year when, in *Wisden*, I revised the career figures of W. G. Grace, for the figures that were compiled by F. S. Ashley Cooper for the 1916 *Wisden* after Grace's death have come to be regarded as having an established niche in cricket records. However, many statisticians have been dissatisfied with the figures over the years and this article is an attempt to illustrate where the discrepancies arise.

They fall into two categories: (a) the inclusion in the past of a number of matches that cannot strictly be regarded as first-class, and, in the opinion of both myself and other statisticians, should never have been included in the first place: (b) the differences in scores in *Wisden* and *Scores and Biographies*.

Dealing with (a) first, Grace in 1871 made the outstanding and undisputed aggregate of 2,739 runs. Although well short of 2,000 runs in 1872, he was close to the target in 1873 in matches whose status is not in doubt. As far as can be ascertained many years afterwards, a journalist-cum-statistician proceeded to add his scores in four minor matches— M.C.C. v. Hertfordshire at Charleywood [*sic*], M.C.C. v. Staffordshire at Lord's, the 1872 North American XI v. 14 Gentlemen of M.C.C. with Rylott at Lord's (in which he scored *152*), and a one day match at The Oval between North and South after the main fixture finished in two days.

Neither Hertfordshire nor Staffordshire has ever had any claims to first-class status, nor to be classified among the leading counties before there was a clear-cut division of First Class and Minor counties. The M.C.C. side which opposed the North American XI was clearly a weak one because it could not play on level terms and it was necessary for it to be strengthened by a professional, and the one-day match at The Oval was obviously a scratch game to fill the time available. However, the addition of these matches gave Grace an aggregate of 2,139 runs for the season, and in retrospect it is difficult to escape the conclusion that it was done deliberately, as his bowling figures in these matches were omitted. Although they did not have a significant effect on his figures, he was also credited with two similar matches in 1872—M.C.C. v. Hertfordshire at Charleywood [*sic*] and another one-day South v. North match at The Oval, to fill the time available after the main match had finished early.

There are four other matches which are perhaps slightly more open to doubt. Three of these were for Gloucestershire v. Somerset, one in 1879, in which Grace scored *113*, and two in 1881. Now the status of Somerset before it became a first-class county officially in 1891 has been open to conjecture over the years. However, the Association of Cricket Statisticians, which has researched nineteenth century cricket in greater depth, through a group of statisticians working in unison, than any individual statistician in the past, has given in its booklet *British Isles First-Class Cricket Matches* contemporary evidence from both *Wisden* and *James Lillywhite's Cricketers Annual* (the *Red Lillywhite*) that Somerset were regarded as first-class only from 1882 to 1885, after which they ceased to play matches against the recognised first-class counties until their re-appearance in 1891. As modern *Wisdens* have stated this for some years under the heading 'Constitution of County Championship', it is obviously inconsistent to credit Grace elsewhere in the Almanack with matches against Somerset before 1882.

The remaining match is Gloucestershire v. M.C.C. at Lord's in 1868. Here again there is contemporary evidence from *John Lillywhite's Cricketers Companion* (The *Green Lillywhite*) that the match was not regarded as first-class and the *Companion* does not grant Gloucestershire this recognition until they began playing against the leading counties in 1870.

In regard to the second category, there has been a tendency among statisiticans in the past to regard *Wisden* in its early years as unreliable, and to work from *Scores and Biographies* until this ended in 1878, though this is due partly to *Wisden* not publishing bowling analyses until its 1870 issue and the difficulty and cost of obtaining the early issues before the facsimile editions were printed. However, the Association of Cricket Statisticians, which is in the process of publishing booklets of the first-class scores of this era, has consulted contemporary newspapers such as *Bell's Life* and also, where available, county scorebooks. These have shown the reverse to be true: i.e. that *Wisden* is more reliable. The discrepancies seem to arise only on bowling analyses, and result in adjustments to Grace's bowling figures for a number of seasons, nearly all in the early part of his career. They are too numerous to mention in this article, but I give below a summary showing how the revised career totals have been compiled:

	Inns	*Not Outs*	*Runs*	*100s*	*Runs*	*Wkts*
Former figures	1,493	105	54,896	126	51,545	2,876
Less matches not accepted as first-class	15	1	685	2	536	68
Bowling adjustments in various matches					—10	+1
NEW TOTALS	1,478	104	54,211	124	50,999	2,809

Thus his bowling figures are 67 runs more than those given in the 1981 *Wisden*, through the Association of Cricket Statisticians finding a further discrepancy in his figures and the more recent discovery of an unpublished analysis for the Gentlemen of England v. Oxford University at Oxford in 1866.

As has already been stated. Ashley Cooper compiled Grace's full career record in the 1916 *Wisden*, and, his stature as a statistician at that time being unquestioned, one feels that it was a great pity that he did not grasp the nettle firmly in the hand and delete the obvious minor matches. Even he himself, in the magazine *Cricket* in 1896, in making the first attempt to summarise Grace's career figures, had referred to the matches in 1873 as not being really first-class, though he had continued to include them.

The first public query that I can trace over these figures was in a letter to *The Cricketer* magazine for June 25, 1927 about the 1873 season. It was followed by letters in two subsequent issues, including the comment that it was unthinkable that anybody should wish to deprive the Old Man of the credit attaching to the feat of scoring 2,139 runs! The matter was again raised by E. L. Roberts in an article in *The Cricketer* for May 4, 1940, when he listed Grace's catches and queried the matches accepted as first-class. He suggested revised batting and bowling aggregates through the deletion of five matches. There was no follow-up in correspondence, possibly because more serious matters at that time were occupying the minds of historians and statisticians.

The first real attempt to provide alternative figures for Grace came from the late Roy Webber in the February 1961 issue of *Playfair Cricket Monthly*. He gave season by season figures, indicating the matches he had omitted as well as certain bowling corrections. His findings were not identical with those of the Association of Cricket Statisticians, as he took a harsher view of what were and were not first-class matches in the 1870s and 1880s. He gave Grace lower totals than those quoted currently, though he did agree with 124 centuries.

Finally, in an article in *The Cricketer Winter Annual (November) 1975* John I. Marder queried the inclusion of Grace's century against Somerset in 1879, giving detailed contemporary evidence that Somerset were not first-class at that time.

Upon this account rests my case for revising the long-established figures of W. G. Grace.

J. M. BREARLEY—SUCCESS THROUGH PERCEPTIVENESS [1983]

BY JOHN ARLOTT

Having enjoyed his finest hour as a captain, Michael Brearley retired from the first-class game. In the years since his only participation has been as an occasional writer on cricketing affairs. To sum up so unusual a professional athlete required the same virtues of high intelligence and perception which are so striking a feature of the subject himself. There was no better choice than John Arlott, who brought to the job the additional asset of an aesthetic sensibility unmatched in cricket literature since the days of Cardus.

The reference to Brearley's benefit fund reminds me that at the climax of his year I spoke for him at a boxing night at the London Hilton. These institutions, which would once have delighted me, feeding the vicarious prizefighter inside me, had by this time come to disgust me. The juxtaposition of prime beef on the plate and more of it in the nearby ring provided a moral too stark to ignore, and, having eaten a good dinner before singing for my supper, I left for home, but not before conversing with the beneficiary of the evening on a variety of subjects. These included the clarinet, the one patch of executive common ground between us. I could see that the classical clarinet, with its cool, pure tone, was perfect for a thinker of Brearley's gentle detachment. He could, I imagine, have made an excellent orthodox clarinettist, but not an improvisor.

As to his curious relationship with Botham, I cannot forget the scene on the television screen when, for the second time in a month, Botham was laying waste the Australian attack with a godlike relish. While the destruction was being wrought Mike Brearley was seen watching from the balcony, a quiet smile of proprietory wonder on his face. I may have been mistaken, but I thought I detected also in his demeanour a tincture of wistfulness. Nobody would understand better than Brearley that when an elemental force is involved, logical perceptions fly out of the window.

COMFORTABLY before lunch on Tuesday, September 14, 1982, at Worcester, J. M.—Mike—Brearley made the final run in Middlesex's ten-wicket win over Worcestershire. He had been applauded on to the field at the start of the match; and he was applauded off it, into the retirement he had planned and announced. He walked into the pavilion for the fourth, and last, time as captain of the county champions.

There is little doubt that he was one of the best—certainly the most sustainedly successful—captains international cricket has known. A shrewd and experienced North country professional and Test selector summed it up in the words: 'This man is as good a captain on the field as Illingworth; off it, he must be far and away the best we have had.' He added: 'If only he could get some more runs there could never be any question about him.' Runs, though, are not a yardstick of captaincy, only a reinforcement of selection.

Mike Brearley's record as a Test captain is excelled only by Sir Donald Bradman who, it will be conceded, had—by comparison with his opponents—stronger sides under his command. In short, Brearley captained England in 31 Test matches, of which they won eighteen and lost four; while, of nine series, seven were won, one drawn and one lost. In his eleven years as captain of Middlesex they won the County Championship three times and shared it once, against five and one shared in their previous 89 years in the competition. They were twice winners and once losing finalists in the Gillette Cup; once Benson and Hedges Cup finalists; once runners-up and twice third in the John Player League.

His achievement that will live in the imagination of all those who lived through it—or who read of it in the future—is the taking over of the 1981 England team, one down to Australia, which had all the look of a beaten side, and transforming it, almost incredibly, into the winner of the rubber by three to one. Much credit, of course, must go to Ian Botham for his amazing all-round cricket. Yet Botham had been in the losing team Brearley took over. After that Brearley stepped down from the England captaincy, as he did from that of his county a year later, on a note of triumph.

The simple explanation for his success was expressed by the Australian fast bowler, Rodney Hogg, not generally known for his perspicacity, when he said 'I reckon Brearley has got a degree in people.' The salient points of his make-up are intellectual quality, clarity of mind and common sense—which are by no means the same thing, nor always found in the same person—and human perception. He would not claim the finest brain cricket has known. Indeed, he has argued that Edward Craig, his contemporary at Cambridge, was superior both mentally and as a batsman. It is, though, as certain as may be that his was the most effective intellect ever closely applied to the game. His clarity of mind enabled him to pierce the woolly romanticism and anachronistic feudalism which for so long obscured the truth of cricket. His common sense was reflected in his recognition of the need for Kerry Packer to be accepted into the body of cricket; and that, if players were not better treated financially, the available talent would ebb even further away.

His understanding—both intuitive and tutored—of human beings proved a major asset in his captaincy. He was able to reach, sympathise with and—in the current term—motivate cricketers as few, if any, others have done. If that capacity proved helpful, it also led to some of his major griefs, for his depth of understanding made his failures in human relationships the more agonising.

His career is absorbing to follow, if only for its many-sidedness. Invariably cricketers who achieve so much have been single-minded about the game. Mike Brearley has never seen it as an exclusive interest so much as the finest of games, set in a world of more important matters. That has enabled him to detach himself mentally from a match in which he was deeply involved and to assess it objectively.

Yet he could not be so detached about his own performance. Throughout his career as captain of England he was deeply—often inhibitingly—concerned about his batting form in Test matches. Clearmindedly recognising his own potential, he was idealist enough to appreciate how far he often fell short of it. Had he played under a captain as sympathetic as himself, the problem might have been solved. In the event, although he often batted freely and fluently in county cricket, when he played for England anxiety drove him constantly into over-care. This frequently cost him his wicket. In short he was, like all good batsmen, basically an instinctive player; not even he could quite impose thought on the high-speed reactions of batting against pace. Thus his best Test innings were defensive; salvage operations conducted with an eye to survival. History, surely, will say that his captaincy and fine slip-catching compensated for the deficiency.

He was born in Harrow on April 28, 1942. His father, Horace Brearley, who came from Yorkshire, was a good enough batsman to play as an amateur for that county once and, after he moved south, twice for Middlesex. He employed encouragement to help his son towards a success in cricket which was soon evident. At fourteen he won a place in the First XI of City of London School, and held it for five years.

He began his 21-year career in first-class cricket for Cambridge University against Surrey, at Fenner's, on April 29, 1961, as wicket-keeper and No. 8 batsman. His 76 was the highest score of the match for Cambridge. Within three weeks he had gained the respect of some stern critics with 73 and 89, by far the highest Cambridge scores, against Benaud's Australians. By the time of the University match he had made his first and second centuries and been top scorer in ten Cambridge innings. Against Oxford his 27, which held the unsteady Cambridge innings together, was bettered only by Jefferson's lusty 54 at No.9. With 1,158 runs at 44.53 he was second to Craig (1,342 at 47.92) in the University averages. Selection for the Gentlemen against the Players at Lord's put an unusual seal of achievement on his first season: but brought him only two—relatively unsuccessful—matches for Middlesex.

Next year he was less successful for Cambridge until his century against Oxford; and he scored 143 for once out for Middlesex. He was praised for his captaincy of the University at Lord's in 1963, when he made 790 runs at 30.38. Then, in 1964, came his best season. The first man since F. S. Jackson in 1892 and 1893 to captain Cambridge in consecutive seasons, he made his second century against Oxford and finished top of the University averages, 25 ahead of the next man, with 1,313 at 57.08. And he set a new Cambridge record individual aggregate of 4,068. He was chosen to captain the President of M.C.C.'s XI against the Australians and, with a top score of 67 out of 179 for seven, saved the match. Over the entire season only Tom Graveney and Eric Russell made more than his 2,179 runs. The Cricket Writers Club elected him Young Cricketer of 1964 and he was, almost inevitably, chosen for the winter's tour of South Africa.

That would have been a considerable series of performances for an undergraduate in the days when they could devote their time to cricket without fear of the examiners. Brearley, however, not only kept wicket through two of those four seasons but, changing academic horses in midstream, he achieved a first in Classics and a two-one in Moral Sciences. In addition he was joint-top in the Civil Service examination.

In South Africa the competition of more experienced players kept him out of the Test team, but he contrived to see those facets of that country and its people which are not usually shown to visiting cricketers. Back in England, he played regularly for Middlesex and, like many before him, found a first full county season as an opening batsman a trying experience. He was, though, not afraid to graft, and in that summer he probably learnt more about going in first against the new ball than in any other phase of his career.

It is possible that, in 1966, Mike Brearley might have advanced from a highly talented and promising batsman to a great one. That was the next logical step in his progress. But he became, once again, preoccupied with studies, and took a post-graduate course in philosophy at Cambridge. He found time to play a few matches for Cambridgeshire, where he was intrigued by keeping wicket to Johnny Wardle's left-arm mixture of finger spin, the Chinaman, and its complementary googly. He turned out twice, too, for the University, for whom he scored a century against a powerful Yorkshire bowling side. Although that was not the hardening process old pros would have prescribed for an aspiring 24-year-old batsman, the selectors were happy to send him as captain of the M.C.C. Under-25 team to Pakistan. There his batting was remarkable. His 312 not out against Northern Zone was one of the rare instances of a triple-century being made in a day; and he scored 223 against Pakistan in the second representative match. He averaged 132 for the tour; more than twice as many as any other member of a side which included Dennis Amiss, Keith Fletcher and Alan Ormrod.

Whatever conclusion may be drawn about his absence from the first-class scene in 1966, it must be virtually certain that the development of his batting lost crucial momentum when research at Cambridge and teaching in the Universities of California and Newcastle kept him out of first-class cricket in 1967, and restricted him to the latter part of the 1968, 1969 and 1970 seasons. That may appear contradictory when the best part of his career lay ahead. He had yet to become the outstanding captain of his, or perhaps any other age, but he was never again such an outstanding batsman among his contemporaries as he had been when he returned from Pakistan.

In 1971 he gave up university teaching in order to take up the Middlesex captaincy. Outside cricket in the following years he developed his long-standing interest in psychotherapy. He set about not merely captaining but rebuilding a Middlesex side which had not had major success since the Championship title of 1949. In 1975, though eleventh in the table, Middlesex performed the then unique feat of reaching both finals—of the Gillette and Benson and Hedges—only to lose both. Brearley's own performance and confidence steadily improved, his average rising through 33, 30, 34 and 44, until, in 1975, he was top of the county's batting figures, in aggregate and average, and sixth in the national averages.

In 1976, in a characteristically perceptive move, he recruited Alan Jones, the former Sussex and Somerset bowler, who provided the extra edge of penetration to give Middlesex their first county title for 29 years. In the same season Brearley was chosen for England—as a batsman, it should be noted. Opening the innings in the first two tests against West Indies he scored 0, 17, 40 and 13. He was picked for the tour to India, Sri Lanka and the Centenary Test of 1977 in Australia, as vice-captain to Tony Greig. First in aggregate and second in average for the entire Indian tour, he made only 215 at 26.86 in the Tests. Still, he made top score in both the third and fifth Test matches and, most valuably, steadied the English second innings in the anniversary game at Melbourne.

Then came the Packer defections, which Brearley probably understood as clearly as and with less bias than anyone else in cricket, though he refused to take part in the operation. Because of his share in it, Greig was dropped from the captaincy, playing under Brearley, who inherited it, in the 1977 home series against Australia, who employed all their Packer men. Brearley played two useful innings; but that mattered little beside the fact that Australia were beaten by three-nothing.

In addition, Middlesex finished equal first in the Championship with Kent and won the Gillette Cup. Brearley, despite his absences at Tests, was top of their averages with a figure of 68.33. After captaining England in the first two—drawn—Tests in Pakistan, Brearley had his arm broken by a ball from Sikander Bakht, who was not more than fast-medium, and returned home without going on to New Zealand.

The injury seemed subsequently to unsettle him and he had an abject batting year. But again results gave his reply: Middlesex finished third in the Championship; England beat Pakistan two-nothing, New Zealand three-nothing, and Australia, on their own pitches but without their Packer players, five-one. In 1979, India were beaten three-one but, although Brearley's batting revived, Middlesex, an unhappy fourteenth, experienced their worst season under his captaincy.

In 1979–80 Australia, at full Packer-reinforced strength, were waiting to take revenge for, above all, the humiliation of a year before. They did so most effectively from a playing point of view. Despite Botham's spirited resistance, the bowling of Dennis Lillee and Geoff Dymock, and the batting of Greg and Ian Chappell and Allan Border, were too much for England. Australia won all three matches of the series. Brearley batted resolutely enough to average 34.20, better than his figures against some substantially less hostile attacks. This was his one real defeat.

Unfortunately Lillee chose to bait Brearley in an offensive and childish manner; while a section of the crowd at Melbourne treated him in a fashion which the Australian manager, in an official statement, said made him 'ashamed to be an Australian'. This was England's first experience of the new, Packer-inspired commercialisation of Australian cricket. Brearley was pressured to accept playing conditions already rejected by the TCCB, and the Australian authorities behaved less than honestly in portraying him, through the media, as a 'whingeing Pom'. Brearley never behaved better nor with more dignity.

The Golden Jubilee Test at Bombay, played on the way home from Australia and lifted to considerable heights by Botham's splendid all-round cricket, did something to wash away the unpleasant taste. More happily, Brearley led Middlesex to yet another championship and the Gillette Cup, and then decided to allow himself another couple of seasons before he retired. Nevertheless, he decided that his studies in psycho-analysis would prevent him from touring in the following winter. The selectors needed to 'blood' his successor; and Botham inherited, with unhappy results for his own playing performances over more than a year. Subsequently, in 1981, after an English defeat at Trent Bridge and an unhappy draw at Lord's, Botham resigned his office and the selectors recalled Brearley. He can hardly have contemplated the task with pleasure, but under his calm, tactically skilful, and friendly leadership, and through the amazing all-round performances of the revived Botham, England won the third, fourth and fifth Tests; at Headingley, Edgbaston and Old Trafford respectively.

So to 1982; another Championship and retirement. He has gone with regret but not bitterness. He realises that he will miss the companionship, the humour and the excitement of the first-class game but he is clear on what he wants to do. He hopes still to play some cricket, preferably of a competitive kind, and he will, surely, contribute much on the cricket committee of the TCCB. For the two years until he completes his studies and qualifies as a psychoanalyst, he will practise as a psychotherapist. He has already worked in a clinic for disturbed adolescents and is convinced of his destiny in this field.

It would be foolish to pretend that Mike Brearley is the usual type of county cricketer. He is a serious man; an idealist in matters of morals, but also a realist. Happy to accept, and content that he had earned, a benefit of £31,000 in 1978, he had always believed that cricketers in general were underpaid in view of the risks their career implies. He has campaigned along those lines; not merely for himself. He was an early, active, and wise member of the Cricketers' Association which is, in effect, the players' trade union.

Much of his influence over his players stemmed from his friendly approach. Physically lean and wiry, even at 40, his hair greying, there is an engagingly boyish quality about his easy smile and a frankness about his expression confirmed by honesty. He remains a most interesting character who has displayed so many facets that one waits, intrigued, for the next.

M.C.C. AND SOUTH AFRICA [1985]

BY MATTHEW ENGEL

The evening of July 13th, 1984, saw one of the most extraordinary off-field events of the postwar years, a meeting of M.C.C. members to debate the issue of South Africa's expulsion from the family of cricketing nations. Ever since the D'Oliveira affair fifteen years before, there had been attempts by assorted pressure groups to lift the ban, defy the ban, evade the ban, bend the ban. These strenuous efforts had met with little success and engendered a succession of crises and broken careers. Those countries which opposed the re-entry of South Africa continued to maintain an attitude of rigid opposition. It was a boom time for hypocrisy, sanctimony, sophistry and humbug, much of which was well in evidence at the great meeting in the Central Hall, Westminster, when a thousand members turned up to fight their corner.

I, perched on the balcony, leaning on its rail to watch the deployment of forces, was fascinated to witness the disclosure of a moral dilemma in all its ramifications which, by the time the vote was taken, had reached positively gothic proportions. It was amusing to watch the tonnage of red herrings being sploshed into the arena, deeply saddening to watch a great many distinguished men producing so deafening a volume of noise in the act of barking up the wrong tree. And it was tragic to see a beautiful game struggling to stay afloat in the treacherous waters of the twentieth century. Matthew Engel's account is certainly accurate in its reminder that already by 1984, M.C.C. had become emasculated through the devious transference of power to the Test and County Cricket Board, that misguided sales force which had already begun aggrandising so lucratively on behalf of the game. The time was soon to come when G. O. Allen, by this time transmogrified into Sir George, was to resign from a governing body which had relegated his club to the fringes of executive authority. It was this irony which made the debate pathetic. None of the members who bared their souls so passionately seemed to have any inkling that whatever they did, forces far beyond their control would settle all the issues.

With apologies to the writer of the piece, I must reject his impression that the debate was of a high quality. On the contrary it rarely rose above the standard of a prep school debating society in an average year. Indeed, it was this aspect of the night which saddened me most of all. I had come anticipating Gladstonian windbaggery, Churchillian rhetoric, Lloyd Georgian insolence. There was none of this, only a succession of uninspired oratorical scuffles, enlivened by the clattering flight across the hall of yet another stuffed owl. Mr. Engel says that John Carlisle's speech was cogent. It is also true that George Eliot was one of the Brontë sisters. He suggests that John Pashley's speech, apart from its length, was effective. In fact it was so awful that it did irreparable harm to his own cause. Somehow it is symbolic of the ineffectuality of the whole business that before any of the casuists had opened their mouths, the issue had been settled by the postal vote. I remember leaving the hall and emerging into the stifling evening heat of Parliament Square deeply distressed that so unique a game should have been so fatally compromised by events. As I waited for a taxi, an image came into my head which would not go away. It was of Garfield Sobers and Graeme Pollock batting together for the Rest of the World.

THE summer of 1983 will mainly be remembered as a time when cricket people could forget their troubles and enjoy the game and the sunshine, if only temporarily. The problem of South Africa was never that far away from anyone's consciousness. But its prime manifestation came in a manner that left little damage, and was even rather quaint.

On July 13, the members of the Marylebone Cricket Club voted to support their committee and reject a proposal to send a touring team of their own to South Africa. In the history of one of sport's most intractable crises, it will probably not be regarded as one of the most momentous decisions; in the history of one of sport's most famous and most powerful clubs, it may well have been.

The idea of trying to use M.C.C. as a locomotive to pull South Africa back into world cricket had been conceived a year earlier at a meeting of the six-man executive of the right-wing pressure group, Freedom in Sport: the Conservative MP John Carlisle, Jeff Butterfield, Tommie Campbell, John Reason, Edward Grayson and Lord Chalfont. All except Mr. Campbell also happened to be members of M.C.C.. The club had not been directly involved in the issue since 1968. On that occasion the committee, in spite of the cancellation of the 1968–69 tour over South Africa's refusal to admit Basil D'Oliveira, was still defending, though with growing unease, the principle of continuing cricketing links. It beat off liberal opposition, led by two of the less conventional men to captain the England team, the Rev. David Sheppard and Michael Brearley, by a margin of more than three to one.

In the fifteen intervening years very little had changed in South Africa's general political outlook. But a great deal had changed in cricket since the formation of the multi-racial South African Cricket Union in 1977. The game was integrated in theory, and sometimes in practice. There was a better case for playing South Africa in the eighties than there ever had been in the totally segregated sixties. But even more had changed in the rest of the world; attitudes had hardened and the sports boycott had become a weapon with a wider purpose.

Something else had changed; M.C.C. no longer had that much authority to do anything about it. 1968 was also the year when it surrendered its role as the ruling body of English cricket and moved into a nebulous position of influence without anything like the same direct power—the house of Lord's in this sense being like the House of Lords. It was associated with the policies made elsewhere in cricket, without being able to change them. As far as the boycott went, cricket was in any case forced largely to comply with policies made elsewhere.

None the less, M.C.C. seemed ideal for Freedom in Sport's purposes. Its supporters could get nowhere with any of cricket's ruling bodies, national or international. But, under Rule 43, it takes only 50 members to demand a special general meeting. Finding 50 was not a problem for Mr. Carlisle and his friends. They set up their own committee including the evocative names of Denis Compton and Bill Edrich. There were brief but hopeless talks with the real committee to see if an accommodation could be reached. In April, Jack Bailey, the secretary of M.C.C., stood at the Grace Gates and received a petition proposing 'that the members of M.C.C. Committee implement the selection of a touring party to tour South Africa in 1983–84'. He has been seen looking happier.

The problem Mr. Bailey—and cricket—now faced was a curious one.

M.C.C., in theory, had become merely a private club. Plenty of private clubs had been taking South Africa and dispensing discreet aid and comfort through the years of supposed isolation. It quickly became clear, because of the sanctions that would almost certainly be applied to any current first-class players who might make the tour, that, if forced to send a team, the committee would have to despatch players not far above customary club level—the men who habitually raise the flag for Marylebone and cricket in places like Bangladesh or the United States. But the very initials M.C.C. have a special power. Few people with a casual involvement in cricket at home and even fewer overseas have cottoned on to the club's diminished role. The last Test-playing tour party to be called M.C.C. had been in 1976–77. After six years the change had still not permeated the consciousness of much of the world's cricketing public. Thus one of the great dangers of the tour would have been mistaken identity. Indeed the most worried man I met before the vote was one of the likely tourists, who thought South Africa might get it wrong and unleash their fastest bowlers at him.

The case put by the 50 members and sent out on their behalf by M.C.C. was that a tour would recognise the progress made by S.A.C.U., 'half the slide of international sport towards total political influence and possible disintegration, and allow long-suffering sports people to get on with sport'. M.C.C.'s rebuttal acknowledged that the resolution would appeal to many members and talked about 'hypocrisy and double standards' among South Africa's opponents. But it then argued that such a tour would achieve nothing in cricketing terms, breach the Gleneagles Agreement, which the British Government was pledged to support, and endanger the club's remaining positions in the game; as custodian of the Laws, as owner of Lord's, which the black countries might refuse to visit, and in I.C.C., for which M.C.C. still automatically provided the president and secretary. Since a number of overseas officials regarded this as an anachronism anyway, Mr. Bailey and the incumbent president, Sir Anthony Tuke, were aware that they might be the first casualties.

The meeting was fixed for the night prior to the first Test—well after the World Cup and the annual I.C.C. meeting. The World Cup was conducted amid constant rumours that the South Africans, having bought their own teams of English and West Indian rebels in successive years, were now trying to sign anything that moved. A S.A.C.U. delegation, led by Joe Pamensky, paid its annual, now ritualised visit to the I.C.C. which in an equally ritualised way refused to see them. Mr. Pamensky's visit was very public but he said little about the impending M.C.C. vote, beyond saying that any team it sent would be very welcome.

The postal votes began to pile up at M.C.C.'s solicitors in the City. There were rumours about these too, most of them saying that the proponents were not far short of the two-thirds majority they would need to carry the motion and well above the simple majority that would be regarded as a huge moral victory and a humiliation for the club's establishment. Everyone Mr. Carlisle met at Lord's, he said later, told him they were voting for him. Since his majority at Luton West had gone up from 200 to

12,000 at the June General election, he may well have been feeling invulnerable. His only moment of discomfort came when the Prime Minister (ineligible to join M.C.C. owing to her sex) came out against the tour in the Commons.

The evening of July 13 turned out to be one of almost unbearable heat. The committee had hired Central Hall, Westminster, the largest available, in the expectation that around 2,000 of the 18,000 members would wish to come. But it was no night for attending meetings voluntarily. Only 1,000 turned up. The meeting was also a little overshadowed. By coincidence, a few hundred yards across Parliament Square, the newly elected House of Commons was debating whether or not to bring back hanging. Some thought that M.C.C. was debating whether or not to hang itself.

Mr. Carlisle proposed the motion. His speech—cogent and well received—made much of the argument that it was unfair to treat sporting and business links differently. He was seconded by John Pashley, a former Yorkshire League cricketer, who emphasised the importance of not being pushed around in a speech that was passionate and effective until, for a hot evening, it went on too long.

The motion was opposed by Hubert Doggart, a former President of M.C.C., who, as in the committee's written argument, conceded part of the case before putting over the official view of the realities of the situation and implying that Mr. Carlisle's motives were political rather than sporting. He was seconded, in similar vein, by Colin Cowdrey who, fifteen years earlier, had been prominent in the 'bridge-building' school of thought. Both went down well, assisted by their known love for the game and their gentle demeanour which enabled them to disguise some sharp debating points. The floor speakers included another Conservative M.P. Andrew Hunter, Denis Compton and Brian Johnston (a popular B.B.C. commentator), all for the motion; the antis included two churchmen— David Sheppard, now bishop of Liverpool, and John Stacey.

But the debate did not matter. As Mr. Bailey knew (though he says he did not tell a soul) the Carlisle forces were already beaten. They had lost the postal vote 6,069 to 3,935; they lost the vote in the hall 535 to 409—an overall total of 6,604 to 4,344 against the resolution, or 60.3 per cent to 39.7.

The expectations that had built up in the past few days now worked heavily against Mr. Carlisle and his supporters. The focus was on the committee victory rather than on the perhaps more remarkable fact that 40 per cent of those who voted and almost a quarter of M.C.C.'s traditionally docile membership had repudiated the committee on a matter on which it had fought furiously to enforce its point of view. This suggested that M.C.C.'s rulers might have many more uncomfortable nights, over all kinds of issues, in the years to come.

Mr. Carlisle felt later, in view of what everyone had told him beforehand, that he must have been defeated by the votes of people who never go to Lord's. He thought too that it had been a mistake to pin down the committee by putting a date to the tour, when the important thing was winning the principle. Mr. Bailey thought the exercise had cleared the air and enhanced the reputation of the club. Everyone agreed that, whether or not M.C.C. debated the matter again, cricket was not going to be able to forget South Africa.

HOW HEADLEY'S GENIUS PAVED THE WAY [1985]

BY E. W. SWANTON

It was becoming noticeable that subtle amendments to the almanack's editorial policy were shortening the length of the essays. With one or two exceptions, it was clear that no theme was considered important enough to be worth more than 1500 words, whereas in the past writers had been encouraged to exfoliate when the occasion suggested it. One of the outstanding essays to appear in the almanack in the 1970s was Grahame Parker's monumental 'The Midwinter File'. Under the new stringencies, that essay could never have appeared at all. The problem was that cricketing affairs were now so multifarious that the editor was finding himself hard put to keep all the vital information within the boards of a single volume. The 1985 edition was approaching the cubic; it contained nearly 1300 pages, the most ever. The 'Cricket Records' section alone was longer than the entire almanack in its inaugural year; so was the section devoted to the one-day game. Understandably, therefore, in approaching the promising theme of the genius of George Headley, E. W. Swanton was obliged to confine himself to a mere 1300 words.

Swanton reminds us that great as Headley's successors in the West Indian side have been, from Worrell, Weekes and Walcott to Sobers, Lloyd and Richards, Headley alone among them was obliged for most of his career to sustain the West Indies batting single-handed. There is no question, from either of the twin viewpoints of the statistical or the testimony of rivals, that Headley was one of the greatest batsmen the game has known. It has always been a deep regret of mine that my first visit to a first-class match took place at Lord's in 1939, that George Headley made history there in that season, and that I was neither lucky enough nor shrewd enough to snatch the chance to watch him batting in his prime.

And yet, in a curious way I did, and if the circumstances do not on first acquaintance seem to have very much to do with cricket, I retain the unshakeable conviction that they do, with particular reference to Swanton's canny observation that Headley showed all the signs of a natural captain of a cricket team, which is another way of saying that he was possibly a natural leader of men. Sometimes the quintessence of an artist, or at any rate some vital aspect of it, can be revealed in a situation so incongruous to the artist's natural habitat that the casual reader might find himself tempted to reject the evidence on the grounds of its being comically irrelevant. In taking the greatest of West Indian batsmen out of his conventional milieu I am not being in any way perverse, but indulging my eagerness to disclose to others a moment of insight I was fortunate enough to stumble into.

In 1953 I was working as a professional jazz musician, touring the four kingdoms with a nine-piece band led by my fellow-saxophonist Ronnie Scott. One of our engagements took us to the town of Rhyl, where we dispensed our art to an audience more intent on its own choreography than on our music. It was a conventional old-fashioned ballroom, complete with bandroom, glitterball, and a balcony for the benefit of spooning couples and dancers with sore feet. After we had been playing for half an hour there came the obligatory marathon drum solo, which always bored me to the point where I was inclined to seek distractions. Happening to glance up at the balcony to our right, I noticed a small group of men intent on our antics. I peered closer and with a pang of delight recognised George Headley, surrounded by, amongst others, Alfred Valentine and Everton Weekes. There were five of them altogether, and they were conducting themselves in the manner of serious students of the music with not much interest in the dancing. Excited by the realisation that we were being observed by great men, I was now exercised by the problem of conveying to my eight companions the degree of their greatness. All my fellow-musicians knew a little about cricket, and their keenness to know more had actually resulted in money being secreted from the band fund for the purchase of bats, stumps, pads and balls, so that having taken lunch in some roadside cafe en route to this or that town, we could find a green space and steal an hour to stage our own Test matches. But as to cricket history, I was alone in my obsession. I knew, however, that the rest of the band were much alive to the idea of greatness in any field, so that once I spread the word, friendly gestures were made to the claque on the balcony, which returned them with broad smiles. During our interval, overtures were undertaken, introductions made, and it was agreed that once the dancing was done, the cricketers would come back to our hotel for a drink, I being even more euphoric by now because I had identified one of the party as Clyde Walcott.

Shortly before midnight there straggled through the moonlit streets of Rhyl a party of five international cricketers, nine well-known musicians, one singer and one road manager. In those days commercial hotels tended to make the assumption that all life on the planet ended at eleven o'clock at night, but we managed to knock up a dropsical porter who refused to serve alcohol but unbent to the extent of pots of coffee and sandwiches. I took the opportunity to engage Headley in conversation. This was not difficult. He was eager to talk of music, and asked me to identify a drummer he had once seen during his time in New York, and whose virtuosity he had remembered ever since. From the description, small, black, with a hump-back, it was obvious that Headley was describing Chick Webb, and I gave him the name.

I assume that the cricketers were abroad in that unlikely part of the world because of involvement in the leagues—Rhyl is not so very far from Lancashire—but the overriding impression which every one of us received was of the unquestioned authority among our guests of George Headley. All the others deferred to him. He was their father-figure, and they all loved him. He made no discernible signs of authority, but when he decided it was time to go, every one of us knew the party was over. There then took place the comic ceremony of George Headley asking me for my autograph, which I gave on condition that he would then give me his. The ceremony was repeated with all the cricketers and all the musicians, after which Headley said good night, wished us well, and led his party into the night.

There is no conclusion to this account. It is not a short story, merely an anecdote, which, for all its casual nature, remains unforgettable, and which confirms for me the gifts of leadership possessed by George Headley. He was the commander of the rest, and with all his smiling humility, even deference, in the matter of the autographs, gave the impression of being in some indefinable way a great man.

There are two postscripts to this memoir. The following summer, I was strolling alone along Oxford Street when I saw approaching me Clyde Walcott, arm in arm with Mrs Walcott. He gave me a brilliant smile, introduced me, and passed the time of day for a few minutes. In 1957, when the West Indies side returned to England for a new series, I sent a telegram to them on the eve of the Lord's Test, wishing them good luck. I signed it 'The Ronnie Scott Band', even though we had long since disbanded. In the event, Trevor Bailey did for them and England won by an innings. I don't know if they ever received the telegram.

THE death, aged 74, of George Alphonso Headley, MBE, whose obituary notice was published in the 1983 *Wisden*, naturally prompts some estimation as to where this indubitably great batsman stands in the cricketers' pantheon, and especially in relation to the fellow West Indians who have followed him.

Headley was not the first West Indian batsman to be designated 'great'. That distinction, according to the sure judgement of the senior West Indian historian, C. L. R. James, belongs to George Challenor, who so impressed the English critics when he came over with the West Indian teams of 1906 and 1923. On this latter tour he delighted everyone with his classical off-side play and finished third in the season's first-class averages with 51. Challenor came also—and I dimly recall him—in 1928 and played in West Indies' first-ever Test series of that year, though by then, at 40, he was past his prime. The cricketers of Trinidad and British Guiana (now Guyana), as well as those of his native Barbados, will have learned by Challenor's example, as also from that of his fellow-islanders, P. H. Tarilton and H. B. G., later Sir Harold, Austin. It was these white Bajans who, practising the batting art on flawless turf pitches and influenced in their method by the successive English sides which visited the southern colonies of the Caribbean, helped in their corner of the world to point the way forward.

Headley was certainly the first great *black* West Indian batsman, and the extraordinary thing is that he learned the game not in one of the traditional strongholds of Bridgetown, Port-of-Spain or Georgetown, where inter-colonial rivalry had flourished for more than half a century, but in far-away Jamaica, cut off from the south by a thousand miles of sea. Until, after the Second World War, they became connected with the rest of the Caribbean by air, the Jamaicans' experience of first-class cricket was confined to visits by M.C.C. and privately organised teams, notably the three brought between 1927 and 1932 by Lionel, Lord Tennyson.

Headley was a genius, almost self-taught, who as an eighteen-year-old suddenly announced himself with a succession of very high scores against Tennyson's second team of 1927–28. As historians know well, he was due to have left Jamaica for the United States in order to be trained as a dentist before the first match against the touring side, and it was only the delay in the issue of a visa that allowed him to play—and to announce himself with an innings of 71. When this was followed by 211 against the Englishmen in the second representative match, dentistry's loss became cricket's gain.

Two years later, in his first Test match, played in Barbados, Headley made 176, the first of the ten Test hundreds he had built up when the war came. In the decade which preceded it, this wiry but short, slight fellow, coming in at No. 3 more often than not with next to nothing on the board, held Test innings after Test innings together. At the end of a tour or a series he had averaged, as like as not, more than double the next man. In England in 1939, aged 30 and at his peak, he scored 1,745 runs, averaging 72. No-one else reached a thousand or averaged more than 30. He stood alone.

Headley's reputation rests on his achievements in the nineteen Tests in which he participated between 1930 and 1939. He played in only the first Test of each of the first three post-war series in which West Indies were concerned. On each occasion injury took over, and he did little except to add to his laurels the distinction of being their first appointed black captain. This was in the Barbados Test in 1948, and it is scarcely to the credit of the authorities that twelve years were to elapse before the next man, Frank Worrell, was to be given the chance in Australia to strike a blow for his race.

Incidentally—or almost—Jeffrey Stollmeyer, no mean theorist himself, wrote of him in his autobiography *Everything under the Sun* that 'in addition to being the "supremo" among West Indian batsmen, he had a greater tactical sense than any cricketer with whom I have played'. In other words, given the opportunity, he might have made a first-rate captain.

In the Lord's Test of 1939 George made 106 and 107 out of totals of 277 and 225. As this was the first Test I broadcast in England, the picture of his batting still remains clear in the mind. His stance was distinctly two-shouldered as he stood there, stock still, sleeves buttoned at the wrist and the plum-coloured cap jauntily askew, a model of wary concentration. Like all the great ones, he played the ball very late yet without any suggestion of hurry. He was almost exclusively a back-foot player, strongest on the on-side. Perfect timing and wrist-work propelled the ball sweetly through the whole segment from mid-on to fine leg with little suggestion of force. But he also had all the off-side strokes at will, being, like nearly all the best of the smaller men, a beautiful cutter.

If the key to his batting was a determined avoidance of risk, it was simply that he—unlike his illustrious successors—knew that he could not afford to get out. If he failed, the end was always in sight. Stollmeyer is quite unequivocal: 'He was the greatest batsman that the West Indies produced. Of this I have no doubt, and my association with Test cricket in the West Indies spans a period from 1939 to the present day, during which I have seen and/or played with the three 'Ws', Gary Sobers and Rohan Kanhai in their prime: also Viv Richards of the present crop, great players all.' To this list of those within measurable distance of Headley, one might perhaps today add Clive Lloyd and Gordon Greenidge but surely no-one else. Whether or not one goes all the way with Stollmeyer's judgement it must be acknowledged that he is in a position to speak paralleled only by his great friend and youthful contemporary in the West Indian side of 1939, Gerry Gomez.

But what of the famous batsmen in Headley's descent who have held the West Indian flag high now for the best part of 40 years? Well, the only sure thing about the batting quality of the immortal trio from Barbados, Frank Worrell, Everton Weekes and Clyde Walcott, is that there was precious little between them in terms of achievement. Between 1949 and 1960, playing around 50 Tests apiece, the three Ws in their widely separated styles scored 39 hundreds; Worrell all grace and elegance; Weekes stocky, punchy, full of the killer instinct; Walcott, towering physically above them both, a driver of awesome power. Throw in Worrell's utility as a bowler and Walcott's as a wicket-keeper, and the cliché 'a host in themselves' scarcely meets the case.

Until Worrell's last glorious phase as a captain, by which time the other two had retired, each drew strength from the presence of the other two. Likewise Sobers was never called upon to bear the weight of the West Indian batting unaided. He began with the three Ws, and played most of his long Test career in tandem with Kanhai. These were latterly joined by Lloyd, who in these last ten years has been fortified by the genius of Richards.

Of the last four mentioned, three are little less easy to place than their predecessors. Kanhai (the only East Indian under consideration although some may well argue that Alvin Kallicharran should be) combined a rare natural talent with an admirable technique. Lloyd hits the ball just about as hard as anyone who ever played, but one sees him predominantly as a fighter whose easy manner belies a degree of determination second to none. Richards possesses an almost unequalled brilliance, and his finest innings are incomparable. If he fails more often than the others under review, it is because he is a victim of the modern over-exposure of the top players. He will make no secret that he and his contemporaries, wearied by perpetual travel and the limelight, are often merely going through the motions.

There remains the inimitable Sobers. That no-one can approach his record as an all-round cricketer goes without saying. What one wonders is, if he had not taken 235 wickets for West Indies over a span of 93 Tests, and if in consequence he had batted a couple of places higher in the order, how many more runs and hundreds he would have scored than the figures of 8,032 and 26 which, as they stand, tower above everyone else's? Not that anyone ever cared less about the arithmetic of his cricket. If I had to choose anyone to play for my life, as the saying is, I would name Gary without hesitation. In him genius based on strictly orthodox principles found almost perfect expression.

To sum up: Headley enjoyed a lonely pre-eminence in his day, though it must be allowed that the bowling opposed to him was less formidable than much that his successors had to face. Paraphrasing Plum Warner, who used to say, 'No-one has ever batted *better* than Jack Hobbs.' I would suggest that no West Indian has ever batted better than Headley and Sobers. And a final reflection: how extraordinary that within modern times a few scattered communities with a combined population roughly akin to the three million or so of Sydney or Melbourne should have produced a string of memorable batsmen at least equivalent to the combined output of England and Australia!

JIM LAKER—A TRIBUTE [1987]

BY ROBIN MARLAR

When you require an acute technical analysis, find a technician. The death of James Charles Laker at the early age of sixty-four prompted Wisden *to invite another off-spinner to explain the nature of Laker's greatness. Robin Marlar's exposition is as logical as it is appreciative of Laker's complete mastery, and illustrates the gulf between the perceptions of an expert and the reflections of the day-to-day cricket reporter. The essay does, however, feature one astonishing omission. That any bowler, having taken nine wickets in the first innings of a Test match against Australia, should then take all ten in the second innings, is, as Marlar writes, incredible. But the facts are more incredible by far. Earlier in that same season of 1956, playing for Surrey against the tourists, Laker returned first innings figures of all ten wickets for 88 runs in 46 overs. No bowler in all the history of first-class cricket has ever taken ten wickets in an innings twice in the same season. No bowler has ever performed the feat twice against a touring side. No bowler in any first-class game, having taken nine wickets in the first innings, has ever added all ten in the second. This is the derring-do of the tuppenny bloods, and yet the hero was a gentle man with the mildest of demeanours.*

My only contact with Jim Laker was at the annual Wisden *dinners, those shining examples of the celebratory occasion at which each guest finds waiting at his set place a copy of the new almanack to be published in a few days. Laker and I were often placed at the same table, and although he was a man of few words, so self-effacing that he might not have been a great*

cricketer at all but one of the representatives of the publishing house, he had
a rich sense of humour, indicated by the hint of a wry grin which often played
about his lips and eyes. I was too shy to address him directly very often, but I
did feed that humorous bent at least once, when I told him that, like him, I
was a Yorkshireman. It was all he could do to stifle his laughter, but he could
not contain the twinkle in his eyes.

Iɴ the early 1950s Everest had not yet been tamed. It stood alone among
the high places of the world. Now, more than thirty years later, its climbs
are still the test for real mountaineers, but even as they prove the efficacy of
their thermal underwear, Everest seems to have shrunk. Hillary and
Tensing have been followed to the top.

Down below, in kinder, greener conditions, the underwear is not for
keeping out the cold but for mopping up the sweat. Even so, on the cricket
field, conditions of wind and wear, of dust and damp still must be watched
and taken into account. There, however, Jim Laker's achievement,
nineteen wickets in a Test match, has not attracted followers. Nor may it
ever be beaten. Twenty wickets in a match is still Everest, far more
significant in a cricket context than any record for batting or even for all-
round excellence.

Laker's nineteen looks less and less repeatable as the seasons pass. Even
if some Caribbean or oriental tyro emerges, as Sobers did to topple Hutton
or Gavaskar to overtake Bradman, there is still that extra air of wondrous
disbelief that Laker should have, could have, taken nineteen Australian
wickets for England in a Test at Old Trafford. And with Lock, most
avaricious of bowlers, bowling 69 overs at the other end for Burke's first-
innings wicket; the one that got away from Laker. Nor should it pass notice
that Statham and Bailey, both unquestioned occupants of the hall of fame,
sent down 46 overs between them without a strike. Even if you accept that
the 1956 Australians were not one of the best sides from that country, there
were great cricketers in that team; Harvey, Miller, Lindwall, Benaud. In
truth, even though it happened, we can describe Laker's feat only as
incredible.

At 34, Laker was at the peak of his powers in 1956. As a slow off-break
bowler in the classical tradition, he was the unchallenged master of his
craft. His confidence soared. Surrey were in their run of seven successive
Championships, then the only pudding for proof at county level. Stuart
Surridge, the captain who made Laker, allowing his bowler the luxury of
being able to live without ever needing to doubt his own ability, had an
unshakeable belief in the destiny of Surrey and its players. Furthermore,
Laker had something of a score to settle with the Australians. In 1948,
during the last chapter in the Bradman saga which had earlier featured
bodyline and all that, England were desperate for a victory; but at Leeds,
where Australia were set to score 404 to win in 344 minutes, he had failed to
bowl them out in the fourth innings. Afterwards he would talk gently about
dropped catches and the lack of spin support, there being only Compton's
occasional chinamen available. At Lord's, though, where this particular

England defeat hurt more than most, there was a suspicion that when the crunch came, Laker was chicken.

After Laker's failure at Leeds, off-spinning was relegated to third place in the spinning hierarchy behind the left-arm spinners and leg-spinners. Not that it would have mattered who had bowled in the next Test in 1948, because at The Oval England were bowled out for 52. Laker won caps in the years that followed, but first Tattersall and then Appleyard kept him out of the England XI. Both were fine bowlers, but neither was orthodox like Laker. Tattersall held his forefinger, a long one, alongside the seam and pushed his off-spinner in a manner that helped him disguise the away-swinger. Appleyard exploded on the scene as a fast-medium bowler with a deadly off-cutter. Later he slowed down and learned to spin while never losing his quick bowler's action. We have seen the same development since in Greig's bowling. Both Tattersall and Appleyard were deadly on wet wickets. Because of their actions, preceded by a longer run than that of Laker and his followers, they had the potential for an increase of pace and therefore penetration. But Laker, too, was a fearsome opponent on a wet wicket. His action, so grooved in its approach, so upright in delivery, was an instrument on which he could play the pace variations that he wanted, although never reaching medium pace.

Laker's principal asset, and the one he looked for first among spin bowlers in his later coaching and commentary career, was power of spin. His action, a slow bowler's action, enabled him to deliver the ball spun by the fingers and snapped forward with the wrist. He charged the ball with more menace than his rivals and, I suspect, almost all his followers. Not that Laker lacked an away-swinger or the ability to use the breeze from long leg. He was always reluctant to switch his slip to lock up the leg-trap, recognising that no matter how responsive the pitch, even the finger-spun ball might hustle on without deviation, taking the outside edge as a batsman played for the turn.

In another important aspect Laker was pre-eminent, certainly among his contemporaries. Not only did he have equal ability over and round the wicket, but he combined this with the shrewdest understanding of which batsman could be better discomforted by a change of angle. On good pitches, on-side players would be attacked from round the wicket on the basis that they would, if they played across the line of that angle, be candidates for a catch at the wicket or slip. Similarly, by using the full crease from over the wicket, he had a chance of getting through the off-side driver, or at least of taking his inside edge. When the ball was turning, the geometry spoke not only for itself but also to umpires, who would give leg-before decisions on the front foot only if the bowler was going round the wicket.

Laker's ability in this respect—and one not given to the leading Test wicket-taker of this type, Gibbs, who could not bowl round the wicket—depended on the position of his body. Operating round the wicket, he clung to the leg stump with his backside, his final stride short enough to give him perfect balance, enabling him to make maximum use of his six-foot frame. Because of this perfect action, he was able to maintain not only his tight control over direction and length but also those subtle variations in trajectory, in the 'loop', which differentiated Laker from one breed of lesser performer. Only his splendid control gave Surridge, his captain, crowding helmetless in the danger zone, the courage to walk forward from short leg. Indeed, Laker was sure that some catches were missed because his close men were too keen.

Generations overlap, but the second overlap will inevitably take the players and their game into new territory, thus rendering comparisons deceptively, dangerously, impossible. In Laker's time pitches were uncovered, albeit progressively less so. Outfields were less like carpets. There was less grass on the squares and what there was, was cut shorter. The science of pitch preparation was in its infancy. Groundsmanship is not so unlike farming that we can fail to notice that in Laker's time there was no embarrassing food mountain. No batsman then wielded heavier willow than 2lb 7oz, and most bats were 2lb 4oz. Pads were less padded, and technique against the off-break was not so well developed that batsmen could avoid opening the 'gate'; with the result that an off-break, when properly spun, could go through to bowl a highly rated player.

Match balls were hand-, not machine-stitched and less well dyed, although they did keep their shape better. If you gripped these balls tight with the fingers across the seam and ripped them across it, the skin on the fingers was eventually torn. Laker soaked his right forefinger in surgical spirit at the start of the season to harden the skin, but even so it tore, the split eventually deepening until it bled. Each spinner had a different solution to the problem, some even stopping giving the ball such a tweak. Not Laker. Never. He would use a concoction called Friar's Balsam, which seemed to give him antiseptic protection until a corn developed, although later in the season that corn would itself split and bleed.

It should not pass notice that in the second innings of that famous Old Trafford Test, Laker bowled 51 overs and two balls with hardly a break. Yet in all of the 1956 season he bowled *only* 959 overs: *only* because it was not uncommon for spin bowlers to break 1,000 or even 1,250 overs a season. Laker's spinning finger thickened with arthritis, noticeably so when compared with the same digit on the left hand, and from time to time, when confronted by these problems, he was, perhaps inevitably, not keen to fill the stock-bowling role as a Surrey match eased gently towards a draw. Like the voice of a Callas, a spin bowler's finger demanded judicious use.

No cricketer could have made an impression on the game as vividly as Laker without having the personality to deploy his talent. He might have gone to Surrey from Catford, but Jim Laker was the archetypal dry Yorkshireman. If his tongue could cut, his eye was keen. His humour depended on the detached observance of the passing scene, never better illustrated than in his story of the journey home after that Test, when he sat in a Lichfield pub alone and unrecognised whilst others celebrated what he had done. Nor were his years in banking wasted, for he invested shrewdly when he finally settled in Putney. After his brief flirtation with industry, commentating for television, together with his articles and books, kept him financially afloat. Cricket apart, he was not looking for the big one.

Not all cricketers travel contentedly through the rest of their lives. To all appearances Laker was one of the lucky ones. Perhaps an inner awareness of his stupendous achievement as a player, the bestest with the mostest, gave him lasting satisfaction. When he came back from his next winter tour in South Africa to pick up yet more awards, he found that the legislators had begun to interfere with the right of captains and bowlers to place their fielders at will. 'They have made it harder for anyone to repeat my success,' he told one audience, and as so often in his cricketing judgement, Laker is likely to be right. When shall we look upon his like again?

SIR GEORGE ALLEN [1987]

A Special Portrait

BY J. J. WARR

The transmutation of G. O. Allen into Sir George was long overdue by the time it took place, in the Queen's Birthday Honours of 1986. In the Wisden *of the following season J.J. Warr, one-time Middlesex and England fast bowler, more latterly an entertaining speaker at cricket dinners and prominent in the affairs of M.C.C., wrote an affectionate study of the old knight. Although no more than a bookmark for the definitive biography published by E. W. Swanton in 1985, Warr's sketch has its moments. Among the insights he offers are the spectacular cloak-and-dagger wartime career complete with American honours, and an account of the moment when Sir George attempted to re-enact the Wellingtonian saw concerning the playing fields of Eton, incidentally adding a priceless item to the stockpot of cricketing arcana by becoming the first England cricket captain to be arrested as an enemy spy. Lord Harris might have invited it, Douglas Jardine perhaps deserved it, but it was Sir George who actually claimed it. And there is at least one moment when Warr's prose is haunted by the ghost of Wodehouse, when Lady Dickson describes her brother as 'married to cricket'. The essay closes with an interesting thought. Sir George filled more administrative posts than any other man. Had he given to playing cricket the time he devoted to its administration, his record might have been even more spectacular than it was.*

As for the cricket-lovers of my generation, he was for so long an element of fixity in a swirling universe that he came in some odd way to be a surety for the future. So long as he went on administering this, arranging that, dictating here and advising there, the world of recollection did not after all seem so very far away. I can still hear the bookie's runners of my childhood talking

*admiringly of 'good old Gubby' when he won the first two Tests of the 1936–
37 series. Then I see him glaring at the ragamuffins in the Nursery nets on a
sun-drenched wartime evening. And, in the very year in which Warr's essay
appeared, one of the ragamuffins was invited into his home, adjoining the
Lord's ground, to be greeted in friendship and treated with courtesy and
humour. I recalled all this when I read the news of his knighthood, and recall
also the feeling that even he could not go on forever.*

S IR George Oswald Browning Allen was born in Sydney, Australia, on
July 31, 1902, being very much in the tradition of England captains who
were not born in England. To name only some, Sir Pelham Warner was
born in Trinidad, F. R. Brown in Peru, D. B. Carr in Germany, E. R.
Dexter in Italy, and M. C. Cowdrey and D. R. Jardine in India. 'Gubby',
aged six, was brought to England with his brother and sister to be
educated, and the family remained here ever after. His contribution to the
national game of cricket has been immense, of which the award of the CBE
followed in 1986 by a knighthood in the Queen's Birthday Honours is a
clear recognition. Most people thought his knighthood was long overdue,
but it did make him the last man in a hat-trick, following his grandfather
and father.

However, there are other aspects of his life to demonstrate that cricket
has not been his sole preoccupation. A highly successful stockbroker in
peacetime, he also rose to the rank of Lieutenant-Colonel in military
intelligence in the War Office in the Second World War, specialising in all
aspects of German ground-to-air defences and particularly their siting; not
unlike deciding on the field placing in a Test match. He saved many
casualties among bomber pilots by his skill and knowledge and was
awarded the Legion of Merit by the Americans.

One of the more colourful incidents of his military career occurred
before he was posted to the War Office; when he was serving in the control
room at Hawkinge during the Dunkirk evacuation. On hearing that his
brother had been seriously wounded, he obtained permission to fly to
break the news to their mother, who was living near Eton, at Datchet, and
the aircraft, carrying Belgian markings, landed on the playing-fields of
Eton as the nearest and most convenient place. Although they had the
consent of Fighter Command to return to Hawkinge, before that
happened, as Gubby found on his return from Datchet, the plane was
surrounded by the Eton Home Guard under the command of Corporal
Lord Porchester, now the Queen's racing manager. And even though
Gubby went to Eton and was in the XI for three years, the intrepid patrol
arrested him as a German spy, making him the only England cricket
captain to suffer such a fate.

The incident did nothing to diminish Gubby's interest in racing, which
was nurtured by all the great Newmarket trainers who regularly went to
Fenner's to see the cricket. He has also known many of the leading
politicians, both domestically and internationally. The foreword to the
book, *Gubby Allen: Man of Cricket*, was written by a former Prime

Minister and close friend in Lord Home of the Hirsel, and pride of place in Gubby's St John's Wood home is a suitably inscribed photograph of another personal friend, Sir Robert Menzies of Australia.

The game of cricket has been a linchpin in his life, however, and it was his own sister, Lady Dickson, who remarked that as a perpetual bachelor Gubby was 'married to cricket'. Whilst Gubby does not deny this, he is adamant that when Sir Pelham Warner proposed him first for the Middlesex committee and then the M.C.C. cricket committee, he was very reluctant to accept. That notwithstanding, his first-class playing career stretched to more than 30 years, and it was only by liberal use of elastoplast and embrocation that he was still playing in the 1950s. Indeed, in those days, when he took the field he resembled the mummified figures of the great Pharoahs of Egypt. He is an authority on every muscle in the human body, having pulled most of them in his time. He has had five operations on his hips and it is said that he got so expert that he did the last two himself. Jim Swanton, his Boswell in *Gubby Allen: Man of Cricket*, once jokingly described him as a hypochondriacal megalomaniac and Gubby did not dissent.

Returning to his first-class career, there were four great highlights. In 1929 he took all ten wickets against Lancashire for Middlesex at Lord's, which has remained a unique feat in county cricket at Lord's to this day. It was only a late fitness test on the Friday that enabled him to play, and as he was delayed in the office on the Saturday, working for Debenham's, he did not take the new ball. His final figures were ten for 40 and eight of them were clean-bowled. Next would be his partnership with Les Ames of 246 in two and threequarter hours against New Zealand at Lord's in 1931; it remains a world record for the eighth wicket in a Test match and is the oldest such record to remain unbroken. Going in when England were 190 for seven, Gubby drove with power and, without making a mistake, finished with 122, his first and only Test century and still the highest innings by someone batting at number nine for England.

Then came his two tours of Australia, in 1932–33 and, as captain, in 1936–37. On the bodyline tour he emerged as a white knight, which was the image presented in the recent Australian television serial. There is a considerable grain of truth in that assessment, but it was spoilt by the totally inaccurate characterisation of people like P. G. H. Fender, who was depicted as a banjo-playing buffoon, and Sir Pelham Warner, as a whisky-swilling nonentity: two images as far from the truth as it is possible to imagine. Gubby is also shown as disagreeing with Douglas Jardine on the field, which is something he never did nor would ever have contemplated. He refused to bowl bodyline—a decision which was made in the dressing-room—but Gubby remained a firm friend of Jardine for the whole of Jardine's life.

The 1936–37 tour with Gubby as captain saw Bradman as something of an ogre. He had had marvellous tours of England in 1930 and 1934, and the memory of him in 1930 must have been one of the reasons why in 1932–33 Jardine was prepared to stretch the spirit and ethics of the game to breaking-point in order to snuff him out. As it turned out, with England bowling in an orthodox manner, the 1936–37 tour was one of the most exciting in the history of the Ashes. It also produced one of the most famous remarks in cricket. Gubby intended to console R. W. V. Robins when, in the second innings of the third Test, he dropped Bradman at 24 off Gubby's bowling: 'Oh forget it, old boy, it will probably cost us the rubber but what the hell.' Robbie recalled that remark endlessly, but always with amusement and not rancour.

The lifelong friendship between Gubby and Robbie is an interesting study in contrasts. R. W. V. was ebullient, volatile, totally unpredictable and much given to instant opinions followed by instant decisions, many of which carried a diplomatic backlash. G. O. A., on the other hand, prefers to weigh things up with great care and achieve his objectives by logical argument and with just a dash of lobbying. They had a close relationship as players, and I recall with particular pleasure the time when Gubby was a regular visitor as a batsman to the perfect wicket at Fenner's to play for the Free Foresters in the early 1950s. He was usually a scorer of a century in one innings or the other, and R. W. V. used to mock him, saying how easy it was to flog undergraduates round Fenner's. He added that if he played himself he would score 50 batting with a walking-stick. Gubby challenged him to turn out and try his luck using a proper bat. He did, and was bowled first ball in each innings: an Imperial pair! The late O. J. Wait bowled him in the first innings and I was the bowler in the second. The joke was enjoyed by all parties except for the same batsman who was on a hat-trick in both innings.

Distinguished as his playing career has been, it is in the administration and think-tanks of the game that Gubby has had his greatest influence. Despite his initial reluctance, he was elected to the M.C.C. committee in 1935 and was at the time ten years younger than any other member of that committee. Subsequently he has been the Club's President, Treasurer and one of its Trustees, serving in one form or another for 51 years. He has been a distinguished chairman of selectors but does emphasise that silk purses cannot be made out of sows' ears: good selectors and good captains are only as good as the material they can choose and the players who play under them. He has held more offices in cricket than anyone in living memory, including being President of the Umpires' Association for more than 25 years. To him, though, his contribution to coaching the young has given him as much satisfaction as anything else. With H. S. Altham he wrote *The M.C.C. Cricket Coaching Book* in 1952. It has remained the 'bible' of coaching and has sold 100,000 copies.

Golf, in his spare time, has always been an abiding passion, and even in his eighties he is still making adjustments to his swing in search of perfection. His early tutor was Leonard Crawley, who had possibly one of the finest golf swings of all time. His lowest golf handicap has been four and, even now, one of his bad shots can produce a stream of verbal criticism of himself which would cause even Freddie Trueman to blush. Over the years he has derived immense pleasure from head to head confrontations with his friends, rather than seeking to put his name on trophies or golf club walls, while among his friends in the County Cricketers' Golf Society there is a term for the world's worst golfer: it is 'Gubby's foursome partner'. He can be seen at his beloved Berkshire or Sandwich outdoing Nigel Mansell at the wheel of his golf buggy, still hitting the ball straight but sacrificing length for accuracy, which is a polite way of saying that he doesn't hit it as far as he used to.

Jim Swanton has pointed out in 'the book' how many cricket crises Sir George has lived through, and they were summed up by Prince Philip in his telegram to the President of M.C.C. on the occasion of Gubby's 80th birthday celebration at Lord's: 'No man has done more for M.C.C. and for cricket over a long period when things have been far from easy. He deserves all the tributes he is bound to get. Philip.'

Gubby spoke at the 150th M.C.C. Anniversary Dinner in 1937 and it is hoped that he will do the same at the 200th in 1987. Like all great sportsmen, he identifies the one key moment of luck or fate which launched him on his career. In his case it was in 1922. Having had no success in the Freshmen's match at Cambridge, he was invited to play for Middlesex against the University and took six for 13 which, needless to say, got him into the University side. One of his victims was Hubert Ashton, the Cambridge captain, bowled by a trimmer, which might have helped his cause. For some reason he has never been one of *Wisden's* Cricketers of the Year, but I suppose that is because he has been more sparing with his activities on the field than off.

M.C.C.—200 YEARS [1987]

A Celebration

BY E. W. SWANTON

In the same edition of the almanack Sir George's biographer, E. W. Swanton, wrote a piece marking the bicentenary of M.C.C. To encompass the history of so vast an organisation in a mere few paragraphs is one of those unreasonable requests which editors cannot always avoid, and, considering the brevity of the essay, it does an excellent job. There is an air about it of apprehension, rooted in the loss of status of the club in the face of the advent of the Test and County Cricket Board. When M.C.C. surrendered part of its authority in order to comply with the rules covering government grants, it did not seem at the time to be much more than a bit of bureaucratic box-and-coxery. In fact it was very much more than that, and speaking as one who has sometimes lost patience with the club's vagaries of administration, I think it was a bad day indeed when M.C.C. was superseded by another organisation. Asperities have already risen to peaks of imbecility, with the T.C.C.B. taking umbrage at the fact that club members are entitled to free entry to the

*ground during Test matches, and threatening to remove Tests from Lord's
and stage them elsewhere, perhaps the London Palladium. While it is a
truism that the members of sporting administrative bodies are selected
according to the degree of their ineptitude and unworldliness, the T.C.C.B.
sounds sometimes like a bunch of lunatics.*

*Perhaps in this regard I could take exception, very mildly, to one
observation of Jim Swanton, when he writes, regarding the grant to cricket
from the government, that Harold Wilson's administration could 'scarcely
treat with a private institution'. He is misled. Governments can treat with
anyone they like, and, regrettably, often do. I cannot help wondering what
might have happened had the club committee appealed to Mr. Wilson's sense
of cricket history. He certainly possessed one, as I discovered once, when he
wrecked a luncheon speech of mine by persistently slipping me torn
fragments of menu on which he had scribbled the names of obscure
Yorkshire villages which possessed good cricket sides.*

THERE is no phrase more neatly expressive of the role of M.C.C. in the
evolution of the game than Sir Pelham Warner's well-worn description:
a private club with a public function. It may well have been 'Plum', too,
who coined the aphorism that 'M.C.C. reigns but does not rule.' In
common parlance, while it has been accepted as the final seat of authority,
it has not thrown its weight about. Pray notice the change of tense. We
must write now in the past tense to the extent that, although Marylebone
Cricket Club remains the maker and custodian of the Laws, just as it has
been since its formation just two hundred years ago, and although it still
provides the ICC, according to custom, with its venue, its Chairman and its
secretariat, the Club has had since 1968 no more than a guiding voice in the
governance of the English game in its various aspects, both amateur and
professional.

When at that time Mr. Harold Wilson's Labour administration agreed at
last to make Government grants available to sports and games, they could
scarcely treat with a private institution, however venerable and respected.
Hence, in consultation with Mr. Denis Howell, the Minister with special
responsibility for sport, M.C.C. made a voluntary devolution of its tacitly
accepted through never explicit powers. The Test and County Cricket
Board, formerly 'The Advisory', would in future manage and control the
first-class game, and a new body, the National Cricket Association, would
be answerable for all aspects of the amateur game, with special emphasis
on the coaching of the young. Both these bodies, along with M.C.C.,
would contribute equal representation, a third each, to a court of appeal
known as the Cricket Council. The gist of all this is no doubt apprehended
more or less by the average devotee of *Wisden*; but it is an outline perhaps
worth defining afresh in this celebratory bicentennial year.

The future of M.C.C. will be what its successive committees make of a
wonderful heritage. Theirs is the ground, unique historically, perfectly
placed geographically to remain, as it has always been, the natural
headquarters of the game. When the spotlight turns on to Lord's this

coming summer, it will show an arena better equipped to accommodate members and public than ever before. The handsome new Mound Stand complements and follows the contours of the recently built Tavern Stand, right up to the open decks of 'free seats' at the Nursery End. As the eye moves anti-clockwise, the Grand and Warner Stands continue the line of the boundary round to the centre-piece of the Pavilion, that four-square monument to Victorian self-assurance which seems likewise to be the very emblem of cricket's permanence as a national institution.

Behind the Pavilion (which itself has been greatly modernised within and to which a library of fitting size and dignity has been appended), and contiguous with the tennis and squash courts and the Memorial Gallery, opened in 1950, the T.C.C.B. and N.C.A. are now comfortably and independently housed. So, alongside the Harris garden and in a separate building, is the Middlesex C.C.C. Away on the Nursery ground stands the M.C.C. Indoor School, through which many thousand cricketers of all ages have passed since its opening ten years ago. Add to the picture the modern Tavern alongside the Grace Gates, and it strikes one afresh how greatly over the last two decades the face of Lord's has changed. What we must be truly thankful for is that the transitions have been wrought without loss of character. One cannot visualise further significant building in the immediate future, and so in 1987 Lord's can face the years ahead confidently as it is. Thank heaven it will always be a cricket ground—surely *the* cricket ground; never a stadium.

So much for 'the plant', but what of the men who have made M.C.C. and Lord's what they are today? The gallery is a remarkable one, starting with Thomas Lord himself whom that small band of noblemen commissioned to procure a ground for the club they were about to form. All that is known about Lord marks him as a man of quality. He had, say Lord Harris and F. S. Ashley-Cooper in *Lord's and the M.C.C.*, a 'handsome presence and possessed a *bonhomie* that was almost irresistible'. Three grounds he had to find as London extended to the north, finally, in 1814, putting down his roots only just in time on the present site.

In those first days, two men of a very different temper held the stage: the Rev. Lord Frederick Beauclerk, reputedly the best cricketer in England around the turn of the nineteenth century, and the first Secretary of M.C.C., Benjamin Aislabie, who doted on the game though much too fat to be any good at it. Thomas Hughes portrayed him affectionately on the occasion in *Tom Brown's Schooldays* when he brought the M.C.C. team to Rugby. In the earliest pavilions (the first was burned down in 1825), Aislabie cast on the scene a benevolence which held the club together, a necessary antidote no doubt to Beauclerk (descended from the union of Charles II and Nell Gwynne), who as a dictator of affairs on the field and off, and a sharp betting man to boot, comes across almost as a villain of old-style melodrama.

Following Aislabie's death in office in 1842, the affairs of M.C.C. declined to a point which brought press agitation for a cricket parliament to depose the club from its position of authority. It was rescued from the hands of reactionaries such as Robert Grimston—who greeted with disgust the advent of the mowing machine—by a character ideally suited to the situation in R. A. Fitzgerald.

Bob Fitzgerald was clearly a popular personality and withal a lively one. 'Whether it was the magnificence of his swagger, the luxuriance of his beard, the fun that rolled out of him so easily, or the power of his swiping, I do not know, but as regards each he could not escape notice,' wrote Lord Harris, who as to the fun tells of Fitzgerald's favourite trick when a wicket fell of pretending to catch a mouse in the grass.

Fitzgerald reigned as Secretary of M.C.C. from 1863 to 1876, having become in that time the first salaried occupant. As an undergraduate, Harris was a member of the team which Fitzgerald in 1872 took on a successful pioneering tour of Canada and the United States, the first ever undertaken by amateurs. He also took sides to Paris and Dublin, and flew the flags of M.C.C. and I Zingari in many unfrequented places. (The M.C.C. colours of red and yellow date from his time.) Fitzgerald was both reformer and innovator. Alas, he perhaps drove himself too hard, for his health completely failed and he died young. A tangible memorial to him in the M.C.C. library is a collection of illustrated scrapbooks, donated by a grandson, T. G. Fitzgerald.

If young George Harris was on the threshold of a leading role in the rapid evolution of cricket, an even greater figure was another of Fitzgerald's North American party, W. G. Grace himself, already a rising star. The 1870s saw the dawn of county cricket, wherein the Graces of Gloucestershire led the way, and the game expanded mightily around the ample frame of W. G., who was, let it be said, ever a loyal M.C.C. man. Middlesex began to play at Lord's in 1877, thus providing Londoners with a regular programme of first-class cricket. The following year came the event that popularised the game more than anything else; the first visit of the colonials from Australia and their defeat of M.C.C. in a single day.

Although for some years yet the financial prosperity of M.C.C. continued to depend greatly on the three classic fixtures, Eton v Harrow, begun in 1805, Gentlemen v Players, from 1806, and the University match, from 1827, the frequent Australian visits, along with the appeal of Middlesex, brought an even wider public to Lord's.

No essay aiming to sketch the M.C.C. story in its bicentenary year should omit mention of the longest-serving of all its officers, Sir Spencer Ponsonby-Fane, whose life was bound up with Lord's almost from his days as a Harrow boy in the mid-1830s until his death in 1915, aged 91. For 36 years he served the club as Treasurer, which was in his time and ever after the key post. Finding only two pictures in the place (admittedly Francis Haymans), he started the now incomparable art collection. Diplomat—he was secretary to Palmerston—and courtier, Ponsonby-Fane personified that close aristocratic involvement with M.C.C. which was continuous from the foundation until after the Second World War.

On this point, a word here in parenthesis. Although its beginnings and the close connections with Eton, Harrow, Winchester, the other major schools and the Universities determined the style and pattern of its membership, M.C.C. has not been, at least in living memory—and contrary to popular belief—a socially exclusive club. Granted a civilised standard of behaviour, good cricketers have always been welcome.

Next, chronologically, comes a very major figure in the story, Francis Lacey, a barrister by training, who took on the secretaryship at the age of 38 in 1898 and held it until 1926, when he was honoured with the first knighthood for services to cricket. Ignoring the advice of his predecessor, Henry Perkins, to 'take no notice of the damned committee', Lacey put the club on a sound administrative footing. Where M.C.C. had been loath to involve itself with the international and county scene, Lacy had a keener eye for the game's welfare and the Club's responsibilities. The Board of Control for Test Matches and 'The Advisory' were formed early in his time, while in 1903 M.C.C. (as the Melbourne CC had been urging it) undertook to choose and manage the tours to Australia.

Plum Warner led the first side out that winter and brought home the Ashes, and M.C.C. has been a household name in cricket ever since. In due course, and over a span of 70-odd years, the M.C.C. colours were flown in South Africa, the West Indies, New Zealand, India, Ceylon (now Sri Lanka) and Pakistan, as well as in many other countries not on the test match circuit.

The post-Great War years saw the formidable Treasurer-Secretary partnership of Harris and Lacey, and it is fascinating if profitless to speculate whether, if old Lord Harris had lived another year or so, he might have scented the coming bodyline trouble in the late summer of 1932 and either scotched it at birth or at least apprehended the situation more swiftly when the first warning signals from Australia came wafting back. The bodyline message for cricket's rulers, so far as Test cricket was concerned, was to beware the sudden onset of unruly passions. There were storms to come, all right, but not yet. M.C.C. was soon marking its 150th anniversary with three very successful matches and a celebratory dinner of many courses and toasts of which the writer, recently elected, retains only a blurred memory.

Through the Second World War—as distinct from the complete 1914–18 shut-down—M.C.C. kept the flag flying admirably with a regular programme of cricket each summer, culminating in the 'Victory Tests' between England and the Dominions. More people (413,856) watched cricket at Lord's in 1945 than in 1939—an augury fulfilled by the vast crowds, in the first post-war years, of people anxious to dull the thought of past horrors and present shortages and discomforts.

M.C.C. was more active than ever before in the period between the war's end and the transitions of 1968, presiding over ever more frequent Test exchanges, setting up enquiries at the behest of the counties—five of these, achieving much less than their labours deserved, sat within 30 years—and, especially, turning its attention to encouraging the young. The present comprehensive structure of School Associations' coaching and competitive cricket must be traced back to the foresight and energy in 1948 of G. O. (now Sir George) Allen and his subsequent partnership with H. S. Altham. Their *M.C.C. Cricket Coaching Book*, regularly updated, has sold 100,000 copies.

Altham and Allen, successive Treasurers, apart from a single year, from 1950 to 1974, both steeped in all aspects of the game, served M.C.C. in the Harris tradition, if using a softer touch, in harness with three Secretaries of contrasting personality but equal dedication, Colonel R. S. Rait Kerr, R. Aird and S. C. Griffith.

An extension of the hierarchy must be mentioned here. The modern President is expected—indeed obliged—to play a far more active role than ever before. What until the late 1940s was almost a sinecure has become highly demanding post involving many hours a week, dealing with the complexities of both M.C.C. itself and the I.C.C. (of which the President of the day is the automatic Chairman), and the evolving relationship with the new bodies.

Whereas in the 40 years prior to the 1939–45 war only eight Presidents had been first-class cricketers, over the last 40 years the figure is 28. Most of these have brought to the job wide experience in cricket administration. When, however, a President has named as his successor a man of distinction outside the game—Lord Caccia, the late A. H. Dibbs, and the present Chairman of Finance, Sir Anthony Tuke, are recent examples—the Club has been invariably well served. It is easy to be too close to the game's problems and even to be insensitive to public opinion.

The most unfortunate instance of this was 'the D'Oliveira Affair' when the Committee had to withstand, in the fateful year of 1968, a vote of no confidence—albeit fairly comfortably defeated—at a Special General Meeting. The Club, in the persons of the Chairman of I.C.C. and its representatives, had come much more favourably from the 'throwing crisis' of 1960. Harry Altham and Gubby Allen were chiefly involved here, ultimately with the decisive backing of Sir Donald Bradman.

When Kerry Packer's intrusion threatened to tear cricket apart in 1977, the I.C.C. were lucky to find as their Chairmen two patient negotiators prepared to travel the world in search of a settlement in D. G. Clark and C. H. Palmer. Who shall say that the business might not have been brought to a less damaging conclusion by them on behalf of I.C.C. than the subservient long-term accommodation suddenly accepted by the Australian Board?

These are waters under the bridge, and the concluding question to be asked is how well equipped is the M.C.C. of 1987 to fulfil its more limited but still crucial stewardship of the game in the future? Writing on the eve of the bicentenary, I take the mood to be of competence and self-confidence. The Club today is a unique sporting institution with a value and annual turnover measured in many millions, run by a President and committee wherein cricket and business expertise are combined in a fairer mix of the generations than in some earlier days. It has 18,000 members and a waiting-list of embarrassing length. We are at the outset of a year marked by an ambitious series of large-scale events: a ball, dinners at Lord's and the Guildhall, a luncheon on the site of the original ground at Dorset

Square, and more besides. Much imagination has gone into the programme, and the news is that everything is over-subscribed.

There remains the culmination of the festivities; the match between M.C.C., its team drawn from current county players regardless of nationality, and the Rest of the World. On this may Providence look kindly; fair weather, a good match worthy of the occasion, and—dare one hope?—something distinguished in the way of English participation.

GRAEME POLLOCK – A RETROSPECTIVE
[1988]
BY CHARLES FORTUNE

Engaging essays seemed to be in a temporary decline in the almanack, which, in 1988, offered only one which commends itself to an anthology. This took the form of a summary of a career broken at its outset by the engines of political strife. Graeme Pollock had by 1965 shown enough of himself to tempt people to regard him as the most gifted left-handed batsman of all time. But then, memories are notoriously short. When Ian Botham was rewriting the record books and comparisons were being made with Sobers, almost no newspaper so much as mentioned the names of Rhodes and Hirst. It was the same scenario repeated when Pollock arrived on the scene. He certainly was a batting genius. But so was Frank Woolley by all accounts, and Clem Hill, and in a different mould, Philip Mead. It must be accounted a tragedy of the modern game that when he was still in his mid-twenties, Pollock found himself excluded from Test cricket. The highest tribute I can pay him is that when he was batting with Sobers in the Rest-of-the-World Tests of the 1970s, the eye kept flicking from one to the other, and not, as was usual in those days, remaining focused on Sobers.

GRAEME Pollock, the great South African batsman who too soon was denied occupation of cricket's more illustrious creases, retired from the first-class game at the end of the 1986–87 season. In January 1961, aged 16 years and 335 days, he scored his first Currie Cup century in Johannesburg, for Eastern Province against Transvaal B. Twenty-six summers later, with a score of 63 not out and now playing for Transvaal, he was there at the finish of the match which saw his team retain the Castle Currie Cup.

Heredity and environment each supposed that the Pollock brothers should go to the top in cricket. Their father, morning paper editor in the seaport where his family grew up, played for the Orange Free State. The mother, an all-round games player of renown, came of a father who rose in cricket administration to a term of office as president of the South African Cricket Association. Frequently the family moved house, but always there was space for a practice wicket to be set down; for the brothers to bat and bowl through sun-drenched days. And should their contests become heated, always there to arbitrate was Mrs. Pollock.

There is a similarity in the Pollock brothers' cricket background and that of W. G. Grace and his brothers. In both, the genes had given a touch of cricket to the blood. Environment lent itself to endless opportunity for practice, and there was a mother who saw only virtue in making her sons proficient. The analogy may be taken further. Right from their early schooldays, matches were played both with and against adult cricketers of some class.

Graeme, as did Peter, went as a day-boy to the Port Elizabeth High School, Grey College. 'The Grey' has ever had a special care for its cricketers, and Graeme soon found himself at the nets where George Cox, a kindly, able and inspiring man from Sussex, was in charge. Just nine, Graeme was picked for the school's Under-eleven team. The venue was Graaff Reinet, a farming centre 150 miles distant. Bowling, he took all ten wickets; and then he scored the first century to come from his bat. Thus, while himself not yet into double figures, as a batsman he reached his first hundred. Peter, seventeen, beat his brother to a Nuffield South African Schools' cap, but junior came alongside a year later, aged but fifteen.

During the school summer vacation of 1960–61, and free from studies he did not relish, Graeme Pollock set out on his first-class cricket career with Eastern Province. His maiden century was entirely in keeping with the massive scores to follow; never once did this lanky, loose-limbed school-boy deviate from the business of scoring runs. On Wanderers, the ground that was eventually to become his cricket home, the Transvaal B bowlers were irked that this 'kid' should calmly and methodically press ever onwards. As he neared his hundred, the bowling became more physical and the batsman more mature. Pollock, in that maiden hundred, moved through the nineties with never a hesitation; as though, as indeed was so, to the manner born. He was not yet seventeen.

He was nineteen when chosen for the 1963–64 South African tour of Australia. On arrival in Western Australia, he was soon to learn that life with the Aussies is ever real. McKenzie bowled him first for 1 and then caught and bowled him for 0. Before the Springboks left Perth, however, Pollock showed his class, reaching a hundred in 88 minutes, with eighteen fours, against a Combined XI. His Test debut came at Brisbane on December 6, 1963, but this was no happy match. Much interrupted by rain, it was the worse troubled by the abrupt end to a long-established Australian bowler's career. The South African innings had reached but the second ball of the second over on the second day when umpire Egar at square leg no-balled Ian Meckiff four times, and he did not bowl again. That rain pouring down unceasingly on the third day somehow seemed appropriate to a wretched episode in what might have been a noble occasion.

Pollock came into his own in the Third Test on the Sydney Cricket Ground. His brother, Peter, having taken five first-innings Australian wickets for 83, Graeme made 122; his maiden Test century. Thus did the Sydney Cricket Ground set the pattern for the brotherly duets that became the hallmark of South Africa's Test matches. That match was drawn, and with the Australians one up from victory at Melbourne, the series moved on to Adelaide, where South Africa won by ten wickets.

All else in that Test gave place to the Barlow-Graeme Pollock third-wicket partnership. Coming together on the Saturday with three hours till close of play, they added 225. Adelaide, most genial of great cricket grounds, was on this Saturday packed to overflowing. No cloud in the sky, his partner well set, the younger Pollock moved through early assurance into total command. McKenzie, Hawke, Benaud could find nothing to halt or hinder his surging strokeplay. My broadcasting companion for the series was the renowned Australian captain, and grandsire of famous Australian cricketers, Victor Richardson. Came the moment when I glanced his way, indicating it was now his turn to talk, his response was a shaking of the head and a murmured 'No, no, you carry on.' So captivated was this veteran stalwart that tiny tears of ecstasy shone in the corners of his eyes. He wanted only to sit back, the more fully to relish that day's batting. Never will one seasoned and long experienced in cricket confrontation pay a more sincere tribute to a young man than Victor Richardson spontaneously paid to Graeme Pollock that day.

Before 1964 had run its course, M. J. K. Smith and his M.C.C. team had arrived in South Africa. Two good teams on slow wickets meandered through a dreary five-match series. England won at Durban, the first of the Tests, and Pollock was out twice to Titmus for 5 and 0. Of his eight dismissals in the five Tests, three went to Titmus and three to Allen; off-spinners both. There were times, bowling round the wicket and pushing the ball across him, when they seemed to be questioning the orthodoxy of his strict adherence to a sideways-on position. Against this, however, they, like all who bowled at him, were met by his marvellous judgement of length. Rarely was he brought forward unless the ball was there to play.

The power and the beauty of his batting came again in the last of the Tests on his home ground in Port Elizabeth. With one defeat and three drawn Tests, Port Elizabeth offered a last chance for South Africa, as in 1956–57, to square the series. Pollock made scores of 137 and 77 not out. Barlow and Bland, both in fine form throughout the rubber, could be kept in check by England's bowlers, but not Pollock. His driving into the covers had fieldsmen occasionally wringing their hands or, more often, groping in vain for the ball travelling hell-bent to the boundary. Several off-drives were self-retrieving. There is a low retaining wall, with a smooth cement surface, just beyond the boundary at long-off for the left-hander. Pollock's drives from it rebounded back towards the stumps at the bowler's end.

Rain put an early end to a scene set for a fighting finish to the series, but in July that year the contest was being resumed in England. Victory at Trent Bridge in the second of the three Tests gave South Africa the rubber; and that victory was a Pollock family affair. Graeme scored 125 and 59 while Peter took five wickets in each England innings: ten for 87 in all.

It is for his batting at Trent Bridge in 1965 that, in England, Graeme Pollock is best remembered; and this was the batting of a player only 21 years old. Of his hundred there, *Wisden* said that following the lunch break '. . . he reigned supreme for seventy more minutes while he lashed the bowling for 91 out of 102 . . . he offered no chance'. The power and the artistry of his strokeplay that day was awesome. Using his height (6ft 2½in) to full advantage, he drove the English bowling, off back foot and front, through the covers, regardless of length. The ball to which other batsmen would have offered a defensive bat was simply struck to the boundary. Ted Dexter later wrote of him: '. . . he could hit the good-length ball, given only a modicum of room outside the off stump, actually harder than he could hit the half-volley. Now that takes some doing.'

Across the world cricket scene, that was pretty much the end for South Africa. Pollock was to play twice more against Australia in South Africa— Bobby Simpson's side in 1966–67 and Bill Lawry's in 1969–70—and he was in England in 1970 for the series between England and the Rest of the World, which took the place of the cancelled tour by South Africa. A century in the fifth 'Test', which incorporated with Garry Sobers a fifth-wicket partnership of 165, was his one big innings. His scores for eight innings averaged 31.25 and were below those of the other Springbok batsmen, Barlow, Procter and Richards.

At home, however, Pollock was consistently a heavy scorer, and in the two series with Australia he was often brilliant. Against Simpson's team came double-century at Newlands. Four years later, when Lawry brought his team on from India, Pollock at Durban made 274 in the only South African innings and established a new record score by a South African in Test cricket. Thereafter, his and South Africa's international cricket were to be restricted to home series against 'breakaway' visitors from England, Sri Lanka, the West Indies and Australia. The innings of 144 against an Australian XI with which he bowed out of international cricket in Port Elizabeth in 1986–87 was both convincing and memorable; it seemed hard to think of him as being 43 in three to four weeks' time.

If it is permissible to attach the word 'genius' to the artistry of a batsman, then Graeme Pollock is such among cricketers. Like others so acknowledged he was ever the master craftsman. Perhaps the all-important factor was that from the start, the bowling he faced was more skilled and demanding than will have come the way of many others. Only Colin Cowdrey among the cricketers I have known has moved so easily up the rungs that take cricket toddlers to a Test match debut. Pollock never underestimated the opposition, nor hesitated to meet a challenge. When thirteen, he became excited, even entranced, by the skill and application of the Australian, Neil Harvey, like himself a left-handed batsman. It was Harvey's dedication to the task of making runs, and still more runs, that determined Pollock never to yield his wicket while runs were there to be taken.

His move from Eastern Province to Transvaal in 1978–79 undoubtedly enriched and extended his playing days. So, too, did the SACU move that brought the 'breakaway' touring teams to South Africa. Graeme Pollock, a supporter of full tours to South Africa by unofficial teams of international standard, is established in cricket administration: president of the South

African Cricket Players' Association, board member and team selector with the Transvaal Cricket Council. We shall not see his like again at the crease, but he may yet become a prominent figure in cricket's council chambers.

FIVE CRICKETERS OF THE YEAR [1988]

A few years ago, after I had completed the four volumes of my anthology of Wisden's *Almanack since its inception in 1864, my publishers innocently inquired after further volumes. There were two possibilities which occurred to me, one obvious, the other less so but more practicable. To compile a volume consisting in its entirety of the essays published as 'Five Cricketers of the Year' sounded a dazzlingly attractive proposition. But in the end I opted for the second, more sensible choice, a book of the* Wisden *obituaries. My reason was that the essays on the outstanding new players of each season are pleasurable to read but must by their very nature be incomplete. Cricketers are selected for the honour the moment they attain a certain pre-eminence over their fellows, a rise which almost always takes place on the threshold of greatness. This means that the essays tell nothing of what happened next, of how the genius burst into full flower, if it withered on the vine. To put it another way, the record is woefully incomplete. Consider the fact that Bradman was given the accolade in 1931, Hutton in 1938, Denis Compton in 1939, Bill Edrich in 1940, Botham in 1978. The most ironic date of all attaches to Harold Larwood, who was included among the 'Five Cricketers of the Year' in 1927, five years before Douglas Jardine so benignly changed the course of his life.*

'Five Cricketers of the Year' is perhaps less a tribute to greatness than an exercise in prediction, and it must be said that in the hundred years covering the feature, Wisden's *score has been very high. However, it is the failures which are often the most intriguing, and the reader of Anthony Bradbury's review of the series can hardly fail to be moved by the sadly obscure fate of H. L. Calder of Cranleigh School, a fast-medium bowler whose father played for Hampshire. Mr. Bradbury mentions a few of the anomalies which have accumulated over the years, but fails to make any reference to the comicality of the most spectacular backhanded tribute ever paid by any almanack to any important, not to say self-important figure. The reader, if he cares to refer to the 1909 almanack, will find, not 'Five Cricketers of the Year', but 'Lord Hawke and Four Cricketers of the Year'.*

JONATHAN AGNEW

The Lancashire and former England opening batsman, David Lloyd, was halfway through a forward defensive push when his off stump was despatched halfway towards the Leicestershire wicket-keeper. It was

August 1978, and with his fourth delivery in county cricket, a gangling eighteen year old just out of Uppingham School had discovered that he had enough pace to bother Test players as well as sixth formers. By the close of the season, that same bowler, Jonathan Agnew, had won a Whitbread scholarship to Australia, and when invited to an England net in Melbourne, he struck the captain, Mike Brearley, a nasty blow in the face. It was, Agnew recalls, merely a gentle delivery off two paces that flew off a wet patch; but it did not deter the headline writers. Such early publicity did him no favours, but when a bowler arrives who is young, fast and English, a quiet settling-in period to one of the more difficult apprenticeships in sport is often denied him.

It was, therefore, only after some seasons of high promise but relatively modest delivery that JONATHAN PHILIP AGNEW realised his early potential and developed into a Test-match bowler. Born in Macclesfield on April 4, 1960, he was capped three times in 1984 and 1985, but it was not until last summer that he fully matured as a bowler. He took 101 wickets, the first Leicestershire player to take 100 since Jack Birkenshaw nineteen years earlier, and in doing so he helped his side recover from a disastrous start to third place in the County Championship. For reasons best known to themselves, the England selectors did not consider this good enough to earn Agnew a place on any of the three separate winter tours—to the World Cup, Pakistan or New Zealand.

Asked about Agnew's omission, the chairman of selectors, P. B. H. May, expressed concern about his fitness—rather a baffling statement to make about someone who bowled more overs than any other fast bowler in the Championship. There had been a time when the air at Grace Road would reverberate not just to the sound of leather upon willow, but also to the twanging of an Agnew hamstring; but the days had long since gone when the names of Agnew and another injury-prone Test player, Les Taylor, together on the same scorecard would startle collectors of memorabilia. ('Swap you an Agnew and a Taylor for a Ward and Shuttleworth?')

After four or five seasons of injury problems, probably the result of trying to bowl too fast, Agnew had by and large remained fit since 1983. But the injury-prone image had unfortunately stuck. He has never, for example, had back problems, although one annual cricket publication last year described that as the reason for long absences in his second season. He has had the occasional pulled muscle, which is a difficult achievement for someone with scarcely a muscle about his person. At almost 6ft 4in, he barely tips the scales at twelve stone, and this despite a gargantuan appetite which involves anything between three and six cooked meals a day. His pace comes from a whippy wrist action and co-ordination.

In the field, Agnew has at times appeared to be moving with his bootlaces tied together, but his long run-up was one of the more graceful in the game. However, it was the shortening of that run-up, and a cutting-down of pace, which led to last season's achievements—and, following James Whitaker, to his becoming the second Old Uppinghamian in consecutive years to be named one of *Wisden's* Cricketers of the Year.

Agnew had more often than not been given choice of ends with the new ball at Grace Road. This was invariably down the slope towards the pavilion, and with the prevailing wind. However, that became less automatic with the signing of the West Indian fast bowler, Winston Benjamin, and the advance of Phillip DeFreitas. An early-season game against Somerset saw Agnew running up the hill and into a gale. He cut down his run, strove for accuracy rather than pace, and took wickets. He has always been able to swing the ball, but he was often wayward off a full run. Now, by adhering to a fuller length, he became more dangerous, knowing that batsmen would remain reluctant to get forward with a full commitment because of his past reputation. And just to remind them of it, he could still produce the quick short delivery to force a sharp reappraisal of footwork. He also developed, and took many wickets with, an extremely effective slower ball.

Like DeFreitas at Middlesex, Agnew slipped through the coaching net at another county. He attended Alf Gover's school at Surrey at the age of sixteen, and played for two seasons during the summer holidays for Surrey's Second XI. Not a lot of interest was shown, he recalled, and it was probably only a coincidence that the coach at The Oval, Fred Titmus, was dismissed soon after Agnew's dramatic start with Leicestershire. He had been recommended to them by the senior coach at Uppingham, Les Berry, himself a former Leicestershire player, and secretary-manager Mike Turner arranged four times to see Agnew play. Because it rained or he did not bowl, he never did; so he signed him anyway on Berry's reputation as a judge of young cricketers.

Agnew was close to giving up the game in 1986, when he discovered that he was not enjoying it as he felt he ought to. He was also considering a career outside the game, preferably in the media, and that winter he joined the sports staff at BBC Radio Leicester, becoming in time a Sports Producer. He approached 1987 as his farewell season, but with the return of success and enjoyment, he has set his mind on attempting to regain an England place.

It will not, in all probability, be as an all-rounder, although he can certainly bat. After a bad injury, sustained in South Africa some years ago, fast bowlers have sometimes needed radar to locate him; but on his day he can destroy anything pitched up around off stump. He did so last season during his career-best 90 at Scarborough, while at the same time demonstrating that the Agnew of old, playing hard but always with a sense of fun, had resurfaced. When Leicestershire's captain, Peter Willey, came in to join his night-watchman, who was by then in the eighties, Agnew waited for him to take guard before walking down for a tactical discussion. 'Now then, Will,' he said, 'just look for the ones and give me the strike. I'm in a bit of nick out here, you know.'—Martin Johnson.

NEIL FOSTER

Although a good enough bowler to make his county debut as an eighteen year old still at school, and then picked for a full overseas England tour three years later, Neil Foster nevertheless took seven years to graduate from being considered a player with Test potential to holding down a regular place in the England side in 1987. In the intervening years there was a brief flirtation with a career in soccer, a serious spinal injury, and sparse Test appearances which gave him too little time to establish himself.

In an age when state-controlled comprehensive schools were devoting more and more time to soccer, and less attention to cricket, NEIL ALAN FOSTER, born at Colchester on May 6, 1962, needed a keen cricketing father to maintain his interest in the summer game. At Philip Morant School in Colchester, Foster in his early teens was a tall, fast centre-forward, later turned central defender, who attracted the interest of the local Football League side. School cricket was, in the main, limited to twenty-over games after lessons, and Foster's development owed more to contacts at the nearby grammar school, who pushed him forward to the Essex Schools Under-14 side, and to his family.

Raised in the Essex village of Wivenhoe, Foster from a tender age was performing twelfth-man duties for the local club, where his father, Alan, was considered the 'Geoff Boycott' of the side. Foster says, 'He was a keen, if somewhat deliberate opening batsman, gentle in-swing bowler and immensely proud of his achievements at club level.' Later they switched to another Essex side, Mistley, where Foster from the age of fourteen began to develop the high upright action that was to become the hallmark of his bowling in the years that followed. Impressive performances for Essex at the 1979 county youth festival at Cambridge, and a handful of Second XI games during the summer holidays, led to his being offered a two-year contact by Essex the following spring, and within weeks he made his first-class debut.

It was on the night of his eighteenth birthday that Foster was summoned to Ilford to join an injury-hit side to play Kent the following day. With insufficient Second XI games under his belt to qualify for a cap or a sweater, he had to borrow equipment, and his career began inauspiciously when his first delivery produced four wides. 'I'd only been used to the soft grounds of club cricket up until then, and on the harder Ilford surface I lost my footing in the delivery stride,' he recalled. Fortunately his confidence did not suffer and he quickly claimed two impressive scalps. England Test batsmen Bob Woolmer and Chris Tavare—the latter fresh from scoring 84 and 115 against Essex in the M.C.C. match at Lord's—both fell to catches behind the wicket. In a later spell he also accounted for century-maker Alan Ealham, but even though he finished the innings with three for 51, it was to be his only Championship match until the start of the 1982 season.

Leaving school with six 'O' levels and one 'A', he was offered a two-week soccer trial the following winter with Ipswich, then managed by Bobby Robson, who was later to take charge of the England side. Eventually the trial lasted nearer three months while Robson tried to make up his mind whether Foster would make the grade as a professional footballer. With no decision forthcoming before Essex returned for pre-season training, he left Portman Road and played very little soccer thereafter. As a diversion from cricket, he later turned to golf with his wife, Romany, and at the end of last season was playing off a handy 16.

His only outing for Essex in 1981 was against the Sri Lankan tourists, but he made a big enough impression while playing for Young England against Young India to be awarded a Whitbread Scholarship, which sent him that winter to the Tasmanian club side, Glenorchy. There he began to suffer the occasional bout of back stiffness, which deteriorated on his return home. Specialists diagnosed stress fractures in two vertebrae near the base of his spine, and for three months he was forced to wear a corset of plaster as doctors hoped the injury would heal by itself. By September 1982, however, there was no improvement, and surgeons opted to insert two six-inch metal plates, secured by four screws, in his back.

Three months later, one of those screws had to be removed after it worked loose, but after supervised rehabilitation at a clinic in Clacton, he was passed fit to start the 1983 season with Essex. In August he was picked for his Test debut against New Zealand at Lord's. By his own admission Foster did not bowl well in the match, claiming only the wicket of Jeremy Coney while conceding 75 runs in two innings. But there were extenuating circumstances. Shortly before the game, X-rays showed that another screw had loosened, and with a blood blister evident he was forced to have fluid drained from his spine twice a day during the Test. The match ended inside four days, and by the following Friday Foster was back in hospital having the plates and two abscesses removed. Fortunately it was to be almost six months before England began their winter tour to New Zealand and Pakistan, so giving Foster time to rebuild the strength in his back, despite the lack of a support.

For the next three years Foster was to be the yo-yo man of English cricket, popping up at home for the Lord's Tests of 1984 and 1985, but at least having the satisfaction of making each winter tour and producing match-winning figures of eleven for 163 against India at Madras on a pitch that had broken the hearts of many other pacemen.

Although with his late movement away from the bat Foster picked up 105 wickets for Essex in 1986, and was picked for England's tour of Australia, he failed to play in a Test and decided to reappraise his attitude towards playing for England. 'I decided at the start of the 1987 series against Pakistan that if I got into the England team, I would simply try to produce my county form. In my early Tests I always felt on trial, and as a result tended to try to bowl defensively. Whereas with Essex I had always been regarded as an attacking bowler.'

Bristling with an aggression which belies the soft burr of his East Anglian accent, Foster finally broke through at Leeds, where he took eight for 107 in 46.2 overs and emerged with credit from a match which England lost by an innings. Retained throughout the series, he finished the summer as England's leading wicket-taker with fifteen victims at an average of 22.60.

Although Essex's fortunes had fallen into sharp decline, Foster still took 86 first-class wickets in 1987, and with Ian Botham unavailable and Graham Dilley unfit, Foster, a mere onlooker in Australia less than twelve months earlier, departed with England for the World Cup in India and Pakistan as the side's leading strike bowler. His place in the side was strengthened by several useful late-order innings, in which he hit hard with a straight bat, and a growing reputation as an athletic outfielder with a strong, low return.—Graham Otway.

DAVID HUGHES

In the middle of the 1986 season David Hughes was considering retiring from first-class county cricket. He was 39, in the second team, and for two years he had felt he was no longer in Lancashire's first-team plans. He held back his letter of resignation as he led the second team to their championship, and within weeks he had been appointed captain of the county, one of the more surprising appointments in the club's 123-year history. It so shocked one former captain that he threatened to return his cap, blazer and sweaters. He described the decision as the worst he had ever known the club make.

It was a bold appointment. There had been no significant change in the team in 1986 under Clive Lloyd, the most successful Test captain of modern times, and Lancashire looked doomed to another season of desperation, another summer among the bottom teams in the County Championship. 'I know I can't be around a long time,' said Hughes at the time. 'I can't go down in history as a great Lancashire captain. All I want is to see Lancashire moving up again, to restore the pride in the county. Too many people consider us a laughing stock.'

As well as making Hughes captain, the committee appointed the second-team coach, Alan Ormrod, as coach/manager. Hughes and Ormrod's approach was positive and clear. Hughes made a point of speaking to each player before the season started and told them what was required. In essence, everybody was to give 100 per cent for Lancashire, and ill discipline would not be tolerated. Before the season started he promised, as many captains do, to play positive, attacking, entertaining cricket, always to be prepared to lose in order to force a win. Unlike most pre-season promises, he managed to stick to his from start to finish, and he led Lancashire in their attempt to become outright champions for the first time in 53 years, a challenge which failed by only four points.

Hughes's contribution as a batsman was disappointing, as a bowler non-existent, but as a captain inspirational and commanding. When he learnt he had been chosen as one of *Wisden's* Cricketers of the Year, he was staggered, 'Perhaps I have underestimated my own contributions,' he said.

DAVID PAUL HUGHES was born in Newton-le-Willows in South Lancashire on May 13, 1947, son of Lloyd Hughes, who had been a professional cricketer in the Bolton League. He was educated at Newton-le-Willows Grammar School, played for the town team in the Manchester Association and later joined Farnworth in the Bolton League. His introduction to the county was through the Club and Ground team in 1965 when he was eighteen, and two years later, when he was leading wicket-taker in the second team, he made his first-class debut, against Oxford

University at Old Trafford. Jack Bond started his successful five-year run as captain in 1968—he was only 35—and gave Hughes the opportunity to establish himself in the side. He took the chance and played in 23 of the 30 first-class matches, a promising left-arm spinner who took 31 wickets at 22.80 each but whose batting average of 14.48 hardly justified a position often as high as No.7 in the order. The veteran off-spinner, John Savage, was his spinning partner that year. In 1969, the start of Lancashire's really successful period, it was Jack Simmons. The two of them quickly struck up a partnership which was to help take Lancashire to two John Player League championships and three Gillette Cup wins, all between 1969 and 1972.

Hughes's best years as a bowler were under Bond's care, his peak coming in 1970 and 1971 when he bowled more than 800 overs and took 82 first-class wickets each season. He took 296 wickets in the five years Bond was captain. Since then, under four other captains, he has only once exceeded 50 wickets in a season in first-class matches. He had taken 585 wickets for Lancashire by the end of the 1982 season, but in the next five claimed only seven. As his bowling declined, so his batting blossomed, enabling him to reach 1,000 runs in a season for the first time in 1981. He followed this the next year with his best all-round season, averaging 48.25 with the bat and topping Lancashire's bowling averages with 31 wickets at 24.45 each. But he was unable to maintain that performance and gradually slipped into a more regular place in the second team than the first . . . until his leadership qualities came through to persuade the committee to give him the daunting task of rejuvenating Lancashire.

Hughes once said he hoped he would not be for ever remembered only for his innings against Gloucestershire in the semi-final of the Gillette Cup in 1971, when he turned the match by hitting John Mortimore for 24 runs in one over. 'I am mainly a bowler and that is how I would like to be remembered,' he said. Perhaps, too, he will be recalled in years to come for his captaincy—Brian Bearshaw.

PETER ROEBUCK

For most of his 32 years, Peter Roebuck has nursed a burning ambition to be a highly successful member of a successful Somerset side. He played an important part in their emergence as a cricketing force when five limited-overs titles were won between 1979 and 1983, the first trophies in Somerset's long, diverting history. And he took a leading role in the rebuilding of the club after the divisive Richards-Garner-Botham controversy of 1986. His performance—as spokesman, batsman and captain—was vital to the 1987 improvement after that sad, vituperative episode.

His commitment stemmed from a fierce, competitive nature, based on a critical analysis of all the factors involved and the determination and talent to put his decisions to the test. His current vice-captain, Victor Marks, a friend of many years, said, 'He seems to thrive on contest, competition and conflict. He rises to the occasion, is very much alive and always reacts in a positive way. He has improved dramatically over the past few years, with the security of his position and the captaincy. He puts a great deal more energy into his job than most people could.' Somerset's coach, Peter Robinson, recalled many hours spent with the bowling machine, ironing out technical faults which he, Roebuck, had found.

Known for some time as a rather dour, studious, and bespectacled batsman, he revealed another side of his nature through his witty, pointed observations in his writings for a number of outlets. And in 1987, as he extended his range of strokes and even hit ten sixes, his batting has displayed a new dimension. 'I now go in trying to take the initiative,' he said, 'instead of waiting for things to develop.' The hundred he scored when his index finger was broken at Headingley in May was his fourth in all competitions in a thirteen-day period, and when he returned to the side after that injury, he took his tally of first-class hundreds to five. Only Hick, Athey, Crowe and Gatting hit more. He missed by a single run averaging 50 for the season.

Born in Oxford on March 6, 1956, PETER MICHAEL ROEBUCK, one of six children of schoolteachers, grew up initially in a third-floor flat in Bath. His father was a cricket enthusiast, his mother kept wicket for Oxford University ladies; one of his sisters later captained that team. Yet when it was apparent how badly bitten he was by the cricket bug—in the 1960s when professional cricket was at a very low ebb—it was felt he should be dissuaded from pursuing cricket as a living. Perhaps, it was thought, if he were hit and hurt by a cricket ball, he might share the view. Consequently, he was taken to Peter Wight's indoor school at Bath, was hit, hurt and taken to hospital. 'When I came back, I wanted to play just as much.' That was the first hurdle overcome.

'I was completely wrapped up in Somerset cricket from about the age of ten, but one way of practising was soon stopped.' Hitting a plastic ball against the wall of an adjoining flat, and giving a running commentary, was useful training. Unfortunately, the adjoining flat was used by a group holding séances ('trying to get in contact with Aunt Doris's poodle', suggested Roebuck), and having quite misinterpreted the tappings and the voice, they were very cross when the real source was discovered.

As his cricket came on in Bath junior circles, his parents decided to seek a scholarship at Millfield School, the nursery of many budding sportsmen. The first thing he saw when opening the study door of the founder, the highly individual R. J. O. Meyer, was an orange coming at him. He caught it. The intelligence test that followed he found totally incomprehensible, but the results were momentous for the family. Peter, his younger brother, and two of his sisters were given free scholarships, his parents were taken on the staff, and they were given a house in Street.

Quickly he appeared in the Somerset Second XI, 'as a four foot two leg-spinner, with a good googly, who batted No. 11 with a sound technique but not enough strength to get runs against far bigger chaps'. He was thirteen. In due course he went to Cambridge, worked hard for a degree (he ended with a First Class Honours in Law) and continued with the cricket he loved. He made 158 in the 1975 University Match, against Vic Marks, and both were in the Oxford and Cambridge side which beat Yorkshire in the Benson and Hedges Cup the next year.

However, 1976 brought another steep hurdle. The pace of the West Indian fast bowler, Andy Roberts, was outside Roebuck's experience at the time. Opening the innings for the Combined side at Fenner's, he ducked into a bouncer and, although feeling fairly well, was taken to hospital. A nurse, shown where he was hit, said, 'Another quarter of an inch the other way and you'd have been a goner.' Roebuck returned to the crease, and soon Roberts knocked his cap off. He went away, and in a dark room, playing a Joni Mitchell record, he realised that if he wanted to play first-class cricket, he had a lot to learn. He reckoned he had the talent, reflexes and ability to do it, so methodically he worked out what to do and how to do it. 'Perhaps the most courageous thing I've done,' he thinks. 'You never know until you've been hit like that—the smell of leather, you know.'

Life with Somerset was not always easy. So many remarkable characters surrounded him, making him even more withdrawn, but his first full season in 1978 was a success. Then came the triumphant Somerset period. He had never thought about captaining Somerset, but in 1983, when the World Cup required Botham, Marks, Richards and Garner, he found himself captaining a young side when Brian Rose was injured. The players reacted well, Roebuck enjoyed it, and subsequently he became involved in the broader issues of the club.

The rumblings of the 1986 row were present even then. 'Too many people taking and not giving,' and 'Too many people putting their heads in too much sand for too long.' He rationalised it, made his decision—'the most difficult and painful I've ever taken'—and helped to carry it through. Now Roebuck's ambitions are simple. 'I want to see Somerset the best club in the land and winning the Championship. Oh, I'd also like to get in the top ten of Somerset run-scorers.'

One of the best rewards of 1987, he said, was to note how great bowlers such as Marshall, Hadlee and Clarke seemed to bowl better at him than at others. 'It can be uncomfortable, but I take it as a challenge—and as a compliment when I see how they look when they've got my wicket.'—Eric Hill.

SALIM MALIK

In recent Test Matches, Headingley has been a proving ground for the techniques of English and visiting batsmen. There the swinging and seaming ball sifts out the orthodox wheat. In 1986, when India defeated England at Headingley, the exposition of classical technique was given by Dilip Vengsarkar; last year, when Pakistan defeated England in the Test which settled the series, it was given by MUHAMMAD SALIM MALIK.

Brought up as they have been on pitches of unswerving rectitude, by no means all Pakistani batsmen have been models of orthodoxy. Zaheer Abbas gladly redirected the straight ball through cover-point, while Javed Miandad has been prone to whip it to leg with his dominant right hand. In the batting of Salim Malik, their heir-apparent as Pakistan's master batsman, there may be found a dedication to playing straight.

Salim gives thanks to his first coach for instilling in him this orthodoxy.

Born in Lahore on April 16, 1963, the son of a Punjabi engaged in exporting linen-wear to Europe, he was taken when twelve by his elder brother to the Victorious Club in Iqbal Park. There he bowled leg-spin until the club coach, Rabb Nawaz, decided he could bat better than he could bowl. The coach then told him that the cut and the hook were the two riskiest strokes in cricket, and advised him to concentrate on hitting the ball in the 'V' between mid-on and mid-off. It has been Salim's guiding principle ever since.

Developing at the precocious rate which seems almost to be the norm in that part of the cricket world, he was selected at sixteen for a Pakistan Under-19 tour of India and Sri Lanka. He made his first-class debut for Lahore against Customs, and in his second match he scored a century against Muslim Commercial Bank. More significant, Salim thinks, was his performance for Pakistan Under-19s when they were hosts to the Australian Under-19s; with the matches being televised, he received wide exposure as Pakistan's leading run-scorer. As one for the future, he was taken on Pakistan's full tour to Australia in 1981–82. 'I was very confused, there were so many senior players,' he explains in improving English, his third language after Punjabi and Urdu. But on returning to Pakistan, those senior players revolted against the captaincy of Miandad and were dropped from the Test side. Salim was chosen as one of the replacements, made his Test debut against Sri Lanka at Karachi, and hit a hundred, at 18 years and 328 days the youngest Pakistani to have done so on debut.

Subsequently he did not score runs in a quantity befitting his technique or talent; yet Salim was still putting together a promising portfolio of Test centuries, with an average in the early forties, when a ball from Courtney Walsh reared from Faisalabad's re-laid pitch and hit him above the left wrist. It was the October 1986 Test match in which West Indies were dismissed for their lowest ever total of 53. Pakistan, having been 37 for five, were being rallied by Salim and Imran Khan when the fracture happened. In Pakistan's second innings, when runs were still vital, Salim batted left-handed at No. 11 for one ball and then right-handed in a stand of 32. He missed the rest of the series and, still bothered by stiffness in his left wrist, never got going in the following Test series in India.

However, on that tour of India, which preceded Pakistan's visit to England, he did play a one-day innings that was a wonder of its kind. In front of a capacity crowd in Calcutta, India were coasting to victory when Salim came in, for Pakistan had to score 78 in less than eight overs. He found it one of those magical days when the bowler pitched exactly where Salim wanted, and he proceeded to hit an unbeaten 72 from 35 balls, the best innings of its length in one-day internationals.

When he came to English pitches, he found he had to modify not his technique but his attitude. 'I have a short temper but I learnt to be patient in England, to be more defensive and wait for the bad ball.' He got out for 99 at Headingley in the last over of the day, he says, because he was nervous after not making a century for eighteen Tests. (He had hit five centuries in his first 21.) It eventually came two Tests later at The Oval, during a stand of 234 with Miandad.

A brilliant out-fielder with a pinpoint throw, Salim had to convert to first slip in England for want of anyone else. He did not like having to do the job with cold hands, but did well enough until the last morning of the series, when an edge from Gatting slipped out. As a slow in-swing bowler he has performed occasionally for Habib Bank, his present team, under the captaincy of Miandad, and he has not forgotten completely his leg-breaks.

An unmarried Muslim, Salim lives in Lahore and prays whenever cricket allows. During the World Cup, one of his prayers was answered by Imran, who let him bat at No. 3, the position he had wanted for a long time. But wherever he bats for Pakistan, Salim Malik has the class to score many runs for many years to come in model style.—Scyld Berry.

WE ALREADY KNEW HE COULD BAT [1989]

Graeme Hick in 1988

BY PETER ROEBUCK

The best writing to be found in the 1989 almanack came from Peter Roebuck, who, one day in the previous summer, had had the mixed blessing of fielding out to Worcestershire while their Rhodesian prodigy Graeme Hick was registering the first quadruple century in the county championship since Archie MacLaren's 424 for Lancashire, again against Somerset in 1895. It is well known that the Worcestershire captain declared with Hick's tally still nineteen short of MacLaren's record. The reason why he declared ought to be a stinging reproach to the Association of Cricket Statisticians, who must have been scandalised to read that nobody knew anything about MacLaren's mark at the time Hick was set fair to pass it.

For some years now, all England has been awaiting impatiently the day when Hick ceases to be Rhodesian and changes magically into an Englishman. This miracle is scheduled for April 1st, 1991, and those who see symbolism in the day and the month will no doubt enjoy a smile. Hick is a player of beauty and correctitude, not at all the insolent swashbuckler that Barry Richards used to be, nor the savage destroyer Vivian Richards still occasionally is. He has apparently infinite composure, and, if he means to go on as he as started, will soon be marching up the list of those who have scored a century of centuries.

IN 1895 one Archie MacLaren arrived in Taunton to meet a Somerset eleven led by Sammy Woods, a local legend. Archie hadn't faced any bowler over fourteen years of age for five weeks, but his dad was in the crowd so he wanted to do well. Only by a squeak did he survive his first ball. A day and a half later he lobbed a catch and walked off. He'd scored 424. Gamlin was the bowler, one of nine tried. Gamlin wasn't much of a cricketer. Sam told his chums at the Clarke's Tap that he was playing 'on account of being good at rugby'. Sam was that sort of bloke. Somerset was that sort of county. And he was very good—at rugby.

MacLaren's score sat in the record books, speaking of the time as might a snuff box in a museum. In a changed world it reminded us of a past of Free Foresters and Devon Dumplings. It could not be done again, could it? Golly, even Somerset rarely fielded total incompetents these days. Besides, the fielding had improved, the ball had shrunk (1927) and the stumps had grown (1931). Big scores were still possible. Gimblett had hit 310 in 1948 and Viv Richards 322 in 1985, but no-one had approached 400 in county cricket since the old Queen died.

Had Worcestershire not declared at tea (there were no tea intervals in Archie's day) on May 6, 1988, MacLaren's record would have been broken. It is not for this writer to decide if Somerset's tactics were quite as sound as those of Mr. Woods, but it can be taken that our selection was rather more conservative. Moreover our fielding was good and the bowling did not flag until the second afternoon when the captain, seeing that the horse had bolted and emptied the yard besides, served up some atrocious swingers to which a tiring and expansive batsman nearly fell. Nothing was given away easily. Yet Hick scored 405 not out.

One thing had changed in 1988. Four-day cricket was being tried. Batsmen could bat for two days. Some were doing so. Already Gooch had plundered 275 off Kent; and that was just in the first innings. Hick was in form too, taking 212 off the Lancashire bowlers at Old Trafford. Around the counties, cricketers were staggered by the new scale of things. These scores were beyond contemplation. As it turned out, Hick was only warming up.

At Taunton, he was nearly out first ball, clipping a drive inches off the ground in front of square leg. Our man was patrolling behind square. I'd considered moving him for Hick but had let it be for a minute, a fatal delay. Only by a narrow squeak did he avoid playing on a few minutes later. On 148 he was dropped in the gully where, ironically, he was to be caught twice in the return gave a fortnight later. He never really gave Somerset a ghost of a chance until he'd passed 300. I never thought 300 could be written as if it were a staging-post. It takes me a month to score 300 runs.

Once or twice his leg shots were lifted, but they were hit with a power that was efficient rather than savage and they thundered through or over the field. Standing erect and immense yet never imperious, Hick boomed drives to mid-off or through extra cover—'not a man moved' shots—and he late-cut delicately. Throughout he ran fast between the wickets, throughout he used a bat so broad that bowlers felt as if they were trying to knock down a tank with a pea-shooter.

Yet there was never any sense of awesome personality in this awesome batting. Hick did not impose himself save as a batsman. From slip I saw a simple, straightforward fellow with a simple technique founded upon straight lines, power and fitness. Whenever possible he put his foot down the wicket and hit the ball hard. He was never as menacing as Viv Richards, whose saunter to the crease can have the effect upon a bowler that a bugle has upon a stag. Nor did Hick coil himself into an intensity of idea, execution and will as might Martin Crowe. No, he strode to the wicket as soon as Gordon Lord was out, took guard and began hitting the ball in order to score runs. He did not say much, and yet he was neither distant nor aloof. I never saw Walter Hammond bat, but I imagine he was something like this—authoritative, commanding, civil and durable.

At the crease Hick avoided flamboyance, eschewed the macho. Discipline was at the core of his game. If he was bowled a good ball he blocked it. Bad balls were hit. Unlike Richards or Botham he does not try to destroy a bowler's length. Unlike lesser batsmen he never gives his wicket away, whatever his score. Watching him, you cannot tell if he is on 10 or 210. He simply carries on. His game is as pure as a punched hole. It is this that frightens bowlers.

Most impressive of all, his 405 was a deeply unselfish innings. On a good pitch and in good weather his team had subsided to 132 for five. One mistake from Hick and they'd have been all out for a poor score. Yet after some hours of run-making Hick ran a fast 3 off the last ball of an over to give Newport an extra run and the strike. It was this sense of being in a team that caught our eye because it said so much about the man. We already knew he could bat.

Apart from its proportions, Hick's innings was not a masterpiece. He has acknowledged this. His hundred against a pounding West Indian attack on a dodgy Worcester wicket must have given him greater satisfaction, because there his technique, courage and temperament were stretched and did not break. And yet I wouldn't say this was his outstanding innings either, however significant it was. Hick's most important innings of the season was his last one, at home against Glamorgan with Kent breathing down Worcestershire's neck and the Championship at stake.

To win the title Worcestershire had to score 300 runs in their 100 overs on an unreliable surface. Glamorgan had scored 244. Their bowlers were in top form. Upon Hick's innings hung the destiny of the Championship. Of course the game was closely followed around the counties. At Taunton, the lunch scores were read over the loudspeaker as we tucked into saddle of lamb in the dining-room. 'Worcestershire 144 for three.' A colleague had time to utter the word 'Hick' before the announcer continued, 'Graeme Hick 74 not out'. A sigh went around the room, a reaction which spoke of the inevitability of things. It was as if we'd been told Liverpool had won the Football League. Whether joyful or sorry, no-one was surprised.

Hick scored 197 and Glamorgan were duly finished off next day. During the season Hick scored 3,684 runs in all cricket; 2,713 of them in all first-class matches, a record since fixtures were cut in 1969, and 2,443 in the Championship. His first-class total of 2,615 (average 79.24) for the county was only 39 runs short of Harold Gibbons's Worcestershire record of 2,654 (average 52.03) set in 1934. He equalled Glenn Turner's Worcestershire record by scoring ten hundreds, several of them on bad wickets, and his century against Glamorgan was the 34th first-class hundred of a young career. His strike-rate of innings per hundred is 5.29. Bradman's was 2.88, Ponsford and Woodfull's 5.00 and Vijay Merchant's 5.20; then comes Hick. Uniquely he holds four partnership records for Worcestershire—the second wicket with Curtis, sixth with Rhodes, seventh with Newport and the eighth with Illingworth. No other player holds more than three records for a county. Statistics trip off the page. And he's only 22. A retiring Somerset captain once said, 'God help my successor.' People bowling to Hick feel like that.

Hick suffered only two humps during the year. After his 405 not out, cameras followed him everywhere to record his reaching of 1,000 runs before the end of May. For a time he failed. Against Somerset at Worcester, he appeared agitated, rushing to the wicket, too aggressive. For once his batting was wild rather than measured. Accordingly he nearly didn't reach his target, and it was only his masterful innings against the West Indians that got him home. He needed 153 runs in that innings, an impossible target and yet, surviving one trenchant appeal, he reached it.

He failed in the NatWest Bank Trophy final. Fraser bowled fastish break-backs, searching for a crack between bat and pad and finding it with a scorcher. It was a good delivery. Fraser had denied Hick his drive, cramping him by banging the ball down the Lord's slope. So Hick did not mark a great occasion with a great innings. In fact, you'd hardly have known he was playing. Hick prefers it this way. Ego has no part in his cricket. He talks with his bat.

For Graeme Hick, though, it was a year of nearly undiluted success. He could have done no more. Yet before he can be regarded as truly great he must take command at Test level. It will not be easy. Even at county level bowlers are probing for an Achilles' heel. Some captains think he occasionally lifts his head as he drives and set a man in gully accordingly. But this involves bowling to his strength, and is a risk economically and, to mid-off, physically. Others try to contain him by angling the ball into his body, restricting his opportunities to hit on the rise, his particular joy. Hick pierces the off side as an arrow pierces a balloon, but his leg-side shots are a shade speculative. It is an area of hope, though the leg side is notoriously difficult to defend. Some consider Hick to be vulnerable to spin. One or two fast bowlers fancy rapping him on the gloves. To be frank it is all, like marriage, a triumph of hope over experience.

Test cricket awaits Hick. At Worcester Viv Richards saw a star on the rise. I wonder what he thought. Imran Khan has said that Hick might not be so effective at Test level because, like Zaheer Abbas, he is fundamentally a front-foot player. Yet maybe Zaheer disappointed for other reasons as well. Hick is a tough, strong character, a man with the courage to meet every challenge. He will, I believe, be a major force in Test cricket. After his final innings of the 1988 season, one Glamorgan player said he was 'Unbelievable. I'd never seen anything like it. He played and missed only three or four times. He didn't seem to get the balls others were getting.'

I don't think he ever will.

THE LAWRENCE AWARDS [1990]

Pioneers of Patronage
BY E. W. SWANTON

*To a schoolboy there cannot be enough whimsicalities, oddities, special-
isations, obscure prizes, to fill a cricket season, and to all of us who grew up
in the 1930s one of the richest delights of each season was the Lawrence
Trophy, awarded to the player who hit the fastest hundred in a first-class
match. We had no idea who Lawrence was, or even if there was such a
person. All we knew was that each year some batsman went mad for an hour
or so and ended up richer by the grace of Lawrence. The benefactor was Sir
Walter Lawrence (1872–1939), a sort of marginally more rational Sir Julian
Cahn, who founded the award out of a love of cricket and a desire to
discourage shillyshallying at the crease. There remains slight ambiguity
about the prize. E. W. Swanton, in his highly readable account of the history
of the award, says that the prize was £100, a sum large enough in those days
to buy a motor car. Sir Walter's obituary in* Wisden *says that the prize was
100 guineas, which means an extra fiver for petrol. But could the recipient
buy a car with the money? The obituary says that the award came in the form
of 'a 100 guineas order on a London store', but omits to say which store.*

M Y recollection of the Lawrence Trophy is that at its inception it
aroused considerable interest as a welcome novelty and a deserved
reward to one or other of the many attractive batsmen who graced the
game in the 1930s. It was pleasant for the annual winners to have a
handsome piece of silverware for the sideboard, and it was even more
agreeable to collect the cash prize of £100. That was quite a tidy sum in
those days. Why, you could just about buy a car with it—or was it that one
would have been able to, had war not diverted the manufacturerers to
more sinister machinery?

Perhaps my own attention derived partly from the fact that I used to go
down to Sawbridgeworth on the Essex-Hertfordshire border to play
against Sir Walter Lawrence's XI at Hyde Hall. Very good, keen stuff it
was, too, with the host in the well-established tradition of country house
cricket possibly even keener to win than his players. Shall I say that the
hospitality was always ample, and when there was a home victory to
celebrate, it was even more so.

Sir Walter's patronage was simply a reflection of his love of the game and
was separate from the building firm which his father had founded and of
which he was the head. Thus came the first instance of cricket patronage on
a national scale, and it deserves to be remembered as such. The Lawrence
Trophy was the pioneer, and many years were to pass before Brylcreem
and Gillette and then many more stamped their names on the cricket
public's consciousness.

The Trophy got away to an auspicious start in 1934, for could there be a more appropriate first winner than Frank Woolley, who probably appropriated for Kent more victories against the clock than any man for any side ever. Kent needed 194 in 100 minutes to beat Northamptonshire at Dover and made them with quarter of an hour to spare. *Wisden* tells us that 'Woolley completed his hundred in sixty-three minutes by dazzling stroke-play all round the wicket.' No mention of the Trophy! Another sort of glamour surrounded the second winner, Harold Gimblett. What could be more dramatic than the story of the twenty-year-old farmer's boy, called up at the last minute by Somerset for his first county match, literally missing the bus and lift-hopping his way to Frome, borrowing Arthur Wellard's second bat, going in at 107 for six, and hitting his first 50 in just under half an hour? The first hundred runs of the 23,007 that he was destined to score over a career of mingled triumph and disappointment arrived (as with Woolley) in 63 minutes.

Leslie Ames's first of two prizes for the fastest came in a Folkestone Festival match in 1936 for an England XI against the Indians. Such games were not taken frivolously in those days, but a draw was almost a certainty when, in the second innings, Woolley reminded his partner of the Trophy and gav' him enough of the bowling for Ames to reach his hundred in 68 minutes. Thereupon Ames gave to His Highness the Rajkumar Sir Vijay Vizianagram the second of the four first-class wickets he took in his career. It happens that the race for the Trophy that year is still clear to me because Roger Kimpton, a warm friend of mine, led the field all summer, having saved the match for Oxford aginst the full Lancashire attack in The Parks by making a hundred in 70 minutes. Lame, he batted with a runner, who had only limited exercise as Roger hit 22 fours. Which, on paper, would seem the more meritorious performance? R. C. M. Kimpton was a brilliant cricketer. He made five fast hundreds that season and might well have gone on to play for Australia but for the war. As it was, he won the DFC as a fighter pilot instead.

After which diversion I may record that I saw Joe Hardstaff's match-winning hundred for Nottinghamshire which finished the 1937 Canterbury Week. The *Evening Standard* having gone to press, I enjoyed simultaneously both the performance and a bag of cherries. Tall and very slim, Joe held his Gunn & Moore bat at the very top of the handle and swung it almost lazily through a high perpendicular arc—the very antithesis of the English short-arm clubbing motion of the 1980s. He needed only 51 minutes, six fewer than Hugh Bartlett's scintillating innings against the Australians at Hove the following year, a performance which a dwindling few in Sussex still recall. By now *Wisden* had deigned to list the annual winners, and in the last pre-war summer duly recorded Leslie Ames's second success when he won Kent's match at The Oval. Surrey's declaration left Kent to make 231 in less than two and a half hours. They needed only two hours thanks to Ames's storming hundred, this time in 70 minutes.

There was now a long hiatus before a member of the family, Mr. Brian Thornton, revived the Trophy, linking it in 1966 with the firm of Walter Lawrence. Finding that Fords had put up a prize for the county game, the Trophy went for five years to the maker of the fastest English Test hundred of the year. When in 1971 Fords dropped out, the original terms of the Lawrence Trophy were restored. So things are today, except that of recent years the criterion is not minutes taken but balls received. This modern method of evaluation is hard for the more elderly to get used to. I suppose a rough rule of thumb might be to equate 60 minutes with 51 balls, assuming that the bowlers deliver at the current required rate of seventeen overs an hour and that the batsman concerned receives an equal share of the bowling. Although the fastest innings under the new system was Vivian Richards's hundred in 48 balls for Somerset against Glamorgan in 1986, in terms of time it took him eight minutes longer than Ian Botham's 50-ball hundred in 49 minutes for Somerset against Warwickshire the previous year.

It was refreshing indeed that the 1989 winner should have been young Darren Bicknell, only 21 at the time, member of a Guildford cricketing family and playing for his native county of Surrey. It was one of four hundreds he made during the summer. But it is a great pity that in two or three cases the prize has been demeaned completely when runs have been offered for the taking by the opposition in efforts to contrive a finish. On the other hand, the award has gone to several famous strikers of the ball, as evidenced by such names on the Trophy as Majid Khan, Sobers, Procter, Botham, Richards, Greenidge and Hick—no mean successors to the heroes of half a century ago.

The Walter Lawrence Swanton Trophy has by contrast a much briefer history, but it could be argued that it rewards not a flash in the pan but protracted toil and sweat. It was initiated in 1982 by the *Daily Telegraph* for the first bowler to 100 wickets, initially in partnership with the batting award. Thus it went successively to four fine bowlers in Marshall, Emburey, Lever and Radford. When the *Telegraph* embarked on a wider policy of rewarding young cricketers, Walter Lawrence in 1988 made the award to Franklyn Stephenson. It was a sad sign of the times that last summer—as twice in the 1970s, when, however, the Championship was confined to twenty matches—not a single bowler, English or otherwise, quite reached three figures.

LAWRENCE CHALLENGE TROPHY WINNERS

1934 F. E. Woolley	Kent v Northamptonshire at Dover	63 minutes
1935 H. Gimblett	Somerset v Essex at Frome	63 minutes
1936 L. E. G. Ames	England XI v Indians at Folkestone	68 minutes
1937 J. Hardstaff	Nottinghamshire v Kent at Canterbury	51 minutes
1938 H. T. Bartlett	Sussex v Austalians at Hove	57 minutes
1939 L. E. G. Ames	Kent v Sussex at The Oval	70 minutes
1966 K. F. Barrington	England v Australia at Melbourne	122 balls
1967 B. L. D'Oliveira	England v India at Leeds	173 balls
1968 T. W. Graveney	England v West Indies at Port-of-Spain	174 balls
1969 C. Milburn	England v Pakistan at Karachi	163 balls
1970 G. Boycott	England v Rest of the World at The Oval	*222 balls
1971 B. F. Davison	Leicestershire v Northamptonshire at Leicester	63 minutes
1972 Majid Khan	Glamorgan v Warwickshire at Birmingham	70 minutes
1973 Asif Iqbal	Kent v M.C.C. at Canterbury	72 minutes
1974 G. S. Sobers	Nottinghamshire v Derbyshire at Ilkeston	83 minutes
1975 R. N. S. Hobbs	Essex v Australians at Chelmsford	44 minutes
1976 A. P. E. Knott	Kent v Sussex at Canterbury	†70 minutes
1977 C. M. Old	Yorkshire v Warwickshire at Birmingham	37 minutes
1978 C. G. Greenidge	Hampshire v Glamorgan at Southampton	82 minutes
1979 M. J. Procter	Gloucestershire v Northamptonshire at Bristol	57 minutes
1980 I. V. A. Richards	West Indians v Glamorgan at Swansea	66 minutes
1981 S. T. Clarke	Surrey v Glamorgan at Swansea	62 minutes
1982 I. T. Botham	Somerset v Warwickshire at Taunton	52 minutes
1983 S. J. O'Shaughnessy	Lancashire v Leicestershire at Manchester	35 minutes
1984 M. W. Gatting	Middlesex v Kent at Lord's	79 minutes
1985 I. T. Botham	Somerset v Warwickshire at Birmingham	50 balls
1986 I. V. A. Richards	Somerset v Glamorgan at Taunton	48 balls
1987 R. O. Butcher	Middlesex v Sussex at Hove	73 balls
1988 G. A. Hick	Worcestershire v Surrey at The Oval	79 balls
1989 D. J. Bicknell	Surrey v Essex at The Oval	69 balls

* *Awarded for the most meritorious innings of the series*

† C. G. Greenidge, West Indians v Nottinghamshire at Nottingham, reached his hundred in 69 minutes, but members of touring teams were not eligible for the award at that time.

Note: There was no award from 1946 to 1965.

WALTER LAWRENCE SWANTON TROPHY WINNERS

1982 M. D. Marshall (Hampshire)	– 100th wicket	August 25.
1983 J. E. Emburey (Middlesex)	– 100th wicket	September 1.
1984 J. K. Lever (Essex)	– 100th wicket	August 18.
1985 N. V. Radford (Worcestershire)	– 100th wicket	September 17.
1988 F. D. Stephenson (Nottinghamshire)	– 100th wicket	August 22.
1989 No bowler took 100 wickets.		

Note: There was no award in 1986 and 1987.

EPILOGUE

Every week, from 1970 to 1980, I contributed a 1000-word book review to *The Spectator*. Usually my subjects were literary. Trollope, Wilkie Collins, Shaw and Wells, Dickens and Thackerary, Byron and Shelley, Morris and Rossetti, Graves and Sassoon, Maugham and Priestley, scattered works on the topography of London, a book about the Thames, books about Gladstone and Disraeli, Scott Fitzgerald and John O'Hara, Edward Lear and Charles Dodgson, Dashiel Hammett and Raymond Chandler, in they poured, week after week, year by year, until I began to wonder by what processes of accounting their publishers could justify the enterprise. A collection of Graham Greene's film reviews which flung me back to the one-and-threes at the Old Paramount; an ingenious purported auto-biography by Jimmy Whistler; theories about Sherlock Holmes, about the Great War, about nursemaids, about houseboats. I recall Priestley's late flowering orchid, 'The Image Men'; and a huge cubic package left on a window-still among the also-rans which I thought I might take a perverse pleasure in reading. It was called *The Raj Quartet*. And once a year, as predictable as any calendar, the latest edition of *Wisden's Cricketers' Almanack*.

The literary editor, a young fellow called Ackroyd, came to know the sort of books I enjoyed reading and reviewing most. He came to know also that I had a quirk for cricket, a subject of which he knew less than nothing. It became a relief to him to fling each new almanack at me and know that he was absolved from all further responsibility in the matter. Each year I would try to review the almanack in a different way. As a work of reference, as a manual of social history, as a diary, as a coded message, once even as a novel. In the early 1970s I reviewed the latest edition only to find I had not used up my 1000 words. So I tacked on a paragraph saying that having supplied us with a comprehensive account of the modern world the proprietors of the annual should now make available to us the wonderful eccentricities of the early volumes, which were virtually unobtainable unless you happened to be lucky enough to locate a full set for sale and rich enough to fork out the ten or twelve thousand pounds a set was fetching in those days. Without stopping to consider the implications, I ended by suggesting that an anthology of the best of *Wisden* should be compiled and published.

About a week later I received a letter from a gentleman whose notepaper told me he was Vice-President in charge of Public Relations at Ford Motors. The note was brief and business-like. It said that if I undertook the compilation of just such an anthology, his company would be pleased to be associated with it by subsidising the enterprise. I was in total disarray, to so great an extent that I returned to my review to see exactly what it was I had said. I now decided to attempt to work out some sort of rational plan, which began with a visit to Haddam Whitaker in Bedford Square. This meeting was profitable to me because Whitaker gave the enterprise his blessing. It was also profitable to him, because he sold me the facsimile editions of the almanack, 1864–78, for fifty pounds. I then went the rounds of publishers and those with some say in matters of copyright. After about a year, during which time the Ford vice-president had moved on to another post and been replaced by a successor who sent a curt note withdrawing his company's offer, I landed up with the House of Macdonald, which contracted me to start work.

I then read all 111 volumes of the almanack, making notes as I went, singling out any game noteworthy for something outstanding, or freakish, or funny, or significant in some way. Long before I reached the Great War it was quite clear that the anthology would be in two volumes; long before I reached the Second World War it was even more obvious that the anthology would have to be like a Victorian novel, in three parts. By the time I came down to our own times, the anthology had split itself into four parts. While one part was being prepared for the printers, I worked on the next. The whole business took five years, from 1979 to 1983, during which time the publishing house changed hands. Three different editors worked on the four volumes with me, but as none of them knew any more about cricket than young Ackroyd, theirs were little more than sinecures. All four volumes were generously received, I sighed a deep sigh, purchased some stronger spectacles, and returned to normal life. Three years went by, at which point there was a political shift at Macdonald's and I was asked if there was any more to come. This request led to the publication in 1986 of *The Wisden Obituaries*.

The franchise for the almanack then changed, and I began to lose the drift of things. None of it seemed any longer to have much to do with me. I was quite wrong. Extricating myself from the siren was almost as difficult as first becoming acquainted with her. Macdonald's gave me the amazing news that Marks and Spencer wished to publish their first cricket book and had decided it was to be an illustrated edition of my four thousand pages reduced to four hundred. It was impossible not to cut vital organs, but the St Michael edition was a magnificent piece of book-making. Once again, I sat back and busied myself with other schemes for other books. At which point there entered the next publisher to become involved.

In his biography of G. O. Allen, E. W. Swanton writes: 'The idea of this biography, and that I should be its author, belongs to Mr. R. B. Bloomfield of Hutchinson. He overcame my initial reluctance.' In 1989 he overcame mine too. By now Bloomfield's company was publishing *Wisden*, and what he wished to know was: was there any more to be done? In 1989 appeared the first volume of *The Wisden Papers*, a collection of the essays commissioned by the almanack between 1888 and 1946. There followed a second volume, 1947–68, a third, which the reader now holds in his hand, bringing affairs up to the day before yesterday, and a supplementary fourth volume, *The Wisden Papers of Neville Cardus*. This makes a total of ten volumes in all. Nor does the matter rest there. The first two volumes are now in their third edition. Perhaps the others will follow. I am astonished and of course delighted by the whole business. There was once a very ancient songwriter who was asked to say something about the passing of time, to which he replied, 'If I'd have known I was going to live this long I'd have taken better care of myself.' So it is with *Wisden's Cricketers' Almanack* and yours truly. I sometimes wonder whatever happened to young Ackroyd.

BENNY GREEN